Hellenic Studies 94

TA-U-RO-QO-RO

𐀲𐀄𐀫𐀦𐀫

Recent Titles in the Hellenic Studies Series

TA-U-RO-QO-RO

𐀲𐀄𐀫𐀦𐀫

Studies in Mycenaean Texts, Language and Culture in Honor of José Luis Melena Jiménez

Edited by

Julián Méndez Dosuna

Thomas G. Palaima

Carlos Varias García

CENTER FOR HELLENIC STUDIES
Trustees for Harvard University
Washington, DC
Distributed by Harvard University Press
Cambridge, Massachusetts, and London, England
2022

TA-U-RO-QO-RO: Studies in Mycenaean Texts, Language, and Culture in Honor of José Luis Melena Jiménez, edited by Julián Méndez Dosuna, Thomas G. Palaima, and Carlos Varias García

Copyright © 2022 Center for Hellenic Studies, Trustees for Harvard University

All Rights Reserved.

Published by Center for Hellenic Studies, Trustees for Harvard University, Washington, D.C.

Distributed by Harvard University Press, Cambridge, Massachusetts and London, England

Printed by Gasch Printing, Odenton, MD

Cover Design: Joni Godlove

Production: Kerri Cox Sullivan

ISBN: 978-0-674-27257-6
Library of Congress Control Number: 2022936187

José Luis Melena Jiménez

Contents

Table of Contents

Photo Section follows

Preface

WORKS OF SCHOLARSHIP, LIKE HUMAN LIVES, move through time and space in ways as unpredictable as the human lives to which they are attached. This Festschrift in honor of José Luis Melena is no exception. What has made the contributors persist in perfecting their papers is the unique individual whom we are honoring.

José Luis Melena is, among philologists, a unique example of wisdom, capacity for work, tenacious determination, a deep and reverent sense of the vocation of being a scholar and a concomitant recognition that it is a rare privilege to pursue scholarly truths as a life's work. Personally—and all of us contributors have felt the effects of José's personality—he is generous towards others and has an unwavering sense of humanity, despite the disappointments, frustrations, sorrows, and miseries we inevitably confront as we live out our lives. In his career life and in his home life, José has been tested as if a modern Job. As William Faulkner put it about one of his most memorable characters, it is often a signal mark of success in the lives we lead to endure and endure and endure. José has done that and done so much more for all of us and for many others with equanimity and with intelligent understanding of human weaknesses.

Born in 1946, while still an adolescent schoolboy in his native San Sebastián at the beginning of the 1960s, during one of his frequent visits to the Reading Room of the Municipal Library, he began to read with great interest a Spanish translation of *The Aegean Civilization* by Gustav Glotz: *La Civilización Egea* (1926). He remembers being captivated by drawings of the Knossos tablets, much like the decipherer of Linear B, Michael Ventris, reading Adolf Erman's *Die Hieroglyphen*. And at once he was clear about where he was going to direct a big part of his studies: the Aegean writing systems.

A few years later, he found on the shelves of the library of the Peñaflorida Institute, where he was studying for the Higher Baccalaureate, a precious book, *Diecisiete tablillas micenicas* by Manuel Fernández Galiano (1959). He read it in full, as well as all the works available about Mycenae during his high school years in

San Sebastián. Such an early and determined sense of vocation in a recondite and complex area of scholarly inquiry that was studied by very few people in those days is very rare. In some ways it parallels the boyhood interests of Michael Ventris, who in young adulthood in the late 40's and early 50's, after his military service in World War II, virtually abandoned the career field of architecture that his mother more or less had dictated that he take up and instead worked intensively toward the decipherment of Aegean scripts, his real passion.

With characteristic intelligence and determination and Delphic self-knowledge, José Luis Melena stayed his course. It is not surprising, therefore, that, in October 1965, having just arrived in Salamanca to begin his university studies, he caught the attention of Manuel García Teijeiro, who was going to teach Mycenaean Greek, and the leading Spanish figure in the understanding of Mycenaean script and language, Martín S. Ruipérez himself. José asked specifically for the two volumes of *Scripta Minoa* (1909 and 1952) and for the run of the journal *Minos*. It was clear why José Luis Melena chose the University of Salamanca to study Classical Philology.

But staying the course was not without investigating seriously other areas of interest. Recently, José reminded us (personal communication August 3, 2021) that "my Master Thesis dealt with the taboo in Ancient Greece (1970) as a preliminary study for my [then proposed] PhD dissertation on the Homeric words for 'strength' which I eventually abandoned for a Mycenaean subject." We can see how far José went down this alternative path by reading his impressive early article that merged intensive study of Indo-European and Homeric vocabulary with what has been his lifelong passion for Mycenology: "El testimonio del micénico a propósito de los nombres de las distintas fuerzas en Homero," *Emerita* 44:2 (1976): 421–436.

From the time he received his diploma (with Extraordinary Award) in 1970 to today, José Melena has done enormous and extraordinary work in virtually all the subfields that make up the field of Mycenaean studies. He has provided all kinds of help, sometimes without due recognition, to hundreds of researchers around the world, beginning with his decisive work in the edition of *Acta Mycenaea*, the proceedings of the Fifth International Colloquium of Mycenaean Studies organized by his teacher Martín S. Ruipérez in 1970. The *acta* were published as separate volumes of the journal *Minos* XI (1971) and XII (1972). This and many other tasks, which include his doctoral thesis ("Estudios sobre las inscripciones de Cnoso," Madrid: Universidad Complutense de Madrid, Facultad de Filosofía y Letras, 1973) and his work on the journal *Minos: Revista de Filologia Egea*, were carried out in a first stage of job instability and regular travel (Madrid, Salamanca, Canarias) until he achieved the position of Professor of Greek Philology at the University of the Basque Country, in 1983.

Mycenology would not have had the strong development that it has had throughout the world in the last fifty years without the tireless cooperative work of José Luis Melena. Among many other major scholarly duties that he performed during all this time, it is worth mentioning first and foremost the journal *Minos*. For over four decades (1970–2011), its enormous international prestige in this field was due almost exclusively to the work of José Luis Melena, first as secretary and then as editor.

It is a pity that, for various reasons, this tribute could not appear in the journal to which José dedicated a large part of his life. We are very grateful to the Center for Hellenic Studies, especially to Gregory Nagy, Leonard Muellner, Kerri Cox Sullivan, and Jill Curry Robbins for their roles in publishing our Festschrift. We thank Charles Delattre, Roser Gómez Guiu, Jörg Weilhartner, Jared Petroll, and Zafeirios Adramerinas, who were of great help with proofing and formatting these complicated texts. Tom Palaima always thanks Garrett Bruner, PASP archivist, for locating needed materials.

José's excellent scientific production and his capacity for work and planning made it natural for José to be chosen Secretary General of the Comité International Permanent des Études Mycéniennes (CIPEM) in 1990, relieving John Chadwick. At the same time he replaced Martín S. Ruipérez as representative of Spain in CIPEM. He went well beyond working dutifully in these two key positions until he voluntarily ceded them to successors twenty years later in 2010.

The scientific prestige of José Luis Melena transcends the scope of Mycenaean and Classical Philology, as is made clear by two important external recognitions. The first is his appointment in 1987 as Cultural Attaché of the Embassy of Spain in Athens and Director of the Instituto Cultural Español Reina Sofía (now known as the Instituto Cervantes) in the Greek capital, a position from which he was ignominiously dismissed in 1990 through political machinations. The second was receiving the Euskadi Research Prize from the Basque Government in 1999.

We would like to close on a personal note beyond the expressions of gratitude that we have made, as have other contributors, in our papers and/or in the section of brief personal comments that closes this volume.

I, Carlos Varias García, would like to highlight the unparalleled kindness of José Luis Melena in guiding my doctoral thesis. In a letter written in January 1991 that I have treasured ever since receiving it, José Melena, having just recently arrived in Vitoria after enduring the shock of being removed from Athens, responded to my letter from Barcelona asking him to direct my doctoral thesis. José not only welcomed my request, at a very difficult time for him, but also proposed a change of thesis topic from one having to do with Mycenaean anthroponymy to another, the joint study of the inscriptions in Linear B of Mycenae.

The letter contains an impeccable argument that later proved to be correct. My thesis, from beginning to end, has the stamp of José Luis Melena, and without him as director it would never have seen the light of day. Such was his continuous support and scientific direction that I received as doctoral student, despite being at a different university. José's support was just as decisive throughout my entire academic career for which I have many times heartily thanked him. Thank you, again, José.

I, Tom Palaima, consider José my second mentor, after Emmett L. Bennett, Jr. José shares with Emmett a sincere sense of the fun in working on problems having to do with the Mycenaean Greeks and the writing system that they used. I was honored that he invited me to serve first on the Comité de Redacción of *Minos* from 1986–2011; then as assistant editor and book review editor 1990–95, and finally as co-editor and book review editor 1995–2011. Working with José, our labors were no burden at all. His open-mindedness, high scholarly standards humanely applied to submissions, and his critical and truly selfless enthusiasm for new ideas were so wonderful to absorb that it is only in recent years that I have come to see how exceptional these attributes were within our field or any scholarly fields. I share fully Carlos's sense that José Melena is a generous person.

There are stories that could be told of how calmly José withstood personal professional attacks and life tragedies that would have caused most human beings to respond by becoming bitter and hateful or by despairing of life itself. I share with Carlos a deep sense of gratitude for the forty-one years now that I have known and cooperated with José. I have asked him many stupid questions. I have always gotten careful, sincere, and kind answers.

We are sure that if life circumstances permitted Julián Méndez Dosuna, who did an enormous amount of work in organizing, collecting, and editing this volume in the first years of work on it, would add reflections similar to ours. Without Julián's work, this volume would not exist. He is truly, not just alphabetically, its first editor.

We, all three of us, are proud to have José Luis Melena as a mentor, a colleague, a guiding spirit, a friend, and a fellow explorer in the often sad and sorrowful pathways of life

We thank all our fellow contributors for making this volume a thank offering worthy of a remarkable scholar and human being.

Carlos Varias García, Universitat Autònoma de Barcelona
Thomas Gerard Palaima, PASP, University of Texas at Austin
Julián Méndez Dosuna, Universidad de Salamanca

Bibliography of
José Luis Melena Jiménez

Books, Book Chapters, and Articles

1972

- "Un mundo nuevo en la antigua Grecia," *Universitas* 20: 89–97.
- "Alejandro Magno," *Universitas* 42: 223–231.
- "En torno al ΣΚΗΠΤΡΟΝ homérico," *Cuadernos de Filología Clásica* 3: 321–356.
- "Tables of Ideograms and Syllabograms of Mycenaean Linear B," in *Acta Mycenaea. Proceedings of the Fifth International Colloquium on Mycenaean Studies, Held in Salamanca, 30 March–3 April 1970*, ed. M. S. Ruipérez, I [= *Minos* 11] (Salamanca: Ediciones Universidad de Salamanca), xvii, xviii, xx, and xxi.
- "Index of Mycenaean Words," in *Acta Mycenaea. Proceedings of the Fifth International Colloquium on Mycenaean Studies, Held in Salamanca, 30 March–3 April 1970*, ed. M. S. Ruipérez, II [= *Minos* 12] (Salamanca: Ediciones Universidad de Salamanca), 451–476.
- "On the Knossos Mc Tablets," *Minos* 13.1: 29–54.
- "Further Comments on *142 and *151," *Minos* 13.2: 259–260.

1973

- *Estudios sobre las inscripciones de Cnoso*, PhD diss., Facultad de Filosofía y Letras, Universidad Complutense de Madrid.
- "Algunas consideraciones sobre las tablillas Ai (2) de Cnoso," *Estudios Clásicos* 69–70: 209–214.
- "Las tablillas del escriba 51 de Micenas y la forma ṭọ-so-ne," *Estudios Clásicos* 69–70: 215–219.

1974

- "Reflexiones sobre los meses del calendario micénico de Cnoso y sobre la fecha de la caída del Palacio," *Emerita* 42.1: 77–102.
- "*ku-pa-ro* en las tablillas de Cnoso," *Emerita* 42.2: 307–336.
- "*ki-ta-no* en las tablillas de Cnoso," *Durius* 2.3: 45–55.
- "A Tentative Identification of the Syllabogram **18*," *Nestor* 3: 8 (Correspondence 1 November 1974): 954–955.

1975

- "*po-ni-ki-jo* in the Knossos Ga Tablets," *Minos* 14 (1973 [1975]): 77–84.
- "El primitivo nombre de Heracles," in *Genethliakon Isidorianum. Miscellanea graeca, latina atque hebraica Isidoro Rodríguez Herrera XIV lustra complenti oblata* [= *Helmantica* 79–81] (Salamanca: Universidad Pontificia), 377–388.
- "Part III: Indexes of Mycenaean Words," in *The Thebes Tablets* II, ed. Th. G. Spyropoulos, and J. Chadwick, Suplementos a *Minos* 4 (Salamanca: Ediciones Universidad de Salamanca), 109–117.
- *Studies on Some Mycenaean Inscriptions from Knossos Dealing with Textiles.* Suplementos a *Minos* 5 (Salamanca: Ediciones Universidad de Salamanca).
- "A Supplement to MY Ge 603.1 and the Identification of *da-ra-ko*," *Nestor* 4: 8 (Correspondence 1 November 1975): 1015–1016.

1976

- "Coriander on the Knossos Tablets," *Minos* 15 (1974 [1976]): 133–163.
- "Aromatics Plants on the Knossos Tablets," *Minos* 15 (1974 [1976]): 226–227.
- "El testimonio del micénico a propósito de los nombres de las distintas fuerzas en Homero," *Emerita* 44: 421–435.
- J. M.ª Otero and J. L. Melena, "La estela inscrita de Siruela, Badajoz," in *Actas del I Coloquio sobre Lenguas y Culturas Prerromanas de la Península Ibérica (Salamanca, 27–31 mayo 1974)*, ed. L. Michelena, F. Jordá Cerdá, and J. de Hoz (Salamanca: Ediciones Universidad de Salamanca), 343–352 + Láminas I-II.
- "La producción de plantas aromáticas en Cnoso," *Estudios Clásicos* 78: 177–190.
- "A Suggestion for the Interpretation of the Couple *no-ri-wo-ki-de/no-ri-wo-ko*," *Nestor* 5: 8 (Correspondence 1 November 1976): 1059–1060.

- *Sobre ciertas innovaciones tempranas del griego (El tratamiento de yod inicial y la alternancia* pt-/p-*). Informe provisional* (Salamanca: Ediciones Universidad de Salamanca).

1977

- "On the New Linear B Inscription from Mycenae," *Minos* 16: 17–18.
- "An Emendation for the Word *te-ra-ni-ja* along with a Tentative Interpretation of Such a Form," *Nestor* 5: 8 (Correspondence 1 November 1977): 1133.

1978

- "En torno a la identificación del silabograma *79 del silabario micénico," in *Actas del V Congreso Español de Estudios Clásicos (Madrid, 20 al 25 de abril de 1976)* (Madrid: Sociedad Española de Estudios Clásicos), 751–757.

1979

- "Note on Spelling with a Dummy Vowel on KH Z 1," *Nestor* 6: 5 (Forum May 1979): 1369.

1981

- "El aceite en la civilización micénica," in *Producción y comercio del aceite en la Antigüedad. Primer Congreso Internacional (Madrid, 4-6 diciembre 1978)*, coord. J. M. Blázquez Martínez (Madrid: Editorial de la Universidad Complutense), 255–282.
- "On the Identification of a Plant Motiv on a Minoan Pin," *Nestor* 8: 7 (Forum October 1981): 1554–1555.

1982

- "The Reading of the Vase Inscription TI Z 30," *Kadmos* 21.1: 95–96.

1983

- "Further Thoughts on Mycenaean *o-pa*," in *Res Mycenaeae. Akten des VII. Internationalen Mykenologischen Colloquiums in Nürnberg vom 6.-10. April 1981*, ed. A. Heubeck and G. Neumann (Göttingen: Vandenhoeck & Ruprecht), 258–286.
- Discussion bei Y. Duhoux, "Les syllabogrammes *34* et *35* du linéaire B," in *Res Mycenaeae. Akten des VII. Internationalen Mykenologischen Colloquiums in Nürnberg vom 6.-10. April 1981*, ed. A. Heubeck and G. Neumann (Göttingen: Vandenhoeck & Ruprecht), 124–125.

- Response to St. Hiller, "Fruchtbaumkulturen auf Kreta und in Pylos," in *Res Mycenaeae. Akten des VII. Internationalen Mykenologischen Colloquiums in Nürnberg vom 6.–10. April 1981*, ed. A. Heubeck and G. Neumann (Göttingen: Vandenhoeck & Ruprecht), 201.

- Response to J. T. Killen, "On the Mycenae Ge Tablets," in *Res Mycenaeae. Akten des VII. Internationalen Mykenologischen Colloquiums in Nürnberg vom 6.–10. April 1981*, ed. A. Heubeck and G. Neumann (Göttingen: Vandenhoeck & Ruprecht), 232–233.

- Response to A. Morpurgo Davies, "Mycenaean and Greek Prepositions: *o-pi, e-pi*, etc.," in *Res Mycenaeae. Akten des VII. Internationalen Mykenologischen Colloquiums in Nürnberg vom 6.–10. April 1981*, ed. A. Heubeck and G. Neumann (Göttingen: Vandenhoeck & Ruprecht), 310.

- "Notas de Filología micénica, III: El silabograma **86*," *Emerita* 51: 255–267.

- "Un nouveau raccord de fragments dans les tablettes de Cnossos," *Minos* 18: 69–70.

- "Olive Oil and Other Sorts of Oil in the Mycenaean Tablets," *Minos* 18: 89–123.

- "Perfiles generales para una historia del ditirambo como género literario," *Tabona* 4: 181–223.

1984

- "Allí donde al macho la hembra marida," in *Apophoreta Philologica Emmanueli Fernández Galiano a Sodalibus Oblata. Pars Prior*, ed. L. Gil and R. M.ª Aguilar [= *Estudios Clásicos* 87] (Madrid: Ediciones Clásicas), 151–158.

- "Dos lecciones sobre el verbo griego," *Tabona* 5: 285–342.

- "Un ara votiva romana en El Gaitán, Cáceres," *Veleia* 1: 233–260.

- *EX ORIENTE LUX. La aportación de las filologías del Oriente Próximo y Medio antiguo a la comprensión de los primeros textos europeos. Discurso pronunciado en la Solemne Apertura del Curso Académico 1984-1985* (Vitoria-Gasteiz: Servicio Editorial de la Universidad del País Vasco).

1985

- *Serta gratulatoria in honorem Juan Régulo*, vol. I: *Filología*, ed. J. L. Melena (La Laguna: Universidad de La Laguna).

- "Notas de Filología micénica, VI: El silabograma *83," in *Serta gratulatoria in honorem Juan Régulo*, vol. I: *Filología*, ed. J. L. Melena (La Laguna: Universidad de La Laguna), 473–486.

- *Symbolae Ludovico Mitxelena septuagenario oblatae quas edidit José L. Melena*, 2 vols., Anejos de *Veleia* 1 (Vitoria-Gasteiz: Servicio Editorial de la Universidad del País Vasco).

- "*Salama*, Jálama y la epigrafía latina del antiguo Corregimiento," in *Symbolae Ludovico Mitxelena septuagenario oblatae quas edidit José L. Melena, Pars prior*, Anejos de *Veleia* 1 (Vitoria-Gasteiz: Servicio Editorial de la Universidad del País Vasco), 475–530.

1987

- "Notas de Filología micénica, II: ¿Qué se asienta en PY Un 1320 [+] 1442?," in *Athlon. Satura grammatica in honorem Francisci R. Adrados*, vol. II, ed. P. Bádenas de la Peña, A. Martínez Díez, M.ª E. Martínez-Fresneda, and E. Rodríguez Monescillo (Madrid: Editorial Gredos), 613–618.

- *Studia Palaeohispanica. Actas del IV Coloquio sobre Lenguas y Culturas Paleohispánicas (Vitoria/Gasteiz, 6–10 mayo 1985)*, ed. J. Gorrochategui, J. L. Melena, and J. Santos [= *Veleia* 2–3 (1985–1986) [1987] (Vitoria-Gasteiz: Servicio Editorial de la Universidad del País Vasco).

- *Studies in Mycenaean and Classical Greek Presented to John Chadwick*, ed. J. T. Killen, J. L. Melena, and J.-P. Olivier [= *Minos* 20–22] (Salamanca: Ediciones Universidad de Salamanca).

- "On the Linear B Ideogrammatic Syllabogram *ZE*," in *Studies in Mycenaean and Classical Greek Presented to John Chadwick*, ed. J. T. Killen, J. L. Melena, and J.-P. Olivier [= *Minos* 20–22] (Salamanca: Ediciones Universidad de Salamanca), 389–457.

- "On Untransliterated Syllabograms *56 and *22," in *Tractata Mycenaea. Proceedings of the Eighth International Colloquium on Mycenaean Studies, Held in Ohrid, 15–20 September 1985*, ed. P. Hr. Ilievski and L. Crepajac (Skopje: Macedonian Academy of Sciences and Arts), 203–232.

- "Una apostilla a *COLVAV*," *Veleia* 4: 371–372.

1988

- "Notas de Filología micénica, I: El ideograma *142," in *Texts, Tablets, and Scribes. Studies in Mycenaean Epigraphy and Economy Offered to Emmett L. Bennett, Jr.*, ed. J.-P. Olivier and Th. G. Palaima, Suplementos a *Minos*

10 (Salamanca and Lejona: Ediciones Universidad de Salamanca and Servicio Editorial de la Universidad del País Vasco), 213–217.

1989

- J. M. Driessen, L. Godart; J. T. Killen, C. Kopaka, J. L. Melena, J.-P. Olivier, and M. Perna, "107 raccords et quasi-raccords de fragments dans *CoMIK* I et II," *Bulletin de Correspondance Hellénique* 112.1 (1988 [1989]): 59–82.
- E. L. Bennett, J. M. Driessen, L. Godart, J. T. Killen, C. Kopaka, J. L. Melena, J.-P. Oliver, and M. Perna, "436 raccords et quasi-raccords de fragments inédits dans *KT* 5," *Minos* 24: 199–242.
- "Πρόλογος," in M. Fernández Galiano, *Πανόραμα της Ελληνικής Φιλολογίας στην Ισπανία: 20ος αιώνας* (Athens: Ισπανικό Μορφωτικό Ίδρυμα «Βασιλίσσα Σοφία»).

1990

- J.-P. Olivier, J. L. Melena, and C. Piterós, "Les inscriptions en linéaire B des nodules de Thèbes (1982): La fouille, les documents, les possibilités d'interprétation," *Bulletin de Correspondance Hellénique* 114.1: 103–184.
- "Notas de epigrafía romana de Extremadura, I: Sobre un pretendido teónimo nuevo en Lusitania," *Veleia* 7: 147–153.
- M. S. Ruipérez and J. L. Melena, *Los griegos micénicos* (Madrid: Historia 16).

1991

- *El Mundo Micénico. Cinco siglos de la primera civilización europea 1600–1100 a. C.*, catálogo de la exposición del Museo Arqueológico Nacional, Madrid, enero–febrero 1992; comisario: José L. Melena (Madrid: Ministerio de Cultura).
- "La Civilización Micénica reflejada en los documentos en Lineal B," in *El Mundo Micénico. Cinco siglos de la primera civilización europea 1600–1100 a. C.*, catálogo de la exposición del Museo Arqueológico Nacional, Madrid, enero–febrero 1992; comisario: José L. Melena (Madrid: Ministerio de Cultura, 1991), 62–73.
- J. L. Melena and J.-P. Olivier, *TITHEMY. The Tablets and Nodules in Linear B from Tiryns, Thebes, and Mycenae. A Revised Transliteration.* Suplementos a *Minos* 12 (Salamanca and Lejona: Ediciones Universidad de Salamanca and Servicio Editorial de la Universidad del País Vasco).

1993

- L. Godart, J. T. Killen, C. Kopaka, J. L. Melena, and J.-P. Olivier, "501 raccords et quasi-raccords de fragments dans les tablettes de Cnossos post-*KT* V," *Minos* 25–26 (1990–1991 [1993]): 373–411.
- J. L. Melena, G. Owens, and M. Serrano, "55 raccords de fragments dans les tablettes de Cnossos," *Minos* 25–26 (1990–1991 [1993]): 413–417.

1994

- "Notas de epigrafía romana de Extremadura, II: Sobre el ara funeraria de Granadilla," *Veleia* 11: 317–318.

1995

- L. Godart, C. Kopaka, J.-L. Melena, and J.-P. Olivier, "175 raccords de fragments dans les tablettes de Knossos," *Minos* 27–28 (1992–1993 [1995]): 55–70.
- "167 Joins of Fragments in the Linear B Tablets from Pylos," *Minos* 27–28 (1992–1993 [1995]): 71–82.
- "224 Joins and Quasi-Joins of Fragments in the Linear B Tablets from Pylos," *Minos* 27–28 (1992–1993 [1995]): 307–324.

1996

- "The Reconstruction of the Fragments of the Linear B Tablets from Knossos," in *Atti e Memorie del II Congresso Internazionale di Micenologia, Roma-Napoli, 14-20 ottobre 1991*, vol. 1: *Filologia*, ed. E. De Miro, L. Godart, and A. Sacconi (Rome: Gruppo Editoriale Internazionale), 83–90.
- M. S. Ruipérez and J. L. Melena, *Οι Μυκηναίοι Έλληνες* [translation of *Los griegos micénicos*, Madrid 1990] (Athens: Ινστιτούτο του Βιβλίου— Μ. Καρδαμίτσα).

1997

- "28 Joins and Quasi-joins of Fragments in the Linear B Tablets from Pylos," *Minos* 29–30 (1994–1995 [1997]): 95–100.
- "133 Joins and Quasi-joins of Fragments in the Linear B Tablets from Pylos," *Minos* 29–30 (1994–1995 [1997]): 271–288.
- "Notas de epigrafía romana de Extremadura, III: Sobre un nuevo nexo de letras," *Veleia* 14: 375–377.

1999

- "40 Joins and Quasi-joins of Fragments in the Linear B Tablets from Pylos," *Minos* 31–32 (1996–1997 [1999]): 159–170.
- "13 Joins and Quasi-joins of Fragments in the Linear B Tablets from Pylos," *Minos* 31–32 (1996–1997 [1999]): 171–178.
- "19 raccords et quasi-raccords de fragments dans les tablettes de Cnossos," *Minos* 31–32 (1996–1997 [1999]): 417–422.
- "Some Thoughts on the Origin of the Knossos Fragments Found in 1984 at the Heraklion Museum," in *Floreant Studia Mycenaea. Akten des X. Internationalen Mykenologischen Colloquiums in Salzburg vom 1.-5. Mai 1995*, vol. 2, ed. S. Deger-Jalkotzy, St. Hiller, and O. Panagl (Vienna: Verlag der Österreichischen Akademie der Wissenschaften), 363–387.

2001

- J. L. Melena and T. G. Palaima, "100 Years of Linear B from Knossos," *American Journal of Archaeology* 105.2: 316–320.

2002

- R. J. Firth and J. L. Melena, "Identifying the Linear B Tablets from the Arsenal and Little Palace at Knossos," in *A-NA-QO-TA. Studies Presented to J. T. Killen*, ed. J. Bennet and J. Driessen [= *Minos* 33–34 (1998–1999)] (Salamanca: Ediciones Universidad de Salamanca), 107–133.
- R. J. Firth and J. L. Melena, "The Knossos Tablets: Genesis of the 5000-Series," *Minos* 35–36 (2000–2001 [2002]: volumen del cincuentenario): 315–355.
- "24 Joins and Quasi-joins of Fragments in the Linear B Tablets from Pylos," *Minos* 35–36 (2000–2001: volumen del cincuentenario): 357–369.
- "63 Joins and Quasi-joins of Fragments in the Linear B Tablets from Pylos," *Minos* 35–36 (2000–2001: volumen del cincuentenario): 371–384.
- R. J. Firth and J. L. Melena, "A Tale of Two Fragments: KN Dl 8216 and 8217," *Minos* 35–36 (2000–2001: volumen del cincuentenario): 451–458.

2006

- "A New Fragment of Linear B Tablet from Pylos," *Minos* 37–38 (2002–2003 [2006]): 111–112 + plate XVIII.

- R. J. Firth and J. L. Melena, "22 Joins and Quasi-Joins of Fragments of Linear B Tablets from Knossos," *Minos* 37–38 (2002–2003 [2006]): 113–120 + plates XIX–XXVI.

2008

- R. J. Firth and J. L. Melena, "The Knossos Linear B Tablets: Genesis of the Listing of the Later Fragments," in *Colloquium Romanum. Atti del XII Colloquio Internazionale di Micenologia (Roma 20-25 febbraio 2006)*, ed. A. Sacconi, M. Del Freo, L. Godart, and M. Negri, vol. I [= *Pasiphae* I] (Pisa and Rome: Fabrizio Serra Editore), 281–307.

2010

- "De leonas y ralladores de queso (Aristófanes, *Lisístrata* 231)," in *DIC MIHI, MVSA, VIRVM. Homenaje al profesor Antonio López Eire*, ed. F. Cortés Gabaudan and J. V. Méndez Dosuna (Salamanca: Ediciones Universidad de Salamanca), 431–440.

2014

- "Filling Gaps in the Basic Mycenaean Syllabary," in *Donum Mycenologicum. Mycenaean Studies in Honour of Francisco Aura Jorro*, ed. A. Bernabé and E. R. Luján, Bibliothèque des Cahiers de l'Institut de Linguistique de Louvain 131 (Louvain-la-Neuve: Peeters), 75–85.
- "Filling Gaps in the Mycenaean Linear B Additional Syllabary: The Case of Syllabogram *34*," in *Ágalma. Ofrenda desde la Filología Clásica a Manuel García Teijeiro*, ed. A. Martínez Fernández, B. Ortega Villaro, H. Velasco López, and H. Zamora Salamanca (Valladolid: Ediciones Universidad de Valladolid), 207–226.
- "Mycenaean Writing," in *A Companion to Linear B: Mycenaean Greek Texts and Their World*, ed. Y. Duhoux and A. Morpurgo Davies, vol. 3 [=Bibliothèque des Cahiers de l'Institut de Linguistique de Louvain 133] (Louvain-la-Neuve: Peeters), 1–186.

2016

- R. J. Firth and J. L. Melena, "Re-visiting the Scribes of Knossos: The Principal Hands 101-123, 125-141," *Minos* 39: 249–318.
- R. J. Firth and J. L. Melena, "Re-visiting the Scribes of the Room of the Chariot Tablets at Knossos," *Minos* 39: 319–351.
- R. J. Firth and J. L. Melena, "The Secondary Scribes of Knossos," *Minos* 39: 353–378.

- "La invocación a las NUBES: Aristófanes, *Nubes* 264–291, 323–325," in *ΕΥΠΟΙΚΙΛΩΝ ΑΝΘΟΣ. Estudios sobre teatro griego en homenaje a Antonio Melero* (= *Studia Philologica Valentina* 18, n. s. 15), 217–228.

2019

- *The Knossos Tablets. Sixth Edition. A Transliteration* by José L. Melena in collaboration with Richard J. Firth (Philadelphia: INSTAP Academic Press).

2021

- *The Pylos Tablets. Third Edition in Transliteration* by José L. Melena with the collaboration of Richard J. Firth [=Anejos de *Veleia*, Series Maior 14] (Vitoria-Gasteiz: Servicio Editorial de la Universidad del País Vasco).

Forthcoming

- "On the Structure of the Mycenaean Linear B Syllabary, I: The Unstraliterated Syllabograms. Preliminary Report," in *Proceedings of the Eleventh International Mycenological Colloquium (Austin, Texas, May 7-13, 2000)* [available at www.ehu.academia.edu/Jose Luis Melena].
- R. J. Firth and J. L. Melena, "The Find-Places of the Knossos Tablets: The 5000-Series," in *Proceedings of the Eleventh International Mycenological Colloquium (Austin, Texas, May 7-13, 2000)* [available at www.ehu.academia.edu/Jose Luis Melena].
- *TITHEMY. The Tablets and Nodules in Linear B from Tiryns, Thebes, Mycenae. A Revised Transliteration* by José L. Melena and Jean-Pierre Olivier. 2nd ed. by José L. Melena, with the addition of Iklaina, Iolkos, Midea.

Reviews

- J.-P. Olivier, *The Mycenae Tablets IV* (Leiden, 1969), in *Minos* 10.2 (1969 [1970]): 186–187.
- D. J. Georgacas, *The Name "Asia" for the Continent: Its History and Origin* (*Names* 17 [1969]: 1–90), in *Minos* 10.2 (1969 [1970]): 193–194.
- P. Åström, *Excavations at Kalopsidha and Ayios Iakovos in Cyprus* (Lund, 1969), in *Minos* 10.2 (1969 [1970]): 195–196.
- L. Drees, *Olympia, Gods, Artists, and Athletes* (London, 1968), in *Minos* 10.2 (1969 [1970]): 197–198.
- E. A. S. Butterworth, *The Tree at the Navel of the Earth* (Berlin, 1970), in *Minos* 10.2 (1969 [1970]): 198–199.

- V. E. G. Kenna, *The Cretan Talismanic Stones in the Late Minoan Age* (Lund, 1969), in *Minos* 10.2 (1969 [1970]): 199.
- J. Raison and M. Pope, *Index du Linéaire A* (Rome, 1971), in *Minos* 13.1 (1972): 101.
- J. Chadwick, J. T. Killen, and J.-P. Olivier, *The Knossos Tablets. Fourth Edition* (Cambridge, 1971), in *Minos* 13.1 (1972): 102–103.
- N. C. Scoufopoulos, *Mycenaean Citadels* (Göteborg, 1971), in *Minos* 13.1 (1972): 108–109.
- D. L. Page, *The Santorini Volcano and the Destruction of Minoan Crete* (London, 1970), in *Minos* 13.2 (1972): 262–264.
- E. L. Bennett, Jr. and J.-P. Olivier, *The Pylos Tablets Transcribed,* Part I: *Texts and Notes* (Rome, 1973), in *Minos* 14 (1973 [1975]): 191–192.
- S. Symeonoglou, *Kadmeia I: Mycenaean Finds from Thebes, Greece. Excavation at 14 Oedipus St.* (Göteborg, 1973), in *Minos* 14 (1973 [1975]): 198–200.
- M. Lindgren, *The People of Pylos: Prosopographical and Methodological Studies in the Pylos Archives.* Parts I & II (Uppsala, 1973), in *Minos* 14 (1973 [1975]): 200–201.
- M. Ventris and J. Chadwick, *Documents in Mycenaean Greek. Second Edition* (Cambridge, 1973), in *Emerita* 44.1 (1976): 217–219.
- P. Ballotta, *Le déchiffrement du Disque de Phaestos* (Bologna 1974); *Le Poème du Disque de Phaestos* (Bologna, 1974); *Ricerche di Susbtrato* (Bologna 1975); *Sémantique des idéogrammes* (Bologna, 1975), in *Minos* 15 (1974 [1976]): 230–231.
- M. Ventris and J. Chadwick, *Documents in Mycenaean Greek. Second Edition* (Cambridge, 1973), in *Minos* 15 (1974 [1976]): 233–239.
- A. Tovar, *Sprachen und Inschriften. Studien zum Mykenischen, Lateinischen und Hispanokeltischen* (Amsterdam, 1973), in *Minos* 15 (1974 [1976]): 240–241.
- A. Sacconi, *Corpus delle iscrizioni vascolari in Lineare B* (Rome, 1974), in *Minos* 16 (1977): 236–238.
- A. Sacconi, *Corpus delle iscrizioni in Lineare B di Micene* (Rome, 1974), in *Minos* 16 (1977): 238–239.
- E. L. Bennett, Jr. and J.-P. Olivier, *The Pylos Tablets Transcribed,* Part II: *Hands, Concordances, Indices* (Rome, 1976), in *Minos* 16 (1977): 239–240.
- N. A. Masouridi, Ἡ μινωϊκή γραφή εἰς τὰς πινακίδας τῆς Πύλου (Athens, 1976), in *Minos* 16 (1977): 240–241.

- *Dal sillabario minoico all'alfabeto greco* [= *La Parola del Passato* 166], in *Minos* 16 (1977): 241–244.
- Y. Duhoux, *Aspects du vocabulaire économique mycénien (cadastre-artisanat-fiscalité)* (Amsterdam, 1976), in *Minos* 16 (1977): 244–247.
- G. Maddoli, *La civiltà micenea: Guida storica e critica* (Rome-Bari, 1977), in *Emerita* 45 (1977): 480–482.
- L. Godart and A. Sacconi, *Les tablettes en linéaire B de Thèbes* (Rome, 1978), in *Minos* 18 (1983): 262.
- J. T. Hooker, *Linear B: An Introduction* (Bristol, 1980), in *Minos* 18 (1983): 263–264.
- F. Vandenabeele and J.-P. Olivier, *Les idéogrammes archéologiques du Linéaire B* (Paris, 1979), in *Minos* 18 (1983): 264.
- J. P. Best, *Supplementum epigraphicum mediterraneum* (Middelie, 1982), in *Aula Orientalis* 2.1 (1984): 159–163.
- J. Chadwick, L. Godart, J. T. Killen, J.-P. Olivier, A. Sacconi, and I. A. Sakellarakis, *Corpus of Mycenaean Inscriptions from Knossos*, vol. III (5000–7999) (Cambridge and Rome, 1997), in *Minos* 31–32 (1996–1997 [1998]): 458–464.

Translations into Spanish

Books

- L. R. Palmer, *Introducción crítica a la lingüística descriptiva y comparada* [=Biblioteca Románica Hispánica II, Estudios y Ensayos 227] (Madrid: Gredos, 1975) [original title: *Descriptive and Comparative Linguistics. A Critical Introduction* (London, 1972)].
- R. P. Stockwell and R. K. S. Macauly, eds., *Cambio lingüístico y teoría generativa* [=Biblioteca Románica Hispánica. II, Estudios y Ensayos 266] (Madrid: Gredos, 1977) [original title: *Linguistic Change and Generative Theory* (Bloomington, IN, 1972)].
- J. M. Anderson, *Aspectos estructurales del cambio lingüístico* (Madrid: Gredos, col. 'Biblioteca Románica Hispánica. II, Estudios y Ensayos' 270, 1977) [original title: *Structural Aspects of Language Change* (London, 1973)].
- J. Chadwick, *El mundo micénico* (Madrid: Alianza Editorial, col. 'Alianza Universidad' 204, 1977) [original title: *The Mycenaean World* (Cambridge, 1976)].

- R. P. Stockwell, *Fundamentos de teoría sintáctica* (Madrid: Gredos, col. 'Biblioteca Románica Hispánica. II, Estudios y Ensayos' 304, 1980) [original title: *Foundations of Syntactic Theory* (New Jersey, 1977)].
- Th. Bynon, *Lingüística histórica* (Madrid: Gredos, col. 'Biblioteca Románica Hispánica. II, Estudios y Ensayos' 314, 1981) [original title: *Historical Linguistics* (Cambridge, 1977)].
- E. Vermeule, *La muerte en la poesía y en el arte de Grecia* (Mexico: Fondo de Cultura Económica, 1984) [original title: *Aspects of Death in Early Greek Art and Poetry* (Berkeley, 1979)].
- P. Faure, *La vida cotidiana en la Creta minoica.* Translation review (Barcelona: Argos Vergara, 1984) [original title: *La vie quotidienne en Crète au temps de Minos* (Paris, 1973)].
- R. Jakobson, *Obras Selectas* I. 40 articles translated by J. L. Melena (those in English, French, and Italian), G. Costas (those in German), and V. Díez (those in Russian) (Madrid: Gredos, 1988).
- E. Vermeule, *Grecia en la Edad del Bronce.* Segunda edición. Translation review (Mexico: Fondo de Cultura Económica, 1990) [original title: *Greece in the Bronze Age* (Chicago, 1964)].
- Z. Zateli, *Y vuelven con el crepúsculo* (Madrid 1996) [original title: *Και με το φως του λύκου επανέρχονται* (Athens, 1993)].

Other Translations and Translation Reviews

- D. Schmandt-Besserat, "El primer antecedente de la escritura," *Investigación y Ciencia* [original: *Scientific American*] 23 (agosto 1978): 6-17.
- Hung-hsiang Chou, "La osteomancia china," *Investigación y Ciencia* 33 (junio 1979): 72–81.
- W. A. Fairservis, "La escritura de la civilización del Valle del Indo," *Investigación y Ciencia* 80 (mayo 1983): 30–45.
- J. Friberg, "Números y medidas en los primeros documentos escritos," *Investigación y Ciencia* 91 (abril 1984): 68–77.
- "Επίλογος,» in *Σύγχρονη ισπανική ποίηση*, ed. H. Ματθαίου (Athens, 1989).
- Review of translation into Modern Greek of Miguel de Cervantes, *Η τσιγγανόπουλα και Η δύναμη του αίματος*, translated by H. Ματθαίου (Αθήνα 1989) [original titles: *La gitanilla y La fuerza de la sangre*].
- Review of all the translations of Modern Greek into Spanish published in Greece in 1988, 1989, and 1990.

- Collaboration with J. Mastoraki to translate into Modern Greek *Soneto IV* of Paravicino dedicated to El Greco.
- T. Taylor, "El caldero de Gundestrup," *Investigación y Ciencia* 188 (mayo 1992): 68–74.
- Translation of some articles included in *El Mundo Micénico. Cinco siglos de la primera civilización europea 1600–1100 a. C.*, Madrid 1991, and general review of book's translation. Translation of the handout and texts of the Exhibition with the same title.
- K. Demakopoulou, "Historia y arqueología del fenómeno cultural micénico," in *Actas del Ciclo 'La presencia micénica en el Mediterráneo: aspectos generales y regionales'* [forthcoming].
- Sp. Iakovidis, "Grecia y el Mediterráneo en la Edad del Bronce Reciente," in *Actas del Ciclo 'La presencia micénica en el Mediterráneo: aspectos generales y regionales'* [forthcoming].

Abbreviations

CoMIK	J. Chadwick, L. Godart, J. T. Killen, J.-P. Olivier, A. Sacconi, and I. A. Sakellarakis, *Corpus of Mycenaean Inscriptions from Knossos*, 4 vols. (Cambridge-Rome, 1986–1998).
DMic.	F. Aura Jorro, *Diccionario Griego-Español*. Anejos I–II: *Diccionario micénico*, 2 vols. (Madrid, 1985, 1993; repr. 1999).
DMic.Supl.	F. Aura Jorro, A. Bernabé, E. R. Luján, J. Piquero, and C. Varias García, *Diccionario Griego-Español*. Anejo VII: *Suplemento al Diccionario Micénico* (Madrid, 2020).
Docs²	M. Ventris and J. Chadwick, *Documents in Mycenaean Greek*, 2nd edition (Cambridge, 1973).
Documents	M. Ventris and J. Chadwick, *Documents in Mycenaean Greek* (Cambridge, 1956).
EDG	R. S. P. Beekes, *Etymological Dictionary of Greek*, Leiden Indo-European Dictionary Series 10 (Leiden, 2010).
KT⁶	J. L. Melena, in collaboration with R. J. Firth, *The Knossos Tablets. Sixth Edition. A Transliteration* (Philadelphia, 2019).
PTT³	J. L. Melena, with the collaboration of R. J. Firth, *The Pylos Tablets. Third Edition in Transliteration* (Vitoria-Gasteiz, 2021).

TA-U-RO-QO-RO

𐂚𐀸†𐍙†

1

Philologia cum Archeologia Procedit

Reflexiones en torno a la demografía y composición de la sociedad micénica

Francisco Aura Jorro

Universidad de Alicante

francisco.aura@ua.es

A José Luis Melena,
maestro y, sobre todo, amigo

Abstract

The paper is an example of an interdisciplinary approach to the ethnic composition of Mycenaean society, based on the analyses of personal names and foreign ethnic adjectives attested on the tablets (particularly, the feminine ethnic adjectives of the Pylian series Aa, Ab, and Ad).

Palabras clave

micénico, sociedad, etnia

Keywords

Mycenaean, society, ethnic group

Introducción

Hace ya más de veinticinco años que en una tarde de mayo afirmaba Chadwick (1999:36):

> The complete Linear B scholar must be not just an epigraphist, not just a linguist, not just an economic historian and archaeologist; ideally he or she (for I must pay tribute to the achievements of the ladies among us) must be all these things simultaneously.

En esencia, Chadwick no hacía otra cosa que constatar una evidencia: la necesidad del enfoque interdisciplinar para desentrañar el contenido de unos textos como los micénicos, documentos burocráticos de gran simplicidad, cuyo texto, rígido y aséptico (listas, inventarios, registros, y cálculos), no es más que una ventana bien estrecha que reduce, a veces hasta sus últimos límites, la visión cabal de ese mundo.

Efectivamente, el análisis textual de los documentos, con ser imprescindible, no es suficiente para su compresión y es necesario recurrir a otras disciplinas y a las comparaciones que puedan establecerse entre los datos documentales procedentes de otros archivos de territorios, más o menos, vecinos y contemporáneos, básicamente, de Mesopotamia y Egipto (cf. Melena 1984), o correspondientes a épocas posteriores de la historia de Grecia.[1] Incluso será posible iluminar hechos no documentados del mundo micénico, como la destrucción por fuego de los palacios y la desaparición de sus estados, mediante la comparación con otros mucho más alejados en el espacio y el tiempo.[2]

No debemos insistir más; queda clara la importancia de la complementariedad de la filología con la arqueología y las disciplinas asociadas. Nos ocuparemos de un ejemplo de esta complementariedad: el caso de la composición étnica del mundo micénico. Para ello puede ser interesante comenzar con una cuestión general: de los datos arqueométricos obtenidos en diferentes enterramientos resulta que, en general, la esperanza de vida, cuando menos de la elite micénica continental, debió estar en torno a los 40 años para los hombres y entre 32.6 y 31 para las mujeres (I. Morris 2006:81, basado en Bisel y Angel 1985), indicando sus marcadores osteológicos[3] y dentales, en relación con los de individuos de épocas anteriores, el consumo de una dieta más rica en proteínas y grasas que en hidratos de carbono.[4] Esta dieta, probable objeto de una preparación más elaborada, evidencia la realidad de una relación estrecha entre cocina y estatus. Parece que el alimento y su preparación se erigen como actores y sostén

---

[1] Es el caso, por ejemplo, de Firth (1994–1995), quien, para su estimación de la población de Creta en el MR IIIA/B, recurre a la comparación y extrapolación de los datos obtenidos de una serie de variables, correspondientes a épocas diferentes de la isla.

[2] Este podría ser el caso de la interpretación de la "cerámica bárbara," cuya aparición en niveles del HR IIIC se aduce como prueba de una invasión, desde los Balcanes o Tracia, con la que habría llegado a Grecia o, por el contrario, sería el resultado de la manufactura que siguió a la destrucción del sistema industrial micénico.

[3] Bisel y Angel (1985) aplican la osteología al estudio de la dieta y su influencia en la salud, en época micénica. Por su parte, e igualmente basado en la osteología, Halstead (1977) apunta a un incremento de la esperanza de vida coincidente con la época micénica.

[4] Sobre la comparación de datos de diferentes disciplinas véase la ejemplificación que de ello hacen Manolisi *et al.* (2001), de la que resulta que los individuos de más estatus eran más altos, con menos desgaste dental y caries, lo que indicaría una dieta más rica en proteínas y grasas que en hidratos de carbono.

de diferencias claras entre las elites y la población en general, diferencias que se interrumpen, solamente, con la participación comunitaria de unos y otros en banquetes rituales o *de estado*, en los que la elite asocia en sus celebraciones a integrantes del resto de la sociedad micénica con la finalidad "de reforzar la cohesión de la comunidad participante" (García Soler 2001). Derivaban de ello la consolidación del poder de las elites, así como el refuerzo y legitimación de las relaciones jerárquicas de esa sociedad, en un contexto de hermandad (Nikoloudis 2001).

Consideramos que en un trabajo de estas características está de más hacer referencia a la estructura de la sociedad micénica que, a buen seguro, no aportaría nada a lo ya dicho por otros con mayor fundamento. Es este un asunto del que prácticamente desde el comienzo de la Micenología se han ocupado con brillantez una nutrida nómina de investigadores, por lo que su relación, aquí y ahora, es innecesaria; baste como muestra la lista de referencias bibliográficas sobre el tema que presenta Shelmerdine (2008). En cambio puede resultar interesante examinar el estado de la cuestión sobre la composición étnica.

La Composición Étnica

El análisis de dos grupos léxicos concretos que aparecen en la documentación en lineal B, ciertos étnicos, en función propia[5] o de antropónimo (*onomastics*, tal como los entiende Nikoloudis 2008:49), y un número considerable de antropónimos masculinos de origen no griego, delatan la presencia en los reinos micénicos de población foránea, de origen anatolio y levantino, según indican los primeros;[6] autóctona, a juzgar por los segundos, que será lógicamente *minoica*, en el caso de Cnoso.[7]

Ambos grupos son un indicador más de las relaciones de todo tipo que mantuvieron los micénicos a lo largo de su historia, tanto entre sí como con otras áreas y pueblos de su entorno. Prueba de ello es, en lo histórico-arqueológico, la asunción de modelos administrativos o la adopción de técnicas productivas ajenas, así como la realidad de un comercio de intercambio que se traduce en la adquisición de materias primas, utillaje u objetos de diferente naturaleza. Este

---

[5] Previene Nikoloudis (2008:46) contra la calificación de "étnicos," a los que prefiere designar como "adjetivos toponímicos," puesto que a veces solo se refieren al origen geográfico de grupos e individuos, tal como son identificados por los administradores micénicos.

[6] Si bien aparecen algunos micénicos en territorios ajenos, como *ra-ke-da-mi-ni-jo* ('Lacedemonio') en Tebas o *ko-ro-ku-ra-i-jo* ('Corcirense') en Pilo, cuyo significado primario, como el del resto de los antropónimos de este tipo, es señalar su *etnicidad* (Efkleidou 2004:66).

[7] Antropónimos minoicos aparecen también en menor medida en el continente. Para un listado completo de antropónimos y teónimos masculinos y femeninos cnosios, así como de su posible origen griego o no griego, véase Landenius-Enegren (2008:97–190).

es el caso, por ejemplo, de ciertos elementos, obviamente importados, como los sellos cilíndricos orientales encontrados en Cnoso o en Tebas, que, sea cual fuere la razón de su origen o finalidad, hacen patente la realidad de estos contactos, establecidos de manera directa o indirecta.

En cuanto a los étnicos y antropónimos mencionados, su aparición en los textos indica dos hechos: uno, que los intercambios alcanzan también a las personas, sin prejuzgar, por el momento, cómo o cuándo se han realizado o a qué se debieron; y dos, una realidad étnica híbrida que tal vez hubiera podido abocar a una sociedad permeable si su historia no se hubiera interrumpido a finales del HR IIIB2. En paralelo, el análisis de esas menciones documentales ayudan al conocimiento del nivel social de estos individuos.

Respecto del reparto de los antropónimos griegos y no griegos, la norma general, tanto para el continente, como para Creta, es que en las capas superiores de la sociedad son mayoría absoluta los de origen griego sobre los no griegos. En cambio, el panorama varía en las capas inferiores, según se trate de una u otra localización. En el caso de Creta, los estudios de Baumbach (1983, 1987, 1992), Firth (1994–1995), Ilievski (1992) o Varias (1998, 1998–1999) ponen de relieve la superioridad numérica de la población con nombre de origen no griego sobre la portadora de nombres griegos, en una proporción aproximada de 70% / 30%, datos que se invierten en el continente.

La superioridad numérica de los antropónimos de origen no griego sobre los griegos en las capas inferiores de la población cnosia alentó la hipótesis de que, durante la dominación micénica de la isla, una parte considerable de esa población sería de origen minoico, lo que, en más de una ocasión, hizo suponer que esta civilización mantuvo su identidad cultural en la Creta del período micénico.

Sin valorar esa hipótesis en su conjunto, sí puede decirse que es esta una idea poliédrica que ha confirmado a lo largo de los años la vigencia de algunas de sus facetas, entre las que destaca, por ejemplo, la percepción de diferencias entre los sistemas administrativos de los estados micénicos continentales y el de Cnoso.

En tablillas cnosias y continentales aparece un grupo minoritario de étnicos, en función de antropónimo,[8] que, como los étnicos femeninos, en función propia, que mencionaremos a continuación, confirma la relación de los micénicos con Egipto, Anatolia, y Chipre. Entre los primeros—muy pocos en comparación

---

[8]   En Pilo, de los 36 que registra Efkleidou (2002–2003:277), son 23 los que reconoce como foráneos. Aparece en las tablillas algún teónimo foráneo: *a-si-wi-ja po-ti-ni-ja* (*Ἀσϝία, Ἀσία / *Ἀσϝιος, hom. Ἄσιος), cuyo culto, probablemente, fue introducido por las mujeres anatolias (S.P. Morris 2001:423). El masculino *a-si-wi-jo* es utilizado como antropónimo en Cnoso, Pilo y Micenas.

con los designados por étnicos en función propia[9]—figuran los muy conocidos *a₃-ku-pi-ti-jo* (Αἰγύπτιος), 'Egipcio'; *mi-sa-ra-jo* (*Μισραῖος) 'Egipcio' (cf. top. Miṣṛ 'Egipto'); *a-ra-si-jo* (*'Αλάσσιος) 'Chipriota' (cf. top. Ἄλασσα, *Alašia*, 'Chipre'); *ku-pi-ri-jo* (Κύπριος) 'Chipriota'; *ki-e-u* (*Χιηεύς) 'Quiota' (cf. Χῖος); *mi-ra-ti-jo* (Μιλάτιος, Μιλήσιος) 'Milesio' (cf. top. Μίλατος); *ra-mi-ni-jo* 'Lemnio' (cf. Λῆμνος); *ru-wa-ni-jo* 'Luvita' (Widmer 2006) o *si-mi-te-u* (Σμινθεύς) 'Esminteo' (cf. top. Σμίνθη en la Tróade; Godart y Sacconi 1999:541).

En cuanto a los étnicos en función propia, en Pilo destaca el grupo de los femeninos foráneos que, junto a autóctonos y nombres de oficio, aparecen en las series Aa, Ab y Ad, referidos a mujeres relacionadas con la manufactura textil de la lana y el lino.[10] Son de sobra conocidos *a-*64-ja*, *ki-ni-di-ja*, *ki-si-wi-ja*, *mi-ra-ti-ja*, *ra-mi-ni-ja* o *ze-pu₂-ra₃*,[11] cuyo número subraya la importancia de las relaciones de Pilo con Asia Menor.

Lo primero que cabe preguntarse respecto de los étnicos, tanto en función propia como en la de antropónimos, es su significado, de qué manera han llegado y, consiguientemente, qué lugar ocupan en el entramado social los así designados.

Respecto de la primera cuestión, parece claro, que unos y otros tienen la función distintiva de identificar a sus portadores como foráneos. Cuestión diferente será la de su valoración social; mayor, sin duda, para las menciones individuales (étnicos en función de antropónimo) que para las colectivas (étnicos en sentido propio) (Efkleidou 2002–2003:264ff.).

Es posible que esa diferencia entrañe cuestiones de género relacionadas con lo laboral, dado que el uso de étnicos en función de antropónimo es mayoritariamente masculino y atiende a diversidad de oficios, puesto que este personal aparece, en igualdad de condiciones, en las mismas áreas de actividad que los autóctonos. Es más, en una ocasión uno de estos, *ku-te-re-u* 'Citereo', es registrado como miembro de la *ke-ro-si-ja* de *a-pi-qo-to* (PY An 261.6), lo que significa que estos foráneos podían llegar a ocupar puestos superiores del organigrama laboral. De cualquier manera, a juzgar por la escasez de étnicos usados como antropónimos que se detectan entre los funcionarios registrados por su nombre,[12] es muy

---

[9] De los 615 étnicos anotados, solo 36 lo son en función de antropónimo que corresponden a 46 hombres. De estos, 23 son foráneos, en su mayoría de Asia Menor y Chipre.

[10] Para una descripción completa de los términos, tanto étnicos como nombres de oficio, que afectan a las mujeres en estas series pilias, véanse Chadwick (1988) y Olsen (2014:60–133). Killen (2001:172) ha calculado su número en unas 750 (Aa, Ab); en tanto que serían unas mil las adscritas a esta manufactura en Cnoso (serie Ak).

[11] '(Mujeres) de ¿Asia? (¿Lidia?: cf. Chadwick 1988, 63s.), Cnido, Quíos, Mileto, Lemnos o Halicarnaso', respectivamente.

[12] Tan solo dos, de entre 84, un *e-qe-ta*, *pe-re-u-ro-ni-jo* (cf. top. *pe-re-u-ro-na-de*), y un *ko-re-te*, *te-po-se-u* (cf. **ti-nwa-to*) (Efkleidou 2002–2003:286).

improbable que los foráneos hayan accedido a responsabilidades superiores, administrativas o no, reservadas a la elite, una de cuyas notas distintivas es el uso de patronímicos, lo que sugiere un estatus basado en la genealogía.[13]

De manera contraria, los grupos (étnicos en función propia) serán exclusivos de mujeres y referidos en todos los casos a la manufactura textil. Tritsch (1958) les negaba a los grupos mencionados de mujeres anotadas en las series pilias Aa, Ab y Ad la consideración de esclavas y las suponía *refugiadas* que, en época de riesgo bélico, habrían encontrado protección en Pilo. Siempre según Tritsch, tales mujeres desempeñarían oficios propios de hombres; un trabajo remunerado con asignaciones alimentarias en contraprestación y por parte de palacio. Era esta una hipótesis que, al margen de otras consideraciones (como por ejemplo, ¿dónde estaban los hombres que también debían haber huido?), no tenía en cuenta la aparición de apelativos o la designación conjunta de grupos de mujeres por étnicos ajenos al mundo micénico, juntamente con otros pilios.

Por el contrario, Chadwick (1988:91–92), las consideraba esclavas de allende las fronteras, bajo la autoridad de supervisores masculinos y con un estatus de dependencia servil (*menial*). Procedentes de guerras o razias, habrían sido trasladadas a Pilo, una vez compradas en sus lugares de origen o en mercados, de manera que *mi-ra-ti-ja* puede significar 'mujeres de Mileto' o 'mujeres (compradas) en (el mercado de) Mileto'. Presenta como refuerzo de su hipótesis el apelativo *ra-wi-ja-ja* ('cautivas') en Aa 807, Ab 586, Ad 686.[14]

Una opinión similar es defendida por Efkleidou (2002–2003:285n38), para quien los grupos de mujeres registrados en Aa y Ab podrían haber sido esclavas, ya que reúnen la mayoría de los condicionantes de este grupo social: carecen de identidad personal respecto de palacio, del que dependen para su manutención; la ausencia de hombres debe entenderse como que son objeto de uniones irregulares y no de relaciones familiares estables y reconocidas (cf. Ad 684); no tienen libertad para disponer de sí mismas, etc.[15] En cuanto a su origen, apunta, asimismo, al argumento de los cambios y las alteraciones regionales. Si bien no hay datos fehacientes de lo que pudo ocurrir, sí se sabe que a finales del s. XIV a. C. (transición entre el HR IIIA / IIIB) Citera, nexo entre Creta y el Continente, pierde dicho papel y sufre un despoblamiento (Broodbank, Kiriatzi,

---

[13] No obstante, en PY Un 443 aparece *ku-pi-ri-jo* ('Chipriota'), identificado por Killen (1995:218) como un *collector*, es decir, un miembro de la elite. Tanto este como el que aparece en la serie Fh de Cnoso pueden llevar este nombre porque ellos o sus padres o abuelos, miembros de la elite, habrían tenido una relevancia especial en el comercio con Chipre.

[14] El hecho de que no sean descritas específicamente como *do-e-ra* es irrelevante para Chadwick (1988:90), puesto que, como afirma, quienquiera que manejara esas tablillas conocería su estatus. Secundariamente, KN B 822 y 988 aseguran la práctica de la adquisición de esclavos en el mundo micénico. Véase *contra* Efkleidou 2002–2003:285.

[15] Para los criterios indicativos de 'esclavitud' véase Efkleidou 2004:208ff.

y Rutter 2005). En estas circunstancias, es posible que habitantes de la isla, de manera global o gradual, se trasladaran a Creta o/y el continente. Una vez allí, mantuvieron su identificación a lo largo del tiempo. Si ello fuera así, no podría pensarse que su dependencia absoluta de palacio, que las convierte en clase servil o incluso esclava, es una singularidad de las foráneas, ya que esta situación sería compartida con la de las autóctonas, que, en las mismas circunstancias, se habrían visto abocadas a aceptarla por causas económicas, administrativas o sociales (Efkleidou 2002–2003:285n38). En general, pues, para Efkleidou no hay diferencias de estatus entre autóctonos y foráneos, en tanto que unos y otros pertenecen por igual a un mismo grupo laboral o se incardinan en una situación socioeconómica similar. Cuestión distinta, como ya se ha indicado, es la diferencia de estatus a favor de los foráneos registrados de manera individual, respecto de los que los son de manera colectiva.

Ergin (2007), por su parte, tras establecer comparaciones con situaciones mesopotámicas anteriores, relaciona el origen de estas mujeres anatolias con el conflicto entre el imperio hitita y Aḫḫijawa, cuyo *dossier* comenta.[16] Al hacerlo, introduce la variable *genealógica*, que ya había apuntado Carlier (1983:17), cuando sugería que estas mujeres serían la generación actual, descendiente de *mujeres extranjeras*, cuyo origen se remontaría al pasado. Es decir (volviendo a Ergin), que las mujeres anotadas en las series pilias Aa, Ab y Ad serían descendientes de quienes llegaron a Pilo como consecuencia del citado conflicto, sucedido durante los reinados de Arnuwanda I, Muršili II y Hattušili III que corresponden, respectivamente, a los períodos 1420–1400 a. C., 1321–1295 a. C. y 1267–1237 a. C. Por tanto, de ser esto así, es imposible que los cautivos mencionados en los textos hititas fueran los trabajadores que anotan las tablillas pilias que, como se sabe, corresponden a la fracción del último año de vida del palacio (HR IIIB2, entre 1200 y 1190 a. C.). En este sentido y como indica Ergin (2007:276), es posible que el reinado de Hattušili III sea una excepción, de manera que algunas de las mujeres registradas en las tablillas podrían haber sido las nietas o biznietas de quienes llegaron durante ese reinado, si bien ni los documentos ni la arqueología (enterramientos, botín de guerra, cambios en la cultura material, etc.) aportan pruebas de la realidad de lo sugerido. Por otra parte, recuerda que una posibilidad alternativa habría sido (como ya apuntaba Chadwick) su adquisición como esclavos en mercados o lugares de contacto entre hititas y micénicos; por ejemplo, Mileto o Ura.

Finalmente, Nikoloudis (2008), respecto de las relaciones de los micénicos con Anatolia, interpreta la *Carta de Tawagalawa* como una prueba del interés de

---

[16] Se trata de: *El desafuero de Madduwatta* (*CTH* 147), *Hazañas de Muršili II en un decenio* (*CTH* 61.1); *La Carta de Tawagalawa* (*CTH* 181); *La Carta de Millawata* (*CTH* 182). Sobre la cuestión de Aḫḫijawa véase el estado de la cuestión de Bernabé (1986) y Bernabé and Álvarez Pedrosa (2004, esp. 295–310).

los pilios por las tierras de Luwia, no solo en cuanto al acopio de materias primas, sino también de personal para sus manufacturas textiles e, incluso, colonos para la nueva provincia (la 'Tramontana'), incorporada al reino a comienzos del s. XIII (Davis y Bennet 1999:115). Es en este sentido como interpreta *wo-ro-ki-jo-ne-jo ka-ma* de PY Un 718, así como explica la etimología de *sa-ra-pe-da*,[17] que sería un enclave habitado por estos colonos. Prueba de su *foraneidad* serían ciertos rasgos lingüísticos presentes en PY Un 718 (*po-se-da-o-ni*, dativo en *-i*, en vez del usual en *-e*), así como en las tablillas relacionadas PY Er 312 y 880 (*pe-ma*, en lugar de *pe-mo*), indicios de un dialecto diferente, ya del escriba, ya de la gente que tiene que ver con la información registrada (Palaima 2002). En cuanto a su estatus, las cantidades de alimento aportadas para un banquete ritual (cf. PY Un 718) y su probable carácter foráneo los sitúa en último lugar, respecto de *e-ke-ra₂-wo*, el *da-mo* y el *ra-wa-ke-ta*, tanto en la tablilla como en el orden social.

Conclusión

En cuanto al componente étnico, la sociedad micénica, en términos generales, se revela como híbrida, integrada, en la que cohabitan micénicos locales, micénicos de otros estados y gentes en principio ajenas étnicamente a ese mundo, llegadas mayoritariamente de Anatolia, no sabemos cuándo (es muy posible que los consignados en las tablillas correspondan a una segunda o tercera generación) y que se han integrado en la estructura social del reino. En ese caso, el étnico ya no es más que una mera referencia identificativa. Una situación que puede compararse, salvando anacronismos de magnitudes y circunstancias sociales diferentes, con lo que, desde hace relativamente poco tiempo, ocurre con los movimientos migratorios en dirección a Europa (desde África, el Oriente Medio o, incluso, Asia) o a USA, respecto de sus vecinos al sur del río Grande.

Su origen está determinado por dos causas posibles: o fueron objeto de botín en *razias* o guerras, o abandonaron sus patrias como consecuencia de alteraciones (sociales, políticas, agresiones, o incluso desastres naturales) o, incluso, del enfrentamiento entre los hititas y Aḫḫijawa. Sea lo que fuere, el resultado es que en algún momento, entre los siglos XV y XIV a. C., se produce un aporte extraordinario de personal como mano de obra en la Grecia continental, más concretamente en Pilo, donde se emplea en especial en la manufactura textil. Es evidente que esta mano de obra, sea o no esclava, formó parte de las clases inferiores y que, a juzgar por la documentación de que disponemos, no se promocionó socialmente a lo largo de su historia. No sabemos si una hipotética

---

[17] Nikoloudis (2008:52) relaciona *sa-ra-pe-da* con el adverbio hitita *šará* 'arriba, hacia arriba' y el nombre *pe-da-* 'lugar, punto, ubicación': 'tierras/llanuras altas'; podría ser un lugar próximo al Aigaleon en la 'Provincia Tramontana'.

prolongación de la vida de los estados micénicos, más allá del HR IIIB2, habría difuminado, primero, y eliminado, al final, esta situación, algo que en nuestros días se está viendo en USA respecto a la población afroamericana o, por el contrario, se habría mantenido el estancamiento como sucede, también hoy, en los *guetos* marginales de las grandes ciudades europeas, residencia de población extracomunitaria.

La manera de ser incluidos en los registros palaciales nos da una idea respecto de su estatus. A los consignados con étnicos en función de antropónimos les corresponde un estatus superior de los registrados *por grupos* (étnicos en función propia).

Bibliografía

Baumbach, L. 1983. "An Examination of the Personal Names in the Knossos Tablets as Evidence for the Social Structure of Crete in the Late Minoan II Period." In *Minoan Society: Proceedings of the Cambridge Colloquium 1981*, ed. O. Kryszkowska and L. Nixon, 3–10. Bristol.

———. 1987. "Names of Shepherds at Knossos." *Acta Classica* 30:5–10.

———. 1992. "The People of Knossos: Further Thoughts on Some of the Personal Names." In Olivier 1992:57–63.

Bennet, J., and J. Driessen, eds. 1998–1999. *A-NA-QO-TA. Studies Presented to J. T. Killen. Minos* 33–34. Salamanca.

Bernabé, A. 1986. "Hititas y aqueos: Aspectos recientes de una vieja polémica." *Estudios Clásicos* 90:123–137.

Bernabé, A., and J. A. Álvarez Pedrosa, eds. 2004. *Historia y leyes de los hititas: Textos del Reino Medio y del Imperio Nuevo.* Madrid.

Bisel, S. C., and J. L. Angel. 1985. "Health and Nutrition in Mycenaean Greece." In *Contributions to Aegean Archaeology: Studies in Honor of William A. McDonald*, ed. N. C. Wilkie, and W. D. E. Coulson, 197–209. Minneapolis.

Broodbank, C., E. Kiriatzi, and J. Rutter. 2005. "From Pharaoh's Feet to the Slave-Women of Pylos? The History and Cultural Dynamics of Kythera in the Third Palace Period." In *Autochthon. Papers Presented to O. T. P. K. Dickinson on the Occasion of His Retirement*, ed. A. Dakouri-Hild and S. Sherratt, 70–96. Oxford.

Carlier, P. 1983. "La femme dans la société mycénienne d'après les archives en linéaire B." In *La femme dans les sociétés antiques: actes des colloques de Strasbourg (mai 1980 et mars 1981)*, ed. E. Lévy, 9–32. Strasbourg.

Chadwick, J. 1988. "The Women of Pylos." In *Texts, Tablets, and Scribes. Studies in Mycenaean Epigraphy and Economy Offered to Emmett L. Bennett, Jr.*, ed. J.-P. Olivier and T. G. Palaima, 43–95. Suplementos a *Minos* 10. Salamanca.

———. 1999. "Linear B: Past, Present, and Future." In *Floreant Studia Mycenaea. Akten des X. Internationalen Mykenologischen Colloquiums in Salzburg vom 1.-5. Mai 1995*, ed. S. Deger-Jalkotzy, S. Hiller, and O. Panagl, 29–38. Vienna.

Davis, J. L., and J. Bennet. 1999. "Making Mycenaeans: Warfare, Territorial Expansion and Representations of the Other in the Pylian Kingdom." In *Polemos: Le contexte guerrier en Égée à l'Âge du Bronze. Actes de la 7e Rencontre égéenne internationale. Université de Liège, 14-17 avril 1998*, ed. R. Laffineur, 105–120. *Aegaeum* 19. Liège.

Efkleidou, K. 2002-2003. "The Status of 'Outsiders' within Mycenaean Pylos: Issues of Ethnic Identity, Incorporation, and Marginality." *Minos* 37–38: 269–291.

———. 2004. "*Slavery and Dependent Personnel in the Linear B Archives of Mainland Greece.*" PhD diss., University of Cincinnati.

Ergin, G. 2007. "Anatolian Women in Linear B Texts: A General Review of the Evidence." In *Vita. Festschrift in Honor of Belkıs Dinçol and Ali Dinçol*, ed. M. Alparslan, M. Doğan-Alparslan, and H. Peker, 269–283. Istanbul.

Firth, R. J. 1994-1995. "Estimating the Population on Crete during LMIIIA/B." *Minos* 29–30:33–55.

García Soler, M. J. 2001. *El arte de comer en la antigua Grecia*. Madrid.

Godart, L., and A. Sacconi. 1999. "La géographie des États mycéniens." *Comptes rendus. Académie des inscriptions et belles-lettres* 143:527–546.

Halstead, P. 1977. "The Bronze Age Demography of Crete and Greece. A Note." *The Annual of the British School at Athens* 72:107–111.

Ilievski, P. H. 1992. "Observations on the Personal Names from the Knossos D Tablets." In Olivier 1992:321–349.

Killen, J. T. 1995. "Some Further Thoughts on 'Collectors'." In *Politeia: Society and State in the Aegean Bronze Age. Proceedings of the 5th International Aegean Conference, University of Heidelberg, Archäologisches Institut, 10-13 April 1994*, ed. R. Laffineur, and W.-D. Niemeier, 213–226. *Aegaeum* 12. Liège.

Landenius Enegren, H. 2008. *The People of Knossos: Prosopographical Studies in the Knossos Linear B Archives*. Uppsala.

Manolisi, S. K., A. A. Neroutsos, E. Andreapoulou-Magou, A. Chasiakou, and G. I. Panagiaris. 2001. "Comparative Study of Cultural Data of Four Mycenaean Locations Using Archaeometric Methods." In *Archaeometry Issues in Greek Prehistory and Antiquity*, ed. Y. Bassiakos, E. Aloupi, and Y. Facorellis, 111–124. Athens.

Melena, J. L. 1984. *Ex Oriente Lux: La aportación de las filologías del Oriente Próximo y Medio antiguo a la comprensión de los primeros textos europeos*. Vitoria.

Morris, S. P. 2001. "Potnia Aswiya: Anatolian Contributions to Greek Religion." In *Potnia: Deities and Religion in the Aegean Bronze Age. Proceedings of the 8th*

International Aegean Conference, Göteborg, 12-15 April 2000, ed. R. Laffineur and R. Hägg, 423–434. *Aegaeum 22*. Liège.

Morris, I. 2006. "The Collapse and Regeneration of Complex Society in Greece, 1500–500 BC." In *After Collapse: The Regeneration of Complex Societies*, ed. G. M. Schwartz and J. J. Nichols, 72–84. Tucson.

Nikoloudis, S. 2001. "Animal Sacrifice in the Mycenaean World." *Journal of Prehistoric Religion* 15:11–31.

———. 2008. "Multiculturalism in the Mycenaean World." In *Anatolian Interfaces: Hittites, Greeks, and Their Neighbours. Proceedings of an International Conference on Cross-cultural Interaction, September 17-19, 2004, Emory University, Atlanta, GA*, ed. B. J. Collins, M. R. Bachvarova, and I. Rutherford, 45–56. Oxford.

Olivier, J.-P., ed. 1992. *Mykenaïka. Actes du IXᵉ Colloque international sur les textes mycéniens et égéens organisé par le Centre de l'Antiquité Grecque et Romaine de la Fondation Hellénique des Recherches Scientifiques et l'École française d'Athènes (Athènes, 2-6 octobre 1990)*. Athens.

Olsen, B. A. 2014. *Women in Mycenaean Greece: The Linear B Tablets from Pylos and Knossos*. London.

Palaima, T. G. 2002. "Special vs. Normal Mycenaean: Hand 24 and Writing in the Service of King?" In Bennet and Driessen 1998–1999:205–221.

Shelmerdine, C. 2008. "Mycenaean Society." In *A Companion to Linear B: Mycenaean Greek Texts and Their World*, vol. 1, ed. Y. Duhoux and A. Morpurgo Davies, 115–158. Bibliothèque des Cahiers de Linguistique Louvain 120. Louvain-la-Neuve.

Tritsch, F. J. 1958. "The Women of Pylos." In *Minoica. Festschrift zum 80. Geburtstag von Johannes Sundwall*, ed. E. Grumach, 406–445. Berlin.

Varias, C. 1998. "Antroponimia micénica en las tablillas de la serie B de Cnoso y en Micenas." *Bulletin de Correspondance Hellénique* 122:440–443.

———. 1998-1999. "The Personal Names from the Knossos B-Tablets and from the Mycenae Tablets." In Bennet and Driessen 1998–1999:349–370.

Widmer, P. 2006. "Mykenisch *ru-wa-ni-jo* 'Luwier'." *Kadmos* 45:82–84.

2

ἐν y ἐνί en micénico

ALBERTO BERNABÉ

Universidad Complutense de Madrid

albernab@ucm.es

Abstract

Analysis of /en/ and /eni/ in Mycenaean (adverb, preposition, first element of a nominal compound, verbal adjective, preverb, and first element of an adverbial compound). Conclusions: (1) Spelling: /en/ as an adverb is written with the preceding word, to avoid a monosyllable; as a preposition or a first element of a compound it is written e- before a vowel or a consonant, but e-nV- before a vowel. (2) Distribution: /en/ and /eni/ are found as adverbs, in the other forms /en/ is the only possible option. (3) Formations: (a) /en/ occurs in nominal compounds of several types: (a₁) compounds with a noun, without a derivational suffix or with *-(a)yo-; (a₂) complex compounds, used as first element of a new compound; (a₃) compounds with a verbal root and a *-ēu- suffix. (b) /en/ as the first component of verbal adjectives in *-to-. (c) There are two verbal compounds with /en/. (d) There is a compound with /en/ as an adverb and another with /eni/.

Palabras clave
vocabulario micénico, preposiciones, compuestos con /en/

Keywords
Mycenaean vocabulary, prepositions, compounds with /en/

1. Propósito

El propósito de este trabajo es reunir el dosier micénico de ἐν(ί) como adverbio, como preposición, como primer elemento de un compuesto nominal o de un adjetivo verbal,[1] como preverbio, y como primer elemento de un adverbio compuesto.[2]

2. Usos como adverbio

2.1 ἐν adverbio

La secuencia *mi-to-we-sa-e* en KN Sd 4404.b se interpreta como /*miltowessa en*/ 'pintado de bermellón por dentro', referido a CUR en .a (cf. Lejeune 1958a:210; Bernabé 2016:534–536). El escriba habría escrito *mi-to-we-sa-e* sin separador para no dejar exento el monosílabo. Da la impresión de que vio la caja del carro por el interior y anotó el color de la parte interna y el logograma CUR, pero se dio cuenta de que por fuera estaba pintado de color púrpura y de que tenía ruedas y añadió *po-ni-ki-ja* BIG 1 en el canto de la tablilla.

2.2 ἔνι adverbio

En varias tablillas, como KN L 593.B, aparece la forma *e-ni-qe*,[3] interpretada por Meriggi (1955:90), Ruijgh (1967:327), y Ventris y Chadwick (*Docs*², 487, 543) como adverbio más la enclítica -*qe*: /*eni kʷe*/ 'y dentro'. Pero Killen (Killen y Olivier 1968:120 y Killen 2015:143ss., 235ss.) cree que es un antropónimo femenino. La cuestión no está resuelta (cf. Landenius Enegren 2008:64).

3. Usos como preposición con dativo

ἐν como preposición con dativo puede aparecer en PY Ub 1315.2 en la secuencia *a-ni-ja-e-e-ro-pa-jo-qe-ṛọ-ṣạ,* interpretada por Bernabé y Luján (2008:339), Bernabé (2011:27–30), y Bernabé y Luján (2016:569) como /*anhiai en ellophaiōi skʷellonsai*/ "riendas que dan la vuelta en la collera."[4]

---

[1] He separado los adjetivos verbales de los compuestos nominales, porque a todos los efectos tienen una formación verbal.

[2] Quiero dar las gracias a Juan Piquero por haberme permitido generosamente usar materiales inéditos de su Tesis Doctoral, que durante el largo trascurso de la edición de esta obra ha sido publicada (Piquero 2019), así como a Eugenio Luján por haberme ofrecido muy interesantes sugerencias.

[3] Para las atestiguaciones, cf *DMic., s.v.*

[4] Sobre */ellopʰaiōi/*, cf. §4.1.5. En PY Xa 1342.2 *e-ni a-pu-ki-ṣị̣*[, *e-ni* podría ser una preposición, pero la falta de contexto no permite asegurarlo.

4. Composición nominal

4.1 ἐν- en compuestos nominales

4.1.1 *e-ka-ra-e-we*

Varias tablillas cnosias de la serie Dm registran el apelativo *e-ka-ra-e-we* referido a corderos. La interpretación más extendida es la de Lejeune (1971:364–367): /engraēwes/ 'animales de cebadero', compuesto de ἐν y el verbo γράω, con sufijo -ηυ-; cf. también Killen 1999:332; Rougemont 2004:22, 2006:123; Perpillou 2004: 165; Weilhartner 2005:92; y Killen 2006:332.[5]

4.1.2. *e-ke-ro-qo-no*

En varias tablillas de Pilo[6] se encuentra el compuesto *e-ke-ro-qo-no* /enkʰerro-kʷoinoi/ 'asalariados'; cf. Rougemont 2009:104 y Olsen 2014:92ss. Está formado sobre */en-kʰerro-/ < **en-kʰeryo-* 'salario', que se interpreta como compuesto de rección preposicional del sintagma ἐν χειρί 'en mano'; cf. Perpillou (2004:182), quien cita como paralelo délf. ἔγχηρα (Schwyzer 1923:325n4, Atenas < Delfos, 380 a. C.), Waanders (2007:54), García Ramón (2014:43), y Melena (2014:35).

4.1.3. *e-ku-se-we-*

En el nódulo MY Wt 501.β se lee *a-ta-ra-qe e-ku-se-we-qe*. La interpretación mayoritaria de *a-ta-ra-* es /antla/ 'vasos para sacar agua' (cf. Risch 1958:98 y Varias 1993: 152; 2008:780, 793), y la de *e-ku-se-we-* /enkhusēwe(s)/ 'embudos' (cf. Varias 1993: 152, Perpillou 2004:166, y Varias 2008:780, 793; 2012a:245n23).[7] Es un nombre de instrumento en -εύς derivado de un nombre de acción */en-kʰusi-/, compuesto de ἐν y de χέω; cf. Leukart (1994:245), quien considera la posibilidad de que sea un compuesto en **es-*, y Meier-Brügger (1995–1996:9).

4.1.4. *e̦-mi-to*

En KN Am 821.1 se lee]*ra-jo,* / *e-qe-ta-e, e-ne-ka, e̦-mi-to* VIR 2. *e̦-mi-to* se interpreta como el genitivo plural /emmistʰōn/, derivado adjetival formado sobre el sintagma ἐν μισθῶι 'asalariados' (cf. Perpillou 2004:183; Rougemont 2009:104s.; y Luján 2012:131s.), aunque puede significar 'mercenarios', cf. gr. alf. ἔμμισθος en Ph.2.19 y Montecchi 2013:119; 2014:88ss.

---

[5] Melena (2014:56) propone ver una forma truncada de un compuesto con *e-ka-ra* 'altar sacrificial' y un segundo término con aspiración inicial.

[6] Aa 777.a, 854, Ab 559.B, 563.B, Ad 691.a; An 199.1.

[7] Cf. bibliografía anterior en *DMic.*, *s.v.*

4.1.5. *-e-ro-pa-jo-*

En PY Ub 1315.2 (cf. §3) *-e-ro-pa-jo-* se interpreta como /*ellopʰaiōi*/ dativo singular de un derivado en -αιο- compuesto de ἐν y de λόφος 'lo que está en la cerviz, collera', cf. Bernabé and Luján 2008:339 y Bernabé 2011:27–30.

4.1.6. *e-to-ki-ja*

En PY Vn 46.6 y 879.3, en un contexto de elementos de construcción, se atestigua la forma *e-to-ki-ja* /*entoikʰia*/, adjetivo sustantivado compuesto de ἐν y de τοῖχος 'muro', con sufijo *-jo-*. Serían piezas 'que se apoyan en el muro', aunque no podamos precisar su significado concreto (cf. Palaima 1991:297; Perpillou 2004:182; y Montecchi 2013:157). En griego alfabético se documenta como sustantivo en Jenofonte *Anabasis* 7.8.1 y como adjetivo en Dionisio de Halicarnaso 16.3.

4.1.7. *e-to-ni-jo*

No incluyo en la lista *e-to-ni-jo*, interpretado por Perpillou (1981; 2004:183) como *ἐν-θόρνιον. Es más verosímil considerarlo un compuesto de ὄνος 'provecho', con suf. *-jo-*.

4.2. ἐνι- en compuestos nominales

La única forma que podría citarse es la que sirve de base al antropónimo *e-ni-to-wo*, un compuesto de rección verbal en el que *e-ni* tiene un claro valor adverbial: /*Eni-tʰowos*/, según propuesta de Leukart (1994:227 y n. 250) '*der hinein (mitten, in die Feinde) springt*', aceptada por García Ramón (2000:208n5).

5. Adjetivos verbales en *-to-*

5.1.]*e-na-ri-po-to*

En KN Sg 884 se lee]*e-na-ri-po-to*, seguido de CAPS[, un nominativo singular o plural /*enaliptos, -oi*/ 'untado', posiblemente con barniz o con una materia grasa destinada a proteger la madera del carro: cf. Plath 1994:53; Bernabé and Luján 2008:209; Luján 2012:144; Killen 2015:179, y Bernabé 2016:536. Es un adjetivo verbal compuesto de /*en*/ y la raíz de ἀλείφω. En griego alfabético se atestigua ἐνάλειπτος, en Hipócrates *De victu acutorum* (*spuria*) 32.4.

5.2. *e-to-ro-qa-ta*

En el archivo cnosio se encuentra *e-to-ro-qa-ta* en las dos tablillas siguientes:

KN Oa 878

.1]   *166+WE   18
.2] e-to-ro-qa-ta   16

KN U 736

.1]na-u-do-mo

.2]93 e-to-ro-qa-ta *181   10

El logograma *166 puede representar una pieza de tela (Melena 1975:56–59; 2014: 144), mientras que la abreviación acrofónica WE puede estar por *we-a-no* y *na-u-do-mo* es ναυδόμος 'constructor de barcos' (cf. Petrakis 2011:207; Montecchi 2013: 112, 209ss.; Weilhartner 2014:204). Melena (2014:152) interpreta el objeto representado por *181 y llamado *e-to-ro-qa-ta* como un lazo utilizado para facilitar la torsión del remo sobre el escálamo; cf. Wachter 2009:217 y Montecchi 2013:210s. En cambio, Lejeune (1971:308, 310, 315) y Perpillou (2004:165) lo consideran un adjetivo verbal en *-to-*, con la preposición **en* y la raíz **terkʷ-* 'torcer', cf. τρέπω,[8] nom. neutr. plu. /entrokʷta/ < **entr̥kʷta*, sustantivado, reconstrucción preferible a la de Heubeck (1958:121s.): /entrōpatai/, plural de un femenino en -α; y a la de Melena (1975:50–63; 2014:39): **/entr̥kʷātai/*, nominativo plural de un nombre de agente en *-tās*.[9]

6. Composición verbal

6.1. *a-pi-e-qe*

García Ramón (2010:79–80; 2012b:436–441) interpreta *a-pi-e-qe* en TH Fq 254.1 como /ampʰi-ʰen-skʷe/, compuesto de los preverbios /ampʰi/ y /en/ con el verbo **sekʷ-* 'decir' y con desplazamiento de la aspiración inicial a /en-/, como en lac. εφ-εν-εποντι (*SEG* 12.368). /en/ habría formado una univerbación con **sekʷ-*, atestiguada en latín *insece*, hom. ἔννεπε, e indirectamente, en céltico (a-irl. *insce* 'discurso', de **eni-skʷii̯ā-*), por lo que podría considerarse como heredada. Es seguido por Melena (2014:39).[10]

Hay motivos para no considerar verosímil la propuesta (cf. Bernabé and Pierini 2017:529–531):

> (a)   Es difícil considerar gr. ἔννεπε como univerbación, si en la épica las formas de aoristo presentan el preverbio en su forma ἐνι-: ἔνισπε *Il.* 2.80, ἐνισπεῖν *Od.* 3.93, Hes. *Th.* 369.

---

[8]   Propuestas menos verosímiles en *DMíc.*, *s.v.* Menos probable por el contexto es la de García Ramón (2000:166–167): un antropónimo /Estʰlo-(k)kʷā(s)tās/, posibilidad que admite Melena (2014:40).

[9]   La transcripción con -r̥- es hija de su tiempo, cuando Ruipérez y su escuela asumieron como indiscutible la propuesta de Heubeck (1972) sobre la conservación de r̥ en micénico. Leukart (1994:92) considera la forma "lautlich und bildungsmäßig unwarscheinlich," mientras que Palaima (1991: 295–296) acepta la interpretación desde el punto de vista del significado, pero no compromete una explicación lingüística, al igual que Waanders (2007:40).

[10]   Pero cf. Melena (2014:118): "without internal aspiration, with a development **-ns- > -nn- > -n-* (before a stop)."

(b) Si no hay univerbación, resulta muy poco esperable una forma con dos preverbios en micénico.

(c) No se atestigua en griego ninguna palabra con ἀμφι- y ἐν.

(d) La trasposición de aspiración en lacon. 3 sg. εφενεποντι se da en una forma con el grado *e* del radical verbal. En la forma micénica habría que suponer una aspiración de -*s*- entre dos consonantes[11] en el grado cero y su traslado a la inicial.

(e) El único verbo de lengua compuesto con ἀμφί en griego, ἀμφιλέγω, significa 'disputar', y rige objeto directo de lo que se disputa; cf. χώρας ἃς ἀμφέλλεγον, "las tierras que se disputaban," *IG* 4².926 (Epidauro, 242–237 a. C.).

Así pues, hay que descontar /amp^{h}i-^{h}enk^{w}e/ de las formaciones con ἐν.

6.2. *e-ke-jo-to*

En PY Aq 218.9 *e-ke-jo-to* es probablemente /enkeiontoi/, 3ª pers. pl. pres. med.-pas. de ἔγκειμαι 'permanecer'; cf. Hajnal (2004:165) y Waanders (2012:565), quien se plantea la alternativa de que sea un subjuntivo prospectivo semejante a hom. κέονται.

6.3. *e-ne-e-si*

En PY En 609.2 leemos *to-so-de te-re-ta e-ne-e-si* VIR 14, /tosoi-de telestai enehensi/ "se encuentran en ella tantos telestas," siendo el verbo[12] un compuesto de /en/ y de /eimi/; cf. el participio]*e-ne-o* de KN As 608 *lat. inf.*

7. Adverbios compuestos

En PY Va 15.1 en contexto poco claro se lee *o-u-qe e-to* *35-ka-te-re* 2̣. La presencia de 2̣ propició la interpretación de *e-to* como dual de un presente de indicativo de εἰμί, /eston/ (*Docs²*, 546). Pero, dado que Melena (*PTT³*, 211) anota en el aparato crítico "2̣ [not complete at right, 4 or more," tal interpretación debe abandonarse. Killen (2000:144s.) sigue la antigua propuesta de Ilievski (1959:115) de leer /entos/ (cf. ἐντός).[13]

---

[11] Hecho que no ocurre en *a₃-ka-sa-ma* /aiksmans/.

[12] Cf. *DMic. s.v.*, Perpillou (2004:165).

[13] De él deriva el compuesto *e-to-wo-ko* KN Fh 462.2 etc., */entoworgos/ 'que trabaja en el interior'; cf. Palaima 1997:14; Killen 2001:437; Weilhartner 2005:118; Killen 2006:93; y Montecchi 2013:127.

8. Conclusiones

8.1. Grafías

Desde el punto de vista gráfico, *en* como adverbio se escribe unido a la palabra anterior en *mi-to-we-sa-e*; como preposición se escribe *e* ante vocal, aun cuando la secuencia está en *scriptio continua* en *-e-e-ro-pa-jo*, mientras que en composición, ante vocal sí se escribe *e-n-* (*e-na-ri-po-to, e-ne-e-si*). La escasez de ejemplos, sin embargo, no permite asegurar que esta distribución fuera la regular en micénico.

8.2. Distribución de /en/ y /eni/

Está claro que /*eni*/ solo aparece como adverbio, independiente o en composición, mientras que /*en*/ admite todo tipo de usos sintácticos.

8.3. Tipos de formación

a) /*en*/ como preposición forma compuestos nominales muy diversos:

(a₁) Compuestos de rección preposicional con un segundo elemento nominal, bien sin sufijo de derivación (/*emmist^{h}ōn*/), bien con sufijos *-(a)yo-* (*/*ellop^{h}aiōi*/ de ἐν λόφωι, /*entoik^{h}ia*/, de ἐν y τοίχωι).

(a₂) Compuestos más complejos, como */*enk^{h}errok^{w}oinoi*/, que está construido sobre un compuesto como los señalados en (a₁) (*en-k^{h}eryo-*), que se usa a su vez como primer elemento de un nuevo compuesto con */*k^{w}oin-*/.

(a₃) Compuestos con un segundo elemento verbal y con sufijo *-ēu-* (*/*engraēwes*/, de ἐν y γράω; */*enk^{h}usēwe(s)*/, este último a través de un nombre de acción: */*en-k^{h}usi-*/, de ἐν y χέω).

(b) /*en*/ como preverbio forma adjetivos verbales en *-to-* (*/*enaliptos*/, de ἐν-αλείφω, */*entrok^{w}ta*/, de ἐν y τρέπω).

(c) En composición verbal la presencia de /*en*/ se limita a dos verbos: /*enkeiontoi*/, /*enehensi*/.

(d) Como adverbio encontramos /*en*/ en /*entos*/ y en composición /*eni*/ en el antropónimo /*Enit^{h}owos*/.

8.4. Pervivencia

De los compuestos con /*en*/ atestiguados en micénico se conservan en el primer milenio /*emmist^{h}ōn*/ (cf. ἔμμισθοι) y /*entoik^{h}ia*/ (cf. ἐντοίχιος), los dos compuestos verbales /*enkeiontoi*/ (cf. ἐγκειμαι) y /*enehensi*/ (cf. ἔνειμι), así como el adverbio /*entos*/ (cf. ἐντός); /*enaliptos*/ se transforma en ἐνάλειπτος. Desaparecen /*engraēwes*/, /*enkhusēwe(s)*/ (no así ἔγχυσις), /*enk^{h}errok^{w}oinoi*/, /*ellophaiōi*/, /*entrokwta*/ y /*enit^{h}owos*/.

Bibliografía

Bernabé, A. 2011. "Some Proposals of Interpretation of PY Ub 1315." In *A Greek Man in the Iberian Street. Papers in Linguistic and Epigraphy in Honour of Javier de Hoz*, ed. E. R. Luján and J. L. García Alonso, 25–34. Innsbruck.

———. 2016. "Testi relativi a carri e ruote." In Del Freo and Perna 2016:511–550.

Bernabé, A., and E. R. Luján. 2008. "Mycenaean Technology." In Duhoux and Morpurgo Davies 2008.1:201–233.

———, eds. 2014. *Donum Mycenologicum. Mycenaean Studies in Honour of Francisco Aura Jorro*. Louvain-la-Neuve.

———. 2016. "Testi relativi a pelle e manufatti in pelle." In Del Freo and Perna 2016:567–587.

Bernabé, A., and R. Pierini. 2017. "What, When, Why: Tablet Functions and *o-te* Expressions in Context." In *Aegean Scripts. Proceedings of the 14th International Colloquium on Mycenaean Studies, Copenhagen, 2-5 September 2015*, ed. M.-L. Nosch and H. Landenius Enegren, 523–536. Incunabula Graeca 105. Rome.

Del Freo, M., and M. Perna, eds. 2016. *Manuale di epigrafia micenea: Introduzione allo studio dei testi in lineare B*. 2 vols. Padua.

Duhoux, Y., and A. Morpurgo Davies, eds. 2008-2014. *A Companion to Linear B. Mycenaean Greek Texts and Their World*, vols. 1 and 3. Louvain-la-Neuve.

García Ramón, J. L. 2000. "Mycénien *qa-sa-ko* /Kʷas-arkʰos/, grec alphabétique Πάσαρχος, Κτήσαρχος et le dossier de **kua(s)*- dans la langue des tablettes." In *Philokypros: Mélanges de philologie et d'antiquités grecques et proche-orientales dédiés à la mémoire d'Olivier Masson*, ed. L. Dubois and E. Masson, 153–176. Salamanca.

———. 2014. "Anthroponymica mycenaea: *e-ke-ra₂-wo* */En-kheriā-wōn/, *ἐγχειρία y ἐγχειρέω 'emprender' (*ʿponer mano en'), ἐγχείρημα, ἐγχείρησις." In Bernabé and Luján 2014:35–49.

Hajnal, I. 2004. "Die Tmesis bei Homer und auf den mykenischen Linear B-Tafeln: Ein chronologisches Paradox?" In *Indo-European Perspectives. Studies in Honour of Anna Morpurgo Davies*, ed. J. H. W. Penney, 146–178. Oxford.

Heubeck, A. 1958. "Griech. βασιλεύς und das Zeichen Nr. 16 in Linear B." *Indogermanische Forschungen* 63:113–138.

———. 1972. "Syllabic ṛ in Mycenaean?" In *Acta Mycenaea. Actes du cinquième Colloque international des études mycéniennes, tenu à Salamanque, 30 mars-3 avril 1970*, ed. M. S. Ruipérez, vol. 2, 55–79. *Minos* 12. Salamanca.

Ilievski, P. H. 1959. "The Adverbial Suffix -θεν in Mycenaean." *Živa Antika* 9: 105–128.

Killen, J. T. 1999. "Mycenaean *o-pa.*" In *Floreant Studia Mycenaea. Akten des X. Internationalen Mykenologischen Colloquiums in Salzburg vom 1.-5. Mai 1995*, ed. S. Deger-Jalkotzy, S. Hiller, and O. Panagl, 325–341. Vienna.

———. 2000. "Two Notes on Linear B." *Živa Antika* 50:141–148.

———. 2001. "Religion at Pylos: The Evidence of the Fn Tablets." In *Potnia: Deities and Religion in the Aegean Bronze Age. Proceedings of the 8th International Aegean Conference, Göteborg, 12-15 April 2000*, ed. R. Laffineur and R. Hägg, 435–443. *Aegaeum* 22. Liège.

———. 2006. "Thoughts on the Functions of the New Thebes Tablets." In *Die neuen Linear-B Texte aus Theben: Ihr Aufschlußwert für die mykenische Sprache und Kultur. Akten des internationalen Forschungskolloquiums an der Österreichischen Akademie der Wissenschaften, 5.-6. Dezember 2002*, ed. S. Deger-Jalkotzky and O. Panagl, 79–110. Vienna.

———. 2015. *Economy and Administration in Mycenaean Greece. Collected Papers on Linear B.* Vols 1–3. Ed. M. del Freo. Rome.

Killen, J. T., and J.-P. Olivier. 1968. "155 raccords de fragments dans les tablettes de Cnossos." *Bulletin de Correspondance Hellénique* 92:115–141.

Landenius Enegren, H. 2008. *The People of Knossos: Prosopographical Studies in the Knossos Linear B Archives.* Uppsala.

Lejeune, M. 1958a. "Essais de philologie mycénienne: (4) Observations sur les composés privatifs, (5) Observations sur le nombre duel." *Revue de philologie* 32:198–217.

———. 1958b. *Mémoires de philologie mycénienne. Première série (1955-1957).* Paris.

———. 1971. *Mémoires de philologie mycénienne. Deuxième série (1958-1963).* Rome.

Leukart, A. 1994. *Die frühgriechischen Nomina auf -tās und -ās: Untersuchungen zu ihrer Herkunft und Ausbreitung (unter Vergleich mit den Nomina auf -eús).* Vienna.

Luján, E. R. 2012. "La moción de género en los adjetivos temáticos en micénico." In Varias García 2012b:127–153.

Meier-Brügger, M. 1995-1996. "Zu griechischen Ableitungen von -si-Abstrakta." *Glotta* 73:9–11.

Melena, J. L. 1975. *Studies on Some Mycenaean Inscriptions from Knossos Dealing with Textiles.* Salamanca.

———. 2014. "Mycenaean Writing." In Duhoux and Morpurgo Davies 2014:1–186.

Meriggi, P. 1955. "I testi micenei in trascrizione (I)." *Athenaeum* 33:64–92.

Montecchi, B. 2013. *Luoghi per lavorare, pregare, morire: Edifici e maestranze edili negli interessi delle élites micenee.* Florence.

———. 2014. "*e-qe-ta* and *e-mi-to* on Linear B Tablet KN Am(2) 821: Military Officials and Soldiers?" *Pasiphae* 8:79–96.

Olsen, B. A. 2014. *Women in Mycenaean Greece: The Linear B Tablets from Pylos and Knossos.* London.

Palaima, T. G. 1991. "Maritime Matters in the Linear B Tablets." In *Thalassa: L'Égée préhistorique et la mer. Actes de la troisième Rencontre égéenne internationale de l'Université de Liège, Calvi, Corse (23-25 avril 1990),* ed. R. Laffineur and L. Basch, 275–310 + plate LXIII. *Aegaeum* 7. Liège.

———. 1997. "Potter and Fuller: The Royal Craftsmen." In *TEXNH: Craftsmen, Craftswomen, and Craftsmanship in the Aegean Bronze Age. Proceedings of the 6th International Aegean Conference, Philadelphia, Temple University, 18-21 April 1996,* ed. R. Laffineur and P. P. Betancourt (= *Aegaeum* 16), 407–412. Liège.

Perpillou, J.-L. 1981. "Discussions mycéniennes. I. *e-to-ni-jo.* II. Abstraits verbaux en mycénien?" *Bulletin de la Société de linguistique de Paris* 76:225–240.

———. 2004. *Essais de lexicographie en grec ancien.* Louvain-la-Neuve.

Petrakis, V. 2011. "Politics of the Sea in the Late Bronze Age II-III Aegean: Iconographic Preferences and Textual Perspectives." In *The Seascape in Aegean Prehistory,* ed. G. Vavouranakis, 185–234. Athens.

Piquero Rodríguez, J. 2019. *El léxico del griego micénico. Index Graecitatis.* Nancy.

Plath, R. 1994. *Der Streitwagen und seine Teile im frühen Griechischen: Sprachliche Untersuchungen zu den mykenischen Texten und zum homerischen Epos.* Nuremberg.

Risch, E. 1958. "Un problème de morphologie grecque: L'accusatif pluriel des thèmes consonantiques en mycénien." *Bulletin de la Société de linguistique de Paris* 53:96–102.

Rougemont, F. 2004. "The Administration of Mycenaean Sheep Rearing (Flocks, Shepherds, 'Collectors')." In *PECUS: Man and Animal in Antiquity. Proceedings of the Conference at the Swedish Institute in Rome, September 9-12, 2002,* ed. B. Santillo Frizell, 20–30. Rome.

———. 2006. "Les porcs dans la documentation mycénienne." In *De la domestication au tabou: Le cas des suidés au Proche-Orient ancien,* ed. B. Lion and C. Michel, 115–129. Paris.

———. 2009. *Contrôle économique et administration à l'époque des palais mycéniens (fin du IIème millénaire av. J.-C.).* Athens.

Ruijgh, C. J. 1967. *Études sur la grammaire et le vocabulaire du grec mycénien.* Amsterdam.

Schwyzer, E., 1923. *Dialectorum Graecarum exempla epigraphica potiora.* Leipzig.

Varias García, C. 1993. "Los documentos en lineal B de Micenas: Ensayo de interpretación global." PhD diss., Universitat Autònoma de Barcelona.

———. 2008. "Observations on the Mycenaean Vocabulary of Furniture and Vessels." In *Colloquium Romanum. Atti del XII Colloquio Internazionale di*

Miceno-logia (Roma, 20-25 febbraio 2006), vol. 2, ed. A. Sacconi, M. Del Freo, L. Godart, and M. Negri (= *Pasiphae* 2), 775–793. Pisa.

———. 2012a. "Micenas y la Argólide: Los textos micénicos en su contexto." In Varias García 2012b:233–257.

———, ed. 2012b. *Actas del Simposio Internacional: 55 Años de Micenología (1952-2007) (Bellaterra, 12-13 de abril de 2007)*. Barcelona.

Waanders, F. M. J. 2007. *An Analytic Study of Mycenaean Compounds. Structure-Types*. Pisa.

———. 2012. "Aperçu des formes verbales dans les textes mycéniens: Remarques sur la morphologie verbale et sur la distribution et les valeurs des thèmes temporels." In *Études mycéniennes 2010. Actes du XIIIᵉ Colloque international sur les textes égéens, Sèvres, Paris, Nanterre, 20-23 septembre 2010*, ed. P. Carlier, Ch. de Lamberterie, M. Egetmeyer, N. Guilleux, F. Rougemont, and J. Zurbach, 563–573. Pisa.

Wachter, R. 2009. "Wort-Index Homerisch–Mykenisch (MYK)." In *Homers Ilias. Gesamtkommentar (Basler Kommentar / BK). Prolegomena*, ed. J. Latacz, 209–234. Berlin.

Weilhartner, J. 2005. *Mykenische Opfergaben nach Aussage der Linear B-Texte*. Vienna.

———. 2014. "Die Teilnehmer griechischer Kultprozessionen und die mykenischen Tätigkeitsbezeichnungen auf *-po-ro*/-φόρος." In Bernabé and Luján 2014:201–219.

3

Mycenaean *wo-ra**

Maurizio Del Freo

CNR-ISPC

maurizio.delfreo@cnr.it

Abstract

It is generally agreed that the term *wo-ra* designated a part of the Mycenaean war chariot. Its interpretation, however, is far from certain, and many different proposals have been advanced so far. The present article suggests a new hypothesis based on the shape of some variants of the CUR logogram.

Keywords

Craftsmanship, Mycenaean war chariots, chariot terminology, Linear B logograms

THE MYCENAEAN TERM *WO-RA* IS attested on two Knossos tablets from the Arsenal (L), which read as follows:

Sp 4451 + 4476 + 8701 + *frr.*   (L; 231)
.a   *vest.*   [
.b wo-ra-e / pa-ra-[•]-we-jo   *253* 2 [

       .a *vest.* perhaps accidental.
       .b Possibly *pa-ra-ḳu-we-jo.*

Sp 4452 + *fr.*   (L; 231)
  [wo-]ra / ka-za   *253* 1 [

* This article is offered to José L. Melena with gratitude and admiration for his invaluable work as editor and interpreter of Mycenaean texts. I thank J. T. Killen and S. Nikoloudis for reading and commenting on a first draft of this contribution. Any remaining errors are, of course, my own responsibility.

The alternation between *wo-ra-e* and]*ra* and the presence of logogram **253* on both tablets make the supplement [*wo-*]*ra* on 4452 virtually certain. *Wo-ra* is written in large characters and is therefore the name of the object represented by **253*, while *ka-za* and *pa-ra-[•]-we-jo* are adjectives of material related to *wo-ra* (see below). The alternation between '2' and '1' suggests that *wo-ra-e* and [*wo-*]*ra* are a nominative dual and a nominative singular, respectively. Moreover, since *wo-ra-e* agrees with the *-ō* dual *pa-ra-[•]-we-jo*, a similar agreement has also to be assumed for [*wo-*]*ra* and *ka-za*. It thus seems reasonable that *wo-ra*, despite the *-a-e* dual, was a feminine noun in *-ā*.[1]

Wo-ra is also indirectly attested on Se 880, a tablet from the Northern Entrance Passage (I3). The text of Se 880 is the following:

Se 880 + 1017   (I3; 127)

.1   ] vac.
.2] , po-ni-ke-a , wo-ra-we-sa   CUR 1

> Possibly [+] Se 9307.
> Cut at right.
> .2 Trace at left (]*jạ*). *wo-* over [[ ]], perhaps [[*wạ*]]. CUR drawn over dividing line.

This tablet records a chariot (CUR 1) described by two terms: *po-ni-ke-a /phoi-nikehā/* 'painted in red' and *wo-ra-we-sa*.[2] The latter is almost certainly the feminine of a *went-* adjective from *wo-ra*. Since *wo-ra-we-sa* 'provided with *wo-ra*'[3] describes a CUR, it is likely that *wo-ra* was a construction part or a decoration of war chariots.

The shape of the logogram **253* clearly shows that the object was some sort of "ring" (Fig. 3.1), but it is of no help in determining its size. As is clear from Sp 4451 and 4452, this object could be made 'of bronze' (*ka-za /kʰaltsā/* vel sim. < **kʰalk-yā*, adjective of material formed with the *io-* suffix instead of the more common *-eio-* suffix[4]) or of another material (*pa-ra-[•]-we-jo*).

The authors of *CoMIK* and *KT*[6], following an old suggestion by J.-P. Olivier,[5] propose for *pa-ra-[•]-we-jo* the reading *pa-ra-ku-we-jo*. As can be seen from the

---

[1] On the feminine dual in *-āe* instead of *-ō*, see Lejeune 1968b (cf. also Sharypkin 2009).
[2] The adjectives *wo-ra-we-sa* and *po-ni-ke-a* describe the logogram CUR and almost certainly refer to *i-qi-ja /ikkʷiā/* 'chariot', a term attested in the Sd and Sf series from the Arsenal and probably implicit in the Se series (cf. Lejeune 1968a:41). If the quasi-join between Se 880 + 1017 and Se 9307 (*pte-rẹ[-wa*) is correct, the chariot recorded on Se 880 was of elm wood (gen. /ptelewās/, cf. πτελέα 'elm'), like those on Se 879, 890, 891, 892, 893, 5729, and 7920.
[3] Cf. Lejeune 1968a:22; Lejeune 1968b:237; Doria 1972:59.
[4] On the adjectives of material, see Ruijgh 1967:237–245 (esp. 238 and 245 for *ka-ki-jo*, *ka-ke-ja-pi*, and *ka-za*) and Risch 1976. For the various possible phonetic interpretations of *ka-za*, cf. DMic. s.v.
[5] Olivier in Killen and Olivier 1968:127.

Sp 4451   Sp 4452

Figure 3.1. The logogram *253 (after *CoMIK* II, drawings by L. Godart).

CoMIK photograph, the faint traces still visible in the lacuna are not sufficient to confirm the reading *ḳụ*.[6] However, in my opinion, Olivier's suggestion can be reinforced by Sp 5102, whose text reads as follows:

Sp 5102   (231?)
    ]ḳọ / pa-ra-ku[

Due to the fragmentary state of the tablet, it is impossible to know whether the *pa-ra-ku*[sequence continued after the break and whether the text had anything to do with chariot construction.[7] The traces visible at the left end seem to exclude that the word before *pa-ra-ku*[was *wo-ra* (or *wo-ra-e*). However, it can be observed that *pa-ra-ku*[occupies the same position as *pa-ra-[•]-we-jo* in Sp 4451 and that, like *pa-ra-[•]-we-jo*, it is written in smaller characters immediately after a word in large characters. Moreover, *pa-ra-ku*[and *pa-ra-[•]-we-jo* seem to have been written by the same scribal hand (*pa* and *ra* are very similar in shape, while *ku* is compatible with the sign [•] of *pa-ra-[•]-we-jo*). Finally, as suggested by R. J. Firth and J. L. Melena, it is likely that the fragment 5102 had been excavated in the Arsenal in 1904 together with Sp 4451 and 4452,[8] which justifies the reclassification of the tablet from Xf (*KT* 5) to Sp (*KT⁶*). Therefore, even if the parallel between 4451 and 5102 cannot definitively confirm the reading *pa-ra-ḳụ-we-jo*, it certainly increases its degree of probability.

Grammatically, *pa-ra-ḳụ-we-jo* is an adjective of material in *-eio-* derived from *pa-ra-ku*, a *-u-* stem attested both at Pylos (str. sg. *pa-ra-ku-we* on Ta 714.1.3, 715.3 and *pa-ra-ke-we* on Ta 642.1)[9] and at Knossos (if [• •]-*ku* on Od(1) 667.B is to be read *pạ-rạ-ku*).[10] Another derivative from *pa-ra-ku* is *pa-ra-ku-ja*, an adjective

---

[6] This explains why the reading is confined to the critical apparatus (cf. Olivier cit. above note 5: "la lecture *pa-ra-ḳụ-we-jo* ne s'impose vraiment pas").

[7] In theory, *pa-ra-ku*[could be *pa-ra-ku* (cf. KN Od 667.Ḅ: LANA), *pa-ra-ku-ja* (cf. KN Ld(1) 575: TELA²), or *pa-ra-ku-we* (cf. PY Ta 715.3, 714.1.3: *to-no, ta-ra-nu, to-pe-zo*).

[8] Firth and Melena 1998–1999:110–112, 114.

[9] On PY Cn 200.1 *pa-ra-ku* is the name of a man responsible for a group of OVIS[x] and has therefore to be distinguished from *pa-ra-ku-we* etc. (for the interpretation /*Brakʰus*/, cf. *DMic. s.v.*).

[10] *KT⁶*: "]*pạ-rạ-ku* not impossible" (cf. Melena in Bennett *et al.* 1989:204).

in -io- documented at Knossos on Ld(1) 575.b (*n. pl.*) and—with the alternative spelling *56-ra-ku-ja—on Ld(1) 587.2 (*n. pl.*). At Pylos *pa-ra-ku* designates a material used in conjunction with *ku-ru-so* /khrūsos/ 'gold' and *ku-wa-no* /kuanos/ 'blue glass paste' to decorate tables, seats, and stools; at Knossos, the adjective *pa-ra-ku-ja* / *56-ra-ku-ja* refers to the color of a number of cloths (TELA), while *pạ-rạ-ku* describes small amounts of wool (LANA).

Among the various interpretations suggested for *pa-ra-ku*,[11] the hypothesis that best fits the evidence is that provided by Melena.[12] According to this interpretation, the adjective *56 / pa-ra-ku-ja*, which refers to the color of some textiles (Ld(1) 575),[13] can be compared with the Hesychius' gloss βαρακίς· γλαύκινον ἱμάτιον and interpreted as /barakuia/ (*n. pl.*) '(textiles) of bluish green color'. According to Melena, this adjective would refer to the color of the precious material called *pa-ra-ku* /baraku/ 'blue-green stone' (perhaps 'turquoise' or 'emerald'), used to decorate the pieces of furniture recorded in the Pylos Ta series.

Melena, considering the alternation *tu-ma-da-ro* / *tu-*56-da-ro* and the consequent possible phonetic value /^{m}ba/ for *56, compares *56 / pa-ra-ku-ja* with Gr. σμάραγδος, μάραγδος and suggests that Myc. /baraku/ could be a loanword from Akk. *barrāqtu* 'emerald', acquired through the mediation of the Minoan language.[14]

Recently, J. Piquero, pointing out the absence of turquoise and emeralds from the Aegean archaeological record in the second millennium BCE, has proposed to interpret /baraku/ as 'blue-green glass paste'.[15]

If one admits that *pa-ra-ku* was /baraku/ 'blue-green stone' or 'blue-green glass paste', *pa-ra-ku-we-jo*, which can be morphologically analyzed as *baraku-*

---

[11] Cf. *DMic. s.vv. pa-ra-ku-we* and *pa-ra-ku-ja* ('green stone, emerald', 'silver', 'tin', 'zinc', 'amber, electron', 'seal stone'); Chadwick 1976:144 ('niello'); and, most recently, Witczak 2000 and Witczak 2009 ('iron').

[12] Melena 1987:224–226. Some of the hypotheses mentioned in note 11 do not take into account the adjective *pa-ra-ku-ja*, which, as mentioned, refers to the color of some textiles; others depend on the interpretation of *wo-ra* as 'wheel rim', which, as will be seen below, is far from certain.

[13] In addition to the *56-ra-ku-ja* textiles, the Ld(1) 575 tablet records a number of other colored textiles: *po-ki-ro-nu-ka* 'with many-colored o-nu-ke', *re-u-ko-nu-ka* 'with white o-nu-ke' and *po-ri-wa* 'grey' (cf. *DMic. s.vv.*). Other color adjectives ending in -io- are *po-ni-ki-ja* '(chariots) painted in red' and *po-pu-ro₂* '(fabrics) of purple color' (cf. *DMic. s.vv.*).

[14] For this hypothesis, see already Ventris 1955:117 and *Documents*, 340.

[15] Piquero 2015a (for a similar hypothesis, cf. Palaima 2004:115: "emerald-color paste"). According to Piquero (287–292), Myc. /baraku/ and Gr. (σ)μάραγδος should not be linked to Akk. *barrāqtu*, but to some other Semitic term derived from the root *wrq* 'green, yellow-green', like, e.g., Eblaite *wa-ru₁₂-ga-tum* 'green stone'. The original concrete meaning ('green stone') would have been replaced by an abstract meaning ('green color'), then again by a concrete one: *pa-ra-ku* 'green glass paste' and *pa-ra-ku-ja* 'green (textiles)' (see also Piquero 2015b).

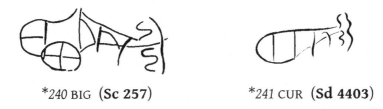

*240 BIG **(Sc 257)***   *241 CUR **(Sd 4403)***

Figure 3.2. The *240 BIG and *241 CUR logograms (after *CoMIK*, drawings by L. Godart).

eio-,[16] can be interpreted as 'made of blue-green stone / blue-green glass paste' or, more likely, 'decorated with blue-green stones / blue-green glass paste'.[17]

Wo-ra seems then to indicate a chariot part made of bronze (*ka-za*) or decorated with blue-green stones or blue-green glass paste (*pa-ra-ku̯-we-jo*).

Unfortunately, the few elements available make it difficult to identify the object. This explains why some scholars only admit the generic interpretation "chariot part."[18] Other scholars, however, have advanced some hypotheses based on the shape of the logogram *253 and/or on the etymology of *wo-ra*. In particular, some have proposed to identify the logogram *253 with a wheel rim,[19] while others have suggested relating it to the lateral curved extensions (or "wings") of the war chariots, a detail that is depicted in the logograms *240 BIG and *241 CUR (Fig. 3.2) as well as in several vases and frescoes.[20]

The etymological analysis of *wo-ra*, for its part, has generated four main hypotheses: /wollā/ (or /wōlā/) 'scratch, abrasion' (< *wol-sā or *wol-nā, cf. οὐλή);[21] /wōrā/ (or /worā/) 'guard, protective device' (< *wer- / *wor- 'to watch, observe, be attentive, care for', cf. ὥρα, ὁράω);[22] /wōrā/ 'leg, support' (cf. Ion. ὥρη, ὤρη, ἄωροι;[23] and /wolā/ (or /wōlā/) 'part of a braided or laced bridle'

---

16. Phonetically, *pa-ra-ku̯-we-jo* can be interpreted as /barakweios/: cf. the two spellings *pa-ra-ku-we* and *pa-ra-ke-we* for instr. /barakwei/ and the parallel formation *do-we-jo* /dorweiōi/ (str. sg.) 'made of wood' (Sd 4413.b etc.) from *doru-eio- (Gr. δούρειος).

17. On the Mycenaean -*eio*- adjectives derived from names of ornaments (like *to-qi-de-jo*, *ko-ki-re-ja*, etc.), see Ruijgh 1967:236, 246, and Risch 1976:314.

18. Lejeune 1968b:237; Duhoux 1975:134; Tegyey 1987:362.

19. *Docs*², 592; Vandenabeele and Olivier 1979:298–299; Plath 1994:57 (but see below note 20).

20. Melena 1972:49 (with reference to Lorimer 1950:316); Plath 1994:57 (but see above note 19); Bernabé 1996:203. On the logograms *240 and *241, see Vandenabeele and Olivier 1979:76, figs. 35–36; for the artistic representations, see Crouwel 1981: pls. 14a–b, 15, 32a–b, 74–75, 77–78, 107 (on the chariot "wings" and their possible function, cf. Crouwel 1981:66–67).

21. *Documents*, 412; Lejeune 1958:22; Ruijgh 1961:209 (with hesitation); Chadwick and Baumbach 1963:230 (*s.v.* οὐλή); Baumbach 1971:177 (*s.v.* οὐλή, with doubts); Georgiev 1979:342; Perpillou 1987:278.

22. Palmer 1957:70 (cf. Palmer 1963:318 and 464, where it is not entirely excluded that *wo-ra* might designate a kind of material or a decoration); Doria 1972:75–76; Bernabé *et al.* 1992–1993:138, 143; Bernabé 1996:203; Bernabé and Lujan 2008:207n5; Piquero 2019:503–504 (*s.v.* ὥρα).

23. Gallavotti 1961:177–179.

(< *wel- 'to turn, roll', cf. εἰλέω, ἴλλω, and perhaps εὐλή, εὔληρα);[24] plus a number of less likely interpretations.[25]

The idea of a wheel rim, however, seems difficult, not only because of the shape of the logogram (which is not perfectly circular), but also because of the materials employed.[26] On the other hand, the hypothesis according to which *wo-ra* would designate chariot wings is problematic. Wings are certainly present in all BIG and CUR logograms,[27] but the adjective *wo-ra-we-sa* is attested on just one tablet.[28] The alternative hypothesis, according to which *wo-ra* would designate not the chariot wings, but a decoration of some sort attached to their ends,[29] is also questionable, as it implies that, in order to represent that decoration, the scribes had recourse to an (inaccurate) depiction of the entire chariot wing.

As regards the etymological hypotheses, the interpretation /wollā/ (or /wōlā/) 'scratch, abrasion' was proposed when the relationship between [wo-]ra, *wo-ra-e*, and *wo-ra-we-sa* had not yet been identified, and it is now untenable for semantic reasons.[30] The second interpretation, /wōrā/ 'leg, support', is uncertain both in form and meaning:[31] not only is it unclear if the root of Ion. ὤρη, ὥρη 'thigh of a sacrificial animal' (cf. Hom. ἄωροι, an epithet describing the twelve πόδες of Scilla in *Od.* 12.89) had an initial w-,[32] but it is also difficult to imagine how the concrete meanings 'pole junction', 'parking brake', 'support for the chariot' suggested by Gallavotti might fit the shape of *253. The third hypothesis, /wōrā/ (or /worā/) 'guard, protective device', is formally acceptable (cf. *wer- / *wor- 'to watch, observe, be attentive, care for'),[33] but none of the concrete meanings proposed—namely 'chariot cover' (Palmer), 'support for a protective tent', 'warrior shield' (Doria), 'side protection of the chariot box',

---

[24] Macedo 2018.

[25] Cf. Georgiev 1956:183–184 (/wo(l)lā/ 'stud', cf. ἧλος, dor. ἇλος, Hsch. γάλλοι· ἧλοι); Milani 1969:646–648 (/wolā/ 'scythe', cf. εἰλύω: the Mycenaean war chariots would have been "scythed chariots"); Petruševski 1979 ('metal part fixed into the hub', cf. Hsch. εὐραί· πλῆμναι and Poll. I, 146 τὰ δὲ τῷ ἄξονι ἐγκείμενα σιδήρια καὶ τριβόμενα ὑπὸ τοῦ τροχοῦ, εὐραί, v.l. of θύραι). All these hypotheses are phonetically or morphologically unlikely.

[26] Wheel rims decorated with bronze or precious stones are conceivable (compare the wheels described as *ka-ki-jo* /kʰalkiō/ 'of bronze' and *ka-ko-de-ta* /kʰalkodeta/ 'bronze-bound' recorded on KN So 894.2 as well as the wheels *ka-ko de-de-me-no* on PY Sa 794), but not very plausible.

[27] Cf. Vandenabeele and Olivier 1979: pls. XLIII–LXVII.

[28] One might think that the adjective *wo-ra-we-sa* was used only when *wo-ra*'s were made of bronze or *pa-ra-ku*, but that would be an *ad hoc* solution.

[29] Bernabé *et al.* 1992–1993:143: "un adorno metálico, quizá en el remate de estas alas, lo que se aviene bien con el ideograma."

[30] In any case, in the chariot production process the scribes of Knossos only recorded the presence or absence of construction parts, never damages or deficiencies (cf. also Gallavotti 1961:178).

[31] The proposal is made by Gallavotti "a puro titolo di ipotesi" (Gallavotti 1961:179).

[32] Cf. Gallavotti 1961:179; *DELG* and *EDG* s.v. ἄωροι.

[33] Cf. *DELG* and *EDG* s.vv. ὤρα, ὁράω.

'chariot wing' (Bernabé, Luján)—is really compatible with the "ring" shape of *253.[34] Finally, the fourth hypothesis is not without problems either. Even if the interpretation /wolā/ or /wōlā/ 'part of a braided or laced bridle' (< *wel- 'to turn, roll') is formally and semantically possible,[35] the shape of the logogram *253 suggests that wo-ra was a sort of 'noseband of a bitless headstall'.[36] Now, while it is conceivable that nosebands were produced and recorded separately from chariots and that they were occasionally decorated with bronze ornaments or precious stones and materials,[37] it is unlikely that chariots were described as 'provided with nosebands'. In our documents, in fact, chariots are always recorded with whole bridles, never with parts of bridles (cf. KN Sd series), and when they are provided with bridles they are described by the phrase a-ra-ru-ja a-ni-ja-pi /araruiā (h)anniāpʰi/, not by a -went- adjective like wo-ra-we-sa.

Under these conditions it is admittedly difficult to propose alternative hypotheses. However, an element which has not yet been duly emphasized can perhaps help formulate a new interpretation. That element is represented by a detail of the logogram CUR in the Se tablets (Fig. 3.3). As observed by Vandenabeele and Olivier, four of the five CUR logograms recorded in the Se series (Se 880, 881, 883, and 7449) show two small semicircles placed on the top of the yoke,[38] a detail that is missing in all the other CUR and BIG logograms of the Knossos S series.[39] Due to their shape and position, these semicircles are interpreted by Vandenabeele and Olivier as terrets, a chariot part often depicted in vase paintings, whose purpose was to guide the reins and prevent them from tangling.[40] Since these semicircles recall the shape of the logogram *253 and are found on the tablet where the adjective wo-ra-we-sa is attested (Se 880), one can

---

[34] It is impossible to say if the meaning of 'decoration attached to the extremities of the chariot wings' (see above) fits the shape of *253, but it is certainly difficult to reconcile with the notion of 'protection'.

[35] As stressed by Macedo (2018:48), even if it is uncertain if εὐλή 'worm, maggot' and εὔληρα 'reins' are Greek words from the i.-e. root *wel(h₁)- or Pre-Greek words (cf. EDG s.vv.), there are some Greek words derived from the root of εἰλέω (< *wel-n-) and ἴλλω (<*wi-wl-) which mean 'rope', 'bond', or 'chain' (cf. ἰλλάς, ἅλυσις, etc.).

[36] Cf. Macedo 2018:48.

[37] Cf. in the Knossos Sd series: e-re-pa-te-jo o-po-qo /elepʰanteiois opōkʷois/ 'horse-blinkers decorated with ivory' and ke-ra-ja-pi o-pi-i-ja-pi /keraiāpʰi opihiāpʰi/ 'horn plaques fixed on the straps' vel sim.

[38] Vandenabeele and Olivier 1979:125, 127, pls. LXVI:2–3, LXVII:1–2. According to Vandenabeele and Olivier, the CUR logogram on Se 8477 would not show these semicircles (cf. 1979:123, pl. LXVII:3). In the CoMIK IV photograph, however, they are clearly visible.

[39] The only possible exception is the BIG logogram on Sc 5165 (cf. Vandenabeele and Olivier 1979:125 pl. LVI:4).

[40] Cf. Vandenabeele and Olivier 1979:128–139, figs. 87–92, and Crouwel 1981:108–109, pl. 77 (cf. also Wiesner 1968:56). The detail on a fresco fragment from Knossos, interpreted as a terret by Vandenabeele and Olivier (132, 136, fig. 84), is probably just one of the two ends of the yoke (cf. Crouwel 1981:97, 108 and n36).

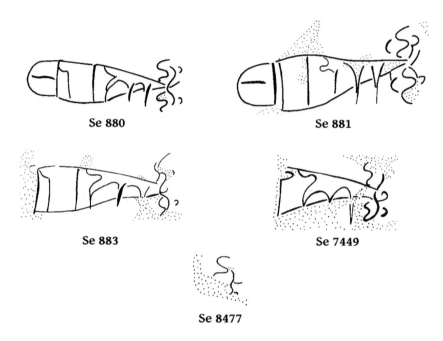

Se 880   Se 881

Se 883   Se 7449

Se 8477

Figure 3.3. The shape of the logogram *241 CUR in the Se series (after *CoMIK*, drawings by L. Godart).

wonder whether *wo-ra* was the name of that accessory. Unfortunately, it is not easy to find confirmation of this hypothesis. The three tablets Se 881, 883, and 7449 are incomplete. It is thus impossible to know if in these cases CUR was preceded by the adjective *wo-ra-we-sa*.

Depictions of Mycenaean war chariots are conventional and not very detailed. It is interesting though that in some vase paintings terrets are represented by one or two concentric circular strokes[41] and that in some cases they have a closed or open oval shape[42] not too different from *253.

The fact that the *wo-ra*'s registered in our documents were made of bronze (*ka-za*) and *pa-ra-ku* is not incompatible with this hypothesis. A number of bronze terrets are in fact known from different places and epochs[43] and some of them are decorated.[44]

[41] Cf. Vandenabeele and Olivier 1979: figs. 89a–b, 92.

[42] Cf. Vandenabeele and Olivier 1979:136 and fig. 88 (craters from Enkomi and Ugarit).

[43] Cf. especially the terrets attached to the chariots buried in the royal tombs of Salamis in Cyprus, dating back to the eighth–seventh centuries BCE (cf., e.g., Karageorghis 1969:27 [T. 1], 80–81 [T. 79]).

[44] Cf. the Sumerian terrets decorated with figurines from Ur and Kiš (see, e.g., Muscarella 1988:329–333) and the Celtic terrets from pre-Roman and Roman Britannia with studs made of bone, coral, or enamel (see Grodecka Lewis 2015 with bibliography). It is not impossible that the *pa-ra-ku-we-jo* specimens were similar to the Celtic terrets, with green stones or glass pieces mounted on

A further detail in support of this hypothesis is perhaps also the fact that Sp 4451 records two *wo-ra*'s, a number identical to the semicircles placed on the yoke of the CUR logograms in the Se series.[45]

From the linguistic point of view, finally, it is not unconceivable that the meaning 'terret' might have developed from /wolā/ 'the thing turned' or /wōlā/ 'turn, turning' (< *wel- 'to turn, roll') or from /worā/ 'watch, guard' or /wōrā/ 'care, concern' (< *wer- / *wor- 'to watch, observe, be attentive, care for'). In the first case the word would describe the shape, in the latter the function of the object.[46]

On the whole, even if, *per se*, none of the elements above is decisive, their combination seems meaningful. The philological, archaeological, and linguistic data converge towards (or are compatible with) the 'terret' interpretation. If that does not necessarily lead us to opt for this solution, it at least makes it plausible. Such a solution clearly implies a lack of lexical continuity between the second and the first millennium BCE.[47] This, however, is not an obstacle, since the analysis of the Mycenaean vocabulary related to chariots and wheels has demonstrated that various technical terms of this sector completely disappeared after the collapse of the palaces.[48]

It must be recognized that this solution leaves a number of details without a clear explanation, e.g., the shape of the logogram *253 (open at the bottom), the registration of a single separated *wo-ra* on Sp 4452, and, in general, the low number of *wo-ra*'s recorded in the tablets.[49] Nevertheless, it seems at least worthy of consideration alongside the other interpretations advanced so far.

---

a base made of bronze or some other material (cf. also the "decorated" terret on the Corinthian crater in Vandenabeele and Olivier 1979:fig. 89a–b).

[45] Unfortunately, the artistic representations do not allow us to determine with certainty how many terrets were used on chariots: see the discussion in Vandenabeele and Olivier 1979:136, and Crouwel 1981:108–109.

[46] For /wolā/ and /wōlā/ there are no clear Greek parallels; for /wōrā/, cf. ὥρα 'care, concern'; for /worā/ one can perhaps cite φρουρά 'watch, guard', if φρουρά is from *προ-hορά < *pro-worā (see discussion in DELG and EDG s.vv. ὁράω, φρουρά, φρουρός). The -ā formations in the ō-grade would present a development from abstract to concrete meaning, similar to that shown by κάπη 'manger', κώπη 'handle', λώπη 'cloak', μύλη 'mill', etc.

[47] In the Homeric poems, the terrets of Priam's ἄμαξα seem to be designated by the word οἴηκες (Il. 24.269). Formally, οἴηκες is the plural of οἴαξ, οἴηξ 'chariot pole'. The interpretation 'terrets' is suggested by the *scholia vetera* (οἰήκεσσιν: κρίκοις, δι' ὧν ἐνειρόμεναι αἱ ἡνίαι). The modern interpreters, however, have suggested other possible meanings ('end of the yoke' and 'hooks for attaching the yoke to the horses' necks'): cf. Wiesner 1968:7, 18. Other terms for 'terrets' attested in the Greek alphabetic sources are: κρίκος, δακτύλιος, and θαιροδύτης.

[48] Cf. Bernabé *et al.* 1990–1991:168–172, and Bernabé *et al.* 1992–1993:154–156.

[49] The open shape of *253 (if it is not accidental) might reflect a construction detail aimed at facilitating the insertion of the reins into the ring. As regards the low number of *wo-ra*'s recorded, as has been suggested by Plath (1994:56), it could be due to the fact that *wo-ra*'s were generally made of less precious materials (cf. the Egyptian terrets, which, as reported by Crouwel 1981:108, were of leather). The hypothesis formulated by Bernabé *et al.* (1992–1993:160 and n140), according to which *wo-ra*'s were rare objects made with precious materials, seems less likely.

Abbreviations

DELG = Chantraine, P. 1968–1980. *Dictionnaire étymologique de la langue grecque: Histoire des mots*. Paris.

KT 5 = Killen, J. T., and J.-P. Olivier. 1989. *The Knossos Tablets*. 5th ed. Salamanca.

Bibliography

Baumbach, L. 1971. "The Mycenaean Greek Vocabulary II." *Glotta* 49:151–190.

Bennett, E. L., Jr., J. M. Driessen, L. Godart, J. T. Killen, C. Kopaka, J. L. Melena, J.-P. Olivier, and M. Perna. 1989. "436 raccords et quasi-raccords de fragments inédits dans *KT* 5." *Minos* 24:199–242.

Bernabé, A. 1996. "Estructura del léxico micénico sobre el carro y sus partes." In *Atti e Memorie del Secondo Congresso Internazionale di Micenologia, Roma-Napoli, 14-20 ottobre 1991*, ed. E. De Miro, L. Godart, and A. Sacconi, 195–207. Rome.

Bernabé, A., J. L. Alonso, L. M. Benito, R. Cantarero, A. Leal, M. L. Marín, S. Moncó, P. Pérez, and P. Rodríguez. 1992–1993. "Estudios sobre el vocabulario micénico 2: Términos referidos a los carros." *Minos* 27–28:125–166.

Bernabé, A., D. Hitos, J. I. Juanes, E. R. Luján, J. A. Negrete, J. G. Rubio, and T. Souto. 1990–1991. "Estudios sobre el vocabulario micénico 1: Términos referidos a las ruedas." *Minos* 25–26:133–173.

Bernabé, A., and E. R. Lujan. 2008. "Mycenaean Technology." In *A Companion to Linear B: Mycenaean Greek Texts and Their World*, vol. 1, ed. Y. Duhoux and A. Morpurgo Davies, 201–233. Bibliothèque des Cahiers de Linguistique de Louvain 120. Louvain-la-Neuve.

Chadwick, J. 1976. *The Mycenaean World*. Cambridge.

Chadwick, J., and L. Baumbach. 1963. "The Mycenaean Greek Vocabulary." *Glotta* 41:157–271.

Crouwel, J. H. 1981. *Chariots and Other Means of Land Transport in Bronze Age Greece*. Amsterdam.

Doria, M. 1972. *Carri e ruote negli inventari di Pilo e di Cnosso*. Trieste.

Duhoux, Y. 1975. "L'ordre des mots en mycénien." *Minos* 14:123–163.

Firth, R. J., and J. L. Melena. 1998–1999. "Identifying the Linear B Tablets from the Arsenal and Little Palace at Knossos." In *A-NA-QO-TA. Studies Presented to J. T. Killen*, ed. J. Bennet and J. Driessen, 107–134. Salamanca.

Gallavotti, C. 1961. "Note sul lessico miceneo." *Rivista di filologia e di istruzione classica* 39:160–179.

Georgiev, V. 1956. "La κοινὴ créto-mycénienne." In *Études mycéniennes. Actes du colloque international de Gif-sur-Yvette, 3-7 avril 1956*, ed. M. Lejeune, 173–188. Paris.

———. 1979. "L'origine des désinences du nominatif-accusatif-vocatif d'après les données mycéniennes." In *Colloquium Mycenaeum. Actes du sixième colloque international sur les textes mycéniens et égéens tenu à Chaumont sur Neuchâtel du 7 au 13 septembre 1975*, ed. E. Risch, and H. Mühlestein, 341–346. Neuchâtel.

Grodecka Lewis, A. S. 2015. "Iron Age and Roman-Era Vehicle Terrets from Western and Central Britain: An Interpretive Study." PhD diss., University of Leicester.

Ilievski, P. H., and L. Crepajac, eds. 1987. *Tractata Mycenaea. Proceedings of the Eighth International Colloquium on Mycenaean Studies, Held in Ohrid, 15-20 September 1985*. Skopje.

Karageorghis, V. 1969. *Salamis in Cyprus: Homeric, Hellenistic, and Roman*. London.

Killen, J. T., and J.-P. Olivier. 1968. "155 raccords de fragments dans les tablettes de Cnossos." *Bulletin de Correspondance Hellénique* 92:115–141.

Lejeune, M. 1958. "Études de philologie mycénienne. III: Les adjectifs mycéniens à suffixe -ϝεντ-." *Revue des Études Anciennes* 60:5–26.

———. 1968a. "Chars et roues à Cnossos: structure d'un inventaire." *Minos* 9: 9–61.

———. 1968b. "Le duel des thèmes en –α." *Revue de philologie, de littérature et d'histoire anciennes* 42:234–239.

Lorimer, H. L. 1950. *Homer and the Monuments*. London.

Macedo, J. M. 2018. "Mycenaean *wo-ra-we-sa*." *Kadmos* 57:45–54.

Melena, J. L. 1972. "On the Knossos Mc Tablets." *Minos* 13:29–54.

———. 1987. "On Untransliterated Syllabograms *56 and *22." In Ilievski and Crepajac 1987:203–232.

Milani, C. 1969. "Note di filologia micenea." *Rendiconti dell'Istituto Lombardo. Accademia di Scienze e Lettere* 103:634–648.

Muscarella, O. W. 1988. *Bronze and Iron: Ancient Near Eastern Artifacts in the Metropolitan Museum of Art*. New York.

Palaima, T. G. 2004. "Feasting in the Linear B Documents." In *The Mycenaean Feast*, ed. J. C. Wright, 97–127. Princeton.

Palmer, L. R. 1957. "A Mycenaean Tomb Inventory." *Minos* 5:58–92.

———. 1963. *The Interpretation of Mycenaean Greek Texts*. Oxford.

Perpillou, J.-L. 1987. "ἐν, ἐνς, ἐξ en mycénien?" In Ilievski and Crepajac 1987: 267–279.

Petruševski, M. D. 1979. "*Wo]-ra, wo-ra-e, wo-ra-we-sa*." *Živa Antika* 29:225–226.

Piquero, J. 2015a. "Incrustaciones con vidrios de colores en Pilo. Análisis lingüístico y arqueológico de micénico *pa-ra-ku-we*." In *Orientalística en tiempos de crisis. Actas del VI Congreso Nacional del Centro de Estudios del Próximo Oriente, Madrid 12-13 de diciembre de 2013*, ed. A. Bernabé and J. A. Álvarez-Pedrosa, 285–296. Saragossa.

———. 2015b. "Micénico *pa-ra-ku-we* y telas *pa-ra-ku-ja*: Una nueva etimología en el contexto del Oriente Próximo." *Aula Orientalis* 33:115–126.

———. 2019. *El léxico del Griego micénico. Index Graecitatis*. Nancy.

Plath, R. 1994. *Der Streitwagen und seine Teile im frühen Griechischen: Sprachliche Untersuchungen zu den mykenischen Texten und zum homerischen Epos.* Nuremberg.

Risch, E. 1976. "Die Stoffadjektive auf *-ejos* im Mykenischen." In *Studies in Greek, Italic, and Indo-European Linguistics. Offered to Leonard R. Palmer on the Occasion of His Seventieth Birthday*, ed. A. Morpurgo Davies and W. Meid, 309–318. Innsbruck.

Ruijgh, C. J. 1961. "Le traitement des sonantes voyelles dans les dialectes grecs et la position du mycénien." *Mnemosyne* 14:193–216.

———. 1967. *Études sur la grammaire et le vocabulaire du grec mycénien*. Amsterdam.

Sharypkin, S. 2009. "Mycenaean Dual Reconsidered." *DO-SO-MO. Fascicula Mycenologica Polona* 8:69–76.

Tegyey, I. 1987. "Scribes and Archives at Knossos and Pylos: A Comparison." In Ilievski and Crepajac 1987:357–366.

Vandenabeele, F., and J.-P. Olivier. 1979. *Les idéogrammes archéologiques du linéaire B*. Paris.

Ventris, M. G. F. 1955. "Mycenaean Furniture on the Pylos Tablets." *Eranos* 53: 109–124.

Wiesner, J. 1968. *Fahren und Reiten*. Vol. I, Chap. F of *Archaeologia Homerica*. Göttingen.

Witczak, K. T. 2000. "Mykeńska nazwa żelaza (**pa-ra-ku*) i jej indoeuropejska geneza." *DO-SO-MO. Fascicula Mycenologica Polona* 1:53–61.

———. 2009. "A Wandering Word for 'Hardened Iron, Steel': A Study in the History of Concepts and Words." *Studia Etymologica Cracoviensia* 14:291–302.

4

Le trait d'union linéaire B[1]

Yves Duhoux

Université Catholique de Louvain (Louvain-la-Neuve)

yves.duhoux@uclouvain.be

Abstract

Presentation of the various forms of the divider in the Linear B script. Description of the way the Mycenaean scribes separated words. Discovery of a new function of the Linear B divider, which could be used as a hyphen, as in the Akkadian and Ugaritic writing systems.

Keywords

Mycenaean script, divider, hyphen

1. Le séparateur mycénien

On utilise souvent l'expression "séparateur (ou diviseur) de 'mot'[2]" pour désigner un signe conventionnellement translittéré par une virgule (",") dans nos éditions du linéaire B. Cette expression mérite une brève mise au point parce qu'elle ne répond pas exactement à la réalité qu'elle est censée dénommer. En effet, un "séparateur de 'mot'" peut être placé non seulement entre deux "mots"[3] comme on s'y attend (c'est le cas le plus fréquent), mais aussi entre:

---

[1] Je remercie les éditeurs scientifiques de ce volume qui m'ont donné l'occasion de revoir cet article, rédigé en 2016. Je reprends les références des tablettes de Cnossos à *KT*[5] et de Pylos à *PTT*[3].

[2] La notion de mot est source de discussions infinies en linguistique. Par commodité, j'emploierai conventionnellement mot dans ce qui suit, mais le mettrai entre guillemets : "mot". Sur le "mot" en linéaire B, voir Melena 2014:15, 123–128, 161.

[3] Ainsi, KN Bk 799.1 (*da-i-pi-ta* , *ke-do-si-ja*; scribe 104).

(a) un "mot" et un idéogramme,[4] ou un idéogramme et un "mot";[5] (b) deux moitiés d'un seul "mot" (voir §§3–4); (c) exceptionnellement, deux idéogrammes.[6] De plus, il peut figurer comme dernier signe d'une rubrique[7] ou d'une tablette.[8] Il vaut donc mieux ne pas employer "mot" et appeler ce signe seulement *séparateur* ou *diviseur*.[9]

Il existe plusieurs formes de séparateur en linéaire B. J'en donne la description ci-dessous. Tom Palaima a bien voulu en commenter épigraphiquement certaines—ses remarques sont signalées par [Commentaire TP] dans les notes. Je l'en remercie.

> (1) Celle qui est de loin la plus courante est un petit trait vertical, comme le premier signe des photos 1a et 1b (§3). En KN Bk 799, le scribe 104 place ce trait entre deux "mots" [l. 1], entre "mot" et idéogramme [l. 2] ou encore entre idéogramme et "mot" [l. 6]. Ce petit trait est généralement placé dans la partie inférieure de la ligne d'écriture, mais peut aussi apparaître dans la zone médiane ou supérieure. On peut parfois avoir l'impression qu'il se dédouble, comme en PY Eo 224.7 (scribe 41) après *do-e-ra*, mais il s'agit d'une illusion.[10]
>
> (2) Il existe un exemple assuré où le séparateur est un petit trait *horizontal* (PY Cn 40.14 après *a-te-re-wi-ja*; scribe 21).[11]

---

[4] Ainsi, KN Bk 799.2 (*u-ra-jo* , VIR). Je définis comme "idéogramme," tout signe rendant un élément intrinsèquement pourvu de sens—par exemple, le signe *1* ou la virgule (,) de l'alphabet latin expriment en eux-mêmes respectivement "une unité" ou "une séparation dans un texte." Contrairement à l'usage, je considère conventionnellement les termes "idéogramme" et "logogramme" comme synonymes. Un "phonogramme" n'a aucun sens propre, mais représente un son dépourvu de signification. Les phonogrammes rendent soit des phonèmes (vel sim.; ces signes sont appelés "lettres," comme *b* ou *y*), soit des syllabes (ces signes sont appelés "syllabogrammes," comme les signes linéaire B ᚼ et ⯊ que nous translittérons respectivement par *de* et *pi*).

[5] Ainsi, KN Bk 799.7 (VIR , *pu-ri*).

[6] Ainsi, KN Ch 896, entre deux abréviations idéographiques (*ne*, *we*; scribe 110); Da 1396, entre OVIS^m et "100" (scribe 117; *KT*⁶ décrit ce signe comme une "deliberate vertical mark"); Dc 1129, entre OVIS^m et "37" (scribe 117; *KT*⁶ décrit ce signe comme une "deliberate mark resembling divider").

[7] Ainsi, PY An 656.9 (scribe 1).

[8] Ainsi, PY An 657.14 (scribe 1).

[9] Sur le séparateur en linéaire B, voir Melena 2014:161–162, qui l'appelle à juste titre "divider."

[10] *PTT*³ édite "*do-e-ra* , ,". [Commentaire TP]: Le scribe H 41 écrit *ra* avec ou sans trait vertical fermant l'horizontale inférieure droite. Et ce petit trait vertical du signe *ra* ressemble à un séparateur de mots (cf. Palaima: 253, deuxième exemple de *ra*). Sur la tablette Eo 224, H 41, le petit trait vertical de *ra* figure à l'intérieur du mot *pa-ra-ko*, en ligne .3. Mais le cas le plus remarquable est le signe *ra* dans le mot *ka-ra-wi-po*[-*ro* sur la tablette Eb 338.1, H 41. Voir aussi à Pylos *ra* chez H 32 (Palaima: 250) et *su* dans la main 43 (Palaima: 256, deuxième exemple de *su*).

[11] *PTT*³ édite une virgule pointée, mais commente "divider after *a-te-re-wi-ja* is horizontal." Partout ailleurs dans cette tablette, le séparateur a la forme classique d'un petit trait vertical.

(3)   Un simple petit point peut régulièrement fonctionner comme séparateur (ainsi, KN De 1136.B entre]*we-ra-to* et *e-ko-so*; scribe 117).[12]

(4)   Exceptionnellement, de longues lignes verticales séparent une tablette en plusieurs parties (ainsi, KN Vd 7545, avec quatre lignes; scribe 124-S). Leur fonction était vraisemblablement d'indiquer l'endroit où une tablette feuille de palmier devait être divisée en "mini-tablettes."[13]

(5)   Sur une autre variante de séparateur, en forme de large point, voir §3.

2. La segmentation des "mots" en linéaire B

Il est de règle que les scribes linéaire B écrivent un "mot" de manière continue, sans le séparer en sous-ensembles.[14] S'ils prévoient que la place disponible sera insuffisante pour l'intégralité d'un "mot," ils laissent généralement un espace vacant et notent ce "mot" en entier à la ligne suivante. Ainsi, PY An 654.7 (scribe 1) se termine par *e-qe-ta,* après lequel viennent un séparateur et une longue zone vierge. Il n'y avait en effet pas de place après *e-qe-ta* pour le "mot" de six syllabogrammes *a-re-ku-tu-ru-wo* qui devait suivre et qui a, en fait, été tracé tout entier l. 8 après le long blanc de la l. 7.

Un autre procédé, bien plus rare, consiste à diviser le "mot" trop long en deux moitiés, sans séparateur entre elles. Ainsi, en PY Ta 709.2, le scribe 2 n'avait pas la place pour noter la séquence "*au-de-we-sa-qe* 1" dans le même module que les signes précédents. Il l'a alors écrite en caractères minuscules, mais en la divisant : *au-de-we-* est au niveau habituel, tandis que *-sa-qe* 1 se trouve au-dessus d'*au-de-we-*; il n'y a aucun séparateur.

On va le voir à l'instant, une nouvelle lecture montre qu'un séparateur a été placé à l'intérieur d'un "mot" en PY An 654.8 à cause d'un manque d'espace (§3; Fig. 4.1a).

Il arrive enfin que le séparateur soit délibérément inséré à l'intérieur d'un "mot" et le divise ainsi en deux moitiés sans que la moindre contrainte de place ait pu jouer: la série PY Ta en donne plusieurs exemples remarquables (§4).

---

[12]   Le scribe 117 affectionne ce séparateur en forme de petit point. [Commentaire TP]: Il est d'ailleurs courant de remplacer un des traits horizontaux du signe *qe* par un petit point lorsque les scribes doivent écrire *qe* plusieurs fois sur la même tablette. Par exemple, PY Eo 276.4 et .8 (scribe 41).

[13]   Duhoux 2012:216–217.

[14]   Duhoux 1999. Il peut pourtant arriver qu'un séparateur soit inséré par erreur à l'intérieur d'un "mot"—ainsi, *po-te-* , *-wo* en PY Eo 268 (scribe 41).

3. Une fonction et une forme nouvelles du séparateur linéaire B

La tablette PY An 654.8–9 (scribe 1) livre un exemple particulier d'emploi du séparateur. Dans ce texte, le long (huit syllabogrammes) adjectif patronymique *e-te-wo-ke-re-we-i-jo*, Etewoklewehios, "fils d'Étéocle," est réparti sur deux lignes consécutives : *e-te-wo-ke-re-we-* (.8) et *-i-jo* (.9), ainsi que l'éditent PTT[1], 52. Après avoir commencé à tracer *e-te-wo-ke-re-we-i-jo* l. 8, le scribe a manifestement vu qu'il ne disposerait pas de l'espace nécessaire pour l'écrire tout entier. Il s'est alors arrêté après le *-we-* et a ajouté *-i-jo* en .9. Le dernier syllabogramme de la l. 8, *-we-*, a un plus petit module qu'*e-te-wo-ke-re-* qui précède (Fig. 4.1a). Cette diminution n'est toutefois pas due au manque de place, car elle s'observe dans d'autres exemples de *we* où il y a assez d'espace dans la tablette.[15] Cependant *-we-* ne constitue pas la fin de la l. 8: il est suivi par un espace qui a été jusqu'ici d'interprétation difficile. E. L. Bennett n'édite aucun signe après *e-te-wo-ke-re-we-* dans le fac-similé de ses *Pylos Tablets*, 70. Une vingtaine d'années plus tard, les PTT[1], 52 font de même, mais signalent dans leur apparat critique la présence d' "an accidental mark or perhaps ... divider."[16] J. L. Melena édite, lui, un séparateur pointé dans son édition des tablettes de Pylos en 2021.[17]

Comment interpréter l'extrême fin d'An 654.8? Une aide précieuse vient d'être fournie par une magnifique photo couleur en haute définition de PY An 654 que Dimitri Nakassis et Kevin Pluta ont pu prendre au Musée Archéologique National d'Athènes pour le compte de l'Université de Cincinnati.[18] Ce cliché a été obtenu en utilisant les techniques de "Reflectance Transformation Imaging (RTI)" et de scanning tridimensionnel à lumière structurée. Je remercie K. Pluta qui a bien voulu me le communiquer, de même qu'une série d'autres photographies de tablettes pyliennes.[19] Cette photo permet de clarifier la lecture d'An 654.8. Après *e-te-wo-ke-re-we-*, on voit un large point qui donne l'impression d'avoir été tracé en enfonçant délibérément le stylet[20] (Fig. 4.1a). Quelle peut être sa fonction? La tablette An 654.1 livre elle-même la réponse avec un

[15] T. G. Palaima me signale ainsi des exemples de *we* de taille réduite en An 654 aux lignes .6 (*ku-re-we*), .11 (*ta-ti-qo-we-wo*) ou .14 (*pe-di-je-we*).

[16] PTT[2], 59.

[17] PTT[3], 39.

[18] Voir Nakassis–Pluta.

[19] Je suis très reconnaissant à l'Université de Cincinnati qui m'a autorisé à reproduire ici les deux clichés de détail des Fig. 4.1a et b. La résolution de ces photos est évidemment de loin moins bonne que celle des clichés originaux dont j'ai pu disposer.

[20] Ne pas confondre ce large point avec le petit cercle (°), soigneusement tracé, qui figure après *po-me* à la hauteur de OVIS^m en KN Dd 1376 (g 117) et dont la fonction reste énigmatique — serait-ce une variante de la "marque de vérification" (checkmark) ✕ (sur laquelle voir Melena 2014:161–162)?

Figure 4.1a. PY An 654.8 (détail) (Courtesy of the Department of Classics, University of Cincinnati, and Dimitri Nakassis–Kevin Pluta).

Figure 4.1b. PY An 654.1 (détail) (Courtesy of the Department of Classics, University of Cincinnati, and Dimitri Nakassis–Kevin Pluta).

deuxième exemple de ce même point. Il figure après *pe-ri-te-u* et ne peut être qu'un séparateur (Fig. 4.1b).[21]

Une nouvelle autopsie de la tablette et des macrophotographies seraient bien sûr utiles pour confirmer définitivement ces lectures.

Ces séparateurs en forme de large point n'apparaissent pas ailleurs en An 654, où l'on trouve toujours le petit trait vertical habituel. Il n'y a toutefois pas lieu d'y voir autre chose qu'une variante apparemment non significative: le scribe 1 a simplement enfoncé délibérément son stylet dans l'argile au lieu d'y tracer un petit trait—le scribe 21 de Pylos a, de même, écrit une fois un diviseur horizontal (§1) dans une tablette où le diviseur vertical est de règle. D'autres exemples de séparateur en forme de large point pourraient peut-être figurer en KN K 740.3–5 (scribe 102?) entre : *255 et "16"; *ku-ru-su-*56* et *207^{VAS}*; *pi-ri-je* et

---

[21] E. L. Bennett (*Pylos Tablets*, 70) représentait en 1955 ce diviseur par une barre verticale. D'après la photo, je me demande si cette barre n'est pas oblique au lieu de verticale et n'est pas accidentelle.

ZE.[22] Par contre, les larges points qui apparaissent quelquefois à Thèbes ne sont probablement pas des séparateurs, mais leur fonction est obscure.[23]

Le large point à la fin d'An 654.8 est donc un séparateur, ce qui livre le texte suivant : [.8] *e-te-wo-ke-re-we-*, [.9] *-i-jo*. Cette nouvelle lecture révèle une fonction inconnue jusqu'à présent du séparateur linéaire B: faire office de *trait d'union* pour indiquer une coupure de "mot," ici en fin de ligne.

Un signe linéaire B correspondant à notre trait d'union moderne n'est-il pas une vue de l'esprit complètement anachronique à l'âge du Bronze ? On pourrait être tenté de le croire, mais il n'en est rien. En effet, des signes équivalant à notre trait d'union apparaissent au Proche-Orient dans les cunéiformes akkadiens (IIIᵉ–IIᵉ millénaires) et dans l'alphabet cunéiforme d'Ougarit (XIVᵉ–XIIᵉ siècles).[24]

4. L'emploi du séparateur à l'intérieur de composés en PY Ta

À Pylos, dans la série Ta, le scribe 2 insère dix fois le petit trait vertical du séparateur classique au milieu de certains "mots."

Cette place inattendue n'est justifiée par aucune contrainte d'espace disponible. Elle se comprend toutefois grammaticalement. Tous ces "mots" sont des composés. Le séparateur disjoint leurs deux membres et montre leur frontière. On trouve ainsi *a-pi* , *to-ni-jo* (Ta 716.1); *a-pu* , *ke-ka-u-me-ṇọ*[(Ta 641.1); *e-ne-wo* , *pe-za* (Ta 642. [1], 3a); *ke-re-si-jo* , *we-ke* (Ta 641.1 [2 ex.]; 709.3 [2 ex.]); *pu-ko-so* , *e-ke-e* (Ta 715.3); etc. La nouvelle lecture de PY An 654.8–9 permet de mieux comprendre cette pratique: c'est le séparateur fonctionnant comme *trait d'union* que le scribe 2 a inséré dans cette dizaine de "mots" afin d'indiquer clairement leur structure morphologique. Les motifs de cette présentation exceptionnelle sont discutés, mais leur réalité n'est pas contestable. D'autres exemples de disjonction de ce type pourraient d'ailleurs peut-être exister, mais sont moins évidents.[25]

---

[22] Toutefois, Melena 2014:162 considère que ces points "seem to play the rôle of substitutes for the logogram for bronze." Il s'agirait alors d'une redondance (que les scribes mycéniens pratiquent régulièrement), étant donné que l'idéogramme du "bronze" figure en K 740.3.

[23] Ces larges points se trouvent en TH Av 100.4–5 (4 ex.; scribe 304), Fq 214.2, 4 (scribe 305), Fq 236.2 (2 ex.; scribe 364), Fq 254[+]255.2 (scribe 305) et Gp 290 (scribe –), le plus souvent au-dessus ou au-dessous de syllabogrammes. En tout cas au-dessus du *-ro* de *pa-ro* en Av 100.4, le point ferait double emploi avec le séparateur classique qui figure après la préposition. Ces points pourraient être accidentels.

[24] Duhoux 2017.

[25] Duhoux 1999:230–232.

5. Note de correction

Je découvre avec plaisir que J. L. Melena lit *e-te-wo-ke-re-we*, *i-jo* en PY An 654.8–9 dans sa toute nouvelle édition des *Pylos Tablets. Third Edition in Transliteration* (avec la collaboration de R. J. Firth), Vitoria–Gasteiz, 2021:39.

Bibliographie

Aegean Scripts = M.-L. Nosch, and H. Landenius Enegren, eds., *Aegean Scripts. Proceedings of the 14th International Colloquium on Mycenaean Studies, Copenhagen, 2-5 September 2015* (Rome, 2017). Incunabula Graeca 105.

Duhoux, Y. 1999. "La séparation des mots en linéaire B." In *Floreant Studia Mycenaea. Akten des X. Internationalen Mykenologischen Colloquiums in Salzburg vom 1.-5. Mai 1995*, ed. S. Deger-Jalkotzy, S. Hiller, and O. Panagl, 227–236. Vienna.

———. 2012. "Les mini-tablettes linéaire B." In *Études mycéniennes 2010. Actes du XIIIᵉ Colloque international sur les textes égéens, Sèvres, Paris, Nanterre, 20-23 septembre 2010*, ed. P. Carlier, C. de Lamberterie, M. Egetmeyer, N. Guilleux, F. Rougemont, and J. Zurbach, 207–225. Pisa-Rome.

———. 2017. "Aides à la lecture à l'âge du Bronze: Égée, Chypre et Proche-Orient." In *Aegean Scripts* I, 209–227.

Melena, J. L. 2014. "Mycenaean Writing." In *A Companion to Linear B: Mycenaean Greek Texts and Their World*, vol. 3, ed. Y. Duhoux and A. Morpurgo Davies, 1–186. Bibliothèque des Cahiers de l'Institut de Linguistique de Louvain 133. Louvain-la-Neuve.

Nakassis–Pluta = D. Nakassis, and K. Pluta. 2017. "Vorsprung durch Technik: Imaging the Linear B Tablets from Pylos." In *Aegean Scripts* I, 285–298.

Palaima = Palaima, T. G. 1988. *The Scribes of Pylos*. Rome.

PTT[1] = Bennett, E. L., Jr., and J.-P. Olivier. 1973–1976. *The Pylos Tablets Transcribed*. Rome.

Pylos Tablets = Bennett, E. L., Jr. 1955. *The Pylos Tablets. Texts of the Inscriptions Found, 1939-1954*. Princeton.

5

Considering the Linear B Tablets in British Museums

Richard Firth

Wolfson College, University of Oxford

richardjfirth4@gmail.com

Abstract

There are forty-five Linear B tablets listed in *CoMIK* IV as being in British museums. The aim of this paper is to consider these tablets and, in particular, how they came to be there.

All of these tablets originated from Knossos, and, with the exception of a small number of fragments, all of the tablets were donations from Sir Arthur Evans, who was responsible for those excavations. It is stated in *Scripta Minoa* II by John Myres that these tablets were presented to Evans by the Greek government. However, this is clearly not accurate, since the most significant series of tablets was presented by the Cretan Assembly, when Crete was still independent of Greece.

This paper considers: (a) the different phases of donations to museums (in respect both of the tablets themselves and of casts made of these tablets); (b) the Royal Academy exhibition of the tablets in 1936; and (c) the publications of the tablets by Evans. The story is rather more complex than might initially be imagined and gives some insight into the *milieu* of the time.

A surprising finding of this work is that the photographs that are nominally of the British Museum tablets Fp 13 and Dd 1171 in *CoMIK* are actually of casts made by Émile Gilliéron.

Keywords

Linear B, Arthur Evans, Ashmolean Museum, Knossos tablets, Émile Gilliéron

1. Introduction

José Melena has been my friend and mentor for many years and I am grateful to the editors for giving me this opportunity to contribute towards this Festschrift.

The aim of this paper is to consider the Linear B tablets in British museums and how they came to be there. Some elements of this topic have already been considered by Firth and Melena (2000–2001). It is now possible to add significantly to that. This is particularly aided by the increased availability of material on the Internet.

The Linear B tablets in British museums can be divided into three different categories:

- the tablets registered in the museums in 1910/11;
- the tablets registered in the Ashmolean in 1938 and 1941;
- the other fragments.

In the introduction to the Minoan section of the Royal Academy exhibition of 1936, Evans explains that he was officially given objects from Crete on three separate occasions. Sometime prior to the union of Crete with Greece in 1913, the Cretan Assembly gave him material and this included a "good representative series of the inscribed clay tablets from the Palace archives." After the union with Greece, duplicate objects were allocated to Evans as excavator. At the conclusion of the excavations, the Greek government presented a further series of objects, including part of a fresco and "an exceptionally fine amphora." It is worth stressing that these objects were given to Evans, as the excavator, rather than to British museums directly. Evans is known to have held a collection of antiquities in his house at Youlbury so, in some cases, there could be a significant delay between the gift to Evans and the subsequent donation by Evans to a museum.[1]

2. The 1910/11 Tablets

In order to comply with the law of antiquities in nineteenth- and twentieth-century Greece, "duplicate," "insignificant," "superfluous," "useless," and "valueless" antiquities could conditionally be legally exported according to the laws of 1834, 1899, and 1932.[2] In the early years of the twentieth century Crete was governed separately to mainland Greece; however, there were also strict laws there and Evans was only permitted to have items that he described as "*duplicates and objets sans valeur.*"

---

[1]   Firth and Melena 2000–2001:456.
[2]   Galanakis, http://wp.chs.harvard.edu/chs-fellows/author/igalanakis/#edn9 (January 2015).

In a letter dated 26 June 1903, Hazzidakis, the Ephor of Antiquities for Central and Eastern Crete, gave Evans permission to transfer a selection of items from Knossos to England. However, at that stage, Evans was specifically denied permission to take any inscribed tablets.[3]

Nevertheless, it is evident that by 1910, Evans had been granted permission to export a small number of inscribed artefacts from Knossos. These included both Linear B tablets and hieroglyphic texts. Evans donated the majority of these items to the Ashmolean Museum in Oxford, but two Linear B tablets were given to the British Museum and one to the Fitzwilliam Museum, Cambridge (see Table 5.1).[4]

Table 5.1

Museum	Registration No. of Tablet	*COMIK / CHIC* no.
Ashmolean Museum	1910.206	CHIC 3
	1910.207	CHIC 5, 159, 160
	1910.208	CHIC 42
	1910.209	CHIC 56
	1910.210	CHIC 59
	1910.211	So 894
	1910.212	Ce 59
	1910.213	Sd 4422
	1910.214	E 777
	1910.215	G 820
	1910.216	Dc 1298
	1910.217	Mc 4455
	1910.218	Ap 639
	1910.219	V 479
British Museum	GR 1910-04-03, 1	Fp 13
	GR 1910-04-03, 2	Dd 1171
Fitzwilliam Museum	GR.1.1911	Ga 676

---

[3] MacGillivray 2000:226.

[4] The Fitzwilliam Musueum accession number (= GR.1.1911) suggests that Ga 676 was given this number in 1911. However, it was actually donated to the museum by Evans in 1922. The implication is that it was on long-term loan to the museum prior to that date.

It is evident from the museum/registration numbers that all of these tablets were received by the museums in 1910 (or 1911 in the case of Ga 676). The British Museum is more specific, showing that the tablets were registered on 3 April 1910.

These tablets cover a wide range of the find-places of Knossos, from an oil tablet from the Clay Chest (Fp 13), one of the earliest tablets found in 1900, to two tablets from the Arsenal, Sd 4422 and Mc 4455, excavated in 1904. They include sheep tablets from the East–West Corridor (Dc 1298 and Dd 1171), a tablet from the Room of the Chariot Tablets (Ce 59), three from the Western Magazines area (Ap, 639, Ga 676, and V 479), and tablets from the North Entrance Passage (E 777, G 820, and So 894). Taken together they could readily be regarded as a "good representative series of the inscribed clay tablets from the Palace archives."

The catalogue of the Royal Academy exhibition of 1936 stated that Desk Case L contained "specimens of original clay tablets from Knossos, presented to the excavator by the Cretan Government, before the Union with Greece." In other words, the display of Linear B tablets shown in 1936 was those identified in Table 5.1.[5] It is worth emphasizing that there is no indication that any of the Linear B tablets that were registered by the Ashmolean in 1938/41 were on display.

It was noted by Firth and Melena (2000–2001:456) that, in principle, these tablets should be marked with Heraklion Museum inventory numbers from their initial entry into that museum in 1904/5. In practice, there are not published photographs of most of the *versos* of these tablets. However, in the case of Ap 639, Dd 1171, and E 777, the *versos* of the tablets are shown in photographs and they are clearly marked with Heraklion Museum inventory numbers (1247, 1257, and 1256, respectively). Similarly, 1254 is written on the obverse of Dc 1298. This demonstrates that these tablets were registered in the Heraklion Museum prior to being given to Sir Arthur Evans.[6]

It is noted by Firth amd Melena (2000–2001:456) that within the Heraklion Museum, the inventory numbers 1247–1257 are now given to replicas of these tablets. The obvious implication is that when the tablets were donated to Evans, they were substituted by casts.[7]

---

[5]   Since there is some ambiguity, it is possible that it could have been a subset of those tablets. In terms of artifacts, this display also contained a replica of the Phaistos Disk and a fragment of a libation table from the Diktaean cave with Linear A script (presumably PS Za 2b or c; i.e., Ashmolean 1923.661 or AE 1).

[6]   <http://sirarthurevans.ashmus.ox.ac.uk/collection/linearb/images.php> [January 2015]; <http://www.britishmuseum.org/research/collection_online/search.aspx?searchText=Knossos+tablet> [January 2015].

[7]   Note that the Heraklion Museum does not appear to have a replica of Mc 4455 (Firth and Melena 2000–2001:456). The Heraklion Museum inventory also notes that 1304 and 1305 were "given to Mr Evans." In the Herakleion Museum inventory, 1268–1303 are hieroglyphic inscriptions from Knossos and 1306–1334 are Linear A inscriptions from Haghia Triada (for which Evans was not the excavator). Thus, it seems likely that 1304 and 1305 were hieroglyphic inscriptions from

It is worth noting the obvious point that these Heraklion Museum inventory numbers (1247–1257) are sequential. When these tablets were transferred from Knossos to the Museum in 1904, it is evident from the inventory numbers that the overwhelming bulk of the tablets were naturally grouped together according to when they had been excavated.[8] However, as already noted, the tablets given to Evans were a representative cross-section of the tablets from Knossos. This suggests that the 1910/11 tablets had already been brought together and earmarked as a donation to Evans prior to being given inventory numbers. Therefore, it seems most likely that Evans himself selected the Linear B tablets that he would like to receive.[9]

It is interesting to consider the replicas. It can be deduced that Gilliéron made these replicas since, in 1927, the British Museum purchased a set of fifteen replicas from Émile Gilliéron (père). These included the twelve Linear B tablets listed in Table 5.1 together with *CHIC* 42, 56, and 59. Replicas of the same tablets are also held by the New York Metropolitan Museum of Art (museum nos. 13.30 4-18, *SM* ii, p. 108). Furthermore, the Spurlock World Heritage Museum in the University of Illinois also has copies of fourteen of these casts (excluding *CHIC* 42). These have the registration numbers 1913.02.0005 to 1913.02.0018, implying that they were acquired in 1913, somewhat earlier than the casts in the British Museum in 1927.[10]

It seems likely that, as part of his efforts to persuade the Cretan government to release the tablets in Table 5.1, Evans asked Gilliéron to make replicas, which could be given to the Heraklion Museum in lieu of the tablets donated

---

Knossos. Furthermore, there are traces of the number 1305 remaining on *CHIC* 56 (Olivier and Godart 1996:108).

8   Firth 2000–2001:80.

9   Firth (2000–2001:84–93) attempts to identify the tablets that were grouped together on the same tray when the tablets were donated to the Heraklion Museum. The inventory numbers 1247–1257 of Linear B tablets now in the British Museums fall within the group labeled as Miscellaneous Batch 1. This is now a small batch within the Heraklion Museum, presumably because a significant number of these tablets were given to the British Museums. It is possible to speculate on the remaining tablets within that batch that Evans might have proposed as part of the donation, following the above line of argument. These are Od 666, M 719, and the sheep tablets Dg 1102, Dg 1185 (both damaged by the heat of the conflagration), Da 1195, Da 1197, and De 1231. Finally, it included the tablet with the "Gem Engraver's Sketch" that Bennett later numbered 5011, which is shown on the dust jacket of *CoMIK* II.

10   <https://www.spurlock.illinois.edu/collections/search-collection/index.php?advsf=0&q=li near+b&or=&g=All&Search=Search> [January 2015]. Replicas of Ga 676 and So 4442 are also held by the Mount Holyoke College Art Museum, Massachusetts (MH 1a.B.F & MH 1b.B.F.): <https://museums.fivecolleges.edu/detail.php?t=objects&type=ext&id_number=MH+1a.B.F>, <https://museums.fivecolleges.edu/detail.php?t=objects&type=ext&id_number=MH+1b.B.F> [January 2015]. From the photographs, it would appear that the Spurlock replicas are much clearer than the later ones created for the British Museum.

to Evans. Then the same molds were reused by Gilliéron to make replicas that could be sold to museums that were not able to display genuine tablets.[11]

SM ii was published in 1952 and was edited by Sir John Myres based on the drawings, text, and photographs left unpublished by Arthur Evans. Following the death of Alice Kober, Myres asked Emmett Bennett to visit Crete, in 1950, in order to match up the drawings and photographs from Evans's archive with the actual tablets. Bennett's work included the drawing up of the tables of inventory numbers that are found in *SM* ii. Within the list of Linear B tablets in the Ashmolean, *SM* ii, p. 108 includes the following:

Tablet	Ashmolean Museum no.
Dd 1171	1910.220[12]
Fp 13	1910.221
L 520	1910.222
Ga 676	1910.223

Although it was not noted in *SM* ii, it is evident that these are all replicas, since three of the original tablets are listed above in Table 5.1 as being in the British and Fitzwilliam Museums. This is perhaps not surprising since the replicas would have been readily available to Evans from Gilliéron.

It is interesting to note that the Ashmolean Museum number 1910.221 is clearly visible on the photograph of Fp 13 shown in *CoMIK* I whereas it is not visible in the photograph of Fp 13 on the British Museum web site. Similarly, the Ashmolean Museum number 1910.220 is clearly visible on the *CoMIK* II photograph of Dd 1171 whereas it is not visible in the photograph of Dd 1171 in the British Museum. Therefore, it would seem that the photographs of Fp 13 and Dd 1171 in *CoMIK* are of of the Gilliéron facsimiles in the Ashmolean Museum, rather than the actual Linear B tablets.

The appearance of L 520 in this list is more surprising as in this case, the original is in the Heraklion Museum. The author is not aware of other copies of this tablet and so it seems unlikely that it was made by Gilliéron.[13]

---

[11] Lapatin (2002:138) notes that, although costly, Gilliéron's facsimiles of ancient artifacts were widely purchased and displayed in museums, although today they are relegated to storerooms.

[12] This is listed as 1910.221 on *SM* ii, 108 but the photograph in *CoMIK* II clearly shows the number as 1910.220.

[13] L 520 = 1938.222 is listed in *SM* ii, p. 108 and is identified as a cast on the web-page <http://sirarthurevans.ashmus.ox.ac.uk/collection/linearb/images.php> [January 2015].

3. References to Casts in Doll's Diary

Christian Doll was the architect employed in 1906/7 to build the Villa Ariadne for Evans. His diaries for that period provide a fascinating insight into life at Knossos during that period. Within these diaries, there are a number of references to casts.

> THURSDAY 26 JULY 1906: Went to camp & got tablet back from Capt. Willett & arranged to have cast made.
>
> FRIDAY 27 JULY 1906: Started Papadákis to make casts of clay inscribed tablet and got four made.
>
> SUNDAY 2 SEPTEMBER 1906: Cameron did not come to tea. Gave him casts of his seal & returned the seal.
>
> WEDNESDAY 6 SEPTEMBER 1906: Gave Papadákis Cameron's two seals to cast.
>
> TUESDAY 19 FEBRUARY 1907: Went to Mess before supper with casts of 3 faced head.[14]

There are three people named in these extracts. Ioannis Papadákis was a professional conservator from the Candia Syllogos who was employed by Evans.[15] Cameron and Willett were officers of the British Army stationed in Heraklion.

They demonstrate that amongst his other responsibilities, Papadákis was required to make casts of Knossos tablets. Furthermore, this was regarded as an unexceptional task, such that casts could simply be requested by Doll for his friends within the British Army.

It seems reasonable to draw a distinction between copies of tablets that were sold to museums around the world, which were made by Gilliéron, and those that were made in small numbers by Papadákis at the request of Evans and his employees.

Thus, on the balance of evidence, it seems likely that the cast of L 520 held in the Ashmolean was made by Ioannis Papadákis.

Finally, it is worth noting that from the twelve Linear B tablets given to Evans in 1910, he chose to use six of them in the illustrations of *PoM* IV.[16] In addition, L 520 is illustrated on *PoM* IV, 663. In practice, Evans had photographs taken of many of the more significant tablets and he had included drawings

---

[14] In his catalogue of the 1936 exhibition, Evans refers to "archaic bead seals ... often three-sided." It seems possible that this extract from the diary should read "3 faced bead."

[15] MacGillivray 2000:181.

[16] The page numbers of *PoM* IV with these illustrations are 675 (Fp 13), 707 (Ap 639), 712 (V 479), 792 (Sd 4422), 795 (So 894), 833 (Mc 4455).

in the Handlist. Furthermore, as such a prominent person, he would have had access to all of the Linear B tablets when he was visiting Crete. Overall, about 10 percent of the tablets in the Handlist are illustrated in *PoM* IV. Therefore, there is a much higher proportion of this 1910/11 group of tablets than of Handlist tablets in general. This may simply be a pragmatic decision by Evans to include more of the tablets that were accessible in Oxford, which could be readily re-drawn to a standard suitable for publication. Alternatively, Evans might have considered publication when he selected the tablets that were donated to him by the Cretan Assembly.

4. The 1938/41 Tablets

The Linear B tablets registered in the Ashmolean in 1938 and 1941 are listed in Tables 5.2a, 5.2b.

According to Horwitz (1981:242), Evans donated his collections to the Ashmolean around 1938, as his health deteriorated. The residual Linear B items registered in 1941 were donated in the year of Evans' death.

The listing of these tablets in *SM* ii, p. 108 is a little confused because of the editing of inscriptions that were not in Evans' Handlist. Myres chose to continue the numbering in the Handlist to include additional tablets found in the Heraklion and Ashmolean Museums and in the drawings and photographs amongst Evans's papers. However, on closer examination a number of these already appeared in the Handlist, and this led to repeated re-numbering of these tablets. Thus, on *SM* ii, p. 108, the Ashmolean tablet 1938.179 (now Dq 8208) is referred to as both 1652 and 1714. The inscription listed as 1653 is now identified as Wm 1817.

It is interesting to note that we have no record of casts being held by the Heraklion Museum or other museums of any of the above tablets. However, a cast was made of K 872 and given to the Ashmolean Museum (1938.713), whereas the original was retained at Youlbury and was probably given to the museum at a later stage. K 872 has the inventory number AE 2031.[17]

It is worthwhile considering the statement in *SM* II, p. 108, that the Greek government gave all of the Linear B tablets in the Ashmolean Museum to Sir Arthur Evans.

Prior to Bennett's visit to Heraklion in 1950, no particular interest had been given to the large number of Linear B fragments that had been excavated at Knossos. Evans had not documented the overwhelming majority of these fragments in his publications or notebooks and they had not been photographed.

---

[17] Firth and Melena 2000–2001:456. For K 872, see *CoMIK* IV, p. 291 and the Ashmolean web site <http://sirarthurevans.ashmus.ox.ac.uk/collection/linearb/images.php> [January 2015].

Table 5.2a

Registration no.	CoMIK / CHIC no.
1938.704	Sc 238
1938.705	Se 883
1938.706	Ra 1540
1938.707	B 799
1938.708	De 1301
1938.709	Dl 47
1938.710	E 1569
1938.711	M 1645
1938.712	Dh 1646
1938.713	K 872 (cast)
1938.848	L 1647
1938.849	Sc 218*
1938.850	De 1648
1938.851	Sg 889
1938.852	L 1649
1938.854	D 1650
1938.855	K 1810 [= SM ii, 776bis]
1938.856	B 8206
1938.858	Wm 8207
1938.859	Sc 1651
1938.860	Sc 1644**
1938.861	Ws 8152
1938.1080	Ws 1703
1938.1152	Ws 8153

Table 5.2b

Registration no.	CoMIK no.
1941.179	Dq 8208 [= SM ii, 1652]
1941.180	Wm 1817 [= SM ii, 1653]
1941.1227	Ag 1654
1941.1247	Dk 8209

*The museum number given here for Sc 218 is based on the Ashmolean web site. This implies that the museum no. of 1938.489 quoted in *SM* ii, p. 108 and repeated in *KTT*[5] p. 284 and *CoMIK* IV, p. 291 is in error.

**SM ii, p. 108 suggests that Ashmolean tablet 1938.860 is Sc 236 instead of Sc 1644. This is clearly in error but the cause of the error is difficult to explain.

They had been given to the museum but they had not received inventory numbers and had simply been stored in containers until 1950 when approximately half of these fragments were shown to Bennett. It can be readily accepted that the museum could have given some such fragments to Evans as *"duplicates and objets sans valeur."* This might account for items such as B 8206, Wm 8207, Dq 8208, Dk 8209.[18]

However, at the other end of the scale, there are four tablets amongst the 1938 group which are illustrated in *PoM* IV, namely: Sc 238 (p. 788); B 799 (p. 705); K 872 (p. 729); Ra 1540 (p. 855). These are clearly interesting tablets for illustration because they contain recognizable ideograms, which would have been of interest to Evans in his struggle to interpret the tablets. For example: Sc 238 has an ideogram of a chariot and a cuirass; B 799 has ideograms of people; K 872 has bull's head rhytons and "Vapheio cup"; and Ra 1540 has a sword. Furthermore, there are an additional six tablets, the tablets D 47, De 1301, E 1569, Sc 218, Se 883, Sg 889 that appear in Evans' Handlist. In principle all of these ten tablets should have been given to the Heraklion Museum in 1904 and received inventory numbers, along with the other Linear B tablets from Knossos. However, there is no indication of them in the Heraklion Museum inventory records and it is worth questioning whether there are signs of Heraklion Museum inventory markings on the tablets themselves. To these we can add De 1648 and Ws 1703, which are fine examples, but for some reason were omitted from the Handlist.

It is evident that Evans obtained some of the Cretan artifacts unofficially, even though there might have been some post hoc arrangement to formalize the situation. MacGillivray (2000:225) gives evidence that Evans did not respect the antiquities laws. Mackenzie's letters to Evans in 1905 describe sending to him Early Minoan pottery fragments from Knossos and other finds via a British officer in the Royal Navy (Captain Tupper of the cruiser *Venus*) to avoid the involvement of Hazzidakis. It also records Evans's disappointment at the quality of these EM fragments.[19] In his diary, Doll writes of British Army officers taking a box of antiquities to England for him (9–10 February 1907). It seems possible that at least some of the more choice examples of the 1938/41 group of Linear B tablets did not pass through the Heraklion Museum before finding their way to Oxford.[20]

---

[18] Although these would have been available to the editors of *SM* ii, only Dq 8208 is briefly recorded in *SM* ii (as 1652 on p. 108).

[19] See Momigliano 1999:170, 172–173.

[20] If there were traces of Heraklion Museum inventory numbers on any of the 1938/41 group of tablets in the Ashmolean, this would clearly demonstrate that those particular tablets had formally entered the museum and been donated to Evans. However, it would not be anticipated that minor fragments would have Heraklion Museum inventory numbers since these fragments were not examined within the museum until they were shown to Bennett and Ventris in the 1950s.

5. The Other Fragments

This final section concerns the remaining Linear B fragments that found their way from Crete into British museums. In practice, these have already been considered in some detail by Firth and Melena (2000–2001) and there is little to add here to that account.

Nevertheless, it is worth drawing attention once again to the story of two fragments, Dl 8216 and Dl 8217, which are in the British Museum. Dl 8216 was donated to the museum in 1920 by Major F. W. B. Willett and has the registration number 1920-04-16, 1. Dl 8217 was donated in 1947 by Mrs J. C. Cameron and has the registration number 1947-09-26, 52.[21]

The account of Firth and Melena shows how these two fragments can be traced back to the friendship between Christian Doll and the officers of the British forces that were stationed in Heraklion at that time. This relatively small group of officers included Captains Frederick W. B. Willett and James S. Cameron of the 2nd Battalion Royal Sussex Regiment. It is these men who are mentioned in the brief extracts of Doll's diaries given above dealing with casts and it was through these men that two fragments of Linear B tablets found their way from Knossos to the British Museum.

6. Concluding Remarks

José Melena's ongoing work on Doll's diaries gives a fascinating insight into Heraklion and Knossos at that time and the above details relating to the Linear B fragments are just a small part of that story.

Bibliographical References

CHIC = J.-P. Olivier and L. Godart, *Corpus Hieroglyphicarum Inscriptionum Cretae*, Études Crétoises 31 (Paris, 1996).

Evans, A. J. 1936. "Exhibition Illustrative of Minoan Culture with Special Relation to the Discoveries at Knossos: Introductory Notice and Guide to Arrangement." In *Catalogue of the Exhibition of British Archaeological Discoveries in Greece and Crete, 1886-1936*. Royal Academy of Arts.

Firth, R. J. 2000–2001. "A Review of the Find-Places of the Linear B Tablets from the Palace of Knossos." *Minos* 35–36:63–290.

Firth, R. J., and J. L. Melena. 2000–2001. "A Tale of Two Fragments: KN Dl 8216 and 8217." *Minos* 35–36:451–458.

---

[21] As part of the same donation Mrs. Cameron gave a fairly large collection of Cretan material, including a number of seals. One of these seals is *CHIC* 216 (GR 1947-09-26, 8).

Horwitz, S. L. 1981. *The Find of a Lifetime: Sir Arthur Evans and the Discovery of Knossos.* London.

Lapatin, K. 2002. *Mysteries of the Snake Goddess: Art, Desire, and the Forging of History.* Boston.

MacGillivray, J. A. 2000. *Minotaur: Sir Arthur Evans and the Archaeology of the Minoan Myth.* London.

Momigliano, N. 1999. *Duncan Mackenzie: A Cautious Canny Highlander and the Palace of Minos at Knossos. BICS* Suppl. 72. London.

6

Anthroponymica Mycenaea 12

Ne-ri-to /*Nērito-*/ 'libre de discordia' (ἔρις), Ἀνήριτος y Ἀνήριστος / Ἀνέριστος frente a hom. νήριτος 'innumerable, incalculable' (**nắrito-*: NP Νήριτος, topón. Νήριτον)

José L. García Ramón

Università Cattolica del Sacro Cuore, Milan

jose.luis.garcia.ramon@gmail.com

Abstract

The Pylian man's name *ne-ri-to* is to be understood as /*Nērito-*/, the phonetic outcome of *$\ast\mathring{n}$-$h_1$ri-to-* 'free of strife, quarrel', i.e. as a privative compound whose second member is a -*to*-derivative of *$\ast h_1ér$-i-* (ἔρις), actually *$\ast h_1ér(h_2)i$-* (PIE *$\ast h_1er(h_2)$-* 'to separate', as per M. Weiss). The name is an antonym of ἐριστός 'which may be contested' (S.), with secondary -στο-. It is not attested in its original shape in Alphabetical Greek, but survives: (1) as the MN Ἀνήριτος and Ἀνήριστος (Ἀ-νήριτος, Ἀ-νήριστος, with recharacterization of *Νήριτος by means of privative ἀ-); and (2) as Ἀνέριστος (Ἀν-έριστος, with ἀν° and °έριστος on the model of ἔρις). The second member °ηρι(σ)το-, with Wackernagel's lengthening, is attested in ἀμφ-ήριστος 'contested (on both sides)' (hom.+), cf. MN Ἀμφήριτος, Ἀμφήριστος.

Myc. *ne-ri-to* /*Nērito-*/ joins therefore MN *na-ne-mo* /*Nānemo-*/ (hom. νήνεμος 'windless': *$\ast\mathring{n}$-$h_2n\partial_1mo$-*), MN *na-pu-ti-jo* /*Nāputio-*/ (hom. νηπύτιος 'young': *$\ast\mathring{n}$-h_2pu-* '*infans*'), and *no-pe-re** /*nōpʰeles-*/ 'out of service, useless' (*$\ast\mathring{n}$-h_3p^heles-*). Myc. *ne-ri-to* /*Nērito-*/ has the same structure as hom. νήριτος (*$\ast n\bar{a}rito$-* 'countless, immense': *$\ast\mathring{n}$-h_2ri-to-*, with *°h_2eri-*, cf. ἀρι-θμός 'number, account'), which underlies Homeric Νήριτον (a mountain in Ithaca and Kephallenia) and Νήριτος (name of a local hero of Ithaca, like Ἴθακος), both created *ad hoc* from the epithet. The second member °αριτος lives on in Alphabetic Greek in non-privative compounds like μεγ-ήριτος (Hsd.), ἐπ-ἄριτος (of selected troops: Arcadia), MN Ἐπ-ήριτος and others. Privative compounds with ἀριθμός as second member, which are surely secondary, have the same formal variants as those with °ἄριτος.

Keywords

Greek, Indo-European, Mycenaean, onomastics, word formation

Resumen

1. *Ne-ri-to* en PY Cn 131 en una lista junto a otros antropónimos griegos: posibilidad de *interpretatio graeca*.

2. Los compuestos privativos en griego: (1) /n$\bar{V}$C-/ (*/n̥-HCV-/), (1a) remodelación /a+n$\bar{V}$C-/; (2) /an-VC-/; los compuestos no privativos: (3) el alargamiento composicional.

3. Los hechos micénicos: coexistencia de los tipos (1) NP *na-ne-mo* /Nānemo-/ y *na-pu-ti-jo* /Nāputio-/, epíteto *no-pe-re-a₂* /nōpʰeleʰa/, *re-e* /-leʰe/; y (2) *a-no-no* /anono-/ 'no sujeto a *o-na-ta*' (gr. alf. ὀνᾱ-), *a-na-mo-to* /an-armo(s)to-/ (: hom. ἀνάρμοστος), NP *a-ne-ra-to* /An-era(s)tos/ (: ἀνέραστος) *et al.* Imposibilidad de reconocer los tipo (1a) y (3) por limitaciones del Lineal B.

4. Hom. νήριτος 'innumerable, incalculable' (*nārito-: *n̥-h₂ri-to-, *h₂eri-, cf. ἀρι-θμός): topón. Νήριτον 'inmenso', NP Νήριτος (formado sobre el topónimo). Mic. */Nārito-/ se habría notado †na-ri-to. Sin datos seguros de las variantes †ἀ-νάριτος, †ἀν-άριτος en el I milenio, solamente μεγ-ήριτος (Hes.), (arc.) ἐπ-άριτος, NP Ἐπ-ήριτος. Las variantes con ἀριθμός: (1) νήριθμος (Theoc.), (1a) ἀ+νήριθμος (A.+); (2) ἀν-άριθμος (Pi.+); (3) ἰσ-άριθμος (Pl.+).

5. Mic. *ne-ri-to* /Nērito-/ (más bien que /Nēristo-/) 'libre de discordia' (*n̥-h₁ri-to-, *h₁eri-: ἔρις; en realidad *h₁erh₂- 'separar' [M. Weiss]). Continuidad en el I milenio de /Nērito-/ como Ἀνήριτος (tipo 1a: /a+nerito-/), y Ἀνήριστος (1a: /a+neristo-/), Ἀν-έριστος (2: /an+eristo-/). El segundo miembro °ήρι(σ)το- pervive en hom. ἀμφ-ήριστος, también en la onomástica: Ἀμφ-ἔριτος, Ἀμφ-ήριτος, Ἀμφ-ήριστος.

6. Conclusiones.[1]

[1] Trabajo realizado en el marco del Proyecto de Investigación FFI 2016-79906-P del Ministerio de Economía, Industria y Competitividad (España): "Estudio diacrónico de las instituciones socio-políticas de la Grecia Antigua y de sus manifestaciones míticas" (AEI/FEDER, UE). Versiones previas han sido presentadas en conferencias en Harvard (Department of Classics, 13.11.2017), Ann Arbor (ECIEC, 17.6.18) y Milán (Sodalizio Glottologico, 10.7.2020). Los textos se citan según las ediciones de José Luis Melena, que ha tenido, como siempre, la amabilidad de poner a mi disposición sus lecturas y materiales. La versión final se ha beneficiado de sus comentarios, así como de los de Julián Méndez Dosuna (Salamanca) y de Carlos Varias (Barcelona, UAB): conste aquí mi agradecimiento. Para la bibliografía relativa a cada forma micénica se remite a *DMic.*; para la etimología e historia de las formas griegas en general a los *lemmata* de Frisk 1960, Chantraine

1. El antropónimo *ne-ri-to* (PY Cn 131(1).4),[2] que aparece precedido de *pa-ro*, se atestigua en un registro de entregas de animales en la localidad de *pi-*82*, especificados mediante el correspondiente ideograma (OVIS^m, OVIS^f, CAP^f) y en cada caso con indicación del origen, concretamente de la persona a cuyo cargo están (*pa-ro* + antropónimo) o un topónimo, sin que sea siempre posible decidir,[3] como hace ver el texto de PY Cn 131(1) (8; H 1, H 21?):

.1 pi-*82 , we-re-ke
.2 pa-ro , pi-me-ta , × OVIS^m 200 pa-ro , o-ku-ka , OVIS^m × 130[
.3 pa-ro , ku-pi-ri-jo , OVIS^m 50 × pa-ro , a-ka-ma-wo OVIS^m 120 ×
.4 pa-ro , ko-ru-no OVIS^m 100 × pa-ro , ne-ri-to OVIS^m 30 ×
.5 pa-ro , po-ro-u-te-we OVIS^m 90 × pa-ro , o-wa-ko CAP^f 54 ×
.6 ma-ro-pi , to-ro-wi OVIS^m 130 × pa-ro , a-no-po OVIS^m 130 ×
.7 pa-ro , ke-ro-wo OVIS^m 130 × pa-ro , ra-pa-sa-ko OVIS^m 91 ×
.8 pa-ro , po-ke-we OVIS^f 27 × pa-ro , a-ri-wo-ne × OVIS^m 100
.9 pa-ro , a-we-ke-se-we OVIS^m 170 × pa-ro , po-ko-ro OVIS^m 100 ×
.10 pa-ro , e-ti-ra-wo OVIS^m 100 × pa-ro , a-ta-ma-ne-we OVIS^m 140 ×
.11 pa-ro , se-no OVIS^f 44 × pa-ro , ko-ro OVIS^f 24 ×
.12 pa-ro , do-qo-no × OVIS^m 80 pa-ro , wo-ki-to × OVIS^m 73
.13 pa-ro , me-te-we OVIS^m 163 × pa-ro , ke-sa-me-no OVIS^f 40 ×
.14]pạ-ro , pu-wi-no CAP^f 55

Entre los antropónimos incontestables, al menos cinco son reconocibles como griegos (i.e. de etimología griega e IE):[4] se trata de *po-ro-u-te-we* .5 /*Plou-*

1999, y *EDG*, ; para las homéricas a Snell-Mette 1955. Para las referencias de los antropónimos se remite, salvo indicación explícita, a Bechtel 1917 y a Fraser *et al.* 1987–2018.

La serie *Anthroponymica Mycenaea* incluye una serie de *Vorarbeiten* para un léxico de los antropónimos micénicos: vid. García Ramón 2000, 2000–2001, 2005a, 2005b, 2012a, 2012b, 2012c, 2016, y 2017.

[2] Se trata de un *hapax*, sin relación ninguna con el oscuro NP *ne-ri-wa-to* en KN Og(2) <4467>.3 (tablilla perdida).

[3] En esta construcción *ne-ri-to*, como todas las formas en -(C)o en la lista, puede entenderse como dat. /-ōi/, como loc. /-oi/ o incluso como instr. /-ō/, que también es posible con *pa-ro* (cf. TH Oq 434 *pa-ro , te-qa-jo*[ ]wị-re-u-pi (J. L. Melena, c.p.): formas como *a-we-ke-se-we* /-ēwei/, *po-ro-u-te-we* /-tēwei/, *po-te-we* /-tēwei/ o *a-ri-wo-ne* /-wonei/, pueden recubrir dativos en /-ēwei/, /-wonei/ o instrumentales en /-ēwē/, /-wonē/. Excepcionalmente el origen se expresa con *pa-ro* seguido de un topónimo (*ma-ro-pi* .6), como en PY Cn 40, donde coexisten *ma-ro-pi* .8.9 y *ma-ro* .10.12 (discusión en Hajnal 1995:167n214, 307, 163–165).

[4] El antropónimo *a-ka-ma-wo* .3 /Alkma(i)wo-/ o /Akma(i)wo-/ es dudoso: Ἀλκμαῖος no se atestigua en griego alfabético y tampoco está clara la presencia de /-aiwo-/ en ἀλκμαῖος· νεανίσκος (Hsch.) o ἀκμαῖος 'vigoroso' (A.) y como antropónimo Ἀκμαῖος. La sílaba final excluye /Alk-māwōn-/ (: Ἀλκμάων, Ἀλκμαίων), que obligaría a suponer un error por *a-ka-ma-wo-ne. Otros nombres del registro, como *ku-pi-ri-jo* .3 /Kuprio-/ (: Κύπριος), *ra-pa-sa-ko* .7 /Lampsako-/ (cf. topón. Λάμψακος), *a-ta-ma-ne-we* .10 /Athamanēwei/ (: Ἀθαμανεύς?), quizás *o-ku-ka* .2

tēwei/, *a-ri-wo-ne* .8 /*Ariwonei*/, *a-we-ke-se-we* .9 /*Aweksēwei*/, *e-ti-ra-wo* .10 /*Ertilāwōi*/, *ke-sa-me-no* .13 part.aor en */-*sameno*-/. Estos antropónimos presentan correspondencias, más o menos exactas, en griego alfabético: para /*Ploutēwei*/, cf. Πλουτίων, Πλούτιος, Πλοῦτις; para /*Ariwonei*/, cf. Ἀρίων; para *a-we-ke-se-we* (*Ἀϝεξεύς), cf. ἀεξί-γυιος (Pi.), ἀεξί-φυλλος (A.), (ἀέξο/ε- 'hacer crecer'); para /*Ertilāwōi*/, cf. Λα-έρτης 'que avanza/se lanza sobre el pueblo'.[5] Por su parte, el part. aor. *ke-sa-me-no* puede recubrir /*Ker-sameno*-/ (κείρο/ε- 'cortar') o */*Kens-sameno*-/ (IE **k̑ens*- 'hablar con autoridad').[6] Todo ello legitima el intento de una *interpretatio graeca* también para *ne-ri-to*.

Ne-ri-to ha sido ocasionalmente identificado con el antropónimo homérico Νήριτος, héroe local de Ítaca, homónimo de un monte Νήριτον, también en Ítaca, y en territorio de los cefalenios.[7] Esta identificación no plantea dificultad formal (hom. Νήριτος, Νήριτον pueden, en principio, recubrir tanto *nērito-como *nārito-), pero implica renunciar, contra toda lógica, a la interpretación de hom. νήριτος 'innumerable, incalculable', 'inmenso' como *νάριτος (: *nārito-, de **n̥-h₂ri-to*-, cf. *h₂eri-: ἀριθμός, ἐπ-άριτος), que se habría notado †*na-ri-to* en Lineal B. La presente contribución intentará hacer ver, sobre la base de una tipificación de las variantes formales de los compuestos privativos, especialmente los heredados de estructura */*n̥-HC*-/ (§2) y su representación en micénico (§3), que mic. *ne-ri-to* recubre /*Nērito*-/ (**n̥-h₁ri-to*- 'sin discordia'; cf. ἔρις, ἐριστός), compuesto privativo cuya estructura con grado cero /°*HC*-/ del segundo miembro es idéntica a la de *νάριτος (*nārito- : **n̥-h₂ri-to*), con el que habría confluido por evolución fonética en jónico-ático, aunque con significados distintos: los pasajes en que aparece hom. νήριτος como epíteto común apuntan inequívocamente a 'inmenso' (§4). El compuesto onomástico /*Nēritos*/, que no se atestigua en esta forma en griego alfabético, pervive en una serie de variantes recaracterizadas como privativas por medio de ἀ-, que son sus continuantes formales: Ἀνήριτος (/*a+nērito*-/) y Ἀνήριστος (analizable como Ἀ+νήριστος o Ἀν-ήριστος, con alargamiento composicional), y Ἀν-έριστος (§5).

2. Recordemos, para mayor claridad, que los compuestos privativos con *n- presentan en griego dos tipos básicos, (1) proto-gr. *nē-, *nā-, *nō- : gr. alf. νη-, νᾱ-, νω- (reflejo fonético de **n̥-h₁*-, **n̥-h₂*-, **n̥-h₃*- respectivamente con términos

---

/*Ōgugāi*/ (cf. topón. Ὠγυγίη), *po-ke-we* .8 /*Pʰōkēwei*/ (cf. étn. Φωκεύς), *pu-wi-no* .14 /*Pur(s)wīno*-/? (: Πύρρινος?) son conocidos como nombres propios en griego, aunque sin etimología IE, mientras que otros permanecen opacos.

5 García Ramón 2017: mic. /*Erti*°/, /°*értēs*/ (cf. ἔρετο· ὠρμήθη, ἔρσῃ· ὁρμήσῃ Hsch.) pertenecen a un lexema diferente del de mic. /*Orti*°/ (: Ὀρτι°/ Ὀροι°), /°*órtēs*/ (ὀρνυ-, ὀρσα-).

6 Igualmente aor. **k̑n̥s-ē*- en el NP *ka-e-sa-me-no* /*Kaʰēsameno*/ y la forma truncada *ka-e-se-u* (García Ramón 1992:241, 255, 251).

7 Landau 1957:88, 221, 264; Masson 1972:290. Contra, con razón, Bader 1972:159 con n52.

60

con laringal inicial como segundo miembro) y (2) proto-gr. *an-e-, *an-a-, *an-o-: gr. alf. ἀν-ε-, ἀν-α-, ἀν-ο- (posteriores a la vocalización de las laringales ἐ-, ἀ-, ὀ-), así como un subtipo mixto, convencionalmente (1a), /a+nV̄-/ (i.e. /a+nē-/, /a+nā-/, /a+nō-/): se trata de una variante de (1) /nV̄-/ recaracterizada secundariamente como privativa con adición de ἀ- (del tipo ἄ+θεος). Los tipos están bien representados en griego del I milenio, así como en micénico (§3), donde los datos son obviamente menos numerosos y, además, la grafía deja un margen de imprecisión respecto a los tipos (1b) y (2). Estos resultados coexisten, por lo demás, con ἀ- privativo, regular en posición anteconsonántica (/a-C-/ de *n̥C-) del tipo ἄ-θεος, ἄ-κτιτος (mic. *a-ki-ti-to*), ἄ-φθιτος (mic. fem. *a-qi-ti-ta*):

(1) /nV̄-/ como tratamiento fonético de *n̥HC-, i.e. *n̥-h₁C- > /nē-/, *n̥-h₂C- > /nā-/, *n̥-h₃C- > /nō-/ en formaciones antiguas:[8]

νῆστις 'que no come, ayuno' (*Il.*): *n̥-h₁d-ti- 'sin comida', cf. ἔδομαι (*h₁ed-*), también νήστης 'id.' (Sem., Arist.).

νήνεμος (*νάνεμος) 'sin viento, calmado' (Hom.+), mic. *na-ne-mo*: *n̥-h₂enə₁mo- 'sin viento' (cf. ἄνεμος: *h₂enə₁mo- §5).

νωφελής* 'sin utilidad' (asegurado por mic. *no-pe-re-a₂* /nōpʰeleʰa/ 'inservibles '): *n̥-h₃bʰel-es-; cf. ὄφελος 'utilidad' Hom.+ (IE *h₃bʰel- §5).

(1a) /a+nV̄-/ (i.e. /a+nē-/, /a+nā-/, /a+nō-/):

νῆστις → ἄ+νηστις (A., Crat.)[9]

νήνεμος → ἀ+νήνεμος (trag.)

νωφελής* → ἀ+νωφελής (A.+, prosa)

(2) /an-V/ (i.e. /an-e-/, /an-a-/, /an-o-/), formaciones recreadas en el interior del griego sobre la correspondiente forma base con vocal inicial breve, que implica que el compuesto no es heredado:

ἀν-έραστος 'no amado' (Call.): mic. *a-ne-ra-to* /Anera(s)to-/ (cf. ἐρατός 'amable' Hom.+, ἐραστός Pl.); igualmente ἀν-ελέητος 'sin piedad' (Arist.) frente a hom. νηλεές, cf. *infra*.

---

[8] Igualmente, para *n̥-h₁-, cf. νήφο/ε- 'estar sobrio' (hiperdor. νᾱφο/ε-, cf. νήφονες· νήφοντες Hsch.): *n̥-h₁gʷʰ-on- (Weiss 1994), IE *h₁e(h₂)gʷʰ- 'beber' (hit. eku-ᵐⁱ, toc.B yok-; Lat. *ēbrius*: *h₁ēgʷʰ-r-, (cf. de Lamberterie 1998:134); νήγρετος 'dormido' ('no despierto': *n̥-h₁gr-eto-), adv. νήγρετον (*Od.*+) (: ἐγείρο/ε-). Para *n̥-h₂-, cf. νημερτής (*n̥-h₂mer-t-) 'sin error, infalible' (*Od.*+), νᾱμερτής (trag.), cf. ἁμαρτάνο/ε- 'errar'. Para *n̥-h₃- cf. νωθής (*n̥-h₃es-) 'vago, inútil' (referido a animales, Hom.+), 'estúpido' (Hdt.+) junto a ἀνόθηρον· νωθρόν, Hsch. (cf. hom. ὄθομαι 'ser/estar atento, preocuparse de', ὀθεύει). Para una clara presentación del material griego cf. Forssman 1966:145–149.

[9] Cf. las glosas ἄνηστις· ἀντὶ τοῦ νῆστις, προσκειμένου τοῦ α, ὡς ἀσταφίς (Hsch. α 5098 Cunningham).

ἀν-άρμοστος 'no ajustado' (Hdt. Ar.+, cf. ἄρμοστος Plb.+): mic. *a-na-mo-to* 'sin *a-mo-ta*' 'sin las ruedas puestas' (de carros, Cnoso).

ἄν-οδος 'no accesible' (Eur., cf. ὁδός), forma sentida en composición como sin aspiración inicial, a diferencia de ἄ-υπνος 'sin sueño' de *ṇ-supno-*.

Por regla general, las posibilidades (1), (1a), y (2) no se atestiguan para todos los lexemas, ni coexisten en el mismo estado de lengua. Es, por ejemplo, el caso de ἄποινα 'rescate, justo pago': se atestiguan (1) νήποινος 'sin justo pago' (*Od.*+, φυτῶν νήποινος 'carente de plantas', Pi. *P.* 9.58)[10] junto a (2) ἀν-άποινον 'sin rescate' (1×: [κούρην …] ἀπριάτην ἀνάποινον, *Il.* 1.99), pero no (1a) †ἀν-ήποινον. Concretamente, las posibilidades (1a) y (2) rara vez se dan juntas, sin que sea posible detectar un *rationale* para la presencia de uno u otro en según qué lexemas: así, (1) νηλεής 'sin piedad' (*ṇ-h₁leu̯-es-*, cf. ἔλεος),[11] νηλεές (Hom.), νηλειής (Hes.+) junto a (2) ἀν-ελέητος 'sin piedad', ἀν-ελεήμων 'id.' (Arist.+), ἀν-ελήμων (LXX), pero (1b) ἀν-ηλεήμων en griego tardío (Nicoch. 20).

Recordemos que los compuestos no privativos, citados convencionalmente como tipo (3) en lo que sigue, presentan el alargamiento llamado de Wackernagel, que es fonético en algunos pocos casos y productivo en el interior del griego (aunque no constatable en micénico por las características del silabario).[12] El resultado del alargamiento de la vocal inicial del segundo miembro es similar al del tipo (1), i.e. /°eC/, /°aC/, /°oC/ → /°ēC/, /°āC/, /°ōC/ y coexiste, incluso en un mismo lexema, con la forma sin alargamiento /e-/, /a-/, /o-/ del simple, como en el tipo (2). Algunos ejemplos:

ὠμ-ηστής 'que come crudo' (Hom.), pero συν-έστᾱς 'comensal' (Acarnania)

ποδ-ηνέμιος 'con pies como viento' (Hom.+), ὑπ-ηνέμιος (Sem., Arist.), pero (2) ἀλεξ-άνεμος (Hom.), ἰσ-άνεμος (E.)

οἰκ-ωφελίη 'provecho de la casa' (Hom.+), πολυ-ωφελίη (Arist.)

εὐ-ώδης 'de buen olor' (Hom.), pero εὔ-οδμος 'id.' (Pi.+)

παν-ώλεθρος 'totalmente fatal' (Hdt.), pero παιδ-ολέτωρ, ἀνδρ-ολέτειρα (A.)

---

[10] Es la forma transmitida (sobre un modelo épico) y preferible a la v.l. νάποινος (cf. νάποινος· μάταιος Hsch.), como hace ver Forssman (1966:143–145). El compuesto νήποινος no es heredado, pero la explicación usual a partir de *νη-ποινή es ciertamente errónea: se forma más bien sobre *ἄποινος (por analogía con el tipo *νάνεμος sobre ἄνεμος), no sobre *ποινή.

[11] O bien 'sin escapatoria' (cf. ἀλέομαι), cf. νηλεὲς ἦμαρ (*Il.*+).

[12] Cf. el trabajo clásico de Wackernagel (1889). El alargamiento es esperable en cualquier tipo de compuesto, al margen de cual sea su origen, aunque no todas las formas lo presenten (cf. la visión de conjunto de Bader [1972]).

3. Los compuestos privativos están desigualmente representados en micéni-co.[13] Del tipo (1) se atestiguan hasta ahora tres formas, dos con /nā-/ (*$n̥-h_2$-) y una con /nō-/ (*$n̥-h_3$-), mientras que las limitaciones del Lineal B hacen impo-sible distinguir el tipo (1a) / *a+nV̄-/ /a+nā-/* y /*a+nō-/* del tipo (2) /*an-V-/*. El tipo de compuesto privativo con /*a-/* anteconsonántica (*#$n̥C$-), bien atestiguado en micénico,[14] no nos retendrá en este punto.

El tipo (1) está reflejado en *na-ne-mo* /Nānemo-/ (Tebas), *na-pu-ti-jo* /Nāpu-tio-/ (Cnoso) y *no-pe-re-a₂* /nōpʰeleʰa/, *no-pe-re-e* /nōpʰeleʰe/ (Pilo).

El antropónimo *na-ne-mo* TH Gp (1) 110.1 (dat.) /Nānemōi/ se corresponde con hom. νήνεμος 'sin viento, calmado', como José Luis Melena observó (y me indicó *per litteras electronicas* en 2001 o 2002) apenas se editaron las nuevas tablillas de Tebas (Aravantinos, Godart y Sacconi 2001).[15] Se trata de un compuesto priva-tivo con °ἄνεμος 'viento' (IE *$h_2enə_1$-mo-, *h_2enh_1- 'soplar', véd. *ánⁱ* 'id.'; cf. mic. *a-ne-mo*, *i-je-re-ja* KN Fp(1) 1.10, *a-ne-mo-i-je-re-ja* 13.3 /anemōn ʰiereiāi/), con el tratamiento regular de *$n̥-h_2nə_1$-mo-. Se atestigua, además, un nombre de mujer Νήνεμον (hipocorístico neutro como Σῖμον o Πιθανόν : σιμή, πιθανή) en una lápida sepulcral ateniense (*IG* 2².12111, s.II/I).[16] El epíteto νήνεμος se aplica en Homero a 'aire, cielo' (νήνεμος αἰθήρ *Il.* 8.556)[17] y a 'calma marina' (καὶ τότ' ἔπειτ' ἄνεμος μὲν ἐπαύσατο γαλήνη / ἔπλετο νηνεμίη *Od.* 5.391–392 ≈ 12.169).[18] Aunque sólo a partir de época clásica se atestigua, aplicado translaticiamente a personas (cf. νήνεμον ἔστησ' ὄχλον, Eur. *Hec.* 533), el MN *na-ne-mo* muestra que la metáfora es antigua. Caso similar es el de los antropónimos *a-me-ro* /ʰĀmero-/ (TH Fq *passim*, Gf 134.2, Gp 215.1), Ἥμερος (Creta, 258+) y Ἥσυχος (*passim* s. IV+) que reproducen ἥμερος 'dócil', ἥσυχος 'tranquilo', aplicados a personas a partir

---

[13] Para lo esencial del micénico, cf. Bader 1972:155–172, y García Ramón 2016b:215–216, 238–239.

[14] Cf. entre otros, *a-ka-ra-no* /a-k(a)ranno-/ (*k(a)ras-n-; cf. hom. κάρηνα 'cabezas, picos'); *a-ki-ti-to* /a-ktito-/ (: ἄκτιτος *HVen.*123), que puede reflejar *ˀsin *ki-ti-me-na* en el sentido técnico 'terreno para uso personal'; antropónimo fem. *a-qi-ti-ta* 'imperecedera' /A-kʷtʰitā-/ (: ἀφθιτον, cf. part. perf. *e-qi-ti-wo-e* 'muertos'); antropónimo *a-qa-to* /A-kʷʰato-/ 'imbatible (*$n̥-gʷʰn̥-tó$-, cf. *$gʷʰn̥-tó$-: véd. hatá-, av. jata, hom. ἀρεῖ-φατος); *a-wi-to** /a-wisto-/ 'invisible', 'que no se puede mirar' (prob-ablemente teónimo en antropónimo *a-wi-to-do-to* /Awisto-doto-/).

[15] Desgraciadamente la idea no fue desarrollada por él mismo, como le propuse. Algún tiempo después volví sobre el nombre y sus aspectos fraseológicos (García Ramón 2006:42–43), pensando también en νήνεμος y sin recordar (y, lo que es peor, sin mencionar) de quién había sido la idea. Aunque involuntaria, fue una fusilada clamorosa, que él perdonó en su momento, pero que querría hacer constar aquí, respetando el *ius suum cuique tribuendi*.

[16] *IG* II² 12111 (y *SEG* 28.341), cf. Masson 1989 (= *SEG* 39.316). El antropónimo femenino no es citado en García Ramón 2006:42–43.

[17] Cf. also Ar. *Av.* 778 κύματά τ' ἔσβεσε νήνεμος αἴθρη. Otros referentes de νήνεμος son el mar (πέλαγος Eur. *Hel.* 1456) o lugares aludidos como no expuestos a los vientos (ἐν νηνέμοις Thphr. *HP* 1.8.1).

[18] Cf. asimismo νηνεμίης 'cuando el viento está en calma' (*Il.* 5.523) 'bonanza, calma chicha'.

de época clásica.[19] El tipo recaracterizado (1a) ἀ-νήνεμος se atestigua en época clásica, cf. φυλλάδα ... ἀνήνεμον (S. *OC* 676–677), πέλαγος ἀνήνεμον (Eur. *Hel.* 1456).[20]

El antropónimo *na-pu-ti-jo* /Nāputio-/ (KN Db 1232.B): hom. νηπύτιος 'niño, chico joven'[21] (cf. μηκέτι ταῦτα λεγώμεθα νηπύτιοι ὥς, *Il.* 13.292),[22] presupone una base *nāpu-* (cf. νήπιος 'joven, pueril', en rigor 'infante', de donde 'inexperto' [Hom.+: *nāpu̯-i̯o-]). Todo apunta a un compuesto privativo *n̥-h₂pu/u̯-, e, indirectamente, a un simple *h₂epu- (: *ἄπυ-, no atestiguado). Dos formas posiblemente emparentadas presentan vocal larga inicial, i.e. ἠπ(υ)- (*āp(u)-): ἤπιος 'favorable, bien dispuesto' [Hom.+]), inseparable de véd. *árya-* 'grupo, unión', *āpí-* 'allegado, amigo'[23] y de ἠπύο/ε- 'llamar a voces' (cf. hom. ἠπύτα κῆρυξ).[24] En esta línea, la forma simple puede subyacer en el antropónimo *a-pu-wa* (TH Fq 229.3 *et al.*), que Neumann interpreta como /Āpuwās/.[25] La identificación de *na-pu-ti-jo* /Nāputio-/ como compuesto privativo es segura, al margen de cómo pueda explicarse la vocal larga inicial de ἤπιος, ἠπύο/ε-.[26]

El adjetivo *no-pe-re-a₂* n. pl. /nōpʰeleʰa/ (PY Sa(1) 682,751,790), du. *no-pe-re-e* /nōpʰeleʰe/ (Sa(1) 794) en los registros de ruedas garantizan la existencia de /nōpʰeles-/* 'inservible' (*n̥-h₃bʰel-es-), sentido técnico a partir de *'sin utilidad'

---

[19] Cf. ἡμερώτεροι γεγόνασι Αἰθίοπες (Hdt. 2.30); τέκτονα νωδυνίας ἥμερον (Pi. *P.* 3.6); ἄνδρες οὕτως ἥμεροι καὶ φιλάνθρωποι (D. 21.49); Ἡμέρα, epíteto de Ártemis en Arcadia (B. 11.37); Ὡς ὧν μεταδεδογμένον μοι μὴ στρατεύεσθαι ἐπὶ τὴν Ἑλλάδα, ἥσυχοι ἔστε (Hdt. 7.11). Los primeros testimonios de ἥμερος se aplican a animales (χῆνα ἥμερον, *Od.* 15.162, ζῷα Pl. *Phdr.* 260b), posteriormente a plantas (ἐλαίη, δένδρεα, Hdt.+), los de ἥσυχος a Helios (Hes. *Th.* 763).

[20] La sinonimia respecto a νήνεμος era clara para los griegos, cf. νήνεμον· ἄνευ ἀνέμου, εὔπνουν, εὔδιον, ἥσυχον, ἄπνουν. καὶ ἀνήνεμον τὸ αὐτό (Hsch.).

[21] Heubeck 1970:21. El testimonio de las glosas avala la pertenencia de νηπύτιος, νήπιος y ἠπύω, ἠπύτα a un mismo lexema (cf. νηπύτιον· νήπιον. ἄφωνον. ἄφρονα, ἀνόητον, ἠπύτα· βοητά. κήρυξ μακρόφωνος Hsch.).

[22] Cf. *Il.* 20.200 ὥς νηπύτιον, Ar. *Nu.* 868 νηπύτιος γάρ ἐστ' ἔτι. Como adjetivo 'pueril', cf. *Il.* 20.211 ἐπέεσσί γε νηπυτίοισιν.

[23] Pinault 1988. *Aliter* Jouanna 2003, que propone para ἤπιος los sentidos "doux, bienveillant" en Homero, posteriormente "apaisant," sobre la base de algunos pasajes de Homero, Solón y Sófocles.

[24] En hom. βρι-ήπυος 'de potente (βρι° 'pesada') voz' (epíteto de Ares), °ήπυος puede recubrir un alargamiento composicional.

[25] Para Neumann (2006:135–136), /Āpuwās/ sería un derivado onomástico del tipo Ἀρτύᾱς (: ἀρτυ°). La posibilidad de interpretar *a-pu-wa* como Ἅρπυια (Hom.+) como proponen Aravantinos, Godart y Sacconi (2001:214) es remota. Al margen de que el contexto no permite decidir si se trata de un receptor divino o humano, la supuesta identificación es incompatible con la grafía *a-pu-wa*, pues se esperaría †*a-pu-ja* o *a₂-pu-ja*, como *a-ra-ru-ja* : ἀραρυῖα. La hipótesis de una renovación formal de fecha post-micénica /-uwā/ → -υῖα por analogía con el tipo ἄγυια (Neumann 2006:126) sería en principio posible, pero la opacidad del término, seguramente no griego, lo deja todo en ámbito de lo nebuloso.

[26] Cabe pensar en un locativo *h₂ēp-i (Pinault 1988) o en la influencia del compuesto privativo */nāp(u)-/. *Aliter* L. Van Beek *apud* EDG, s.v. ἤπιος.

(cf. ὠφελέο/ε- 'ser útil, de provecho').[27] La forma no pervive en el I milenio, si bien se continua a partir de época clásica en ἀ+νωφελής (tipo 1a), aplicado, entre otros referentes,[28] a personas (e.g. Pl. *R.* 496d σύμμαχος ... ἀνωφελὴς αὐτῷ τε καὶ τοῖς ἄλλοις ἂν γένοιτο).

El tipo (2) con /an-V-/ está bien atestiguado en micénico, en la medida en que la transliteración con vocal breve está apoyada por las formas alfabéticas correspondientes:

> *a-na-mo-to* /an-armo(s)to-/ 'no ajustado' (: hom. ἀνάρμοστος) o 'sin ruedas' (cf. *a-mo* 'rueda').
>
> *a-na-pu-ke* /an-ampukes/ 'sin bandas' (: ἀνάμπυξ).
>
> *a-ne-ta* /an-⁽ʰ⁾eta/ (ntr. pl.): ἀνετός 'liberado' (cf. ἀν-ίημι 'liberar (tasas)', ἄνεσις).
>
> antropónimo *a-ne-ra-to* /An-era(s)to-/[29] (: ἀνέραστος 'no amado', cf. ἀνεραστότατον (Call. fr. 32.3) frente al simple ἐρατός 'amable' (Hom.+), ἐραστός 'id.' (Pl. *Symp.* 204c ... πάγκαλος ἐφαίνετο ὁ Ἔρως. καὶ γὰρ ἔστι τὸ ἐραστὸν τὸ τῷ ὄντι καλόν), atestiguado en el antropónimo *e-ra-to* /Era(s)tos/ (KN Dc 1359.B) y en Ἔρατος (Atenas, Heraclea s.IV+), Ἐρατώ (Corinto, 570+), Ἐρατά (Tesalia, s. IV+), así como Ἔραστος (Delfos, 301+).[30]
>
> *a-no-no* /an-ono-/ 'no sujeto a *o-na-to*' (/onāton/ 'derecho de beneficio', cf. ὀνητός 'beneficioso' Sud., ὀνητά· μεμπτά Hsch.).[31] La familia de *ὀνίνᾱ- en griego alfabético no presenta forma ninguna con (°)ὠνᾱ-, lo que hace suponer que el simple *o-no* 'provecho, pago' (pl. *o-na*?) recubre /onon/.

Al tipo (2) pertenece asimismo el adjetivo verbal *a-na-to*, fem. *a-na-(i)-ta* /an-ai(s)to-/, /an-ai(s)tā-/ 'sin incrustación' (KN, cf. part. perf. *a-ja-me-na* PY), con psilosis (como en cretense del I milenio) a partir de *an-ʰai(s)to-, que no pervive en el griego alfabético.

---

[27] No se entrará a discutir en este punto la coexistencia de formas con ὀφείλο/ε- 'deber', ὀφέλλο/ε- '(hacer) prosperar' (ὠφελέο/ε-) que apuntan a la existencia de más de una raíz (de Lamberterie 1992).

[28] Entre otros, ἁβροσύναι (Xenoph. fr. 3.1), γόοι (A. *Pr.* 33), σκιά (S. *El.* 1159), πάντα ἀνωφελῆ ἦν (Thuc. 2.47), también en la acepción 'perjudicial' (e.g. ἀλλ' ἔγωγε πολλὰ οἶδ' ἃ ἀνθρώποις μὲν ἀνωφελῆ ἐστι, Pl. *Prot.* 334, en oposición a τὸ παράπαν ὠφέλιμα; †ἀναμνήσθητε† ὡς ἀλγεινὸν καὶ ἀνωφελὲς ἤδη ἐστί, X. *HG* 1.7.27).

[29] *Aliter* Plath 2002: /anᵒ/ por ἀνά con sentido supuestamente aumentativo.

[30] Ambos nombres están bien atestiguados (Ἔρατος 25×; Ἔραστος 44× en las listas de Fraser *et al.* 1987–2018), no así el antónimo.

[31] Se trata del adjetivo verbal en -το- de *ὀνίνᾱ- (ὀνίνη-) 'ayudar, beneficiar' (IE *h₃neh₂-, cf. véd. *nāthá-* 'refugio, ayuda'), con *nomen agentis* mic. *o-na-te** /onātēr/ (pl. *o-na-te-re*) y ὀνήτωρ, dor. ὀνάτωρ (P.+), ὄνησις 'uso, provecho' (Hom. +) y otros derivados.

Los compuestos *a-no-we* 'sin asas' y *a-no-wo-to* 'id'. pueden pertenecer tanto al tipo (1a) (/*a-nŏwwes*-/, /*a-nŏwwoto*-/ como reflejo de **n̥-Hŏu̯s-es*-, **n̥-Hŏu̯s-n̥-to*-) como al (2) (/*an-ŏwwes*/, /*an-ŏwwoto*-/), sin que sea posible una decisión en un sentido con exclusión del otro: en griego alfabético οὖς / ὦς, ὠτός (lesb. οὔατος) presenta vocal larga inicial, tanto en compuestos privativos ("lesb." ἀν-ούατος Theoc.) como de otro tipo, e.g. ἀμφ-ώης (Theoc.), ἄμφ-ωτος (*Od.* 22.10), ἀπ-ούατος (Call.), ἐν-ώτιον (A.). Ello hace suponer /°*ōwwes*-/ en mic. *o-wo-we* /*oiw(o)°*/ 'con una asa', *ti-ri-jo-we* /*tri(o)°*/, *qe-to-ro-we* /*kʷetr(o)°*/ y en el antropónimo *o-tu-wo-we* /*Ortʰwōwwēs*/ 'de orejas erguidas', i.e. 'atentas'?: de */*Wortʰwōwwēs*/ con caida de /*w*-/ por disimilación).

Se observará, por lo demás, que el alargamiento de Wackernagel puede ser admitido para una forma micénica cuando la vocal larga está asegurada en griego alfabético (e.g. *ka-ka-re-a₂* /*kʰalk-āreʰa*/: χαλκ-ήρης 'ajustado en bronce' o los compuestos con °/(*C)ānōr*/: °ήνωρ).[32]

4. El antropónimo mic. *ne-ri-to* tiene una estructura, al margen de cual sea la etimología de la forma que recubre y sus continuantes en el I milenio (§5), idéntica a la de hom. νήριτος 'incalculable, innumerable'. Es, pues, de suponer que la consideración de esta forma sea de ayuda para la interpretación de mic. *ne-ri-to*.

Hom. νήριτος (*nārito-) es el resultado fonético de un compuesto **n̥-h₂ri-to*-, de IE *h₂eri, **h₂rei̯*- 'contar';[33] cf. ant. irl. *renaid* 'vende, cambia', ant. nord. *rím* [n.] 'cuenta', a.a.a. *rīm* [m.] 'número, serie', ant. irl. *rím* 'número', lat. *rītus* 'rito' (**h₂rei̯-tu*-). La familia de ἀρι-, que no parece atestiguada en micénico,[34]

---

[32] Cf. la discusión de Bader (1972:155–163).

[33] Quizá *h₂er-i- (o *h₁ar-i), i.e. *h₂er- (o *h₁ar-) 'ajustar' con una ampliación -*i*-. Una variante **h₂reh₁(i)*- puede subyacer en lat. *reor*, *rērī* 'considerar', protogerm. *rē-d- (ant.ingl. *raēdan* 'opinar').

[34] Hay dos oscuras formas *a₂-ri-e* (PY An 724.5) y *a₂-ri-sa* (PY Eq 213.1) que, de no ser por la aspiración inicial, podrían recubrir ἀρι-, concretamente dos formas verbales, inf. pres. /ʰ*ariʰen*/ e inf. aor. /ʰ*arisai*/ o part. aor. /ʰ*arisan(t)s*/ respectivamente. Sin embargo, la aspiración inicial arruina, en mi opinión, dicha posibilidad. Además, los textos son de estructura y sentido oscuros, en especial PY An (4) 724 (7; H1 / Cii):

1. *ro-o-wa*, *e-re-ta*, *a-pe-o-te*,
2. *me-nu-wa*, *a-pe-e-ke*, *a-re-sa-ni-e* [[ ]]
3. *o-pi-ke-ri-jo-de*, *ki-ti-ta*, *o-pe-ro-ta*, [[ ]]
4. *e-re-e* VIR 1 VIR
5. *e-ke-ra₂-wo-ne*, *a-pe-e-ke*, *a₂-ri-e*, [[ ]]
6. *o-pe-ro-te*, *e-re-e* VIR 5
7. *ra-wa-ke-ta*, *a-pe-e-ke̜*[ ]e̜ VIR 1[

En línea .5 *a-pe-e-ke* /*ap-e-ʰēke*/ (cf. hom. aor. ἀφέηκε), también atestiguado sin aumento *a-pi-e-ke*, podría regir un infinitivo *a₂-ri-e* /*ariʰen*/ 'calcular', pero esta posibilidad presenta serias dificultades: el sentido de 'envió a calcular' (!), al margen ya de que no coincide con el usual de 'dejar libre, despedir' (Hom.+), no se ajusta bien al contenido de la tablilla, que trata del envío de colonos (*ki-ti-ta*) para hacer de remeros, expresado con un infinitivo (*ki-ti-ta o-pe-ro-ta e-re-e* /*ktitān opʰellonta ereʰen*/) y, sobre todo, el paralelo con la línea 3 apunta a una equivalencia de *a₂-ri-e* con la críptica forma *a-re-sa-ni-e*, que no deja reconocer un infinitivo—ni, en realidad, ninguna otra forma del griego. Solo en PY Eq 213.1-2 *o-wi-de*, *a-ko-so-ta*, *to-ro-qe-jo-me-no*, *a-ro-*

está representada en griego por ἀριθμός 'número' (*Od.*+), con el denominativo ἀριθμέο/ε- 'contar' (Hom.+.), ἀρίθμημα (A.), ἀρίθμησις (jónico) 'cuenta, pago', ἀριθμητικός (Pl.+) *et al.* En nuestro caso son interesantes los compuestos privativos con ἀριθμός, de los tres tipos: (1) νήριθμος (Theoc.), (1a) ἀνήριθμος (poet.), (2) ἀνάριθμος (Pi.+), que coexisten con los no privativos (3) ἰσήριθμος (Lyc.+), ἰσάριθμος (Pl.+).

El sentido básico de νήριτος es reconocible en Hesíodo (*Op.* 511 νήριτος ὕλη 'inmenso bosque'), si bien en las escasas atestiguaciones en autores tardíos (A.R. 3.1288 νήριτα ταύρων ἴχνια 'las innumerables huellas de los toros') y, en particular, en la *interpretatio homerica* el sentido del epíteto parece haberse difuminado:[35] así, en el caso de νηριτό-φυλλος 'de innumerables hojas' (νηριτόφυλλον· πολύφυλλον, Hsch. ν 525 Latte), νηριτό-μυθος glosado como ὑπὸ τῷ γήρᾳ πεπτωκώς ἢ <οὗ> οὐκ ἄν τις ἐρίσειε πρὸς <τοὺς> μύθους (Hsch. ν 524 Latte) o εἰκοσι-νήριτος, compuesto artificial que equivale a εἰκοσάκις 'veinte veces', como muestra la comparación entre *Il.* 22.349–350 οὐδ᾽ εἴ κεν δεκάκις τε καὶ εἰκοσινήριτ᾽ ἄποινα / ... ἄγοντες y 9.379 οὐδ᾽ εἴ μοι δεκάκις τε καὶ εἰκοσάκις τόσα δοίη.[36]

Lo esencial de los diferentes tipos de compuestos, privativos y no privativos, con °*ārito*-, °*arito*- se concreta como sigue:

Tipo (1): El antropónimo Νήριτος y el orónimo Νήριτον, que podrían, en términos puramente formales, recubrir tanto *nārito- (: hom. νήριτος 'innumerable, incalculable', translaticiamente 'espeso', 'denso' en el caso de un bosque) como *nērito- (: mic. *ne-ri-to*; cf. §5), ambos del tipo heredado (1), se explican bien *ex Homero ipso* como idénticos a hom. νήριτος en su relación con Ítaca. El sentido del orónimo Νήριτον,[37] en Ítaca (*Il.* 2.632, *Od.* 9.22, 13.351), es obviamente

---

u-*ra* , *a₂-ri-sa* / ... *to-so-de* , *pe-mo* GRA 8 es posible entender *to-ro-qe-jo-me-no* y *a-ro-u-ra* como /trok^{w}eomenos/ (o /strok^{wh}eomenos/) 'al hacer la ronda' y /arourān(s)/ 'la(s) tierra(s) cultivable(s)', pero la aspiración inicial de *a₂-ri-sa* (inf. /^{h}arisai/ o part. /^{h}arisan(t)s/?) hace imposible cualquier relación con ἀριθμός, ἀριθμέο/ε-.

[35] Para una discusión del dosier cf. Leumann 1950:243–245, Ruijgh 1957:161–162. Parece claro que el significado de νήριτος escapaba a los lexicógrafos griegos, que le atribuían significados inventados a partir del contexto. Es, como me indica Julián Méndez Dosuna (*per litteras*), el caso de Hsch. ν 522 Latte Νήριτον· ὄρος Ἰθάκης, ἀντικρὺ τῆς Ἠπείρου (ν 351) ... ὑγρόν. θαλερόν. ἁπαλόν. ἀεὶ ῥέον.

[36] Hom. εἰκοσινήριτος es glosado como sinónimo de εἰκοσάριθμον en Suda (εἰκοσάκωπον πλοῖον καὶ εἰκοσινήριτον καὶ εἰκοσάριθμον). Un análisis alternativo como εἰκοσιν-ήριτ(α) "compté vingt fois, vingtuple" ... εἰκοσι-νήριτ(α) "vingt fois innombrable" (Ruijgh 1957:162) me parece innecesario.

[37] El topónimo está atestiguado en las fuentes latinas como *Neritus*, orónimo (*ab ea Ithaca distat, in qua mons Neritus*, Plin. *NH* 4.55), también como *Neritos*, nombre de una isla en el mar Jonio próxima a Zacinto (*Neritos ardua saxis*, V. *Aen.* 3.271, P. Mela 2.110). Se trata obviamente del término con vocalismo homérico más que de un topónimo ilirio (*pace* Von Kamptz 1982:151), tan imaginario como el concepto mismo de "ilirio."

el de νήριτος, como subraya καταειμένον ὕλη 'revestido de bosque' (τοῦτο δὲ Νήριτόν ἐστιν ὄρος καταειμένον ὕλη *Od.* 13.351; cf. νήριτος ὕλη Hes. *Op.* 511): el epíteto (ntr.) da nombre al monte (ὄρος), que es mencionado como boscoso. Por su parte, el *hapax* Νήριτος,[38] nombre de un oscuro héroe local de Ítaca (κρήνην ... τὴν ποίησ' Ἴθακος καὶ Νήριτος ἠδὲ Πολύκτωρ *Od.* 17.207), aparece precisamente junto a otro héroe local, Ἴθακος, inseparable de Ἰθάκη, a la que, a su vez, se vincula el propio topónimo Νήριτον:[39] se trata, pues, de un nombre inventado *ad hoc*, formado sobre el orónimo Νήριτον como Ἴθακος sobre Ἰθάκη.[40]

Tipos (1a) y (2): No se atestiguan formas recaracterizadas de νήριτος (*nārito-*) del tipo (1a) *ἀ+νήριτος ni (2) *ἀν-άριτος como epítetos comunes. Sólo en la onomástica cabe mencionar el enigmático antropónimo <Ανεριτος> (Atenas, *ca.* 700–650), para que el que se ofrecen dos posibilidades: si <ε> nota /ē/, puede tratarse de un compuesto del tipo (1a), i.e. *ἀ+νάριτος (: át. ἀ+νήριτο-) o bien ἀ-νήριτος (°*érito-*); si, por el contrario, <ε> nota /e/, se trataría de un compuesto del tipo (2) *ἀν-έριτος (*°*érito-*) comparable a Ἀνέριστος.

Tipo (3): Los compuestos con segundo miembro °άριτο-, frecuentes en la onomástica,[41] son en principio ambiguos: si <α> nota /a/, se trata de compuestos con °άριτος, creados en griego; si, en cambio, <α> nota /ā/ en territorio no jónico-ático se trata de °ᾱριτο- (jon., át. °ηριτο- y át. °έριτο- en alfabeto epicórico) con alargamiento de Wackernagel.

Son inequívocos a favor de *nārito-* solamente los compuestos en °ηριτο- con dobletes en °άριτο- fuera del ámbito jónico-ático. Es, entre otros, el caso del *hapax* μεγ-ήριτος 'numerosísimo' (μεγήριτα τέκνα θεάων Hes. *Th.* 240)[42] y el del apelativo ἐπάριτοι (Xen. *HG* 7.4.33-36), designación de los soldados arcadios

---

[38] Que hom. νήριτος, que nunca se aplica a animados, se utilice como nombre es perfectamente posible, dada la libertad de la onomástica griega para utilizar como antropónimos epítetos poéticos no adecuados para humanos, como Ἄσπετος : ἄσπετος 'indecible, imposible de expresar' (Hom+, dicho del αἰθήρ 'aire', κρέα 'trozos de carne', ῥόος 'corriente') o Ἀφθόνητος : ἀφθόνητος 'invulnerable a la envidia' (Pind.+, dicho de αἶνος 'elogio' Pindaro). Con todo, un antropónimo Νήριτος solo se atestigua (3×) a partir del s. II d. C. en onomástica romana (Νόβιος Νήριτος, Κορν. Νήριτος, Κλ. Νήριτος).

[39] Cf. οἵ ῥ' Ἰθάκην εἶχον καὶ Νήριτον εἰνοσίφυλλον (*Il.* 2.632), ναιετάω δ' Ἰθάκην εὐδείελον· ἐν δ' ὄρος αὐτῇ, / Νήριτον εἰνοσίφυλλον, ἀριπρεπές (*Od.* 9.22–23).

[40] Cf. Von Kamptz 1982:41, 44, y Russo en Russo *et al.* 1992:27, con referencia a la tradición de que Ítaco y Nérito fundaron Ítaca (y Cefalenia) y dieron su nombre al monte, mientras que se presenta a Πολύκτωρ (cuyo nombre evoca simplemente la riqueza (πολύ, κτέαρ 'posesión') como epónimo de un desconocido Πολυκτώριον (*Schol. in Od.* V, y BQ), también inventado *ad hoc*.

[41] Así, ya Bechtel 1917, *s.v.* "-ήριτος zu ἀριτός 'gezählt' (vgl. Νήριτος)," que incluye, además de los nombres que serán tratados en §5, Καλ-ήριτος (Maronea, Ródope) y Τιμ-άριτος (próxeno de Cleitor, Arcadia), que no están recogidos en Fraser *et al.* 1987-2018, vol. III/1.

[42] La pertenencia de esta forma al dosier de °άριτο- me ha sido señalada por J. Méndez Dosuna (*per litteras*).

de la Liga Aquea (año 371).[43] El compuesto se atestigua también como nombre ('Επάριτος, Cime, ca. 350–250+), lo que permite suponer °ἄριτο- para el nombre Ἐπήριτος con el que Odiseo se presenta a su padre Laertes (*Od.* 24.306).[44] Lo mismo cabe decir de Μετάριτος (Mitilene, s. III) : Μετήριτος (Tasos, año 510) y, con πεδά (: μετά), Πεδάριτος (Esparta s. V,[45] Tegea, s. III). En cambio, Θεάριτος (nombre de un arcadio en Ática, s. IV) y Κλεάριτος (Arcadia, año 279) pueden recubrir tanto °ἄριτο- como °ἄριτο-.

Recordemos que en el caso de ἀριθμός se atestiguan los compuestos en las variantes esperables, desarrolladas en el interior del griego:

(1) νήριθμος, formado artificialmente sobre el modelo de νήριτος (no procedente de $*\underset{.}{n}$-h_2ri-d^hmo-): νήριθμος (*sc.* κτῆσις) [Ps.-Theoc.] 25.57; νήριθμος ἑσμός (Lyc. 415); νηρίθμους· ἀναριθμήτους, ἀπείρους (Hsch.).

(1a) ἀ+νάριθμος, ἀ+νήριθμος: ἀργύρᾳ τ᾽ ἀνάρ[ι]θμα [ποτή]ρ[ια] κἀλέφαις (Sa. fr. 44.10), ποντίων τε κυμάτων / ἀνήριθμον γέλασμα (A. *Pr.* 90);[46]

(2) ἀν-άριθμος: ἀναρίθμων ἀνδρῶν χαλαζάεντι φόνῳ (Pi. *I.* 5.50).[47]

(3) con y sin alargamiento, e.g. ἰσ-ήριθμος (Lyc. 1258, Nonn. 1.241) además de ἰσ-άριθμος (Pl. *Ti.* 41d).

En conclusión, las variantes de los compuestos privativos (y no privativos) con segundo elemento °ἄριτο- y °ἄριθμο- (ἀριθμός) se concretan como sigue:

---

[43] Cf. ἐπάριτοι· τάγμα Ἀρκαδικὸν μαχιμώτατον. καὶ οἱ παρὰ Ἀρκάσι δημόσιοι φύλακες (Hsch. ε 4231 Latte), sinónimo de ἐπίλεκτοι 'selectos' (Xen. *HG* 7.1.19, 7.2.10; D.S. 15.62.2). Discusión en Schulze 1890:1406: ἐπάριτοι "erlesene"; Von Kamptz 1982:82.

[44] La posibilidad de un segundo miembro ἔρις es unánimemente rechazada por los estudiosos modernos (Wackernagel 1916:250; Heubeck en Russo *et al.* 1992:395), pero no así por los antiguos. Así, ὑποστολὴν ἔπαθε τοῦ <σ>, ὁμοίως τῷ Ἐπήριτος κύριον, ὅπερ ἐν Ὀδυσσείᾳ κεῖται δοκοῦν παρῆχθαι ἐκ τοῦ ἐριστός [κατὰ τὸ Νήριτον ὄρος τὸ οἷον ἀνέριστον διὰ τὸ δασὺ τῆς ὕλης (Eust., *Comm. ad Iliadem* 2, p. 622); ἢ καὶ ἄλλως κατὰ τοὺς παλαιοὺς ἐριστὸν μὲν εἴη ἂν τὸ ἀντιλεγόμενον τίμημα τοῦ νεκροῦ, νήριστον δὲ καὶ ἀποβολῇ τοῦ <σ> νήριτον, ὅπερ καὶ ἐπὶ τοῦ γνωστός καὶ γνωτός γίνεται, τὸ ἀνέριστον καὶ ἀναντίρρητον καὶ ἤδη τυπωθὲν καὶ ὁρισθὲν καὶ δίκαιον. δεκάκις οὖν νήριτον ἀπὸ κοινοῦ κατὰ παράθεσιν καὶ εἰκοσινήριτον κατὰ σύνθεσιν τὸ δεκαπλοῦν καὶ εἰκοσαπλοῦν ἄξιον τίμημα. ἔστι δὲ ἡ τοῦ εἰκοσινηρίτου σύνθεσις ὁμοία τῷ εἰκοσίπηχυ (Eust., *Comm. ad Iliadem* 4, p. 630).

[45] Thuc. 8.28.5. La variante con Πεδα° puede deberse al sustrato predorio? ("substrat achéen," Ruijgh 1957:161).

[46] Cf. asimismo ἀνήριθμος δέ οἱ εἴη ἄργυρος (Theoc. 16.64), μύρμακες ἀνάριθμοι (Theoc. 15.45).

[47] Cf. asimismo ἐρέται δεινοὶ πλῆθός τ᾽ ἀνάριθμοι (A. *Pers.* 40), ἀνάριθμα γὰρ φέρω πήματα (S. *OT* 167).

Tipo (1): /nārito-/ (*n̥-h₂ri-)	νάριτος	*νάριθμος, νήριθμος
Tipo (1a): /a+nārito/	ἀνάριτος?	ἀνάριθμος, ἀνήριθμος
Tipo (2): /an-aritoº/		ἀν-άριθμος
Tipo (3):	μεγ-ήριτος, ἐπάριτος, Ἐπ-ήριτος	ἰσ-άριθμος, ἰσ-άριθμος

5. Una vez establecido que *nárito- 'innumerable' (hom. νήριτος, topónimo Νήριτον, antropónimo Νήριτος) es resultado fonético del privativo *n̥-h₂ri-to-, es obvio que la forma micénica correspondiente se notaría †na-ri-to. Por su parte, el antropónimo pilio ne-ri-to, de estructura similar a la de *nárito-, debe reflejar el resultado fonético de *n̥-h₁ri-to-, compuesto privativo que presupone un derivado *h₁eri-to- de *h₁eri-: ἔρις 'discordia, distanciamiento, disputa'[48] (Hom., Hes.+), con los denominativos ἐρίζο/ε- (aor. ἐρισ(σ)α-), ἐριδαίνο/ε- 'id.' y ἐριδμαίνο/ε- 'provocar, irritar'. Se observará, aunque no es crucial para la interpretación de ne-ri-to /Nērito-/, que ἔρις 'discordia' refleja *h₁érh₂-i- 'división, separación', de IE *h₁erh₂-/*h₁r̥h₂- 'dividir': hit. arḫa- 'frontera, límite' [*h₁erh₂-o-], hit. rec. irḫa-, luv. cun. irha-, luv. jerogl. /irha-/ 'id.'; lit. ìrti (inrù) 'disolverse' y ìrti (iriù) 'rasgar', en la interpretación concluyente de Weiss 1998.[49]

La interpretación de micénico ne-ri-to como /Nērito-/ (o /Nēristo-/) 'libre de discordia, disputa', i.e. 'plácido, apacible' como antónimo de ἐριτός* (no atestiguado), como subrayaba Wackernagel,[50] está garantizada por las formas en ºήριτος (cf. *infra*) y ἐριστός 'objeto de discordia' (S. *El.* 220), así como por el antropónimo Ἔριστος (Dicearquia-Puteoli, *aet. imp.*), con un tema ἐρισ-, probablemente creado sobre el aor. ἐρισ(σ)α- (hom. ἔρισμα '(objeto de) disputa' *Il.* 4.38,

---

[48] El ac. ἔριν frente a ἐριδ- en el resto de los casos demuestra que originalmente se trataba de un tema en -i, que se ha adaptado secundariamente al tipo -ίδ-.

[49] Como señala Weiss (1998:47 "tentatively"), los derivados nominales presuponen un nombre raíz atemático *h₁órh₂-/*h₁érh₂- 'frontera, límite', subyacente, además, en lat. ōra 'límite, costa' (*h₁órh₂-eh₂- sustantivado como colectivo a partir de *h₁órh₂-o- 'relativo al límite', ant.irl. or (m.) 'id.' (*h₁orh₂-ó- 'divisor'). La explicación (recogida en Watkins 2011, s.v. **erə-³** 'to separate, adjoin') es preferible a las que asocian ἔρις como emparentado con véd. ári-, arí- [m.] 'enemigo, extranjero' (Porzig 1942:351; Haudry 1993) o con ὀρίνο/ε- 'excitar, agitar', con ἐρέθο/ε-, ἐρεθίζο/ε- 'provocar, irritar' (cf. Chantraine 1999, s.v. "sans étymologie"; EDG, s.v. "unknown etymology").

[50] Wackernagel 1916, 250: "ἐριτός 'der Bestrittene, Angefeindete," "von ἔρις gibt es sonst keine Bildungen auf -ιτος"; Bechtel 1917 s.vv. -ήριστος, -έριστος zu ἐριστός y -ήριτος "zu einem verlorenen ἐριτός." La existencia de ἔριτος no presupone la de un presente *ἐρίω (pace Bechtel 1917, s.v. -ήριτος: "ήριτος beweist, daß neben ἐρίζω ein Präsens ἐρίω (aus *erijō) bestanden hat"; EDG, s.v. ἔρις: "ἐρίζω ... enlarged from *ἐρί-ω?").

ἀμφ-ήριστος 'objeto de discordia por ambas partes' *Il.* 23.382, ἐριστικός 'pendenciero, discutidor' Pl., Arist.). El compuesto pervive en los antropónimos del tipo Ἀ-νήριτος, Ἀ-νήριστος, Ἀν-έριστος "der, gegen den keine ἔρις möglich ist" en la correcta interpretación de Jacobsohn, que sigue Bechtel.[51] Partiendo de la base de que el antropónimo *ne-ri-to* puede recubrir /*Nērito-*/ o /*Nēristo-*/ 'libre de ἔρις', compuesto del tipo (1), es posible reconocer sus continuantes formales en los compuestos con °ḗrito-, °erito- y °ḗristo-, °eristo- en el I milenio:

(1a) Tipo ἀ+νήριτο-: Ἀνήριτος (Delfos, año 343). Un testimonio muy anterior podría ser <Ανεριτος> (Atenas, 700–650), si <ε> nota /ē/ (i.e. Ἀνήριτος), aunque no se excluye ni que se trate del resultado dialectal de un antiguo *Ἀνάριτος (cf. §4.4), ni tampoco que <ε> note /e/, con lo que tendríamos un Ἀν-έριτος del tipo (2). — Tipo ἀ+νήριστο-: Ἀνήριστος (Esparta, s.VI–V, Orcómeno, año 250–225, Gonnos s. III–II), también fem. Ἀνηρίστα (Ática, s. III). Queda descartado que Ἀνήριστος en ámbito jónico-ático recubra *a-nāristo-, pues en los compuestos con ἀρι- sólo se atestigua la forma °ā̆rito-, sin -s-, no °ā̆risto (§4). Ἀνήριστος aparece en Heródoto como nombre de dos espartanos, el padre de Espertias (Σπερθίης τε ὁ Ἀνηρίστου 7.134.2) y el hijo del mismo personaje (ἐς Ἀνήριστον τὸν Σπερθίεω 7.137.2; Thuc. 2.67.1), quien, como era costumbre, llevaba el nombre de su abuelo.[52]

(2) Tipo ἀν-έριστος: Ἀνέριστος, nombre de un ciudadano de Larisa que es nombrado próxeno por los focidios (*IG* IX/1.99.1 Elatea, s. III). La variante se atestigua también en Eustacio (con explicaciones *e Graeco ipso*)[53] y en los lexicógrafos: ἀνήριστα· ἀνέριστα (Hsch.), ἀνέριστα· ἀφιλονείκητα (Suda).

(3) Tipo °ήριτο- con alargamiento de Wackernagel (°ηρι-)[54]: hom. ἀμφ-ήριστος 'disputado *por ambas partes*' (*Il.* 23.382 [≈ 527] καί νύ κεν ἢ παρέλασσ' ἢ ἀμφήριστον ἔθηκεν "le hubiera pasado delante o ... hubiera conseguido que la victoria quedase indecisa" [Segalà Estalella]), que reaparece en poesía clásica y prosa postclásica.[55] El compuesto está bien atestiguado en la onomástica: Αμφε̄ριτος (Tebas, 400–370, alfabeto epicórico), Ἀμφήριτος (Tasos, s. V; Atica, s. IV; etc.), Ἀνφήριτος (Pition, 27 a. C.–14 d. C.).– Tipo °ήριστο-: Ἀμφήριστος (Tespias, 170 d. C.; Ancona, *aet. imp.* [J. Méndez Dosuna, c.p.]).

---

[51] Jacobsohn 1905:295: "der, gegen den es ein ankämpfen nicht giebt."

[52] Bechtel 2017, *s.v.* -ήριτος conecta el antropónimo Σπερθίας con véd. *spárdh-a-*[te] 'disputar, concurrir' y subraya el contraste de la semántica de los nombres de padre e hijo.

[53] Ἐπήριτος κύριον, ὅπερ ἐν Ὀδυσσείᾳ κεῖται δοκοῦν παρῆχθαι ἐκ τοῦ ἐριστός [κατὰ τὸ Νήριτον ὄρος τὸ οἷον ἀνέριστον διὰ τὸ δασὺ τῆς ὕλης (Eust. *Comm. ad Iliadem* 2, p. 622), κατὰ τοὺς παλαιοὺς ἐριστὸν μὲν εἴη ἂν τὸ ἀντιλεγόμενον τίμημα τοῦ νεκροῦ, νήριστον δὲ καὶ ἀποβολῇ τοῦ <σ> νήριτον (Eust. *Comm. ad Iliadem* 4, p. 630).

[54] Cf. asimismo δύσ-ηρις (P. O. 6.19) junto a át. δύσ-ερις 'de ingrata/mala discordia' (Isoc. 1.31, Arist. EN 1108ᵃ30, Pl. *Lg.* 864a *et al.*).

[55] Aplicado a γένος (Call. *Iou.* 5), νεῖκος (A.R. 3.627), ἐλπίδες (Plb. 5.85.6).

6. En conclusión:

(1) El antropónimo pilio *ne-ri-to* /*Nērito-*/ 'libre de discordia', resultado fonético del compuesto privativo **n̥-h₁ri-to-* (**h₁ér(h₂)i-*: ἔρις) o /*Nēristo-*/, antónimo de ἐριστός (S.), pervive en el I milenio en los continuantes formales Ἀνήριτος y Ἀνήριστος (con remodelación /*a+nēri(s)to-*/) y Ἀν-έριστος (/*an+eristo-*/). El segundo miembro °έρι(σ)το- pervive, con alargamiento de Wackernagel, en ἀμφ-ήριστος (Hom.+), también antropónimos Ἀμφ-ήριτος, Ἀμφ-ήριστος.

(2) La estructura de *ne-ri-to* /*Nērito-*/ es paralela a la del compuesto privativo hom. νήριτος 'innumerable, incalculable' (**nārito-* de **n̥-h₂ri-to-*, cf. **h₂eri-*: ἀρι-θμός), que, de atestiguarse en micénico (*/*Nārito-*/), se notaría †*na-ri-to*. El epíteto subyace en el topónimo Νήριτον y en el antropónimo Νήριτος (formado sobre el propio topónimo), ambos en Homero. A falta de testimonios seguros de las posibles variantes *ἀ-νάριτος, *ἀν-άριτος, el segundo miembro °ἄριτος subsiste en compuestos no privativos, como μεγ-ήριτος (Hes.) o arc. ἐπ-άριτος (: antropónimo Ἐπ-ήριτος). En cambio, en los compuestos secundarios con ἀριθμός como segundo elemento se atestiguan las diferentes variantes: νήριθμος (Theoc.), ἀ+νήριθμος (A.+), ἀν-άριθμος (Pi.+) e ἰσ-άριθμος (Lyc.), ἰσ-άριθμος (Pl.+).

El antropónimo *ne-ri-to* /*Nērito-*/ (**n̥-h₁ri-to-*) o /*Nēristo-*/ viene a sumarse a otros tres compuestos del mismo tipo atestiguados en micénico: *na-ne-mo* /*Nānemo-*/ (**n̥-h₂nₐ₁mo-*: hom. νήνεμος 'sin viento' → clás. ἀνήνεμος), *na-pu-ti-jo* /*Nāputio-*/ (**n̥-h₂pu-*: hom. νηπύτιος 'joven'), *no-pe-re-a₂* /*nōpʰeleʰa*/ 'inservible', *no-pe-re-e* /*nōpʰeleʰe*/ (**n̥-h₃pʰeles-*, → clás. ἀ-νωφελής).

Bibliography

Aravantinos, V. L., L. Godart, y A. Sacconi, eds. 2001. *Thèbes: Fouilles de la Cadmée* I: *Les tablettes en linéaire B de la Odos Pelopidou. Edition et commentaire.* Pisa.

Bader, F. 1972. "Le traitement des hiatus á la jointure des deux membres d'un composé nominal en mycénien." *Minos* 12:141–196.

Bechtel, F. 1917. *Die historischen Personennamen des Griechischen bis zur Kaiserzeit.* Halle.

Chantraine, P. 1999. *Dictionnaire étymologique de la langue grecque. Histoire des mots, avec un Supplément sous la direction de A. Blanc, Ch. de Lamberterie, J.-L. Perpillou.* Paris.

Deger-Jalkotzy, S., y O. Panagl, eds. 2006. *Die neuen Linear B-Texte aus Theben: Ihr Aufschlußwert für die mykenische Sprache und Kultur. Akten des internationalen Forschungskolloquiums and der Österreichischen Akademie der Wissenschaften 5.-6. Dezember 2002.* Vienna.

Forssman, B. 1966. *Untersuchungen zur Sprache Pindars.* Wiesbaden.

Fraser, P. M., E. Matthews, M. J. Osborne, S. G. Byrne, R. W. V. Catling, T. Corsten, J-S. Balzat, É. Chiricat, y F. Marchand, eds. 1987–2018. *A Lexicon of Greek Personal Names.* 6 vols. Oxford.

Frisk, H. 1960–1972. *Griechisches etymologisches Wörterbuch.* 3 vols. Heidelberg.

García Ramón, J. L. 1992. "Mycénien *ke-sa-do-ro* /*Kessandros*/, *ke-ti-ro* /*Kestilos*/, *ke-to* /*Kestōr*/: Grec alphabétique Αἰνησιμβρότα, Αἰνησίλαος, Αἰνήτωρ et le nom de Cassandra." In *MYKENAÏKA. Actes du IXᵉ Colloque international sur les textes mycéniens et égéens organisé par le Centre de l'Antiquité Grecque et Romaine de la Fondation Hellénique des Recherches Scientifiques et l'École française d'Athènes (Athènes, 2–6 octobre 1990),* ed. J.-P. Olivier, 239–255. Athens.

———. 2000. "*Anthroponymica Mycenaea 3.* Mykenisch *to-wa-no* /*Tʰowānōr*/, homerisch Πρόθοος und Προθοήνωρ*." *Živa Antika* 50:205–212.

———. 2000-2001. "*Anthroponymica Mycenaea 1.* Mykenisch *o-ki-ro,* alph.gr. ὀρχίλος. 2. Mykenisch *da-te-wa* /*Dāitēwās*/ und *e-u-da-i-ta,* alph.gr. Δαίτας, Πανδαίτης." *Minos* 35:431–442.

———. 2005a. "*Anthroponymica Mycenaea 4.* Mic. *pe-ra-ko* /*Pʰerakos*/, gr. alf. Φέρακος y el topos ἄκος φέρειν, ἀκεσφόρος." In *De Cyrène à Catherine: Trois mille ans de Libyennes. Études grecques et latines offertes à Catherine Dobias-Lalou,* ed. F. Poli y G. Vottéro, 101–110. Nancy.

———. 2005b. "*Anthroponymica Mycenaea 5.* *a-wi-to-do-to* /*Awisto-dotos*/ und die unsichtbaren Götter im Alph.-Griechischen. 6. *we-re-na-ko* und Myk. */wrēn/*: alph.-gr. °ρρην-, ἀρήν." *Živa Antika* 55:85–97.

———. 2006. "Zu den Personennamen der neuen Texte aus Theben." In Deger-Jalkotzy and Panagl 2006:37–52.

———. 2012a. "*Anthroponymica Mycenaea 7.* Los nombres con primer elemento *e-ri°* (: Ἐρι°) y *a-ri°* (: Ἀρι°)." In *Actas del Simposio Internacional: 55 Años de Micenología (1952-2007) (Bellaterra, 12-13 de abril de 2007),* ed. C. Varias, 107–125. Bellaterra.

———. 2012b. "*Anthroponymica Mycenaea 8.* Micénico *qe-re-ma-o* /*Kʷēlemaʰo-*/ 'que busca desde lejos', τηλόθε μεταμαιόμενος … ἄγραν (Píndaro)." *Annali del Dipartimento di Studi Letterari, Linguistici e Comparati. Sezione linguistica* 1:149–164.

———. 2012c. "*Anthroponymica Mycenaea:* *e-ti-me-de-i* (dat.) /*ʰEnti-mēdēs*/ '(the one) who accomplished his plans', Homeric ἐξήνυσε βουλάς." In *Donum Natalicium Digitaliter Confectum Gregorio Nagy Septuagenario A Discipulis Collegis Familiaribus Oblatum.* http://nrs.harvard.edu/urn-3:hul. ebook:CHS_Bers_etal_eds.Donum_Natalicium_Gregorio_Nagy.2012.

———. 2016a. "*Anthroponymica Mycenaea 9.* Compound Names in °*me-de,* °*me-ta* and Pylian *me-ti-ja-no*." In *Tavet Tat Satyam. Studies in Honor of Jared S. Klein*

on the Occasion of His Seventieth Birthday, ed. A. Miles Byrd, J. de Lisi, y M.
Wenthe, 52–64. Ann Arbor.

———. 2016b. "Il greco miceneo." In *Manuale di epigrafia micenea: Introduzione allo
studio dei testi in lineare B*. 2 vols., ed. M. Del Freo and M. Perna, 211–244.
Padua.

———. 2017. "*Anthroponymica Mycenaea 10*. The Name *e-ti-ra-wo* /Erti-lāwos/
(and Λᾱ-έρτης): ἔρετο· ὠρμήθη (Hsch.), Hom. ὁρμήθησαν ἐπ' ἀνδράσιν,
and Hom. ἔρχεσθαι μετὰ φῦλα θεῶν, Cret. MN Ἐρπετίδαμος." In *Usque
ad Radices. Indo-European Studies in Honour of Birgit Anette Olsen*, ed. B. S. S.
Hansen *et al.*, 161–177. Copenhagen.

Hajnal, I. 1995. *Studien zum mykenischen Kasussystem*. Berlin.

Haudry, J. 1993. "Altindisch *arí-*, griechisch ἔρις, ἐρι-, ἀρι- und der Gott Aryaman."
In *Indogermanica et Italica. Festschrift für Helmut Rix zum 65. Geburtstag*, ed. G.
Meiser, 169–189. Innsbruck.

Heubeck, A. 1970. "Griechisch-mykenische Etymologien." *Studi Micenei ed Egeo-
Anatolici* 11:63–72.

Jacobsohn, H. 1905. "Miscellen." *Zeitschrift für Vergleichende Sprachwissenschaft* 38:
294–296.

Jouanna, J. 2003. "La douceur en médecine: Les emplois médicaux de ἤπιος."
Révue des Études Grecques 113:54–61.

Lamberterie, C. de. 1992. "Le problème de l'homonymie: Les trois verbes ὀφέλλω
en grec ancien." In *La langue et les textes en grec ancien. Actes du colloque
Pierre Chantraine (Grenoble, 5–8 septembre 1989)*, ed. F. Létoublon, 201–217.
Amsterdam.

———. 1998. "νῆστις", "νήφω." *Chronique d'étymologie grecque, 3. Révue de
Philologie* 72:133–134.

Landau, O. 1957. *Mykenisch-griechische Personennamen*. Göteborg.

Leumann, M. 1950. *Homerische Wörter*. Basel.

Masson, O. 1972. "Remarques sur quelques anthroponymes mycéniens." *Minos* 12:
281–293.

———. 1989. "Quelques noms de femmes au neutre dans les inscriptions atti-
ques." *Horos* 7:45–52.

Neumann, G. 2006. "... Gans und Hund und ihresgleichen ..." In Deger-Jalkotzy
and Panagl 2006:125–138.

Pinault, G.-J. 1988. "ἔρις: Védique *ári* — 'Le proche, l'intime'." *Lalies* 6:111–128.

Plath, R. 2002. "Der mykenische Männername *a-ne-ra-to*." In *Novalis Indogermanica.
Festschrift für Günter Neumann zum 80. Geburtstag*, ed. M. Fritz, y S. Zeilfelder,
381–396. Graz.

Porzig, W. 1942. *Die Namen für Satzinhälte im Griechischen und im Indogermanischen*.
Berlin.

Ruijgh, C. J. 1957. *L'élément achéen dans la langue épique.* Amsterdam.

Russo, J., M. Fernández-Galiano, and A. Heubeck. 1992. *A Commentary on Homer's Odyssey.* Vol. 3: *Books XVII–XXIV.* Oxford.

Schulze, W. 1890. "Reseña de: R. Meister, *Die griechischen Dialekte auf Grundlage von Ahrens' Werk: 'De Graecae linguae dialectis'.* 2 vols. Göttingen 1882–1889." *Berliner philologische Wochenschrift* 1402–1408.

Von Kamptz, H. 1982. *Homerische Personennamen.* Göttingen.

Wackernagel, J. 1889. *Das Dehnungsgesetz der griechischen Komposita.* Basel.

———. 1916. *Sprachliche Untersuchungen zu Homer.* Basel.

Watkins, C. 2011. *The American Heritage Dictionary of Indo-European Roots.* Boston.

Weiss, M. 1994. "On the Non-verbal Origin of the Greek Verb νήφειν 'To Be Sober'." *Historische Sprachwissenschaft* 107:91–98.

———. 1998. "*Erotica*: On the Prehistory of Greek Desire." *Harvard Studies in Classical Philology* 98:31–61.

7

Figs and Fig-Trees at Knossos[1]

JOHN T. KILLEN

Jesus College, Cambridge

Abstract

This paper suggests that the three ideograms hitherto read as *NI* on KN F(2) 841 should in fact be read as ARB, with ARB here denoting 'fig-tree'.

Keywords
Linear B, ideograms, figs, fig-trees

I N AN APPENDIX TO MY PAPER IN *Tractata Mycenaea* (1987:174–177) I write as follows:

The text of KN F(2) 841 reads:

.1	]-ti-ja , sa-pi-ti[-ne-]we-jo [
.2	]a-di-*22-sa GRA + *PE* T 5̣ *NI* 8[
.3	]ṇọ-di-mi-zo-jo[ ] , GRA + *PE* 2 *NI* 34[
.4	pa-i-to , mi-sa-ra-jo , sa-pi-ti-ne-we-jo[
.5	su-za , *NI* 75 ka-po , *e*-[
.6	]wa , OLIV 46 e-ra-wa[
.7.8	] *vacant* [

---

[1] To José, in gratitude for his many kindnesses over the years, and with fond memories of shared pizzas between sessions working on the Pylos tablets in the National Museum, Athens.

What is the purpose of this document? An important first step is to determine the function of the entries at the beginning of line 5 and the end of line 6: (i) *su-za* NI 75; (ii) *e-ra-wa*[. As J. Chadwick and others have seen, the most likely explanation of these is that they are references to *trees*. *su-za* is certainly 'fig-tree(s)' on its appearances in the Gv series at Knossos, where it is followed by the ARB (TREE) ideogram; and since on KN Gv 863 *su* (doubtless standing for *su-za*) ARB stands in parallel to *we-je-we*, evidently /*huiēwes*/, 'vine-shoots', the *su-za* standing in parallel to *we-je-we* on PY Er 880 is also likely to denote 'fig-tree(s)' rather than 'figs'. It is true that on the present tablet *su-za* is followed by NI, which normally elsewhere denotes the fruit of the fig, rather than the tree itself; but, as Chadwick points out in support of the hypothesis that NI here denotes fig-tree, "the annotation [*su-za*] would seem superfluous if the fruit were meant" (*Documents*[2] 440). (As Chadwick also notes, the NI sign is doubtless a simplification of the 'tree' sign.) Moreover, *e-ra-wa*[at the end of line 6 readily 'etymologizes' as /*elaiwā*/, 'olive tree' (Gr. ἐλαῖαι: *Od.* XI 590 +). It is true that, at first sight at least, other elements on the record might seem to point in a different direction: *ka-po* following *su-za* NI, which could readily be interpreted as καρπός 'fruit'; the OLIV ideogram before *e-ra-wa* on 1.6, which normally denotes the fruit of the olive; and the wheat (GRA + PE) and fig (NI) ideograms in lines 1 and 3. As we shall see in a moment, however, these apparently contrary indications may well in fact be illusory.

But what of the entries earlier in the tablet? I repeat the text of lines 1–3:

.1   ]-ti-ja , sa-pi-ti[-ne-]we-jo   [
.2   ]a-di-*22-sa   GRA + PE   T 5 NI 8[
.3   ]ṇọ-di-mi-zo-jo[   ] , GRA + PE 2   NI 34[

It has generally been assumed that the GRA + PE and NI entries on both lines 2 and 3 refer to rations or similar allocations of wheat and figs: in *Documents*, for instance, VC discuss F 841 under the heading of records of "mixed rations and consignments at Knossos." The conclusion is an understandable one: records of rations of wheat and figs do occur widely in the tablets. There must, however, be some real doubt as to whether this is the correct explanation of these entries. If NI denotes fig-tree(s) later on the tablet, there must be some question whether it does not have the same value on lines 2 and 3; and it is also surprising, if GRA and *NI* denote rations, that the amounts of the former are so much smaller than those of the latter: in the Ab records of rations of wheat and figs at Pylos, for instance, the two commodities are always recorded in exactly equal amounts.

With these points in mind, I should like to suggest an alternative explanation of the document. The record as a whole is, I believe, one of *landholdings* and of trees on those holdings. Its closest parallel on the records is, I believe, PY Er 880, the text of which runs as follows:

.1	]ke-ra$_2$[ ]ti-me-no , e-ke
.2	sa-ra-pe-do[ ]pu$_2$-te-me-no
.3	to-so [ ]GRA 30[ ] *vacat*
.4	to-so-de , [ ]to , pe-ma GRA 4̣2̣[
.5	to-sa , we-je[ ]1100[
.6	to-sa-de , su-ẓạ[ ]1̣0̣0̣0̣[
.7	*vacat*
.8	ku-su-to-ro-qa , to-so , pe-ma 94
.9	*vacat*

It is now generally agreed that this tablet shows both the dimensions of a piece of land held by *e-ke-ra$_2$-wo* and the number of vines and fig-trees which stand on it. Lines 2–4 are concerned with the dimensions of the two subsections of the land, expressed (as normally in the E tablets) in terms of seed-corn (*pe-ma* GRA); line 5 states the number of vines on the land; and line 6 shows the number of fig-trees. Line 8, finally, is a totaling entry, giving the overall dimensions of the plot: *ku-su-to-ro-qa , to-so , pe-ma* 94: "Aggregate: so much seed-corn: 94 units."

I believe it is attractive to interpret lines 2 and 3 of KN F 841 along precisely similar lines. As we have already noted, it is attractive to interpret the *NI* entry on both these lines as a reference to fig-trees, given that this is likely to be the value of the ideogram later on the tablet; and it is equally attractive to interpret the GRA + PE entries that precede the *NI* entries as indications, similar to the GRA entries that precede the *su-zạ*[entry on PY Er 880, of the surface area of the plots on which the fig-trees stand. Not only does this neatly account for the PE ligatured to the GRA—this will stand for *pe-ma* (or *pe-mo*) and indicate that GRA is here being used as a unit of land-measurement (cf. *pe-ma* GRA on Er 880.4, and *pe-ma/pe-mo* GRA widely elsewhere in the E series)—it will also explain the relatively small amounts in the GRA + PE entries. On PY Er 880, the *pe-ma* GRA figure for the part of the land described as *pe-pu₂-te-me-no*, evidently 'planted with trees', is plausibly restored as 50 and stands therefore in a relationship of 50:1100[, or 1:22[, to the number of fig-trees listed. Here, the ratios between GRA + PE and NI are not only similar in both entries, and thus consistent with the view that the fig-trees stand on the plots whose dimensions are indicated by the GRA + PE entries: they are also similar to the ratio on PY Er 880. On line 1, the GRA + PE figure is T 5 and the FIG figure almost certainly 8, which gives a ratio of 1:16 (T 5 = half a complete wheat unit). On line 2, the GRA + PE figure is 2 and the FIG figure a minimum of 34 and a maximum of 38, giving a ratio of between 1:17 and 1:19.

Thus, taking the tablet as a whole, I would suggest that this is a record of land, probably in two different areas (see *pa-i-to* line 4,]-*ti-ja* line 1 (possibly *do-ti-ja*)) in the 'ownership' of one *sa-pi-ti-nu-wo* (see *sa-pi-ti*[-*ne-*]*we-jo* line 1, *sa-pi-ti-ne-we-jo* line 4). (*sa-pi-ti-nu-wo* recurs on KN As 1516, where a different person may well be intended.) For possessive adjectives derived from personal names indicating 'owner-ship' of land, cf., e.g., *wo-ro-ki-jo-ne-jo* qualifying *ka-ma* (a type of land-holding) on PY Un 718 (and *e-re-mo*, also referring to land, on PY Er 312): as I have suggested in *TPhS* 1983, this is most plausibly interpreted as an -*e-jo* (-*eios*) possessive adjective derived from a MN /*Wroikiōn*/.

The terms immediately preceding the GRA and NI entries on lines 2 and 3 (*a-di-*22-sa*,]*ṇọ-di-mi-zo-jo*) may well be personal names, and may refer to the actual holders of the land, as distinct from its overall 'owner'; and a similar explanation may hold good for *mi-sa-ra-jo* before *sa-pi-ti-ne-we-jo* in line 4. It is attractive to surmise that the entry on lines 4–6 followed a similar pattern to those on lines 2 and 3, viz., that a GRA + PE entry stood to the right of *sa-pi-ti-ne-we-jo* in the area now broken away. Finally, if this record does deal with landholdings, it is attractive to wonder whether the term *ka-po* on line 5 stands for /*kāpos*/, 'garden,' rather than /*karpos*/, 'fruit.' (A possible restoration of the entry in which *ka-po* stands would be as a heading to the olive entries which follow it on line 6 (where OLIV presumably indicates the olive *tree*), e.g., *ka-po* e[-*ra-wa-o* GRA + PE x: 'olive garden: size: x units of seed-corn: forty-six olive-trees, &c.' [Given that OLIV is here likely to represent the tree rather than the fruit, it is tempting to wonder whether the]*wa* that stands before the sign should be restored as *e-ra*-] *wa*, and whether the *e-ra-wa* that follows OLIV is part of a reference to olive trees of a different kind than those that are indicated by this *e-ra-wa*.])

***

The purpose of this paper is to add a footnote to this discussion. As we have seen, the explanation of KN F(2) 841 appears to require the assumption that in three entries on the tablet the ideogram *NI* denotes 'fig-tree' rather than as universally elsewhere on the tablets 'fig' viz. the fruit of the fig-tree. How can we explain this seeming anomaly?

I begin by examining the ideograms on the records that certainly denote 'fig-tree' (*su-za, su*) (see Fig. 7.1).

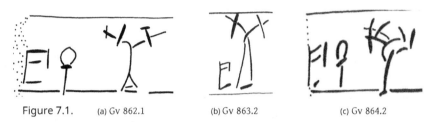

Figure 7.1.   (a) Gv 862.1   (b) Gv 863.2   (c) Gv 864.2

The entries in question read as follows: (a) *su-za* ARB; (b) *su* ARB; (c) *su-za* ARB. As will be seen, ideograms (a) and (b) are very similar. Both show a triangular "trunk" at the bottom of the sign, and a top closely similar to the top of *ni* whether syllabic (*ni*) or ideographic (*NI*); see Figure 7.2.

Figure 7.2.   (a) *ni*: Lc(1) 547   (b) *NI*: Uc 161

The third ideogram (Fig. 7.1(c)), however, takes a different form. Here, there is no triangular "trunk" but a single upright stroke at the bottom; and instead of the single stroke crossing the oblique "arms" at either side, which is characteristic of all examples of *ni* and *NI*, there are two strokes crossing each "arm" (which may be intended to represent branches or foliage).

But what of the supposed *NI*s on KN F(2) 841? I show beneath each of the ideograms in question.

Figure 7.3.   (a) F(2) 841.2   (b) F(2) 841.3   (c) F(2) 841.5

These can hardly be examples of *NI*; as we have seen above, *ni* and *NI* always show one stroke crossing each "arm." What, however, they do resemble is the third example of ARB shown in Figure 7.1(c), with its single upright at the base and its two strokes crossing each "arm." And since ARB on Gv 864.2 is preceded by *su-za*, and since the third *NI* on KN F(2) 841 is preceded by the same word—and, moreover, since ARB will also fit the context in lines 2 and 3 of KN F(2) 841 (see earlier)—it is difficult to doubt that we should read all three of these signs, not as *NI*, but as ARB, here indicating a fig-tree.

One further point should perhaps be added. In the discussion quoted at the start of the paper I suggest that OLIV on l. 6 of KN F(2) 841, which follows]*wa*, perhaps *e-ra-*]*wa*, indicates 'olive trees' rather than 'olives'. Given what we have concluded above, and the disappearance of evidence elsewhere on the record for 'fig' denoting 'fig-tree', this suggestion must clearly come into question. Is it possible, the thought comes to mind, that the ideogram here (see Fig. 7.4) is a form of ARB denoting 'olive-tree'?

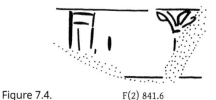

Figure 7.4.   F(2) 841.6

Though the sign has not survived complete, it has little in common with the one example of ARB which seems certain to denote 'olive-tree' (Fig. 7.5(a); see *Docs*^{2}, 276) and has much more in common with the standard form of OLIV, with its three 'leaves' or 'spikes' at the top; see Figure 7.5(b), (c):

Figure 7.5.   (a) ARB: Gv 862.2   (b) OLIV: E(2) 669   (c) OLIV: TH Ft 140.2

There are, however, slight differences: the "leaves" at the top lie flatter than the "spikes" on normal OLIV, and there is an extra stroke between the first and second "leaves" from the left. In the absence of more evidence for the forms that ARB = 'olive-tree' could take, it would clearly be unwise to conclude from these differences that this is an example of that sign, and not OLIV; equally, however, the possibility that this is not OLIV but ARB should clearly be borne in mind.

One final point: In my discussion of the new Thebes tablets in *Texte aus Theben* (2006) I note that the entries on TH Ft 140, which involve GRA + PE entries (with the + PE understood in all registers but the first) followed by OLIV entries resemble those on KN F(2) 841.2.3, where, as we have seen, GRA + PE entries are followed by *NI* (now ARB) entries. I suggest, however, that although it might be tempting to conclude from this similarity that OLIV here denotes 'olive-tree', this is unlikely, given the ratios in the two cases, with the figures for *NI* (now ARB) relative to GRA + PE on KN F(2) 841 much higher than those for OLIV relative to GRA + PE on TH Ft 140. From this I conclude (*Texte aus Theben*, 81) that "it may well be ... that OLIV does not denote olive trees, but is a record, rather like GRA + PE, of the (taxable) productive capacity of the land, in this case in olives." Now that we know that the second ideogram on KN F(2) 841.2.3 and the ideogram on KN F(2) 841.5 is not *NI* but ARB, and that we have no certain evidence for an ideogram denoting fruit indicating the tree from which the fruit comes, this conclusion is clearly reinforced.

Addendum

Since writing the above, I have noticed that one of the points I make in my discussion has already been noted in *Scripta Minoa* II: that the form of *NI* (or rather ARB) which follows *su-za* on KN F(2) 841.5 and KN Gv 864.2 has "four branches" viz. a double stroke crossing each of the two side elements of the sign. The passage concerned reads as follows (*SM* II.60), with the drawings of the original replaced by (deciphered) Linear B signs. "A variant of *NI* with four branches occurs only preceded by *ta-za* and is followed by numeral on KN Gv 864.2." *ta-za* here is a misreading of what we now know to be *su-za*.

Bibliography

Killen, J. T. 1983. "Mycenaean Possessive Adjectives in -e-jo." *Transactions of the Philosophical Society* 81: 66–99.

Scripta Minoa II = A. J. Evans and J. L. Myres, *Scripta Minoa*, vol. II: *The Archives of Knossos* (Oxford, 1952).

Texte aus Theben = S. Deger-Jalkotzy und O. Panagl, eds., *Die neuen Linear B Texte aus Theben: Ihr Aufschlusswert für die mykenische Sprache und Kultur. Akten des internationalen Forschungskolloquiums an der Österreichischen Akademie der Wissenschaften 5.-6. Dezember 2002* (Österreichische Akademie der Wissenschaften, Phil.-Hist. Klasse, Denkschriften 338) (Vienna, 2006).

Tractata Mycenaea = P. Hr. Ilievski and L. Crepajac, eds., *Tractata Mycenaea. Proceedings of the Eighth International Colloquium on Mycenaean Studies, Held in Ohrid, 15-20 September 1985* (Skopje, 1987).

8

Accounts, Values, Futures, Options
Production, Finance, and the End of the Late Bronze Age World Economy

MICHAEL F. LANE

University of Maryland, Baltimore County
mflane@umbc.edu

Abstract

Reviving the position that Linear B scribes shared accounting practices that involved proportions of materials for manufacturing certain quantities of goods, I argue that these proportions were realized through accounts receivable and payable, reflected in scribal terminology. I maintain that the scribes shared an understanding of equivalences among certain classes of basic materials. They were thus able to control both staple and prestige commodity production and to monitor both rewards for obligations fulfilled and investment in diplomatic gift exchange typical of Late Bronze Age elite economies. The cyclical delays between assessment of crops or materials and their final product could transform the understanding of equivalence into a notional system of prices, insofar as expectations of standardization and exchangeability of certain commodities were projected indefinitely into the future. A hierarchy of production, circulation, and consumption interdependencies would arise at multiple scales, offering incentives for expanding and investing in this network of relationships. However, investment strategies and institutional constraints on consumption created weak links in the network. When enough links failed, not only were expectations negated but confidence in the system was also undermined. Such events could have contributed to the rapid demise of palace economies toward the end of the LBA.

Keywords

Wealth finance, prestige goods, *o-no*, *qe-te-(j)o*, end of Bronze Age

Michael F. Lane

THIS OFFERING TO PROFESSOR MELENA harks back both to his interest, early in his career, in proportional contributions of plant materials to palace workshops[1] and to his abiding interest in the manufacture, character, and distribution of honor-gifts and prestige goods, some of which use these materials. Resuming the stance that scribes of the separate archives shared accounting practices involving grids of proportions for the manufacture of certain quantities of certain goods, I argue that these proportions were realized through accounts receivable and payable, reflected in the scribes' precise terminology. Furthermore, I maintain that they shared an understanding of equivalences among some (but not all) classes of basic materials. They were thus able both to control staple and prestige commodity production and to monitor the rewarding of obligations fulfilled and investment in alliance-building gift exchange so typical of Late Bronze Age (LBA) elite economies. The annual or longer cyclical delay between assessment of crops or materials and their final product[2] would begin to transform the likely actual tables of equivalence into a notional system of prices, insofar as the expectations of formal standardization and exchangeability of certain commodities within and between palace economies were projected indefinitely into the future, sometimes irrespective of pragmatic or specific symbolic values originally imbued in them. Thus, a hierarchy of production, circulation, and consumption interdependencies arose at multiple scales that offered incentives for investing in and expanding the network. However, investment strategies and institutional constraints on consumption created weak links in the network. Thus, when enough links failed in their presumed role, not only were expectations negated but confidence in the whole system was also deeply shaken. Such an event could contribute to the observed rapid demise of the palace economies toward the end of the LBA.

Premises

The assumption that Mycenaean scribes generally assessed commodities proportionally and maintained standards of equivalence, when recording palace interests, is associated closely with total political-economic surveillance and is compatible with systems of general redistribution[3] that comparative anthropologists of archaic states and staple versus wealth finance have roundly criticized.[4] Nonetheless, certain relevant observations are widely, if quietly, accepted among Linear B scholars. Some scholars have recently taken more nuanced

---

[1]   Melena 1972, 1974, 1975, 1976, 1983a and b, 2002:380–384.
[2]   See Bennet 2001:27–33.
[3]   *Pace* Bennet and Halstead 2014:272.
[4]   Most notably in Galaty and Parkinson 2007.

views of finance in the Mycenaean palatial economy. I mean to promote the latter on the basis of the former.

Decades ago, Shelmerdine explained the Pylos Ma set as the product of precise calculation of assessments of nested groups of locales, districts, and provinces.[5] Similar proportions evident in the Knossos Mc set,[6] as well as parallel terminology and toponymy in the KN Ga and Nc series, comparable also with the Mycenae Ge series,[7] indicate that the separate archives shared at least general procedures over as much as a century.[8] In 1977, De Fidio's analysis of the *dosmoí* 'assessments' in the Pylos Es series and, by extension, the Er–Un 718 triptych, linked total landholding of a group of named or titled individuals to total *dosmós* from it.[9] Despite later criticism of her assuming equivalence between certain primary and secondary agro-pastoral products, the statistical probability of the results of her calculations being coincidental is very low.[10] Shelmerdine's conclusions concerning methods of assessment could therefore be linked to De Fidio's concerning size of cultivated areas, if the latter are not simply dismissed as the exception to the rule.

De Fidio observed that both Pylian Hands 11 and 24 have whole-unit target totals for a group's landholding, particularly totals in multiples of *spérmo* GRA 5, from which either Hand 1 or 24 assesses *dosmós*. Both Halstead and Killen have also observed target totals for the constitution and allocation of flocks for producing exact amounts of wool or hair,[11] while Killen and Nosch have confirmed that the cycle of targets for assessment extends to palatial textile manufacture.[12] Animals are sometimes kept on land closely associated with assessed locales, many expressly *dãmoi*,[13] literally lands 'distributed [among some people]',[14] the constitution of the latter expressed in Pylos E– and KN F(2) and Uf landholding series. Therefore, even discounting the luxury purposes to which the PY Ma and KN Mc materials or KN Ga and MY Ge non-staples are put

---

[5]   Shelmerdine 1973.

[6]   *Docs²*, 301–303.

[7]   Killen 1983b. The major exception may be the Pylos Na assessments, but these texts also have peculiar terminology and are closely associated with "watcher," "settler," or "cultivator" men (De Fidio 2008; Lane 2012b:160–170).

[8]   See Driessen 2008 on chronology, Nosch 2008 on commonality.

[9]   De Fidio 1977.

[10] For example, R. Palmer's observation (1989:97–98) that PY An 128 *verso* contradicts the "GRA equivalent to *NI*" inference is not fatal, being a unique counterexample that could reflect a simple scribal error. A simple *chi*-square test of actual versus De Fidio's independently calculated values of *dosmós* in PY Un 718 reveals that the probability of the *difference* being stochastic is about 97.5 to 99 percent. This is not true without the equivalences observed.

[11] Halstead 1996–1997, 1999; Killen 1993.

[12] Killen 1976, 1979; Nosch 2011.

[13] KN C(4) 911.6, F(2) 845.b; PY Ea–, Eb–Ep, also *o-pi-da-mi-jo* (PY Cn 608.2, An 830.12).

[14] *EDG*, 325.

(see above), a link may exist between land assessments and prestige goods via the elaboration of certain linen and woolen textiles. Target totals probably also exist for groups of men engaged in relevant 'settling' (*metaktítaị̯*), 'cultivating' (*ktítaị̯, pʰutéres*), and connected military service.[15]

Lately, Nakassis has plotted goods recorded in Linear B on two axes, "staple" versus "non-staple" and "more convertible" (exchangeable) versus "less convertible."[16] He concludes that staples are most "convertible"—but only for themselves—and have little part in recorded forms of recompense. Less exchangeable are provisions for feasts, *géraha* 'honor-gifts', and "prestige goods." He admits that we lack positive evidence of their exchange for staples or any direct evidence of exchange of prestige goods abroad. He concludes that the latter and *géraha* are employed in "accumulation of symbolic profit."[17] More recently, Bennet and Halstead have developed a model of the nature and extent of palatial redistribution, underscoring not just the "shadow" of unrecorded economies but also the importance of *ónon* 'payment', which adumbrates exchangeability of various goods and services.[18]

I agree that no evidence exists for the exchange of prestige goods directly for staples, although exchange for productive land is possible. Nonetheless, careful apportionment of staples is entirely likely both for sustaining dependent labor and for religious festivals. Certainly, there is no demonstrable equivalence of metal to agro-pastoral products (but see Table 8.2). Metals are durables and accumulate over a longer term. There should be no target maximum for them in a non-totalizing economy. Rather, as PY Jn 829 indicates, there may be target minima for certain metal products.

I have explored the possibility that all the Pylian landholding series aim at target totals and that their assessment is made with standard formulas.[19] I concluded that a target is demonstrable for the *dãmos* of the place *pa-ki-ja-na* (Eb–Ep, Ed, Eo–En series) and probable for the place described in the Ea set. I furthermore concluded that *pa-ki-ja-na*'s total GRA 120 can account, through a series of equivalences, not just for its actual Ma and Cn 3 'fatted hog' contributions, but also for the palace's reciprocal wine distribution.[20] The same holds true if one attributes whole-unit totals of landholding to each of the other well-known sixteen tributary places, some of which are expressly or implicitly *dãmoị̯*.

[15]   Del Freo 2002–2003; Killen 1983a, 2006.
[16]   Nakassis 2010.
[17]   Nakassis 2010:139.
[18]   Bennet and Halstead 2014.
[19]   Lane 2012a.
[20]   Lane 2012a:95–100.

Finally, I asserted that a correlation exists between one's individual contribution to *dosmós* and the *onātón* 'profitable'[21] part of the land one enjoys.

In other words, places are assessed and compensated according to the size of relevant landholdings. This does not imply palatial total surveillance of the realm, only a hierarchy of widespread but discrete interests. The apparent restriction of Pylos landholding records to the Hither Province (HP) need not mean interest only in nearby cultivation.[22] Nor do the Na records prove greater interest in the HP, as they probably pertain particularly to colonization of land to be awarded for military service.[23] At issue is the mobilization of portions of primary and secondary products from periphery to center, not whole harvests of bulky staples. One should expect still more Linear B texts to be found at secondary sites.[24]

Account Receivable

The Linear B archives have in common precise metrology, targets of easily calculated fractions and multiples, and everywhere attention to *ópʰelos* 'debt'.[25] The scribes' lexicon is precise too. The trope of assessment by and payment to the palace is one of 'giving' (stem *do-/dō-*). *Dosmós* is the amount of the assessment, and *apúdosis/apudosmós* is the actual payment.[26] The commodities paid are qualified as *dósmii̯a*, 'things pertaining to *dosmós*'. One finds various inflections of *dídōmi* 'I give' with respect to the palace (*dídonsi, dídontoi, dōsei, dōsonsi, dōke, dedoména*) whose subjects or agents are persons and communities.[27] Specifically one finds *apédōke/apúdōke*, literally 'gave from [something]', the object being either assessed or unassessed goods. At least twice, a palace official 'received' (*déksato*) such commodities; in one instance the verb is juxtaposed against *apúdosis*.[28] The exceptional use of *do-/dō-* is Pylos' *dōra* 'gifts' on Tn 316. However, these are presumably donations of prestige goods (and persons), voluntarily, and probably regularly, to *pa-ki-ja-na*.

The pivotal verb in Tn 316 could be *hii̯entoi̯* 'they are being sent'.[29] The palace's—or, at least, named persons', rather than whole communities'—trope

---

21 Incorrectly quoted in Olsen 2014:218.
22 Killen 2008:162–171.
23 Lane 2012b:160–170.
24 For example, lately, see Shelmerdine 2012.
25 Killen 2008:189–191; Nosch 2008.
26 Duhoux 1976:153–161; De Fidio 1977:7–12.
27 KN Og(2) <4467>.1, So(1) 4429.a, U(1) 7507, Ws 1707.β, 8493.βb; PY Jn 829.1, Ma–, Na–, Ng 319.2, 332.2, Un 267.1 (non-technical usage?), Un 718.3.9, Vn 10.1; MY Oi 701.6, 703.3.
28 On KN Lc 642.1, a quantity of TELA + TE textile may be *de-ko-to /dektós/* receivable'.
29 Lane 2016 on this and other possible inflections of *hii̯ēmi* in Mycenaean Greek.

for moving commodities or people is arguably either one of 'sending' (*he-*) or one of 'distributing' (*epi-da-*; cf. *dãmos*). An inverse relation between 'sending' and 'giving' is evident in PY Ma 393, where certain quantities of *dósmiįa* are *án-eta* 'to be sent back, remitted'.[30] Reflexes and derivatives of *híįēmi* 'I send' may be reserved for movements that do not correspond directly to assessed collective *dosmós* and may instead be *ad hoc* disbursements. On PY Cn 3, either groups of unnamed men—albeit under the command of men named in the "coastguard" texts—*hiįénsi* 'are sending' bulls (BOS) to the "inspector, *Diųiįeús*" or, more syntactically awkwardly, plural inspectors are sending bulls to groups of men at separate locales.[31] Persons named at Pylos *apéhēke* 'dispatched' (literally 'sent from [the available]') unnamed men to *Enkʰērráųōn* (the *ųánaks* or his surrogate), the *lāųāgétās* 'war leader', and other named officers for rowing and other duties (An 724).[32] Something similar may obtain on PY An 607, where female servants "have been sent" to *hekᵘétaį* "Companions" (if *e-e-to* is read, plausibly, as /[h]éhento/).[33] *A-pi-e-ke* on PY Un 2.2 is probably best read as a false start of /*aphíįēsi/ 'he is dispatching' finishing as aorist *apéhēke*, describing the goods disbursed for *pa-ki-ja-na* "upon the initiation of the *ųánaks*."[34] Finally, "sending" may be specifically used in the context of elaborating prestige goods, such as armor, chariots, textiles, and fatted animals, if, in rather obscure text PY Vn 15, together with *(h)ármo* 'wheel'. *o-u-qe* , *e-to* is to be read /ou-kᵘe hénto/ "it was not sent" (line 1) and *-i-je-to* /híįetoį/ as "it is being sent" (*verso* a).[35] Wheels are among products of *hopã* 'finishing work' and sent to named persons who presumably have the expertise and tools to return them duly embellished.[36]

"Distributing" is specified when the palace disburses certain quantities of material and finished goods to be divided rationally among several places, particularly if they are directly proportional to these places' productive capacity—for example, the cultivated extent from which *dosmós* is calculated or the number of resident smiths. Wine *epidédastoį* 'has been distributed' to the nine tributary HP places[37] in exact proportion to the actual number of hogs "the *dãmos*-inhabitants will fatten."[38] PY Jn 389.7 and 601.7 each record an extra amount of *kʰalkós* 'bronze' *epídastos* 'distributable' among the bronzesmiths at two different places.

[30] Killen 1984.

[31] *Docs*², 206–208, 435–436.

[32] Del Freo 2002–2003.

[33] *DMic.* I, 203–204.

[34] *DMic.* I, 80–81.

[35] *DMic.* I, 58–59.

[36] For example, KN So-.

[37] PY Vn 20.

[38] Cn 608.

In summary, one palace official may "send" goods or persons to another palace official, elite persons of the recognized *nomenklatura* may send each other the same for meeting palace-prescribed quotas, and palace officials 'send' gifts to cult sites on certain occasions. Palace officials may also 'send' commodities, including animals, for the *hopā́* they need to become honor-gifts, prestige goods, or victuals for feasts.[39] The latter may be the fate of the BOS listed on Cn 3, if the inspectors are sending them to men in the countryside, and the condition of the animals listed in Un 2, if the *opiteu̯kʰeheú̯s* 'provisioner' has dispatched them for a special occasion at *pa-ki-ja-na*. However, the palace's provision from stores of bronze or luxury consumables under its control to places in its administrative ambit—whether for outsourced *talasī́ā* 'stint' manufacture or in reciprocity for commodities 'given'—is 'distributed'. In short, the palace distributes material for making commodities, such as textiles and bronzes, which may be sent for finishing as prestige goods. It seems recompense for the former is staples, in the case of work groups of unnamed women and children,[40] and small amounts of raw material for named men and sometimes their "servants,"[41] comprising *óna* 'benefit payments'.

Accounts Payable

The link between "giving," "sending," and "distributing" or "paying" is work. 'Working' (*u̯erg-*) seems to be a scribal generic term: one can *u̯ór^dzei̯* land[42]; but textiles can also *u̯órgen* 'be worked',[43] and some vessels are *krēsii̯ou̯ergḗs* 'Cretan-style-work'.[44] Some types of work are specific: *telei̯áhen* is connected with services as *telestā́s*,[45] and *(epi)tʰerapískei̯* may refer to some secondary sort of working land.[46] There is *hopā́* work, which appears to be voluntary, and *talasī́ā* work, which appears to be linked to dependency or obligation. Here I discuss types of work as investment for return.

Halstead early recognized the potential for such a transaction. He hypothesized that owners of breeding rams and non-wool flocks could enter into profitable relations with the palaces' official wool flock "collectors," annually earning male lambs and old unproductive sheep for their services and loans of animal

---

[39] Killen 1992, 1994; Melena 1983a.
[40] Chadwick 1988:67–75; R. Palmer 1989.
[41] Killen 1999.
[42] PY Ea-, Eb–Ep.
[43] Lane 2011:85; Lejeune 1971:118n109; also *wo-zo-me-no/-na* of *a-mo-ta* 'wheels', KN So(2) 4433.b, 4438.
[44] PY Ta 641, 709.
[45] L. R. Palmer 1963:195–196; Lane 2012a:75–85.
[46] PY Eb 842.B, Ep 613.8, possibly *in tmesi;* cf. ἐπιθεραπεύω *sensu* "to apply again."

and land capital.[47] Similarly, persons *hékʰei̯/hékʰonsi* 'have' *onátá* of measured land plots, because of prerogative, execution of duties (*ktiménā* land, especially), or 'working' the land itself.[48] Whatever is not *dosmós* from the product of these possessions is effectively the *ónon* 'payment' that realizes an *onātón*. An inducement is offered to maximize yields through this relationship too.

Talasíi̯ā work is more complicated. Groups of women and children appear to receive only rations or payments of staples, not my focus here.[49] The work is therefore at least dependent, if they are native inhabitants, and strictly obligatory, if they are foreign migrants.[50] Some of their work appears to be connected with unnamed contingents of men performing rowing duty under the command of a named man.[51] This embeds them in a more intricate system of obligations and schedules of labor allocation. The system involves bronze-working *talasíi̯ā* assigned to individual named men, presumably to be worked in shops with labor they control.[52] There are remittances for such worked bronze provision, as well as for other specialized duties, in assessments of agricultural products, especially flax.[53] I have argued that some of the same named men are granted land, on which flax is produced, for executing military or naval commands. However, the contingents of unnamed men, some also rowers, actually bring the land into cultivation (*ktii̯énsi*, cf. *ktiménā*). The recompense for men's various *talasíi̯ā* seems to be in kind too—staples or usufruct for the nameless, landed capital for the *nomenklatura*—the latter reminiscent of *onātón* and livestock arrangements described above.[54] The palace would carefully calculate the relationship of work to benefits, especially because new *ktiménā* land is subject to *dosmós*.

The discussion above excludes *óna* in name. Their textual loci are collected in Table 8.1. In most cases, they are juxtaposed against the sort of commodity that could be a *géras* 'honor-gift' or prestige object: oil for perfuming or already perfumed, *démnii̯a* 'couches', and quantities of wool (LANA) and tunics (*146) that are about the size Nosch defines as typical of distributions to workshops or households for manufacturing a few small textiles or a very large

---

[47] Halstead 1990–1991:359–363.

[48] Lane 2012a:74–93; 2012b:154–170 ; Palaima 2012; 2015:621–629.

[49] R. Palmer 1989.

[50] Killen 2001; Nosch 2006.

[51] PY Ad 684 *lat. sup.*, 686.a (where they may be *talantopʰóroi̯* 'burden-bearing'), 697.a; see Chadwick 1988:87–88, Killen 2006.

[52] Killen 1987; Smith 1992:206–208.

[53] Killen 1984.

[54] Lane 2012b:160–170.

Table 8.1. Loci of *o-no* in the Linear B Corpus

Text	Commodity and Amount	Remarks
KN Fh 347	OLE 1	
KN Fh 348	OLE 1 S 1	Above *qe-te-o* OLE 1 (see Table 8.2)
KN Fh 361	OLE 3 V 3	*zo-a* 'for boiling' (for infusion); recipient *ku-pi-ri-jo*
KN Fh 372	OLE 150	Recipient *ku-pi-ri-jo*
KN Fh 5431	OLE 2 S 2	For *de-mi-ni-jo* 'couch'
KN Fh 5447	OLE 9 S ? *MU* 7	Recipient *ku-pi-ri-jo*
KN M(1) 559	LANA 2	
KN Od 5558	LANA ?	
PY An 35	LANA 2 CAP^f 4 *146 3 VIN 10 *NI* 4	To *a-ta-ro* for 'alum'
PY An 615	?VIR	Hand 1, like An 724 below; beside *e-qo-te* on *lat. inf.*, possibly 'fulfilled'
PY An 724	VIR 10	Beside *e-qo-te* (see above) on last line
PY Un 443	LANA 10 *146 10 LANA 3	Equal portions of wool and tunics to *ku-pi-ri-jo* for 'astringent' Likely three units of wool for the '*po-re-no*-girding' (pl.)
PY Un 1322	GRA 6 *NI* [6]? GRA 2 *NI* 2 GRA 12 *146 GRA 5 *146 GRA 15	Likely equal portions of wheat and figs and multiples of rations of each on lines 2–4
MY Oe 108	LANA 4 LANA 3	For *sa-pa* textile (cf. KN L 693 *qe-te-o*, Table 8.2)
MY Oe 109	]*wo-no* ?	Wine (cf. PY An 35 above)

one, as well as for clothing workers.[55] Wheat (GRA), if not wine,[56] may also be distributed toward such ends. At Thebes, wool allocations to individuals are usually of a quantity PA 1 (ca. 1 kg).[57] Thus, *ónon* commodities are tokens of value in themselves and may permit the manufacture of others. They also sometimes provide for feeding and clothing groups of people. They are not *talasíiā*, since the payments may consist of both staples and raw materials and sometimes are made to persons unconnected with a relevant industry. Two Pylian loci indicate that *óna* are paid for *struptēríiā* 'astringent', an ingredient required for "finishing" textile unguent.[58] Thus, it seems reasonable to assume that *ónon* is paid principally for *hopá*. The exact portions and proportions of some *óna*, particularly if we include the wool payments recorded at Thebes, suggest careful calculation of disbursements, which include commodities that have equivalences at the level of *dosmós*.[59] *Óna* may even be investments for future production. In other words, the scribes appear to be tracking both accounts receivable and payable, including investments, in order to maintain or increase production in the next cycle.

Futures

Target totals mean future expectations. The palace expects a certain amount of land to be cultivated over a certain period, so that it will yield a certain amount of primary or secondary agricultural products. Expectations of wool and hair yields for textiles are related to land available for pasture, including *dãmoi*. Cultivators expect to realize *onātá*. There must be enough staples to fund *talasíiā* and to cover certain *óna* for *hopá*. Wine, oils, and couches are needed not only for *óna* but also for festivals. Production of honor-gifts, in the form of textiles or gold vessels (not to mention *géraha* of land) and *hek^{u}ésiia* ('Companion' appropriate) and *ksénu̯iia* ('guest-gift' appropriate) prestige goods is expected for regional and interregional distribution. Local officials presumably expect deliveries for awards at a certain date and cost. Likewise, more distant places presumably need commodities produced according to agro-pastoral or metal-working schedules, on time and in the right amount, for distribution of awards, periodic or special occasions, and investment in local projects. They may well reciprocate with an eye on complementary or supplementary goods in return.

---

[55] Nosch 2009. The exception seems to be the "benefit" of men, possibly *e-qo-‹je-›te* /*ekk^{u}ojēt^{h}ē/ (= ἐξεποιήθη) 'fulfilled', on PY An 615's *lat. inf.* and PY An 724.14 (Hand 1) perhaps totaling the payment.

[56] MY Oe 109.

[57] Nosch 2009:90–92.

[58] Shelmerdine 1986:13–15, 136–137.

[59] See De Fidio 1977:85–88; Lane 2012a:96–100.

We know already that the ever-widening circles of LBA elite exchanges resemble a financial pyramid scheme with multiple apices. Competitive gift-giving among monarchs, whose exclusive domain is diplomacy, makes the constellation among the pinnacles. Providing a certain quantity on some occasion instigates repayment with as much or more in the next cycle.[60] Resources are therefore moved upward for the production of non-staples, so that they can be distributed and paid downward to others, sometimes far away, with the implicit or explicit promise that everyone at each level of the distribution hierarchy will receive greater wealth if (likely gender) he uses it to recruit more people into the manufacture or finishing of more luxuries, supply of basic materials, or provision of cultivable or pastoral land.[61] In other words, at some point, presumably, the allure and distinction that comes from having these commodities can be "cashed in" for non-luxuries, although staples—representing the consumption for production that maintains the basic workforce—seem to be off the table. The net effect in the short term is few people trying to collect real capital with prestige goods but trying instead to capitalize on them.

Pyramid schemes are notoriously unprofitable if they extend mainly vertically. Not only is there the problem of having fewer *Átukʰoi̯* (aka Peters) to rob in order to pay *Onāseús* (aka Paul), but one also eventually runs into a social stratum that cannot provide the labor, materials, or landed capital one requires, especially where great inequalities of wealth or claims to it already exist. Furthermore, sumptuary customs may control the inflation of values attributed to prestige goods by selectively taking them out of circulation, while warfare—like diplomacy, principally a monarchical affair—may control deflation with treasure and land seized.[62]

Options

Before proceeding to trying to link the Mycenaean model outlined above to broader LBA prestige goods economies, I consider the term *qe-te-(j)o* (neuter plural *qe-te-a[₂]*; Table 8.2). It may hold the key to how both palace and non-palace actors bet on the future growth of wealth. The *communis opinio* is that the string represents /*kʷeité(i̯)os/ (vel sim.) 'to be paid,' 'payable,' or 'payment' (cf. τιμητέος 'to be honored').[63] Killen has suggested, on the basis of one collocation with *o-no*,[64] that it represents the balance of a palace's payments still owed to

---

[60] Liverani 1990: esp. 218–229.
[61] See D'Altroy and Earle 1985:188, 194.
[62] Liverani 1990:117–125.
[63] Killen 1995. This is the most logical contextual meaning (*DMic.* II, 201–202), though the hypothetical Mycenaean Greek rendering suffers from morphological irregularities (see Hutton 1990–1991 for discussion).
[64] KN Fh 348; Killen 1979:176–179.

somebody.[65] Although the kinds of commodities listed a *kʷeitéa* are similar to those paid as *óna*, one may wonder why a term sharing the stem of *ónon* and *onātón* is not used, if Killen is right.[66] While some evidence exists that *óna* are precisely apportioned for certain goods or services, the *kʷeitéa* on PY Un 128 appear to be a huge, motley assortment of subsistence and luxury comestibles, including fatted animals, in contrast also with the proportionate *dosmós* for Poseidon or *pe-re-*82* on PY Un 6, 718, and 857. Furthermore, while the palace seems to send some *kʷeitéa* to distant places or persons, the palace clearly also receives *kʷeitéa* from other persons or places. Finally, while *óna* are sometimes given to recognized collectors, including the "international" kind,[67] *kʷeitéa* are nearly as often bestowed by someone uniquely attested or peripheral to the existing complex of obligations and rewards.

I hypothesize that *kʷeitéa* are investments or reinvestments in economies by persons or institutions who may not be regular participants in a region's political-economic hierarchy. Their prospect is a return of at least commensurate exchange value, in addition to the potential for deploying this return as a sign of one's upward allegiance to a palace or cult center and downward as a token that promises exchangeability and increasing rewards from above. Such tokens of value also attract further loyalty to oneself. They are pieces in a confidence game. Through *kʷeitéa*, one can enter the game with a discrete interest in the financial order, farther advanced than if one had opted for leading army and navy expeditions, colonizing, or doing *téleia* on land—although the different investment options might be combined.

Therefore, the *du-ni-jo páró* 'from'[68] whom *kʷeitéa* come in PY Un 138 may, thanks to the agencies of Hands 42 and 43, be the same who has land on which men attend to livestock in some manner[69] and has *onátá* in various locales.[70] He is not, however, in the circle of named men connected with military service, livestock husbandry, or bronze provision. *Du-ni-jo* may refer to a certain special *d(u)már* 'intendant',[71] unless otherwise specified at Pylos, remote from the usual administrative ambit.[72] He may be trying to buy into a network of potentially increasing reciprocation, not just with Pylos but also with the personage

---

[65] Killen 1995:218–220.

[66] 'Promise' of payment is probably *o-u-ko* /*oʉkʰon*/ (MY 108.2, 111.1, 113.1, 120); cf. *e-u-ke-to* /*eʉkʰetoi̯*/ 'she solemnly declares' (PY Eb 297.1, Ep 704.5); DMic. II, 56.

[67] Olivier 2001.

[68] *Pa-ro* surely reflects a fossilized ablative ending. Use as 'chez', as though παρά with the dative or accusative, is unproved. See DMic. II, 85–86.

[69] PY Ae 8, 72, 264.

[70] PY Ea, Eb–Ep series.

[71] An 192.3, possibly On 300.6; cf. KN As(2) 1516.21. DMic. I, 195–196.

[72] Nakassis 2013:121, 237–239.

Table 8.2. Loci of *qe-te-(j)o* or *qe-te-a(₂)* in the Linear B Corpus

Text	Commodity and Amount	Remarks
KN Fh 348	OLE 1	[[*te-o*]]; beneath *o-no* OLE 1 S 1 (see Table 8.1)
KN Fp (2) 363	OLE ? ... S 2	*te-re-no* likely masc. name in gen. (/*Terḗnos/ vel sim.*), *hapax*
KN L(5) 513	TELA²	*po-po* on line b is masc. name elsewhere assoc. with supervising wool and textile production (e.g., KN L(1) 567.1 *o-pi* / *po-po*); here dat. "for *po-po*"?
KN L 693	*ri-no re-po-to ki-to* AES M 1 *sa-pa* P 2 Q 1 *e-pi-ki-to-ni-ja* AES M 1	"Fine linen" for several types of textile (cf. *sa-pa* on MY Oe 108); juxtaposition of same amount of 'bronze' beside both 'khitons' and 'over-khitons' curiously suggests pairing if not equivalence
KN L(5) 5092	TELA¹ ?	
KN L(5) 7380	TELA¹ 2, TELAˣ 4 *po* TELAˣ ?	
KN L(5) 7834	TELAˣ 10	
KN L(5) 8441	TELA 1	
PY Fr 1206	OLE + *PA* V 4	For *po-ti-ni-ja a-si-wi-ja*
PY Fr 1241	OLE 1 S ?	
PY Un 138	HORD 18 T 5 *po-qa* OLIV 4 T 3 V 5 VIN 13 OVISᵐ 5 WE 8 OVISᶠ 1 CAPᵐ 13 SUS 12 SUS+*SI* 1 BOSᶠ 1 BOSᵐ 2 HORD 4 T 8 V 1 *ka-pa* OLIV 7	*pa-ro du-ni-jo*; first four lines pertain to Pylos, last line to person *me-za-wo*
TH Gp 109	VIN 2 V 5	*63-te-ra-de di-wi-ja{-}me-ro*
TH Gp 147	VIN 4	*tu-ka-ta*?]-*si-qe* (cf. disbursement of eight units of wool on MY Oe 112.2)
TH Wu 49	OVISᵐ ... *a-ko-ra*	
TH Wu 50	CAPᶠ ... *a-ko-ra*	
TH Wu 51	SUSᵐ *te-qa-de*	
TH Wu 53	BOSᵐ	*i-ri-ja* on face γ
TH Wu 63	SUSᶠ ... *a-ko-ra*	
TH Wu 65	OVISᶠ *te-qa-de*	
TH Wu 96	SUSᶠ *te-qa-de*	

Me^dzáu̯ōn.[73] Thus, it is intriguing that the *k^uei̯téa* animals recorded on Thebes sealings that are not destined for Thebes (hand γ) are mostly *qe-te-o | a-ko-ra(-jo) k^uei̯téa* 'of the herd' (hand β), the second word /ʰagorā́/ referring specifically to palace animals mixed with non-palace.[74] These could represent payments of sheep, goats, and pigs, even deferred profit therefrom, presuming the palace will accept them, in the hope of converting their value into some other form of wealth. TH Wu appears to record *k^uei̯téa* bulls/oxen from *i-ri-ja*, possibly a personal name.[75]

Much *k^uei̯téa* not destined for scribal centers seems to be sent from them to religious centers, some of which may be in palatial territory, others not. On KN Fh 348, the *k^uei̯téon* of *we-we-ro* is recorded with *te-o* /tʰehōi̯/ 'for the god' *sub rasura* (but not overwritten). The *k^uei̯téon* oil of *te-re-no* on KN Fp 363 is destined for the shrine at *da-*83-ja* and *k^uei̯téos* wine on TH Gp 109 is sent from the palace to **63-te-ra* as "*Díu̯ia*'s portion," both places named being peripheral. The large oil *k^uei̯téon* on PY Fr 1206 is destined for *Pótnia Asu̯íi̯ā* 'Asian/Anatolian Potnia', who may be even farther afield, as Bendall recently argued.[76] *K^uei̯téa* would thus be distinct from *dōra* regularly presented (PY Tn 316).

How were future purchase and optional selling conducted in the wider world economy at the time? Recall that the Linear B *nomenklatura* exhibit communication with the Eastern Mediterranean LBA world system. A flock owner is named 'the Asian' (*Ásui̯os*) at both Pylos and Knossos,[77] and one is recorded at Knossos as 'the Egyptian/Memphite' (*Aigúptii̯os*).[78] In addition to at least one owner at Pylos named *Kúprii̯os* 'the Cypriot'[79] an "international collector" with that moniker trades supplies for very large *óna* at Knossos (see Table 8.1). Killen has suggested he is a commissioned Aegean *tamkārum*.[80] Moreover, women and children work groups, mainly at Pylos, are described as 'Asian', 'Knidian', 'Milesian', 'Lemnian', and possibly 'Halikarnassian', indicating the power to remove and employ labor from the fringes of the Hittite Empire, something also intimated in the Hittite *Aḫḫiyawa* Letters.[81] Elaborated *hopā́* (and *tʰouk^hā́* 'preparation') type prestige goods include *KE* textiles, arguably *géraha* for regional service,[82] and

[73] Cf. An 601.2; KN B(5) 8206 v.2, Sc 202.
[74] Docs², 200; Godart 1972.
[75] Cf. *i-ri-de̞*, MY V 659 lat. dex.
[76] Bendall 2014:147.
[77] PY Cn 285.12, 1287.1; KN Df 1469.B; also Eq 146 (holder of *o-na-to*), and spelled *a-*64-jo*, PY Cn 1287, Fn 324 (recipient of personal barley ration), Jn 832 (bronze-smith); cf. MY Au 653.5, 657.11.
[78] Db 1105.B
[79] Cn 131.3, 719.7. Whether *ku-pi-ri-jo* is the same as the one receiving *o-no* on PY Un 443 is unclear.
[80] Killen 1995:221.
[81] Beckman, Bryce, and Cline 2011; Bendall 2014:150–156.
[82] Melena 2002:380–382.

hekᵘésiįa textiles and chariot parts, as well as *ksénuiįa* textiles of quality expressly similar to *hekᵘésiįa*, and guest-gift perfumed oil too. Additionally, there is tangible evidence of elite "gift exchange" between Mycenae and Egypt,[83] Tiryns and Amurru,[84] and Thebes and Hatti.[85]

The textual and archaeological evidence together point firmly at Mycenaean palace economies' involvement in the world of competitive "gift" giving intimated in the Amarna Letters.[86] This too is a world of precise accounting, purchased alliances, investment of exotic materials and elaborately crafted commodities in regional projects (bringing prestige through implicit worldly connections), and, not least, "gifting" to test one's would-be adversary's ability to reciprocate or up the ante. The Amarna archives not only attest to precise measures of prestige goods, usually in easily calculated multiples, but also hint at standard kinds and measures for certain occasions, even appropriate equivalences. The commodities include textiles, perfumed oil, chariots, and quantities of gold, silver, and bronze, inter alia, as well as persons. Chariots, chariot parts, related teams of horses, and equipment for horses—also attested in the Linear B records—are generally sent in fives or tens.[87] When Assyria is *reestablishing* diplomacy with Egypt, it sends two chariots, one of them of royal type, and two horses (cf. *kᵘeįtéa* above).[88] The Assyrian king reminds the pharaoh of prior generations' gift giving.[89] Other occasions for gifting include accession to kingship,[90] marriage,[91] and religious celebrations.[92] Materials exchanged are invested in elite building projects.[93] The exact weights, often total, of metals and precious stones are emphasized.[94] There is concern with genuineness and weight equivalence for building especially,[95] presumably because such wealth consumption was most conspicuous. Rulers stress matching or exceeding one another's gifts, framing gifting also in terms of mutual "honor."[96] The Assyrian king asserts that it is royal prerogative to consume more than his subjects (not just differently).[97] All

---

[83] See Cline 1987.
[84] For example, Cohen, Maran, and Vetters 2011.
[85] For example, Kopanias 2009.
[86] Moran 1992, also for English translation of the letters (EA) that follow.
[87] EA 3, 7, 9, 11, 17, 19, 22, 37.
[88] EA 15.
[89] EA 16.
[90] EA 33.
[91] EA 2, 3, 11, 13, 14, 24, 31.
[92] EA 3, 23, 34.
[93] EA 4, 5, 16, 19.
[94] EA 7, 14, 22, 25, 31.
[95] EA 3, 4, 7, 10.
[96] EA 3, 4, 9, 19, 20, 42.
[97] EA 16.

these transactions speak of insatiable consumption of materials and labor in and between the aforementioned prestige goods pyramid schemes. They must have required careful accountancy, including targets for agro-pastoral production and minimum requirements for metal production, as is evident in Linear B.

Great Houses of Cards

Although it was a formality for LBA "great kings" to wish each other 100,000 years of rule,[98] the hyperbole still betrays how little thought they had for the sustainability of the prestige goods economy. In Egypt and Hatti, the sources of material and production and, conversely, of distribution of rewards would mainly be Amarna and Hattusa, respectively, governors' or vassals' cities, and possibly subject allies' capitals. While secondary and tertiary sites are often difficult to discern in records, they might be represented in Egypt by a fairly well distributed network of forty-two nome capitals, each with a few major estates,[99] and occasionally another forty-odd cities in the Levant,[100] not including innumerable villages and farmsteads. At Pylos, however, there are sixteen secondary places and easily scores of tertiary places around each of these.[101] Thebes may have about as many second-order places, and Knossos not quite twice this.[102] There would be fewer secondary places still if some archives are subordinate to others (e.g., Pylos and Knossos to Mycenae or Thebes),[103] leaving weak links in the political-economic hierarchy. Incentives existed to move wealth and its promise horizontally, probably among elites around secondary centers. People not entitled to prestige goods, on the one hand, and restricted consumption of *u̯anáktera* 'royal' or *hek^{u̯}ésii̯a*[104] goods, on the other, formed the lower and upper limits for transferal.

These consumption limits, alongside weak links in primary agriculture, livestock, and *talasíi̯ā* production, created conditions wherein the productive failure of any primary or secondary site could lead rapidly to the collapse of the system of prestige goods equivalence, the vacuum sucking promissory value out of the lower tiers. That is, when tokens of legitimacy, reward, and reciprocity could not be consumed as expected, then confidence in the producing institutions would be sapped. This effect could have been particularly acute in the Aegean, where network contingency was high. The test of institutional reliability would

[98] EA 21, 23.
[99] Kemp 2006:165–167, 330–335
[100] Topic of EA 45–382.
[101] Lang 1988.
[102] Bennet 1985:238–242; Aravantinos, Godart, and Sacconi 2001:357.
[103] For example, see Carlier 2008, Kelder 2010.
[104] Perhaps like Mitannian *maryannu* awards.

be attempts finally to "cash in" for the promised accrued benefits—an LBA run on the palace-bank. When prestige goods proved unexchangeable, either for another kind or such capital as land and raw materials, then the emergent framework of standards and pricing would be voided. Alternative systems of exchange, such as those that had arisen on the margins of the pyramid schemes or among *tamkārū*, where equivalences could be negotiated on unsupervised terms, could expand partly into the breach. Increase in such exchanges would further erode the official economy.

While LBA rulers did not expect the collapse, the present model can explain one contributory cause and the contours of its effects. Manufactures specifically for palace consumption or awarding to retainers, such as some textiles, embellished chariots, uniform palace-style ceramics, and certain bronze armaments, should quickly disappear.[105] The last would have been further diminished if new tin could not be procured: witness Tudhaliya IV's revision of a treaty with Amurru that denies Aḫḫiyawa access to crucial Levantine ports.[106] Fresco painting and writing could soon fade away or shift to different media. However, other prestige value objects could have been sustained, such as titles to land and commodities typical of *tamkārum* networks (e.g., certain forms of metalwork, ivory).[107] Traffic on the sea could have increased, encouraging the inclusion of iron metallurgy and diversification of fine ceramics for both local and foreign consumption.

The disruption of rations and payments in staples would have left dependent workforces vulnerable. Only some could be successfully reemployed with respect both to the quality and quantity of goods in demand and to who would support them, especially if disparities in agricultural wealth persisted. The lack of massive engineering projects, including the palaces themselves, is direct evidence of loss of confidence in the prestige goods economy. Growing political strife would follow, alongside decimation of populations through war, childhood death, and adult infertility. All this future past should sound familiar. None of the options it entailed should remain mysterious.

Bibliography

N.b.: Transliterations are taken from Bennett *et al.*, forthcoming, Killen and Olivier 1989, and Melena and Olivier 1991.

---

[105] Deger-Jakoltzy 2008:399–401; Mee 2008:372–379.
[106] Beckman, Bryce, and Cline 2011:50–68.
[107] The persistence of these and Linear scripts in Cyprus may be testimony to how well placed it was to weather the widely flung arms of the sudden economic typhoon.

Aravantinos, V. L., L. Godart, and A. Sacconi, eds. 2001. *Thèbes, fouilles de la Cadmée I: Les tablettes en linéaire B de la Odos Pelopidou*. Biblioteca di "Pasiphae." Pisa.

Beckman, G. M., T. Bryce, and E. H. Cline. 2011. *The Ahhiyawa Texts*. Writings from the Ancient World 28. Atlanta.

Bendall, L. M. 2014. "Gifts to the Goddesses: Pylian Perfumed Oil Abroad?" In Nakassis, Gulizio, and James 2014:141–162.

Bennet, J. 1985. "The Structure of the Linear B Administration at Knossos." *American Journal of Archaeology* 892:231–249.

———. 2001. "Agency and Bureaucracy: Thoughts on the Nature and Extent of Administration in Bronze Age Pylos." In Voutsaki and Killen 2001:29–37.

Bennet, J., and P. Halstead. 2014. *"O-no!* Writing and Righting Redistribution." In Nakassis, Gulizio, and James 2014:271–282.

Bennett, E. L., Jr. *et al.* Forthcoming. *The Palace of Nestor at Pylos in Western Messenia*, volume IV: *The Inscribed Documents*. Austin.

Carlier, P. 2008. "Réflexions sur les relations internationales dans le monde mycénien: Y a-t-il eu des hégémonies?" In Sacconi *et al.* 2008:121–130.

Carlier, P., C. de Lamberterie, M. Egetmeyer, N. Guilleux, F. Rougemont, and J. Zurbach, eds. 2012. *Études mycéniennes 2010. Actes du XIIIᵉ Colloque international sur les textes égéens, Sèvres, Paris, Nanterre, 20-23 septembre*. Pisa.

Chadwick, J. 1988. "The Women of Pylos." In Olivier and Palaima 1988:43–95.

Cline, E. H. 1987. "Amenhotep III and the Aegean: A Reassessment of Egypto-Aegean Relations in the 14th century BC." *Orientalia* 56:1–36.

Cohen, C., J. Maran, and M. Vetters. 2011. "An Ivory Rod with a Cuneiform Inscription, Most Probably Ugaritic, from a Final Palatial Workshop in the Lower Citadel of Tiryns." *Archäologischer Anzeiger* 2010(2):1–22.

D'Altroy, T. N., and T. K. Earle. 1985. "Staple Finance, Wealth Finance, and Storage in the Inka Political Economy." *Current Anthropology* 26(2):17–207.

De Fidio, P. 1977. *I dosmoi pilii a Poseidon: Una terra sacra di età micenea*. Incunabula Graeca 65. Rome.

———. 2008. "Miceneo *ki-ti-ta* e *me-ta-ki-ti-ta*." In Sacconi *et al.* 2008:159–177.

Deger-Jalkotzy, S. 2008. "Decline, Destruction, Aftermath." In *The Cambridge Companion to the Aegean Bronze Age*, ed. C. W. Shelmerdine, 387–415. New York.

Del Freo, M. 2002-2003. "La tablette An 724 de Pylos." *Minos* 37–38:143–171.

Driessen, J. 2008. "Chronology of the Linear B Texts." In Duhoux and Morpurgo Davies 2008:69–79.

Duhoux, Y. 1976. *Aspects du vocabulaire économique mycénien: Cadastre, artisanat, fiscalité*. Amsterdam.

Duhoux, Y., and A. Morpurgo Davies, eds. 2008. *A Companion to Linear B: Mycenaean Greek Texts and Their World*, vol. 1. Bibliothèque des Cahiers de Linguistique Louvain 120. Louvain-la-Neuve.

Galaty, M. L., and W. A. Parkinson. 2007. "1999 Introduction: Putting Mycenaean Palaces in Their Place." In *Rethinking Mycenaean Palaces II: Revised and Expanded Second Edition,* ed. M. L. Galaty and W. A. Parkinson, 21–28. Cotsen Institute Monograph 60. Los Angeles.

Godart, L. 1972. "Les tablettes de la série Co de Cnossos." In *Acta Mycenaea. Actes du cinquième Colloque international des études mycéniennes, tenu à Salamanque, 30 mars–3 avril 1970.* Vol. 2. Ed. M. S. Ruipérez, 418–424. Salamanca.

Halstead, P. 1990–1991. "Lost Sheep? On the Linear B Evidence for Breeding Flocks at Mycenaean Knossos and Pylos." *Minos* 25–26:43–65.

———. 1996–1997. "Linear B Evidence for the Management of Sheep Breeding at Knossos: Production Targets and Deficits in the KN Dl(1) and Do Sets." *Minos* 31–32:187–199.

———. 1999. "Missing Sheep: On the Meaning and Wider Significance of O in the Knossos Sheep Records." *Annual of the British School at Athens* 94:145–166.

Heubeck, A., and G. Neumann, eds. 1983. *Res Mycenaeae: Akten des VII. Mykenologischen Colloquiums in Nürburg vom 6–10 April 1981.* Göttingen.

Hutton, W. F. 1990–1991. "The Meaning of *qe-te-jo* in Linear B." *Minos* 25–26: 105–131.

Kelder, J. M. 2010. *The Kingdom of Mycenae: A Great Kingdom in the Late Bronze Age Aegean.* Bethesda.

Kemp, B. J. 2006. *Egypt: Anatomy of a Civilization.* 2nd ed. New York.

Killen, J. T. 1966. "The Knossos Nc tablets." In *Proceedings of the Cambridge Colloquium on Mycenaean Studies,* ed. L. R. Palmer and J. Chadwick, 33–38. Cambridge.

———. 1976. "Linear B *a-ko-ra-ja/-jo.*" In *Studies in Greek, Italic, and Indo-European Linguistics Offered to Leonard R. Palmer on the Occasion of His 70th Birthday, June 5, 1976,* ed. A. Morpurgo Davies and W. Meid, 117–125. Innsbruck.

———. 1979. "The Knossos Ld(1) Tablets." In *Colloquium Mycenaeum. Actes du sixième Colloque international sur les textes mycéniens et égéens tenu à Chaumont sur Neuchâtel du 7 au 13 septembre 1975,* ed. E. Risch and H. Mühlestein, 151–182. Geneva.

———. 1983a. "PY An 1." *Minos* 18:71–79.

———. 1983b. "The Mycenae Ge Tablets." In Heubeck and Neumann 1983:216–233.

———. 1984. "Last Year's Debts on the Pylos Ma Tablets." *Studi micenei ed egeo-anatolici* 25:173–188.

———. 1987. "Bronzeworking at Knossos and Pylos." *Hermathena* 143:61–72.

———. 1992. "Observations on the Thebes Sealings." In *MYKENAÏKA. Actes du IXᵉ colloque international sur les textes mycéniens et égéens organisé par le Centre de l'Antiquité Grecque et Romaine de la Fondation Hellénique des Recherches Scientifiques et l'École française d'Athènes (Athènes, 2-6 octobre 1990)*, ed. J.-P. Olivier, 365–380. Athens.

———. 1993. "Records of Sheep and Goats at Mycenaean Knossos and Pylos." *Bulletin on Sumerian Agriculture* 7:209–218.

———. 1994. "Thebes Sealings, Knossos Tablets, and Mycenaean State Banquets." *Bulletin of the Institute of Classical Studies* 39:67–84.

———. 1995. "Some Further Thoughts on Collectors." In *Politeia: Society and State in the Aegean Bronze Age. Proceedings of the 5th International Aegean Conference, University of Heidelberg, Archäologisches Institut, 10-13 April 1994*, ed. R. Laffineur and W.-D. Niemeier, 213–224. *Aegaeum* 12. Liège.

———. 1999. "Mycenaean *o-pa*." In *Floreant Studia Mycenaea. Akten des X. internazionalen mykenologischen Colloquiums in Salzburg vom 1.-5. Mai 1995*, ed. S. Deger-Jalkotzy, S. Hiller, and O. Panagl, 325–341. Philosophisch-historische Klasse, Denkschriften 274. Vienna.

———. 2001. "Some Thoughts on *ta-ra-si-ja*." In Voutsaki and Killen 2001:161–180.

———. 2006. "Conscription and Corvée at Mycenaean Pylos." In Perna 2006: 73–87.

———. 2008. "Mycenaean Economy." In Duhoux and Morpurgo Davies 2008: 159–200.

Killen, J. T., and J.-P. Olivier. 1989. *The Knossos Tablet, Fifth Edition*. Suplementos a *Minos* 11. Salamanca.

Kopanias, K. 2009. "The Late Bronze Age Near Eastern Cylinder Seals from Thebes (Greece) and Their Historical Implications." *Mitteilungen des Deutschen Archäologisches Insituts, Athenische Abteilung* 123:39–96.

Lane, M. F. 2011. "Linear B *pe-re-ke-u*, *pe-re-ke*, and *pe-re-ko*: Contextual and Etymological Notes." *Kadmos* 50:75–100.

———. 2012a. "Landholding at *Pa-ki-ja-na*: Toward Spatial Modeling of Mycenaean Agricultural Estates." *Pasiphae* 6:59–116.

———. 2012b. "Linear B *wo-wo/wo-wi-ja*." *Pasiphae* 6:117–184.

———. 2016. "Returning to Sender: PY Tn 316, Linear B *i-je-to*, Pregnant Locatives, **perH3-*, and Passing between Mycenaean Palaces." *Pasiphae* 10: 39–89.

Lang, M. 1988. "Pylian Place-Names." In Olivier and Palaima 1988:185–212.

Lejeune, M. 1971. *Mémoires de philologie mycénienne, deuxième série*. Rome.

Liverani, M. 1990. *Prestige and Interest: International Relations in the Near East ca. 1600-1100 B.C.* History of the Ancient Near East, Studies 1. Padua.

Mee, C. 2008. "Mycenaean Greece, the Aegean, and Beyond." In *The Cambridge Companion to the Aegean Bronze Age*, ed. C. W. Shelmerdine, 362–386. New York.

Melena, J. L. 1972. "On the Knossos Mc Tablets." *Minos* 13:29–54.

———. 1974. "*Ku-pa-ro* en las tabillas de Cnoso." *Emerita* 42(2):307–336.

———. 1975. "*Po-ni-ki-jo* in the Knossos Ga Tablets." *Minos* 14:77–84.

———. 1976. "La producción de plantas aromáticas en Cnoso." *Estudios Classicos* 20(78):177–190.

———. 1983a. "Further Thoughts on Mycenaean *o-pa*." In Heubeck and Neumann 1983:258–286.

———. 1983b. "Olive Oil and Other Sorts of Oil in the Mycenaean Tablets." *Minos* 18:89–124.

———. 2002. "63 Joins and Quasi-joins of Fragments in the Linear B Tablets from Pylos." *Minos* 35–36:371–384.

Melena, J. L., and J.-P. Olivier. 1991. *Tithemy: The Tablets and Nodules in Linear B from Tiryns, Thebes, and Mycenae*. Suplementos a *Minos* 12. Salamanca.

Moran, W. L, ed. 1992. *The Amarna Letters*. Baltimore.

Nakassis, D. 2010. "Reevaluating Staple and Wealth Finance at Mycenaean Pylos." In *Political Economies of the Aegean Bronze Age: Papers from the Langford Conference, Florida State University, Tallahassee, 22–24 February 2007*, ed. D. J. Pullen, 127–148. Oxford.

———. 2013. *Individuals and Society in Mycenaean Pylos*. Mnemosyne Supplements 358. Boston.

Nakassis, D., J. Gulizio, and S. A. James, eds. 2014. *Ke-ra-me-ja: Studies Presented to Cynthia W. Shelmerdine*. Prehistory Monographs 46. Philadelphia.

Nosch, M.-L. B. 2006. "More Thoughts on the Mycenaean *ta-ra-si-ja* System." In Perna 2006:161–182.

———. 2008. "Administrative Practices in Mycenaean Palace Administration and Economy" In Sacconi *et al.* 2008:595–604.

———. 2009. "Les allocations de laine des tablettes en linéaire B de Thèbes." *Kadmos* 48:77–92.

———. 2011. "The Mycenaean Administration of Textile Production in the Palace of Knossos: Observations on the Lc(1) Textile Targets." *American Journal of Archaeology* 115:495–505.

Nosch, M.-L. B., and M. Perna. 2001. "Cloth in the Cult." In *Potnia: Deities and Religion in the Aegean Bronze Age. Proceedings of the 8th International Aegean Conference, Göteborg, Göteborg University, 12–15 April 2000*, ed. R. Laffineur and R. Hägg, 471–477. *Aegaeum* 22. Liège.

Olivier, J.-P. 2001. "Les 'collecteurs': Leur distribution spatiale et temporelle." In Voutsaki and Killen 2001:139–160.

Olivier, J.-P., and T. G. Palaima, eds. 1988. *Texts, Tablets, and Scribes: Studies in Mycenaean Epigraphy and Economy Offered to Emmett L. Bennett, Jr.* Supplementos a *Minos* 10. Salamanca.

Olsen, B. A. 2014. *Women in Mycenaean Greece: The Linear B Tablets from Pylos and Knossos.* New York.

Palaima, T. G. 2012. "Security and Insecurity as Tools of Power in Mycenaean Kingdoms." In Carlier, de Lamberterie, Egetmeyer, Guilleux, Rougemont, and Zurbach 2021:345–356.

———. 2015. "The Mycenaean Mobilization of Labor in Agriculture and Building Projects: Institutions, Individuals, Compensation, and Status in the Linear B Tablets." In *Labor in the Ancient World,* vol. V: *A Colloquium Held at Hirschbach (Saxony), April 2005,* ed. P. Steinkeller and M. Hudson, 617–648. Dresden.

Palmer, L. R. 1963. *The Interpretation of Mycenaean Greek Texts.* Oxford.

Palmer, R. 1989. "Subsistence Rations at Pylos and Knossos." *Minos* 24:89–124.

Perna, M., ed. 2006. *Fiscality in Mycenaean and Near Eastern Archives. Proceedings of a Conference Held at Soprintendenza Archivistica per la Campania, Naples, 21-23 October 2004.* Studi egei e vicinorientali 3. Paris.

Sacconi, A., M. Del Freo, L. Godart, and M. Negri, eds. 2008. *Colloquium Romanum. Atti del XII Colloquio Internazionale di Micenologia, Roma 20-25 febbraio 2006.* Pasiphae 2. Pisa.

Shelmerdine, C. W. 1973. "The Pylos Ma Tablets Reconsidered." *American Journal of Archaeology* 77:261–275.

———. 1985. *The Perfume Industry of Pylos.* Studies in Mediterranean Archaeology, Pocket-book 34. Gothenburg.

———. 2012. "Iklaina Tablet IK X 1." In *Études mycéniennes 2010. Actes du XIIIᵉ Colloque international sur les textes égéens, Sèvres, Paris, Nanterre, 20-23 septembre,* ed. P. Carlier, C. de Lamberterie, M. Egetmeyer, N. Guilleux, F. Rougemont, and J. Zurbach, 75–78. Pisa.

Smith, J. S. 1992. "The Pylos Jn Series." *Minos* 27–28:167–259.

Voutsaki, S., and J. T. Killen, eds. 2001. *Economy and Politics in the Mycenaean Palace States. Proceedings of a Conference Held on 1-3 July 1999 in the Faculty of Classics, Cambridge.* Cambridge Philological Society Supplementary Volume 27. Cambridge.

9

Mycenaean *ka-ra-te-ra, ka-ra-ti-ri-jo,* Related Terms, and the Rise of Diminutives in Early Greek

Alex Leukart

Route de Malagnou 50, 1208 Geneva (Switzerland)
alex.leukart@gmail.com

Abstract

First (§§1–5) it is shown that *ka-ra-te-ra* (MY Ue 611.2) is to be read with quasi-certainty as /krātér/, i.e., *nominative* singular written *plene*.

Secondly (§§6–18) *ka-ra-ti-ri-jo* (MY Ue 611.4, together with *ka-ra{-se}-ti-ri-jo* on the sealing MY Wt 507.β–γ) is analyzed as the nom.pl.masc. of a substantivated relational adjective /krā-tr-io-/, i.e., /krā́trioi/ 'vessels like/resembling craters', derived directly from /krā-tér/ 'mixer', but with the agent suffix in the zero-grade form /-tr-/. This reveals that the formation is not of the period of the tablets (where the suffix would be /-tĕr-io-/) but definitely earlier (probably proto-Greek, parallel to the derivatives in *-io-* from kinship terms) and might represent what could be called a quasi- or pre-diminutive, existing before the lexicalization of the neuter diminutives in /-ion/, already present as such in Linear B (for some more—still summarized—details see §19).

Keywords

Mycenaean *ka-ra-te-ra, ka-ra-ti-ri-jo,* early Greek, diminutives

1. Both of these words are found written on the obverse (recto) of MY Ue 611, one of the most discussed tablets from Mycenae.[1]

---

[1]   For a detailed discussion and interpretation see Duhoux (2008:285–289 and 2013:59–60) and Varias García (2008:779–781, with tables 2 and 3, 791–793). Knowledge of these passages is presupposed for what follows. I am indebted to Lorenz Baumer, Julien Beck, Patrizia Birchler, Hedvig Enegren, Ivo Hajnal, Michael Lindblom and Carlos Varias for information, discussion or having made relevant literature available, as well as my wife Naki-Muriel for typing and substantial support.

Inscribed by Hand 60, it reads as follows:

MY Ue 611

```
.0    ] vacat
.1    ]pe-ra 4  a-po-re-we 2  pe-ri-ke 3
.2    ]ka-ra-te-ra 1  po-ro-ko-wo 4  a-ta-ra 10
.3    ]pa-ke-te-re 30  ka-na-to 5  qe-ti-ja 10
.4    ]qẹ-to 2  ti-ri-po-di-ko 8  ka-ra-ti-ri-jo 7̣
.5                                ]vac.[
                inf. mut.
```

This represents a catalogue of vessels, listed in the *nominative* (mostly plural) as shown by the unambiguous forms of nouns in consonant stems (*pe-ri-ke* /*pelikes*/,]*pa-ke-*/*tĕr-es*/) with which the rest of the forms should then be compatible. This is in fact the case, including the two dual forms *a-po-re-we* /*amphorēwe*/ and *qẹ-to* /*kʷetʰō*/ (cf. πίθος 'wine-jar'), both indifferently nom. or acc.

2. At first sight, then, the only exception would be *ka-ra-te-ra* in line 2, the stem of which, obviously, should be /*krātēr-*/ 'mixing bowl'. From the beginning this form was considered odd because it would be in the *accusative* (singular, given the numeral '1') and thus prompted, e.g., the authors of *Documents* (331, taken up in *Docs²*): "possibly for a derivative *kratēriā*?," or Palmer (1963a, 425): "N.sg. ... κρατηρα by-form of κρατήρ" (apparently /*krātḗr-ā*/ fem., as also given by Milani [1966:425]) to propose these rather strange interpretations.[2]

3. On the other hand, in order to regularize *ka-ra-te-ra* as an accusative form, Risch (1958) proposed to consider *all* the vessel names listed on Ue 611 as accusatives, comparing PY Vn 10 and An 724 and later dialectal forms of accusative plural in ες in consonant-stems (since the fifth century BC), concluding that the Mycenaean acc.pl. of this declension ended in /*-es*/ (written *-e*). He was followed by Lejeune (1968:742); *Docs²*, 496 remained skeptical. Later on Risch admitted (1976:26) that this theory had not been confirmed by later material but nevertheless remained a possibility.

4. The first person to introduce a new perspective on this problem was Georgiev (1958:158) by changing from the morpho-syntactical level to that of *spelling*. He took *ka-ra-te-ra* as /*krātēr*/ nom.sg. masc. with the final /*-r*/ written

---

[2] See the critical remark on the proposal of *Documents*, 331, by Risch (1958:99n2), with misspelling κρᾱτρίᾱ instead of κρᾱτηρίᾱ, corrected by him in the addenda [Nachträge] of his *Kleine Schriften* (Risch 1981:764). κρατηρία 'bowl for compounding drugs, etc.' is attested in Dioscorides (first century AD) and Zosimus the Alchemist (third/fourth century AD) and as variant (cod. Θ) of κρατήριον (cod. M) in Hippocrates, *De natura muliebri* 34b (cf. also below note 12).

with -*ra* (*scriptio plena*, wherein -*a* is a dummy or dead [i.e., not pronounced] vowel, necessary for any syllabic script of the type *CV* [consonant-vowel] to express word-final consonants). For the choice of the vowel here having fallen on -*a*, not only because, e.g., **ka-ra-te-rę* could have likely been read as **/krātĕr-es/* nom.pl. (or also **/krātĕr-ei/* dat.sg.?, cf. Hajnal 2006:60–61), see Meissner 2008:518–519.

5.   In our opinion this is the only satisfactory approach to integrate *ka-ra-te-ra* into the text of MY Ue 611. Duhoux (2008:288 and 2013:60) has given it his clear preference in his anthologies. But above all, Meissner (2008:515–519 [§§7–9]) has offered us a remarkable study on Mycenaean spelling I cannot but follow, in which he reviews all the characteristics of *plene* writing in a very differentiated manner and decisively argues for *ka-ra-te-ra* as a nom.sg. written *plene*.

We can now be confident that this is the right way of understanding *ka-ra-te-ra*. And also our colleague and friend, José Luis Melena, after having first considered it as possibly a derived feminine /*krātēr-ā*/ (Melena 2014a:80), seems now to be rather convinced (Melena 2014b:112 with n148: "/*krātērā*/ is a very odd formation," and 115n151).

6.   *Ka-ra-ti-ri-jo* stands at the end of the last inscribed line (.4) of Ue 611 (obverse), followed by the numeral 7 (or perhaps only 5).

A very similar form is found on the sealing (MY) Wt 507.β–γ, also from the House of the Sphinxes:[3] *ka-ra-se | ti-ri-jo*, written in two parts on the faces β–γ of the sealing.[4] John Chadwick (1959:1–2) states that "it is clear that the sign ‹*se*›

---

[3]   For the correspondences between the names of vessels registered on the recto of Ue 611, those on the Wt sealings, and the concrete vessels found in Room 1 of the House of the Sphinxes see Shelmerdine 1999:571–572, Sacconi 1999:545–546, and Varias García, forthcoming. The extant Wt sealings 501–507, all by Hand 65, are most likely not those which would have served to compile the tablet Ue 611, but an analogous set; see also Pluta 2011:213–218.

A detailed description of all the Mycenae clay sealings, including a new one at that time (Wt 712, inscribed: *a-pe-we-kę* (rather than -*dę* [?], see below) with photographs and drawings, is given in Müller, Olivier, and Pini 1998. The inscribed sealings are discussed by Olivier in pp. 13–17; his text, translated into German, is flawed by several errors/inconsistencies, so on p. 15 (third paragraph), p. 16 (third through to end of fifth paragraph), p. 17 (end of first paragraph); p. 14n73, read: "(1991) 74f." (not "78"). On p. 39 emend ".β–γ vielleicht emendieren zu *ka-ra{-se}-ti-ri-ja*" to "*ka-ra{-se}-ti-ri-jo*."

Concerning Wt 712: If the drawing can be trusted, the last sign is rather -*kę* (because of the two long vertical lines in the lower part with a short vertical line in between, higher up) than -*dę*; the latter is preferred by Olivier, who builds his commentary on this, without considering -*kę*.

[4]   For the idiosyncrasy of Scribe 65 to extend a single word over two faces of a sealing see Pluta (2011:215–217); the purpose was apparently to keep the seal impression inviolate (not to super-scribe it, as in other cases, except on Wt 506.a, where because of lack of space the last sign of the word (.γ *pa-ke-te-ri)-ja* is written on the right part of the seal impression [face .α]). On p. 217 (middle) emend "Hand 57" to "65"; in note 500, second line, emend Oe 611 to Ue 611.

there is larger than the rest[5] and may be an additional annotation not intended to be read as part of the word." Thus, he proposes the *emendation* to *ka-ra{-se}-ti-ri-jo*, which renders this word on the sealing parallel to *ka-ra-ti-ri-jo* on the tablet Ue 611.4, as much as the other corresponding vessel names on Ue 611 and the Wt sealings (see above note 3).

At the same time Chadwick (1959:2) shies away from associating this term with /krātḗr/:

> The word cannot be a simple diminutive from κρατήρ since κρατήριον would require the spelling **ka-ra-te-ri-jo* (cf. *pa-ke-te-ri-ja*), and neuter gender is excluded by the numeral 7 in Ue 611.4. It is therefore most likely a substantivized adjective in -ιος formed from a stem in -τρ-, -τλ-, -θρ- or -θλ-. No likely candidate presents itself among the known Greek vocabulary.[6]

7. On the other hand, Risch (1958:98) considers it as probably a diminutive, "peut-être κρᾱτριο- de κρᾱτήρ (?)," whereas Milani (1966:425 [l. 7: *karateijo* misprinted for *karatirijo*]) takes it as nom. or acc.pl.: "*κρᾱτριοι «vasi» ('vessels'), cfr. κρᾱτήρ," both without any further comment on the form of the derivative.

Finally, Ruijgh (1967:116) takes *ka-ra-ti-ri-jo* as a vessel name in the nom. pl.masc., and thinks that, in the last resort, one could read κρᾱτριος (sg.), derived from a hypothetical word **κρᾱτρός* or **κρᾱτρον* comparable to κρᾱτήρ (cf. ἰᾱτρός : ἰᾱτήρ, ζῶστρον : ζωστήρ) and adds: "noter cependant que κρᾱτήρ est probablement attesté sur la même tablette (l. 2 *ka-ra-te-ra*, si on admet l'accusatif)." The motive, here too, is implicitly but obviously to avoid a direct association with κρᾱτήρ, for the same reason as given by Chadwick (cf. §6).

---

5   This is confirmed by the photograph in Müller, Olivier, and Pini (1998:38), where it is clearly *taller* than the two preceding signs; in the drawing, however, it is less tall, so the vertical stroke from the middle towards the lower edge of the sealing: 18 mm on the photograph vs. 13 mm on the drawing; and the overall height: 30.5 mm on the photograph vs. 26 mm on the drawing. The height of the preceding signs on the photograph is: *ka* = 16.5 mm, *ra*: 21.5 mm. The height of the signs on the following side (.γ) on the photograph is: *ti* = 25 mm, *ri* = 17 mm, *jo*: not significantly measurable. N.B.: The photographs and (adapted) drawings are here enlarged 2.5 times.

6   Chadwick's idea (*ibidem*) to associate *ka-ra-ti-ri-jo* with *ka-ra-re-we* (KN, PY), the name of stirrup-jars destined to contain olive oil, should be abandoned; see Bennett (1958:40). The same holds for Lejeune's speculation (1968:742: adjective χαλάστριος [??] *vel sim.*), for two reasons: (a) This purely hypothetical form has no semantically likely cognate: χάλαζα 'hail' (< **-dya*) is inappropriate; (b) If the [s] should be written in what Lejeune transcribes as *kara‹se›tirijo*, but also for any other interpretation assuming a cluster -str- on Wt 507, we must note that it would be contrary to the spelling rules: one would expect either *ka-ra-sa-ti-ri-jo* (with progressive spelling) or *ka-ra-si-ti-ri-jo* (with regressive spelling), but not *-se-*. Moreover, this can be taken as a *supplementary argument* in favour of *athetizing* the sign ‹se› on Wt 507. (For the terms "pro-" vs. "re-gressive spelling" cf. Meissner 2008:516; Melena [2014b:106–115] uses "tauto-" vs. "heterosyllabic dummy vowels.")

Concerning the meaning of /krā̆trio-/, for Ruijgh it could be 'vessel for drawing or pouring (liquid) from/into a κρᾱτήρ', i.e., implicitly as a substantivized relational adjective (like Chadwick, cf. §6). While it might be interesting on a more general level to remind us of these other formations, for our case it rather makes things more complicated than necessary, as we shall see (*entia non sunt multiplicanda...*, cf. §18).

8. The essential common denominator in the proposals reviewed in the preceding paragraph, even if not explicitly mentioned, is clear: A derivational base /krā-tr-/, with the agent suffix in the *zero* ablaut-grade, i.e., precisely the element which kept Chadwick from associating /krā̆trio-/ directly with /krātḗr/ (cf. §6), but seemed apparently self-evident to the first two scholars (linguists) evoked above (cf. §7).

Now it is precisely this element, too, which should bring us nearer to a solution. The *normal* derivative in -io- from an agent noun in -tēr in Mycenaean at the time of the tablets would have the form -tĕr-io-, i.e., most probably -tēr-io- with long ē-grade by leveling with the nom.sg. -tēr, or possibly -tĕr-io- by leveling with corresponding case forms, but at any rate with e-grade vowel as exemplified by *pa-ke-te-ri-ja pa-ke/-tĕr-ia/* on the sealing Wt 506.γ–α, nom.pl.ntr., diminutive of *pa-ke-te-re* on Ue 611.3 *pa-ke/-tĕr-es/* (cf. §1).[7]

The essential difference in the case of /krā̆-tr-io-/ is, as said, its derivation from a base with the suffix in the zero-grade: -tr-. Rather than keeping us from associating /krā̆trio-/ directly with /krātḗr/, this should incite us to find a specific and at the same time productive answer to this situation.

9. In our opinion it would be as follows:

By its suffix in the zero-grade, /krā̆trio-/ reveals that it was formed at a period *earlier* than that of the tablets, and more precisely at a period of early Greek when zero-grade forms were still prevailing in the declension (in all the oblique cases except the accusative) and when it was normal to form derivatives from the least marked base, i.e., the zero-grade stem, we might dare say in proto-Greek (roughly the period of the arrival of the Greeks on the continent and the immediately following one, presumably).

10. On the formal level, fortunately and in an almost unexpected way, the pertinent proof has survived into classical times in the archaic niche of the *kinship* terms, e.g., πατήρ (with four oblique cases still remaining: πατρ-ί, πατρ-ός, pl. πατρά-σι [< *-tr̥-si], πατρ-ῶν): the relational adjective here is πάτρ-ιος

---

[7]   For the various paradigmatic and apophonic forms of *-t(ĕ)r- in early Greek see Hajnal 2006:60–61, Tichy 1992:411ff., Panagl 1971: (also for spelling questions), esp. 130–132, Risch 1987:282.

(inherited, cf. Lat. *patr-ius*, Ved. *pítr-ya*), not †πατήρ-ιος,[8] as opposed to the other, mostly agent nouns in *-tḗr* which have their corresponding adjectives in -τήριος (e.g., ἐλατήρ *Iliad*+, ἐλατήριος Aeschylus+; σωτήρ *Homeric Hymns*+, σωτήριος Aeschylus+; not in Homer except substantivized θελκτήριον 'charm, spell' *Iliad*+, cf. θελκτήρ 'soother, charmer' *Homeric Hymns*), and as *pa-ke/-tĕrija/* (§8) shows, already at the time of the tablets (in Mycenae).

This, incidentally, is also an *additional* argument in favor of leveling in the declension paradigm having already taken place at the same period; see the table of Hajnal, quoted above, note 7.

11. On the archaeological level, the pristine derivation of /*krā́trio-*/ would show that the Greeks came to know the /*krātḗr*/ at a relatively early time. This, in itself, is not surprising for such an important societal utensil in the new cultural surrounding.

As Michael Lindblom (Uppsala) kindly informs me, the type of vessel that has been designated as *krātḗr* by prehistorians appears in the transition between MH III and LH I, i.e., around 1700–1650 BC.[9]

Comparatively, MY Ue 611 and the sealings Wt 501–507 are from LH IIIB1-late (~1260/50 BC [the Pylos archives are from LH IIIB2/C-early ~1190/80 BC, i.e., about sixty–seventy years younger, still]). This should leave more than enough time back (at least four hundred years if not much more) for an early formation of /*krā́trio-*/.

12. On the syntactic and semantic level we have to recall (cf. §6, end) that *ka-ra-ti-ri-jo*, as it is followed by the plural numeral 7 (or just 5), cannot sensibly be taken as a nominative singular of a normal neuter diminutive in *-ion*, like the neuter plural nominatives *qe-ti-ja* 10 (Ue 611.3) /*kʷetʰ-ia*/ besides .4 *qe-to* 2 /*kʷetʰ-ṓ*/ (nom.dual masc.) or *pa-ke/-tĕr-ia/* (Wt 506) besides *pa-ke/-tĕr-es/* 30 (Ue 611.3). The contrary would require us to postulate a nom.sg.ntr. *of rubric*, which would be completely incoherent on this tablet, for two reasons:

---

[8] A similar archaic formation, also in the semantic field of kinship terms, is ὁμο-γάστρ-ιος *Iliad*+ (γαστήρ; rare) 'from the same belly (: womb), having the same mother', cf. ὁμο-μήτρ-ιος Herodotus+ '*id.*' (from μήτηρ, secondarily associated with μήτρ-ᾱ 'womb'); or also φρᾱ́τρ-ιος Pl.+ (originally from *φρᾱ́τηρ 'brother', then exclusively associated with φρᾱ́τρ-ᾱ collective 'brother-hood' > 'clan' Il.+).

[9] For the form, see Lindblom (2001:26, fig. 4:11); painted pictorial Mycenaean craters appear during LH IIIA1 (~ 1420/10–1390/70 BC), which corresponds to the beginning of the palatial period. Grapes were present on the continent at least since Early Helladic II (~ 2800/2700 BC), so other vessel types would have been used for wine-mixing from this period onwards.
  For the chronology see Driessen 2008:69–79 and de Fidio 2008:82–85. We adopt the absolute dates as proposed by de Fidio ("middle" chronology).

a) all forms followed by plural numerals on Ue 611 are in the plural
themselves (cf. §1).

b) Exactly the same form *ka-ra-ti-ri-jo* recurs on the sealing Wt 507,
in the set of which (Wt 501–507) the *other* sealings also have
plural forms of vessel names, mostly unambiguous: /antla-k^we
enkhusēwes-k^we/ (cf. /antla/ 10 on Ue 611.2), /k^her-nik^{w}t-ēwes/,
/k^wet^h-ia/ and pa-ke/-tĕr-ia/ (see above), /kana(s)thoi/ (ka-na-to 5
Ue 611.3).[10]

13. We would rather need to find a way to understand *ka-ra-ti-ri-jo* as a substantivized relational adjective in the nominative plural masculine in *-ioi*, i.e.,
/krắtr-ioi/.

We have already mentioned Ruijgh's opinion (cf. §7): He does so, but by
reluctantly deriving κρắτριος (sg.) from *hypothetical* base words *κρᾱτρός or
*κρᾱτρον (in order to avoid direct association with κρᾱτήρ, like Chadwick, cf.
§6). For the meaning, he proposes 'vessel for drawing or pouring (liquid) from/
into a κρᾱτήρ' as possible, thus remaining in a relational sense but with a concrete application.

In our opinion there is no need nor even interest to avoid direct association
with κρᾱτήρ (§8f.).

14. By admitting one of the slight semantic variations due to the substantivation of the relational adjective in *-io-*, i.e., "a sort of x, something *like* x,"[11] we
would reach the goal: /krắtr-ioi/ would basically be 'a sort of craters' or 'vessels
like/resembling craters', at the same time sufficiently different from the latter
to be categorized separately. This *could* include that they were smaller than the
normal models, but on the formal level it is not expressed as such, contrary to
the neuter diminutives in *-ion*, plural *-ia* (*qe-ti-ja*, *pa-ke-te-ri-ja* from *qe-to, pa-ke-
te-re* §12).

The reason would be that at the early time of the (: zero-grade) formation of
/krắtrios/, diminutives did not yet exist as a formal-semantic/lexical category of
their own (with objectifying-concretizing neuter gender as their mark), so that

---

[10] The remaining *pa-kọ-to* (Wt 505), considering the preceding examples, can be interpreted as
such, too, or possibly as a dual (as in PY Ta 709.1), or in the last resort as nominative singular
(cf. DMic.); on the whole see Duhoux (2008:288 f.; 2013, 59 f.) and Varias García (2008:781 f. and
forthcoming).

[11] Cf. Debrunner (1917:147 f. [§§291–293]) and Schwyzer (1939:470). These nuances do not show
up in Chantraine (1939:35–38 [§§30–32]). In our opinion the slight semantic shift here depends
primarily on the substantivation (rather than on the neuter gender, which serves to objectify/
concretize, cf. Chantraine 1939:15 f. [§14], Risch 1974:115 [§41a] and, e.g., θελκτήριον [cf. above
§10]).

the substantivized masculine could serve in this capacity—among others. At the best, we might think of a *quasi-* or *pre-*diminutive in *-ios*.

On the other hand, the attested Mycenaean neuter diminutives in *-ion* would be of more recent development, not much earlier than the period of the tablets (which would be LH IIIB1-late for MY Ue 611 and sealings Wt 501–507, i.e., ~1260/50 BC).[12] Those among these with the agent suffix in *e*-grade, like *pa-ke-te-ri-ja* and perhaps *ko-te-ri-ja*, could thus qualify as modern viz. contemporary and possibly spontaneous formations.

15.   On the evolutionary level this correlates well with the fact that there is *no* trace of *assibilation* to be found, neither in Myc. diminutives in ...-*t*$^{(h)}$-*ion* (cf. in our case *qe-ti-ja* from *qę̄-to*, not †*qe-si-ja*) nor in later ones (from the fifth century onwards), as the assibilation *t*$^{(h)}$*i* > *si* is a process that took place and ended at a period prior to the extant tablets; see Lejeune 1968:733–743 (with our remark p. 743).[13] Lejeune (1968:738 [§68a] and 742f.) also rightfully criticizes Ruijgh's (1967:136) refusal to acknowledge the existence of veritable diminutives in *-ion* in Mycenaean (Lejeune 1968:738: "MY Ue 611 ... mentionne à la suite *qe-ti-ja* 10 et *qe-to* 2; il est difficile de voir là autre chose que «dix petits *qe-to*, et deux *qe-to* de taille normale», c.à d. le pluriel d'un diminutif en -ιον"). We would add: all the more when right after "*qę̄-to* 2" figures "*ti-ri-po-di-ko* 8" 'eight /*tri-pod-iskoi*/ ~small tripods', also a clear diminutive, formed with the alternative suffix *-isko-*, and recognized implicitly by Ruijgh (1967:168n356) as such.[14]

Nevertheless Ruijgh (1967:136) maintains that for the corresponding forms in *-ion*, an interpretation as diminutives is never necessary and that he would not admit it, because the use of diminutives is only attested since Epicharmus (i.e., late sixth century) and that it is absent not only in Homer, where stylistic reasons could have played a role, but also in the lyric poets.[15]

---

[12]   Cf. above §11 with note 9. Two further derivatives in the domain of utensils with *e*-grade suffix in *-te-ri-ja*, this time from Pylos (viz about 60 years more recent than Ue 611 and consorts), figure on Ta 709.1: *...po-ro-e-ke-te-ri-ja* **228*^{VAS} 1 *ko-te-ri-ja* 6. The first cannot be a diminutive: the numeral 1 implies a nom.sg.fem., hence in /-*tēr-íā*/ (which recalls κρᾱτηρίᾱ, cf. above note 2). The second, nom.pl.fem. or ntr., is ambivalent. I expect to come back to these lemmata in more detail on a later occasion.

[13]   *Pace* Thompson (2008:753–763).

[14]   Contrary to the reluctance of Chantraine (1966, 165), *Ti-ri-po-di-ko*, name of a swineherd on PY Cn 599.8, could well be a nick-name ("nom parlant"): 'he who has/is on three feet/legs, the two of his own and the third being his (herdsman's) stick'. In this case, though, it could be interpreted not only as /*Tripód-iskos*/ (hypocoristic diminutive, as Chantraine l.c.) but also and as well as /*Tripód-ikos*/ (rather than /-*ikós*/) 'the one on three feet/legs', "Three-Footy" (not diminutive, but characterizing nick-name).

[15]   Here he refers to Chantraine (1939, 64), considerably more differentiated, though (§§50–52). In our opinion certain lyric poetry, namely if in relation to cult and myth, could also have avoided diminutives for stylistic reasons.

For the vessel names, he prefers to take them as substantivized relational adjectives denoting accessory functions in connexion with the basic vessel term, as we have already seen with /krātrio-/ (cf. §7): 'vessel for drawing or pouring (liquid) from/into a κρᾱτήρ'. And in the same way, *pa-ke-te-ri-ja* "could designate, for example, small [*sic*] vessels used for drawing (liquid) from the *pa-ke-te-re*" (Ruijgh 1967:113) and "one can admit, between *qe-to* and *qe-ti-ja*, a relation comparable to the one existing between *pa-ke-te-re* and *pa-ke-te-ri-ja*" (p. 122).

In fact, Ruijgh would not accept that substantivized relational adjectives in -*ion* had already been lexicalized as a new category, i.e., substantival diminutives. Lejeune, on the other hand, has convincingly shown that this is already the case in Mycenaean.

16. What we have argued above with regard to *ka-ra-ti-ri-jo* /krátrioi/ (§8ff.) could *bridge* the gap between the two opposed but not completely irreconcilable positions (and Ruijgh's own terms "small vessels" for *pa-ke-te-ri-ja* shows that he is not far from it ...). In fact, the two points of view diverge only by their chronological (and concomitant factual) positioning: Ruijgh remains on an earlier level, with masc.pl. /krátrioi/ as crown witness (although not recognized as such by himself), whereas Lejeune stands on the level of the tablets, with ntr.pl. diminutive /kʷétʰia/ beside masc.du. /kʷétʰō/ and also *pa-ke/-těria/* besides *pa-ke/-těres/* (§12) as crown witnesses. More precisely, Ruijgh situates himself nearer to the level, a definite time before the tablets, we have postulated for the derivation of /krátrio-/, the status of which we have called *quasi-* or *pre-* diminutive (§14).

17. On the sociolinguistic level, it is interesting to see that diminutives in -*ion* existed already in Mycenaean and that these have their roots in the domain of household articles and craftsmanship with concomitant accountancy, which of course goes with the specificity of the tablets as administrative means. This, however, does not exclude the possible simultaneous existence of corresponding diminutives in the domain of hypocoristic-familial/-iar language or that of depreciative diminutives (*nomen est multifarium*, cf. Chantraine 1939), the *common denominator* being 'small(er) entity' with the three branches:

1) small(er) object (esp. utensils),

2) small (and thus cute) entity,

3) entity not up to normal standards.

18. On the methodological level, finally, after all we have argued, we would retain that Ruijgh's hypothetization of *κρᾶτρον or *κρᾱτρός as bases for the derivation of /krátrio-/ (cf. §§7, 13) is not necessary (if not deviatory) and thus asks for the application of the so-called principle of "Occam's razor": "*entia non sunt multiplicanda praeter necessitatem.*"

19. To sum up: The comprehension of /krā́trio-/ as an archaic formation with the first suffix in the zero-grade (-tr-, vs. full/long grade -tĕr-), dating from a period passably earlier than the tablets, probably proto-Greek, permits us to appreciate and follow the rise of diminutives in -io- in Mycenaean, going through a first phase of substantivized relational adjectives (of any gender), probably originating in part from noun+adjective phrases by ellipsis of the noun phase represented by /krā́trios/, which we have characterized as *pre-* or *quasi*-diminutive.

In a second phase, relatively near to the period of the tablets (because they do not show any trace of assibilation), veritable diminutives appear, as a new lexical class in the form of neuter substantives in -ion, specifically in the semantic field of household utensils (and, more largely, banqueting).[16] Derived from an agent noun in -tĕr, these have the first suffix in long (or full?) grade i.e., -tĕr-ion, by analogy to the stem form in the nominative and/or accusative singular (etc., cf. §8).

This new perspective also enables us to bridge the opposing views of Ruijgh (remaining with the first phase only) and Lejeune (rightly advocating the second phase, too), considering them as representing two consecutive chronological and organically evolutionary levels, perhaps even overlapping/coexisting in different sectors for a certain time.

Bibliography

Bendall, L. M. 2008. "How Much Makes a Feast? Amounts of Banqueting Food-stuffs in the Linear B Records of Pylos." In Sacconi, Del Freo, Godart, and Negri 2008:77–101.

Bennett, Jr., E. L. 1958. *The Olive Oil Tablets of Pylos. Texts of Inscriptions Found, 1955.* Salamanca.

Chadwick, J. 1959. "Inscribed Sealings from Mycenae." *Eranos* 57:1–5.

Chantraine, P. 1939. *La formation des noms en grec ancien.* Paris [repr. 1979].

---

[16] See Varias García (2008 and forthcoming, with nn1–4 [cf. also above note 3]), as well as Bendall 2008.

————. 1966. "Finales mycéniennes en -*iko*." In *Proceedings of the Cambridge Colloquium on Mycenaean Studies*, ed. L. R. Palmer and J. Chadwick, 161–179. Cambridge.

Debrunner, A. 1917. *Griechische Wortbildungslehre*. Heidelberg.

de Fidio, P. 2008. "Mycenaean History." In Duhoux and Morpurgo Davies 2008: 81–114.

Deger-Jalkotzy, S., S. Hiller, and O. Panagl eds. 1999. *Floreant Studia Mycenaea. Akten des X. Internationalen Mykenologischen Colloquiums in Salzburg vom 1.-5. Mai 1995*. Vienna.

Driessen, J. 2008. "Chronology of the Linear B Texts." In Duhoux and Morpurgo Davies 2008:69–79.

Duhoux, Y. 2008. "Mycenaean Anthology." In Duhoux and Morpurgo Davies 2008: 243–393.

————. 2013. *Paradeigmata: Recueil d'Inscriptions Grecques Dialectales I: Le mycénien*. Nancy.

Duhoux, Y., and A. Morpurgo Davies, eds. 2008. *A Companion to Linear B: Mycenaean Greek Texts and Their World*, vol. 1. Bibliothèque des Cahiers de Linguistique Louvain 120. Louvain-la-Neuve.

————. 2014. *A Companion to Linear B: Mycenaean Greek Texts and Their World*, vol. 3. Bibliothèque des Cahiers de l'Institut de Linguistique de Louvain 133. Louvain-la-Neuve.

Georgiev, V. 1958. "Kretisch-mykenische Wortdeutungen." In *Minoica. Festschrift zum 80. Geburtstag von Johannes Sundwall*, ed. E. Grumach, 149–161. Berlin.

Hajnal, I. 2006. "Die Tafeln aus Theben und ihre Bedeutung für die griechische Dialektologie." In *Die neuen Linear B-Texte aus Theben: Ihr Aufschlusswert für die mykenische Sprache und Kultur. Akten des internationalen Forschungskolloquiums an der Österreichischen Akademie der Wissenschaften, 5.-6. Dezember 2002*, ed. S. Deger-Jalkotzy and O. Panagl, 53–69. Vienna.

Lejeune, M. 1968. "L'assibilation de l'aspirée sourde dentale devant 'I'." In *Atti e memorie del Primo Congresso Internazionale di Micenologia, Roma 27 settembre-3 ottobre 1967*, ed. C. Gallavotti *et al.*, vol. 2, 733–743. Rome.

Lindblom, M. 2001. *Marks and Makers: Appearance, Distribution and Function of Middle and Late Helladic Manufacturers' Marks on Aeginetan Pottery*. Jonsered.

Meissner, T. 2008. "Notes on Mycenaean Spelling." In Sacconi, Del Freo, Godart, and Negri 2008:507–519.

Melena, J. L. 2014a. "Filling Gaps in the Basic Mycenaean Syllabary." In *Donum Mycenologicum. Mycenaean Studies in Honour of Francisco Aura Jorro*, ed. A. Bernabé and E. R. Luján, 75–85. Louvain-la-Neuve and Walpole, MA.

———. 2014b. "Mycenaean Writing." In Duhoux and Morpurgo Davies 2014: 1–186.

Milani, C. 1966. "L'apofonia nel Miceneo." *Aevum* 40:397–427.

Müller, W., J.-P. Olivier, and I. Pini. 1998. "Die Tonplomben aus Mykene." *Archäologischen Anzeiger:* 5–55.

Palmer, L. R. 1963. *The Interpretation of Mycenaean Greek Texts.* Oxford.

Panagl, O. 1971. "Eine 'Interferenz' von nominaler Stammbildung und Linear B-Schrift: Zur anomalen Schreibung der Kasusformen von mykenisch *WANAKA.*" *Kadmos* 10:125–134.

Pluta, K. M. 2011. "Aegean Bronze Age Literacy and Its Consequences." PhD diss., University of Texas at Austin.

Risch, E. 1958. "Un problème de morphologie grecque: L'accusatif pluriel des thèmes consonantiques en mycénien." *Bulletin de la Société de Linguistique de Paris* 53:96–102.

———. 1974. *Wortbildung der homerischen Sprache.* Zweite, völlig überarbeitete Auflage. Berlin.

———. 1976. "Il miceneo nella storia della lingua greca." *Quaderni Urbinati di Cultura Classica* 23:7–28.

———. 1981. *Kleine Schriften,* ed. A. Etter and M. Looser. Berlin and New York.

———. 1987. "Die mykenischen Personennamen auf -*e.*" In *Tractata Mycenaea. Proceedings of the Eighth International Colloquium on Mycenaean Studies, Held in Ohrid, 15-20 September 1985,* ed. P. Hr. Ilievski and L. Crepajac, 282–298. Skopje.

Ruijgh, C. J. 1967. *Études sur la grammaire et le vocabulaire du grec mycénien.* Amsterdam.

Sacconi, A. 1999. "Quelques remarques sur les séries W- des textes en linéaire B." In Deger-Jalkotzy, Hiller, and Panagl 1999:543–547.

Sacconi, A., M. Del Freo, L. Godart, and M. Negri eds. 2008. *Colloquium Romanum. Atti del XII Colloquio Internazionale di Micenologia Roma, 20-25 febbraio 2006.* Vols. I–II. Pisa and Rome.

Schwyzer, E. 1939. *Griechische Grammatik.* Vol. 1. Munich.

Shelmerdine, C. 1999. "A Comparative Look at Mycenaean Administrations." In Deger-Jalkotzy, Hiller, and Panagl 1999:555–576.

Thompson, R. 2008. "Mycenaean Non-Assibilation and Its Significance for the Prehistory of the Greek Dialects." In Sacconi, Del Freo, Godart, and Negri 2008:753–765.

Tichy, E. 1992. "Zur Rekonstruktion der Nomina agentis auf *-tér-* und *-tor-.*" In *Rekonstruktion und relative Chronologie. Akten der VIII. Fachtagung der Indogermanischen Gesellschaft, Leiden 31. August-4. September 1987,* ed. R. Beekes *et al.,* 411–420. Innsbruck.

Varias García, C. 2008. "Observations on the Mycenaean Vocabulary of Furniture and Vessels." In Sacconi, Del Freo, Godart, and Negri 2008:775–793.

———. Forthcoming. "Banqueting in Mycenae: The Textual Evidence." In T. G. Palaima *et al.*, eds., *Proceedings of the 11th International Mycenological Colloquium, Austin (Texas, 7–13 Mai 2000)*.

10

Mycenaean *o-pi-ke-re-mi-ni-ja*

Eugenio R. Luján and Juan Piquero

Universidad Complutense de Madrid
erlujan@ucm.es
Universidad Nacional de Educación a Distancia
jpiquero@flog.uned.es

Abstract

The meaning of the Mycenaean word *o-pi-ke-re-mi-ni-ja* is reexamined, taking into account the contexts in which it occurs and with reference to the previous relevant literature. On the basis of the archaeological evidence and of the linguistic data provided by a number of words and glosses in the first-millennium Greek, it is argued that this word must be rendered as *ὀπικελεμνίᾱ and that it referred to chairbacks consisting of vertical slats with one or more cross-pieces. The alternation between singular and plural forms of the word can be accounted for as a difference in the description of the ornamentation of the objects, and it can be arguably explained by the number of cross-pieces that made up the chairbacks.

Keywords
Mycenaean, lexicon, furniture, chairs, PY Ta series

THE WORD *O-PI-KE-RE-MI-NI-JA* OCCURS FIVE TIMES ON THE MYCENAEAN TABLETS, specifically on three tablets: PY Ta 707, 708, and 714.[1] The contexts in which it appears are the following:[2]

[1] This paper was a result of the research projects FFI2012-36069-C03-02 and FFI2013-41251-P, which had the financial support of the Spanish Ministry of Economy and Competitiveness. We are very grateful to Professor J. Méndez Dosuna for his comments and suggestions.

[2] We follow the edition of *PTT*³. The text in the other current editions of the Pylos tablets (Godart and Sacconi 2020 and Olivier and Del Freo 2020:235), which were not available when we wrote

Ta 707[3] (S641 H 2)

.a   ku-te-ta-jo

.1   to-no , ku-ru-sa-pi , o-pi-ke-re-mi-ni-ja-pi , o-ni-ti-ja-pi 1
      ta-ra-nu-qe , a-ja-me-no , e-re-pa-te-jo , au-de-pi 1

.2   to-no , ku-te-se-jo , e-re-pa-te-ja-pi , o-pi-ke-re-mi-ni-ja-
      pi , se-re-mo-ka-ra-o-re , qe-qi-no-me-na , a-di-ri-ja-te-qe ,
      po-ti-pi-qe 1

.3   ta-ra-nu , ku-te-so , a-ja-me-no , e-re-pa-te-jo , au-de-pi

   .1a   *ku-te-ta-jo* continues on *latus superius*

   .1   *ku-ru-sa-pi* over erasure; *-ja-* in *o-ni-ti-ja-pi* over ⟦*pi*⟧, , *au-de-*
          over erasure ⟦*au*⟧

   .2   *ku-te-se-* over erasure, possibly ⟦*ku-te-ta*⟧; *se-re-mo-ka-ra-o-re*
          possibly over erasure

   N. B.:   a PUNCT in stem of *mo*

Ta 708 (S641 H 2)

.1   to-no , ku-te-se-jo , a-ja-me-no , o-pi-ke-re-mi-ni-ja , e-re-pa-
      te 1 ⟦

.2.A to-no , ku-te-se-jo , e-re-pa-te-ja-pi , o-pi-ke-re-mi-ni-ja-pi ,
      se-re-mo-ka-ra-a-pi , qe-qi-no-me-na , a-di-ri-ja-pi-qe[ ] *vac.*

.2.B ta-ra-nu , ku-te-se-jo , a-ja-me-no , e-re-pa-te-jo , a-di-ri-ja-pi
      , re-wo-pi-qe 1[ ] *vac.*

   .1   ⟦*ta-ra-nu-we, ku-te-se-jo , a-ja-me-no , e-re-pa-te-jo , au-de-pi*⟧⟦

   .2.B   *e-re-pa-te-jo* over ⟦*a-di-ri-ja-pi*⟧

Ta 714 (S641 H 2)

.1   to-no , we-a₂-re-jo , a-ja-me-no , ku-wa-no , pa-ra-ku-we-qe ,
      ku-ru-so-qe , o-pi-ke-re-mi-ni-ja

.2   a-ja-me-na , ku-ru-so , a-di-ri-ja-pi , se-re-mo-ka-ra-o-re-qe ,
      ku-ru-so , ku-ru-so-qe , po-ni-ki-pi 1

.3   ku-wa-ni-jo-qe , po-ni-ki-pi 1 ta-ra-nu , a-ja-me-no , ku-wa-no
      , pa-ra-ku-we-qe , ku-ru-so-qe , ku-ru-sa-pi-qe , ko-no-ni-pi 1

   .1   *-jo* over erasure, possibly ⟦*ja*⟧; *ku-wa-no* possibly over erasure

   .2   *se-re-mo-ka-ra-o-re-qe , ku-ru-so,, vacat* over ⟦*ku-wa-no*[
          se-]*re-mo, ka-ra-o-re*⟧; 1 after *po-ni-ki-pi* possibly divider

---

this paper, is basically the same, but we will mention the slight differences in the relevant
place.

³   For line 1 of this tablet Godart and Sacconi (2020 vol. II:192) edit *a-ja-me-no* and Olivier and Del
    Freo (2020:235) *a-ja-me-no*. Concerning line 2, both editions mention the following in their crit-
    ical apparatus: "⟦*e-re-pa*⟧ PTT pas impossible, ⟦*ku-te-ta*⟧ peu vraisemblable."

According to the syntax of the text, *o-pi-ke-re-mi-ni-ja* must be an accusative of respect at PY Ta 708.1 ("a chair inlaid with ivory *in its back*")[4] and, most probably, a dative-instrumental singular at PY Ta 714.1–2 ("a crystal chair inlaid with blue glass paste and green glass paste[5] and gold, *with a back* inlaid with golden human figures and a golden siren head").[6] According to its morphology, *o-pi-ke-re-mi-ni-ja-pi* must be an instrumental plural in its three occurrences, and this interpretation is consistent with the syntax of the tablets.

As the contexts show, the word *o-pi-ke-re-mi-ni-ja* is attested only in the description of a number of chairs of an especially high quality, as proven by the precious materials employed in their ornamentation. We are dealing without a doubt with a compound with the preposition *o-pi-*, which could have the meaning 'adhered to', 'on'.[7] Its most likely interpretation, according to Aura Jorro (*DMic.*, *s.v.*), is that it is a part attached to the *to-no*, most probably the 'back'.[8]

Nevertheless, different proposals have been put forward in order to explain this word. Since the first moment, Ventris (1955:120) suggested an interpretation related to Hesychius' glosses ἀμφικελεμνίς and ἀμφικέλεμνον (see *infra*), but he concluded that "the root meaning of **kelemn-* is hard to deduce ('shoulder'?, 'carrying pole'?)" and finally favored an alternative possibility: **opikrēmniāphi* "from κρημνός, 'an overhanging lip'." He concluded that "in either case the meaning would appear to refer to the edges of the back or arms, which the Tutankhamen parallels suggest as the most favored place for decorative treatment." All of the following papers dealing with this word are indebted to Ventris's arguments, and, in general, Mycenaean scholars prefer the interpretation **ὀπικρημνία* with different meanings (cf. *DMic.*, *s.v.*). However, according to Beekes (*EDG*, 777, *s.v.* κρημνός), the interpretation of this word as **ὀπικρημνίᾱ* is problematic, because the root of κρημνός is unrelated to κρεμάννυμι.

Ruijgh (1967:107–108)[9] preferred an interpretation based on the root **κελεμνο-*, "'*planche*' (ou '*chaise*'?)," and suggested that "on pourrait à la rigueur expliquer *o-pi-ke-re-mi-ni-ja* comme pluriel de **ὀπικελεμνίᾱ*, dérivé de ὀπὶ

---

4   Alternatively, it has been suggested that in Ta 708.1 the term must be interpreted as an instrumental singular or an accusative plural (*DMic.*, *s.v.*, n. 1). But if this were the case, an adjectival form *e-re-pa-te-jo* or *e-re-pa-te-ja* (and not the noun *e-re-pa-te*) would be expected instead.

5   See Piquero 2015 for this interpretation.

6   As we argue in this paper, this hypothesis seems more likely than an accusative of respect (*Docs*[2], 344, 565), a nominative plural (Risch 1986:67–68n16.), or "einer jüngeren Instrumental Form des Plurals auf <- (C)a> /-ǎis/" (Hajnal 1995:22), as Hajnal himself acknowledged.

7   See Rodríguez Somolinos 2013:206–207 for an analysis of the meaning of ἐπί 'adhered to', 'in close contact with the surface of'.

8   See *DMic.*, *s.v.* for a complete list of bibliographical references.

9   Followed by Duhoux (1975:49) and Hajnal (1995:22).

*κελέμνοι et désignant 'ce qui se trouve sur la siège', c'est-à-dire le dossier et le bras."[10]

Although there is no agreement on the interpretation of this term, we think, following Ruijgh (1967:107–108), that its rendering as *ὀπικελεμνίᾱ is the most likely possibility, and we will try to provide evidence for this in what follows.

As pointed out by several scholars,[11] *o-pi-ke-re-mi-ni-ja* must be related to the following words:

a) ἀμφικέλεμνον· ἀμφιβαρές· οἱ δὲ τὸν βασταζόμενον ὑπὸ δύο ἀνθρώπων δίφρον, ἄλλοι δὲ ἀμφίκοιλον ξύλον (Hesychius.). The gloss can be translated as follows: "heavy on both sides; for some, chariot-board borne by two men, but for others, wood hollowed on both sides."

b) ἀμφικελεμνίς· κατ' ὀβελῶν περικρέμασις ἰσορρόπως (Hesychius).[12] There is no straightforward interpretation of this gloss. Liddell, Scott, and Jones 1968, *s.v.* (followed by Rodríguez Adrados *et al.* 1986, *s.v.*) rendered it as 'hanging evenly on both shoulders', accepting a conjecture κατ' ὤμων based on the κατωμένων occurring in one of the manuscripts. However, the reading κατ' ὀβελῶν 'from the skewers' is preferred by Cunningham in his recent edition (2017) and this would seem to fit better with the meaning of the whole family of words. Discussing this difficult gloss in depth is, however, far beyond the scope of the present paper.

c) The word κελέοντες is glossed by Harpocration (K 37 Keanney) as follows:

Κελέοντες· Ἀντιφῶν (*Fr.* 11 Thalheim) ἐν τῇ πρὸς Δημοσθένους γραφὴν ἀπολογίᾳ "ἵνα τοὺς κελέοντας κατέπηξεν." κυρίως μὲν κελέοντές

---

[10] A different view was favored by Perpillou (2004:176). He proposed that the thrones mentioned on the PY Ta tablets were "sièges cérémoniels et processionnels" and that *o-pi-ke-re-mi-ni-ja(-pi)* referred to the cross-pieces which made transporting possible. However, this hypothesis does not explain the alternation between singular and plural forms, and it does not take into account the fact that the *o-pi-ke-re-mi-ni-ja(-pi)* was the part of the chair where the decoration was placed. In accordance with the archaeological evidence, such a part was precisely the 'back' of the thrones, as we will see below.

[11] Ventris and Chadwick (*Documents*, 343 and *Docs*², 565) already mentioned ἀμφικέλεμνον and ἀμφι-κελεμνίς. Chantraine (1999:512, *s.v.* κελέοντες) added the reference to κελέοντες. For further references, see *DMic., s.v.*

[12] The word is also mentioned by Herodianus Grammaticus 3(1).512.3 and Theognostus *Canones* 989 (p. 163.15) in a discussion of the accentuation of the words ending in -ις, but no information on its meaning is provided.

εἰσιν οἱ ἱστόποδες, ὡς καὶ παρ' Ἀριστοφάνει δῆλον τῷ κωμικῷ (*Fr.* 835 Kassel-Austin). μεταφορικῶς δὲ νῦν ὁ ῥήτωρ λέγοι ἂν τὰ ὀρθὰ ξύλα.

It also occurs in the following passage by Theocritus (Theoc. 18.34):

οὐδέ τις ἐκ ταλάρω πανίσδεται ἔργα τοιαῦτα,
οὐδ' ἐνὶ δαιδαλέῳ πυκινώτερον ἄτριον ἱστῷ
κερκίδι συμπλέξασα μακρῶν ἔταμ' ἐκ κελεόντων.

No other winds such reels of thread from her basket,
No other cuts a closer weft from the weaver's beam,
After plaiting it with her shuttle.

The word further occurs in Antoninus Liberalis (Ant. Lib. 10.2):

πρὸς δὴ ταῦτα χαλεπήνας ὁ Διόνυσος ἀντὶ κόρης ἐγένετο ταῦρος καὶ λέων καὶ πάρδαλις καὶ ἐκ τῶν κελεόντων ἐρρύη νέκταρ αὐτῷ καὶ γάλα.

Getting angry for that, Dionysos, instead of a girl, became a bull, a lion, and a panther and nectar and milk flowed for him from the beams.

The older scholia to Theocritus (Sch. Theoc. 18.34) already provide a translation as the 'vertical beams of the loom':

<ἔταμ' ἐκ κελεόντων:> ἐκ τῶν ἱστοπόδων· τέμνεται γὰρ τὸ ὕφασμα ἐκ τοῦ ἱστοῦ, ὅταν τελεσθῇ.

Similar information is provided by the ancient lexicographers:

- κελέοντες· ἱστόποδες. τὰ ὁπωσοῦν μακρὰ ξύλα, δοκοί, ἱστοί (Hsch.) "the vertical beams in the upright loom. Wood that is long in some sense, beams, masts or looms."

- <Κελέοντες·> κυρίως μὲν κελέοντες καλοῦνται οἱ ἱνόποδες· Ἀντιφῶν δὲ ἐν τῇ πρὸς τὸν Δημοσθένην γραφῇ τὰ ὀρθὰ ξύλα οὕτως ὠνόμασεν (*Suda* K 1296) "properly speaking, they call κελέοντες the ἱνόποδες; Antiphon, in his discourse against Demosthenes thus called the upright beams."

- κελέοντες·οἱ ἱστόποδες καὶ πάντα τὰ μακρὰ ξύλα (Aelius Dionysius *Fr.* 19 Erbse).

- κελέοντες·οἱ ἱστόποδες καὶ τὰ λεπτὰ καὶ πηνοειδῆ τῶν ξύλων (Pausanias Grammaticus *Fr.* 23 Erbse).

The interpretation of this whole family of words is problematic. Frisk (1931:97–98) explained κελέοντες from an original present *κέλεω, which would be a denominative of *κέλος and mean 'rising up.' The derivation seems to be accepted by Chantraine (1999:512, *s.v.* κελέοντες), although he also considers the possibility that this is a loanword, an interesting possibility in view of the -μν-suffix found in other formations, such as ἴαμνος, βασυμνιάτης, etc. (see *EDG*, 10). Furnée (1972:245 and n69) stated, "κέλεμνος m. oder -ον n., etwa 'Tragholz.'" and he proposed a relation with κελέοντες and a possible variation μ/ϝ with a ν-suffix vacillation (cf. δίκταμνον / δίκταμον) from an original form *κέλεμος (with two variants: *κέλεμνος / *κελεϝόντες), which is unlikely.[13] Both Chantraine (1999:512, *s.v.* κελέοντες) and Beekes (*EDG*, 95, *s.v.* ἀμφικέλεμνον) appear to accept the relationship among all these words and Myc. *o-pi-ke-re-mi-ni-ja*.

If *o-pi-ke-re-mi-ni-ja* is related to these words, then its phonetic interpretation must be *ὀπικελεμνίᾱ, as stated above. Furthermore, we might probably add yet another gloss to this set: κλέμμιν· δίφρον ἀνακλιτόν (Hsch.) 'seat for reclining'. A relation to κλίνω is unlikely for κλέμμιν, because a form in κλι-/ κλει- (and not in κλε-) would be expected instead.

Although the meanings of all these words seem to be quite different, there are at least two common features to all of them: the objects referred to are in general made of wood, and the idea of verticality is somehow present, especially in the word κελέοντες. All of the objects referred to by these words appear to have the shape of a #, that is, two vertical beams crossing two horizontal ones. This fact will prove to be crucial later. The meaning 'added vertical wood [pieces]' could be a preliminary approximate translation of *o-pi-ke-re-mi-ja*.

Ruijgh (1967:107–108), however, pointed out that it is difficult to understand why *o-pi-ke-re-mi-ni-ja* appears in the plural if it refers only to the 'back of the chair'. In his opinion, the use of the plural could mean that the word refers, in fact, to both the back and the arms of the chair. On the basis of the information provided by the documents, we cannot know exactly how the layout of the decoration of the chair was. However, if we analyze the extant representations of thrones in the Aegean iconography, we can confirm that there were no arms in the models (according to the thrones shown in Rehak 1995b: pls. 32–40 and Younger 1995: pls. 55i and 60–66). It would follow then that the term *ὀπικελεμνίᾱ can only refer to the back of the seat, and it was there that the decoration was placed. However, this still leaves us with the difficulty of understanding why the scribe made this difference between singular and plural forms when describing the 'back' of the chair.

Let us analyze first the two instances in which the word appears to be in the singular. PY Ta 708.1 is the only occurrence in which ivory is mentioned as

---

[13] Beekes (*EDG*, *s.v.* ἀμφικέλεμνον). According to him, an alternation between a suffix -μν- and another formation is more likely.

merely inlaid material (like, for example, *pa-ra-ku-we*) and not as the material in which a given decorative motif was carved, as is usually the case. And PY 714.1 is the only other case in which there is no specification of the material of which the *o-pi-ke-re-mi-ni-ja* was made; it is only stated that it was inlaid with golden human figures and a golden siren head. Most probably, both chairs had wooden backs, but it would appear that when the back of the chair was not decorated with ivory plaques having ornamental motifs, the scribe would use the singular, whereas he would use the plural otherwise.

The instrumental plural *o-pi-ke-re-mi-ni-ja-pi* is always accompanied by an adjective that refers to the precious material that the *o-pi-ke-re-mi-ni-ja* were made of: *ku-ru-sa-pi* on PY Ta 707.1 and *e-re-pa-te-ja-pi* on PY Ta 707.2 and 708.2A. This strongly suggests that we are dealing with chairbacks consisting of ornamental plaques of ivory or gold (as in PY Ta 707.1). The scribe must have used the plural form *o-pi-ke-re-mi-ni-ja-pi* possibly because the number of slats making up the back of the chair was higher than in the cases in which it did not have ornamental plaques, but ivory inlays (Ta 708.1) or golden items (Ta 714).

According to the above-mentioned glosses and words, it is likely that the chairback consisted of two or more vertical slats and probably one or more cross-pieces. This is, in fact, the usual shape of some Mycenaean chairbacks according to the archaeological models preserved, such as certain terracotta throne models with three sloping legs (Richter 1966:6 and figs. 12–14 and 18; Jahn 1990:302 [numbers 132 and 133], 514 with fig. 25; Vlassopoulou-Karyde 2008) (see Fig. 10.1).

We do not intend to identify the terracotta thrones with the thrones recorded in the Pylos Ta series; we would just like to point out the similarities of their backs. Anyway, although a few thrones in Vlassopoulou-Karyde 2008 do have arms (type B), some of the preserved elements seem to be an attempt made by the craftsman to represent the decoration on the back of the chair and not in the arms themselves (Richter 1966:6 with figs. 8–11 and 15–17; Vlassopoulou-Karyde 2008:89) (see Fig. 10.2).[14] As Vetters (2011:324) remarked, "the finials of this miniature throne end in spirals, perhaps emulating the decoration of real thrones, though the Linear B texts only refer to the motif in the contexts of inlays." Some of these terracotta thrones, either of type A or of type B, show some lines painted on the back whose function is possibly to depict

---

[14] Younger 1995:191 drew attention to the fact that on the gypsum throne from Knossos the "impressed string lines formed a grid, presumably to guide painting," but perhaps it was a way to depict this type of back with vertical slats and cross-pieces. Cummer and Schofield 1984:73, no. 479 and pl. 45 also showed a throne model of type A with incised spirals and quirks on the exterior and interior of the back, "which are not paralleled in any Mycenaean throne models to date" (Vetters 2011:323).

Figure 10.1. Myceneaean terracotta three-legged chair with female figure.
Late Helladic IIIB, thirteenth century BCE, provenance unknown.
Part of the Cesnola Collection, now in the Metropolitan Museum of Art, NY
(https://www.metmuseum.org/art/collection/search/241266).

Figure 10.2. Mycenaean terracotta thrones. Late Helladic III,
ca. 1400–1150 BCE, provenance unknown. The George Ortiz Collection, no. 66.
Photo reproduced thanks to the courtesy of the George Ortiz Collection.

the slats referred to earlier (Vlassopoulou-Karyde 2008: figs. 32, 34, and 37).
Moreover, some models of ivory plaques inserted in some chairbacks from Fort
Shalmaneser SW 7 at Nimrud provide evidence of the method followed in these
cases for the insertion of the ivory plaques (Mallowan and Herrmann 1974:3).

***

Summing up, the contemporary archaeological evidence shows that chairbacks
in Mycenaean times consisted of vertical slats with one or more cross-pieces.
And the linguistic evidence provided by a number of words and glosses in the
first-millennium Greek that can be related to Mycenaean *o-pi-ke-re-mi-ni-ja* can
be used as proof that this word must be rendered as *ὀπικελεμνίᾱ* and, in fact,

referred to such #-shaped chairbacks. The alternation between singular and plural forms of the word in the tablets of the Pylos Ta series written by Hand 2 mentioning these *o-pi-ke-re-mi-ni-ja* can be accounted for as a difference in the description of the ornamentation of the objects, and it can be arguably explained by the number of cross-pieces that made up the chairbacks.

Bibliography

Beekes, R. S. P. 2014. *Pre-Greek: Phonology, Morphology, Lexicon*. Ed. S. Norbrius. Leiden.

Chantraine, P. 1999. *Dictionnaire étymologique de la langue grecque. Histoire des mots. Avec un Supplément* sous la direction de A. Blanc, Ch. de Lamberterie, J.-L. Perpillou. Paris.

Cummer, W. W., and E. Schofield. 1984. *Keos 3. Ayia Irini: House A*. Mainz.

Cunningham, I. C. 2017. *Hesychii Alexandrini Lexicon*, vol. I (A–Delta), Berlin.

Duhoux, Y. 1975. "L'ordre des mots en mycénien." *Minos* 14:123–163.

Frisk, H. 1931. "I. Aufsätze. Griechische Wortdeutungen." *Indogermanishe Forschungen* 49:97–104.

Furnée, E. J. 1972. *Die wichtigsten konsonantischen Erscheinungen des Vorgriechischen: Mit einem Appendix über den Vokalismus*. The Hague.

Godart, L., and A. Sacconi. 2020. *Les archives du roi Nestor. Corpus des inscriptions en linéaire B de Pylos*. 2 vols. Pasiphae XIII, XIV. Rome.

Hajnal, I. 1995. *Studien zum mykenischen Kassussystem*. Berlin.

Jahn, B. 1990. *Bronzezeitliches Sitzmobiliar der griechischen Inseln und des griechischen Festlandes*. Frankfurt.

Krzyszkowska, O. H. 1996. "Furniture in the Aegean Bronze Age." In *The Furniture of Western Asia: Ancient and Traditional*, ed. G. Hermann, 85–103. Mainz.

Liddell, H. G., R. Scott, and H. St. Jones. 1968. *A Greek–English Dictionary*. Oxford.

Mallowan, M., and G. Herrmann. 1974. *Furniture from SW.7 Forth Shalmaneser. Commentary, Catalogue, and Plates (Ivories from Nimrud 3)*. London.

Olivier, J.-P., and M. del Freo. 2020. *The Pylos Tablets Transcribed. Deuxième édition*. Padua.

Perpillou, J. L. 2004. *Essais de lexicographie en grec ancien*. Louvain.

Piquero, J. 2015. "Incrustaciones con vidrios de colores en Pilo: Análisis lingüístico y arqueológico de micénico *pa-ra-ku-we*." In *Orientalística en tiempos de crisis. Actas del VI Congreso Nacional del Centro de Estudios del Próximo Oriente*, ed. A. Bernabé and J. A. Álvarez Pedrosa, 285–296. Zaragoza.

Rehak, P. 1995a. "Enthroned Figures in Aegean Art and the Function of the Mycenaean Megaron." In Rehak 1995b:95–118.

————, ed. 1995b. *The Role of the Ruler in the Prehistoric Aegean. Proceedings of a Panel Discussion Presented at the Annual Meeting of the Archaelogical Institute of America. New Orleans, Louisiana, 28 December 1992. With Additions.* Aegaeum 11. Liège.

Richter, G. M. A. 1966. *The Furniture of the Greeks, Etruscans, and Romans.* London.

Risch, E. 1986. "Die mykenische Nominalflexion als Problem der indogermanischen und griechischen Sprachwissenschaft." In *Festgabe für Manfred Mayrhofer*, 63–77. *Die Sprache* 32 Vienna.

Rodríguez Adrados, F., *et al.* 1986. *Diccionario Griego-Español*, vol. II. Madrid.

Rodríguez Somolinos, H. 2013. "What Does ἐπί Really Mean? Contact and Dimensionality of the Landmark as Basic Semantic Categories in the Locative Prepositional Phrases with ἐπί." *Journal of Latin Linguistics* 12:199–230.

Ruijgh, C. J. 1967. *Études sur la grammaire et le vocabulaire du grec mycénien.* Amsterdam.

Ventris, M. 1955. "Mycenaean Furniture on the Pylos Tablets." *Eranos* 53:109–124.

Vetters, M. 2011. "Seats of Power? Making of Miniatures. The Role of Terracotta Throne Models in Disseminating Mycenaean Religious Ideology." In *Our Cups Are Full: Pottery and Society in the Aegean Bronze Age. Papers Presented to Jeremy B. Rutter on the Occasion of His 65th Birthday*, ed. W. Gauss, M. Lindblom, R. Angus K. Smith, and J. C. Wright, 319–330. Oxford.

Vlassopoulou-Karyde, M. 2008. *Πήλινα μυκηναϊκά ομοιώματα καθισμάτων και καθιστά ειδώλια.* Athens.

Younger, Y. 1995. "The Iconography of Rulership: A Conspectus." In Rehak 1995b: 151–211.

11

"Thematic" 3sg. impf. ἦεν 'He Was' and ἦε(ν) 'He Went'

Julián Méndez Dosuna

Universidad de Salamanca

mendo@usal.es

Abstract

The forms ἦεν 'he was' and ἦε(ν) 'he went' (for expected ἦς and *ἦ) have been explained as evidence of ancient (semi)thematic inflections of the verbs εἰμί and εἶμι. I argue that both forms are more likely to have resulted from the reanalysis of 3pl. ἦεν and ἦεν (with subsequent depluralization).

Keywords

Ancient Greek morphology, (semi)thematic inflection, depluralization

Iₙ the third-person plural of the imperfect of the verb εἰμί, the reconstructed PIE augmented protoform *h_1e-h_1s-*ent* evolved via *ἦhεν into Greek ἦεν, which was eventually contracted to ἦν.[1] Uncontracted 3pl. ἦεν is attested in Thessalian as εἶεν (pronounced [eːen]): ὅσσα παρλελιμ[μέ]να εἶεν (Tziafalias and Helly 2004–2005:378–402 no. 1 = *SEG* 55.605, ll. 9–10, Larisa, shortly after 190?), [τοῦμ π]ρούταμ μὲν ἐψαφισμένοι Λασαίοις εἶεν (*ibid.* ll. 13–14), ὅσσα ἀναγκαῖα εἶεν (Tziafalias, García Ramón, and Helly 2006:472–473 = *SEG* 56.633, l. 10, Larisa, 179–172?). This form had already been postulated by Hoffmann (1893:319); Brugmann (1900:352–353); Bechtel (1921:192); Schwyzer (1939:664),

---

[1] This paper forms part of the project FFI2012-35721-C02-022 of the Spanish Ministerio de Economía y Competitividad. It owes much to the helpful corrections and insightful suggestions of Alcorac Alonso Déniz and David Pharies. All dates are BCE.

and Buck (1955:112) as one of the sources of the secondary 3pl. ending –εν in forms such as, e.g., ὀνεθείκαεν, ἐκρίνναεν, ἐνεφανίσσοεν (= Att. ἀνέθεσαν, ἔκριναν, ἐνεφάνιζον).[2]

Contracted ἦν functions as a third-person plural in West Locrian, Delphian, and literary Doric:[3] e.g., ἦν τ᾽ ἐρῳδιοί ‹τε πολλοὶ› μακροκαμπυλαύχενες (Epich., fr. 461 *PCG*), WLocr. ηόπō ϝέκαστος ἐν (*IG* 9².718.9, Chaleion, 500–450),[4] παρῆν ναοπ[ο]ιοὶ τοίδε (*CID* 2.32.30, Delphi, late fourth century).

In Attic-Ionic, ἦεν and ἦν were ousted early on by a new form ἦσαν (unaugmented ἔσαν), which was re-characterized with a 3pl. ending borrowed from the sigmatic aorist. Table 11.1 summarizes the data found in archaic epics (numbers in parentheses indicate occurrences in compounds):

	Homer, Iliad	Homer, Odyssey	Hesiod, Theogony	Hesiod, Works and Days	[Hesiod], Shield	Homeric Hymns	Total
ἦσαν	46 (+ 1)	24	3	1	1 (+ 1)	2	77 (+ 2)
ἔσαν	34 (+ 3)	30 (+ 3)	2		4	3	73 (+6)

Table 11.1. 3pl. impf. of εἰμί in early epics

A parallel innovation is Boeot. *εἶαν (< *ἦαν): cf. παρεῖαν (Att. παρῆσαν) in several manumission records.[5] Lesbian has a thematized form ἔον (Schwyzer 1939: 644.12, Aigai, third century).

As regards the third singular, there can be little doubt that PIE 3sg. impf. *h_1e-h_1es-t regularly evolved into ἦς in Greek (cf. OAv. ås). A few occurrences of this form, which synchronically did not look like a typical third-person singular, survived in several literary and non-literary dialects.[6] A variant εἶε (< ἦε) occurs

---

[2] On this ending see below.
[3] A putative example in Herodotus 5.12.1 is illusory (Wilson 2015:94).
[4] For singular ἔκαστος with a plural verb, cf., e.g., ἔβαν οἶκόνδε ἔκαστος (*Iliad* 1.606).
[5] E.g. *IThesp.* 56.22, 26, 32, 36 (Thespiai, ca. 220).
[6] Arc. ἦς (*IPArk* 3.37, Tegea, ca. 350), Cypr. *e-se* /ēs/ (*ICS* 398.4, Abidos, early fourth cenetury), Dor. ἔς (*IG* 9².882.2, Corcyra, early sixth century; *IG* 9².390.9, Stratos, late fifth century) and ἦς (Alcman 16.1, Sophr. 59.1, Epich. 101, Theocr. 2.78, 90, etc.; *IG* 4².121.21, 118, etc. Epidaurus, fourth century; *FD* III 5.20.38, Delphi 341–314; *ICr.* 1.22.4C.26, Olous, early third century). Lesb. ἦς (Sapph. 44.28 Voigt, Alc. 67.1 Voigt), Boeot. παρεῖς (e.g., *IThesp.* 56.41, 43, 45, Thespiai, ca. 220 BC), παρῖς (ibid. 48), Thess. εἶς (*SEG* 56.636.46, Larisa, late second century); see Masson 1978 and García Ramón 2008:197–198. A new instance (ἡ πεπρωμένον ἦς ἀποθανεῖν;) in an oracular inquiry from Dodona probably composed in Doric (see Dakaris, Vokotopoulou, and Christidis 2013: 461A, early fourth century?) is to be added to the list of occurrences.

in Thessalian in an inscription from Skotousa (*SEG* 43.311, 197–185): ἐπειδεὶ πλείουν τόπος εἶε{ς} (A 71),[7] ἐπιδεὶ πλείουν τόπος εἶε (B 59).

In Attic-Ionic, ἦεν and contracted ἦν are attested as early as Homer. The relevant data are summarized in Table 11.2:

	Homer, *Iliad*	Homer, *Odyssey*	Hesiod, *Theogony*	Hesiod, *Works and Days*	[Hesiod], *Shield*	*Homeric Hymns*	Total
ἦεν	51 (+ 4)	46			2	3	102 (+ 4)
ἦν	45	32 (+ 2)	4	1 (+ 1)	5		87 (+ 3)
ἔην	37	26	2	2	3	1	71
ἤην	1	3					4

Table 11.2. 3sg. impf. of εἰμί in early epics

As Chantraine (2013:279, §134) points out, ἤην and ἔην are in all probability artificial variants for ἦεν and unaugmented *ἔεν (significantly, ἔην mostly occurs in preconsonantal position).[8] Contracted ἦν is general in Attic and in Doric choral lyric.

There is no consensus as to the origin of 3sg. impf. ἦεν, but the crucial role played by 3pl. impf. ἦεν in the elimination of ἦς in Attic-Ionic is in one way or another universally accepted. Basically, two different approaches to the problem have been proposed. According to a line of explanation favored by Schwyzer (1939:663n8, 677n6), Rix (1976:243), and Chantraine (2013:278), among many others, 3sg. ἦεν and ἦν are exactly what they look like: ancient 3pl. forms recycled as singular.

Sihler (1995:551) objects to this explanation, stating that "the reassignment [...] of 3pl. to 3sg. [...] is hard to fathom on any functional grounds," but this objection is easily dismissed. As Schwyzer and Chantraine did not fail to note, the reanalysis may have started in contexts that offered room for syntactic ambiguity between a singular and a plural: e.g., sentences with a multiple subject

---

[7] Thess. εἶε{ς} is probably a blend of εἶε and εἶς (see note 6), as Dubois (2012:49) suggests.

[8] There are only two exceptions in the *Iliad*. Prevocalic ἔην is more frequent in the *Odyssey* (12 occurrences), in Hesiod's *Works and Days* (1 instance) and in Ps-Hesiod's *Shield* (1 instance).

(ἔνθα μάλιστα μάχη καὶ φύλοπις ἦεν, Homer *Iliad* 13.789), a neuter subject (ἄ δὴ τετελεσμένα ἦεν, Homer *Iliad* 18.4) or a singular subject with plural reference (e.g., above-mentioned WLocr. hόπō ϝέκαστος ἔν).

Moreover, the coalescence of 3sg. and 3pl. forms of the verb εἰμί is well attested in later stages of Greek. Thus, like other forms in the Classical paradigm of εἰμί, 3sg. impf. ἦν borrowed the middle past secondary ending and became ἦτο in the early Byzantine period. This form was blended with 3pl. ἦσαν to give rise to 3pl. ἦταν, which survives in Modern Greek. In time, ἦταν began to be used as a 3sg. In the present tense the merger of the 3sg. and 3pl. took place in reverse direction so that, in Modern Greek, 3sg. εἶναι, which derives via ἔναι from the ancient locative adverb ἔνι reanalyzed as a verb form, is also used as a 3pl.

These facts notwithstanding, Sihler (1995:551) explains 3sg. ἦεν as follows:

> [A]n original (unattested) perf. *ἦε would, with ν-movable, have been homophonous with inherited imperf. ἦεν (with fixed -ν). When clearly-marked 3pl. forms like ἦσαν started to become current, ambiguous ἦεν was free, as it were, to be exclusively 3sg.

In other words, the preexistence of 3sg. perf. *ἦε(ν), which must have somehow replaced original 3sg. impf. ἦς, paved the way for the reanalysis of 3pl. ἦεν as a 3sg. If this hypothesis is true, the reconstructed form *ἦε, which supposedly has a cognate—or rather, a lookalike—in Ved. 3sg. perf. *ása* and YAv. *ā́ŋha* might be actually attested as Thess. 3sg. impf. εἶε. Dubois (2012:48) toys with this idea, but rightly rejects it on the grounds that the evidence of the 3sg. imperfect of εἰμί in Thessalian is too meager to postulate a PIE protoform or an innovation shared by Indo-Iranian and Greek.

Sihler's theory is problematic on several counts. First, as he himself acknowledges, the evidence of Indo-European languages suggest that, for semantic reasons, the root *h_1es- lacked a (resultative) perfect tense in Proto-Indo-European (Sihler 1995:550–552). The Vedic perfect is "an innovation based on the model of inherited perfects," which "is hardly vigorous."[9] The evidence of Greek is still weaker, since the presumptive 3sg. perf. *ἦε is posited on the basis of the reconstructed 3sg. impf. *ἦεν, which is a patently circular argument.[10] A similar criticism can be directed at the secondary and

---

[9] For the perfect as a Proto-Indo-Iranian innovation, see further Kümmel 2000:111–113 and 618–620.

[10] *Pace* Sihler 1995:551, 571, 2sg. impf. ἦσθα 'you were' cannot be regarded as evidence of a PIE perfect, in spite of its exact lookalike Ved. 2sg. perf. *ásitha*. The ending –(σ)θα in ἦσθα and a few forms like ἔφησθα, ἤεισθα, was secondarily imported from οἶσθα (formally a perfect); cf. also Hom. 2sg. pres. εἶσθα 'you go', διδοῖσθα, plpf. ᾔδησθα, aor. opt. βάλοισθα, etc. (Rix 1976:243; Kümmel 2000:113).

more recent thematic form *ē̆s-e-t reconstructed by García Ramón (2008:197–198) (for Proto-Greek?) to account for aforementioned Thess. εἶε. Bader's (1976) idea of a PIE 'semi-thematic' inflexion is all the more unnecessary for Greek. The existence of a few scattered thematic forms like 1sg. ἔον (Homer *Iliad* 11.762, 23.643, Sappho 63.7 Voigt), and Lesb. 3pl. ἔον, mentioned above, need not be projected back onto PIE. In all likelihood, they were secondarily modeled on *ἔεν.

Second, if 3sg. impf. ἦεν consistently exhibits a non-movable –ν (with the only exception of Thess. εἶε), the odds are that this was, from the very beginning, a non-movable –ν.[11] Even though the creation of the new 3pl. form ἦσαν dispelled any possible ambiguity with 3pl. ἦεν,[12] 3sg. ἦεν was anomalous in that it looked like a plural. Put in this perspective, Thess. 3sg. εἶε can be explained as the result of the 'depluralization' of 3pl. εἶεν.

In a previous paper (Méndez Dosuna 2018), I criticize the standard view advocated by Morpurgo Davies (1965), Blümel (1982:195–198), and García Ramón (2008:197; 2017), according to which the Thessalian secondary 3pl. endings –εν (e.g., ὀνεθείκαεν, ἐκρίνναεν, ἐνεφανίσσοεν = Att. ἀνέθεσαν, ἔκριναν, ἐνεφά-νιζον) and –ιεν (e.g., ἐδώκαιεν, ἐστάσαιεν, εἴχοιεν = Att. ἔδοσαν, ἔστησαν, εἶχον) were borrowed from 3pl. forms of the optative such as εἶεν (pronounced [ei̯(j)en]) or ἔχοιεν.

As indicated above, Thess. –εν is best explained as a generalization of the ending of Thess. 3pl. impf. εἶεν < ἦεν (Att. ἦσαν). By the same token, 3pl. –ιεν must have been taken over from 3pl. *εἶεν (pronounced [e:ien], [e:i̯en], or [ei̯en]). This is the expected phonetic outcome in Thessalian of an earlier *ἥιεν or *ἦεν (Att. ἦσαν). Crucially, at the time when the analogy took place, the diphthong /ei̯/ cannot have undergone contraction in prevocalic position, as this would have blocked the segmentation *ε-ιεν.[13]

---

[11] Paradoxically, Rix (1976:243) views 3sg. ἦεν as the source of the movable νυ added to 3sg. –ε in the imperfect, the aorist, and the perfect.

[12] Interestingly, Boeotian had a re-characterized form *εἶαν (cf. παρεῖαν) instead of expected *εἶεν, in spite of retaining the original 3sg. form εἶς (cf. παρεῖς). This indicates that the main function of –σαν in Att.-Ion. ἦσαν was not to differentiate 3pl. *ἦεν, *ἦν from 3sg. ἦεν, ἦν.

[13] The monophthongization of /ei̯/ before consonants must have been completed by the fourth century (see Scarborough 2014). Morpurgo Davies (1965:245) inferred from the available evidence that "the pronunciation of the original /ei/ underwent the same changes [i.e., monoph-thongization and raising to /e:/] both in preconsonantal and prevocalic position." García Ramón (1987:121–122) wonders whether this /e:/ was further raised to /i:/ in prevocalic position. To my mind, neither of these conclusions is compelling, but the resolution of this issue is largely irrelevant to our present concerns.

The form *$\varepsilon\tilde{\iota}\varepsilon\nu$ 'they went' remains as yet unattested in Thessalian, but this is not a serious drawback, since evidence for the imperfect of εἶμι in general and for its 3pl. forms in particular is very scarce in Greek inscriptions.[14]

Augmented *h_1e-h_1j-ent should have evolved into *$\mathring{\eta}\varepsilon\nu$ or *$\mathring{\eta}\iota\varepsilon\nu$. Similarly, unaugmented *h_1jent and its hypothetical Lindemann variant *h_1ijent should have resulted in *$\mathring{\varepsilon}\nu$ and *$\mathring{\iota}\varepsilon\nu$ respectively.[15]

The assessment of the forms *$\mathring{\eta}\varepsilon\nu$ and *$\mathring{\eta}\iota\varepsilon\nu$ crucially depends on what one considers to be the regular outcome of *$(-)Hj$- in Greek.[16] Some may consider *$\mathring{\eta}\iota\varepsilon\nu$ (probably via *$\bar{e}ijent$) to be the expected reflex of *h_1e-h_1j-ent, dispensing with *$\mathring{\eta}\varepsilon\nu$ altogether. Others may consider the latter form to be the regular outcome, viewing *$\mathring{\eta}\iota\varepsilon\nu$ as a secondary variant with an -ι- borrowed from zero-grade forms like, e.g., ἴμεν, ἴσαν, etc. This remodeling would have served to remove the homonymy with 3pl. ἦεν of εἰμί.

The ancient epics document the following data:

	Homer, *Iliad*	Homer, *Odyssey*	Hesiod, *Theogony*	Hesiod, *Works and Days*	[Hesiod], *Shield*	Homeric *Hymns*	Total
ἤισαν	3	4 (+ 1)	—	—	1	1	9 (+ 1)
ἦσαν	—	(+ 1)	(+ 1)	—	—	—	(+ 2)
ἴσαν	22 (+ 1)	13	1	—	(+ 1)	—	36 (+ 2)
ἤιον	—	2 (+ 3)	—	—	—	—	2 (+ 3)

Table 11.3. 3pl. impf. of εἶμι in early epics

All these forms are evidently variants of augmented *$\mathring{\eta}\iota\varepsilon\nu$ and unaugmented *$\mathring{\iota}\varepsilon\nu$. The most frequent variants ἤισαν (ἦσαν) and ἴσαν incorporate the ending –σαν of the sigmatic aorist. Rare ἤιον and isolated 1pl. ἤομεν (*Odyssey*

---

[14] There may be a possible instance of a 3pl. or 3sg. of the imperfect of εἶμι in an oracular inquiry from Dodona (see Dakaris, Vokotopoulou, and Christidis 2013:1360A, mid-fifth century?): πῦ τ' ἔρια ἔιεν; 'Where did the stocks of wool go?'. A potential optative ἔιεν ('Where would the stocks of wool be?') cannot, however, be ruled out (see Méndez Dosuna 2016:129).

[15] For the phonetics of εἶμι, cf. Peters 1980:103–105.

[16] For a discussion of the disputed issue of the development of *-Hj- in Greek, see Barber 2013: 122–124.

10.251, 10.570, 11.22) seem to be thematized variants of unattested *ἤιεν and *ἤιμεν (Att. ἦσαν, ἦμεν).

In the third singular, augmented *h_1e-$h_1ei̯$-*t* and unaugmented *$h_1ei̯$-*t* should have evolved into *ἦι and *εῖ respectively (cf. Ved. *áit*, YAv. 3sg. (*up*)*āit̰*), though no traces of such outcomes are found anywhere in Greek. The following are the forms actually attested in the epics:

	Homer, Iliad	Homer, Odyssey	Hesiod, Theogony	Hesiod, Works and Days	[Hesiod], Shield	Homeric Hymns	Total
ἤιε	9	2	—	—	—	1	12
ἤιεν	2 (+ 1)	6 (+ 1)	—	—	—	—	8 (+ 2)
ἦε	1	1	—	—	—	—	2
ἦεν	—	3	—	-	(+ 1)	—	3 (+ 1)
ἴε	1	1	—	—	—	—	2
ἴεν	1	7	—	—	—	—	8

Table 11.4. 3sg. impf. of εἶμι in early epics

The form ἤιε also occurs in Herodotus (39 occurrences)[17] and in a Cretan inscription from Gortyna (*ICr.* 4.72.2.47, ca. 480–450): ἄτι ἔκονσ᾽ ἔιε πὰρ τὸν ἄνδρα "with whichever possessions she had when she moved into her husband's [abode]."[18]

At first blush, all these forms appear to be thematic (cf. ἔ-φερ-ε < *h_1e-b^her-*e-t*), but they are not necessarily ancient. According to Chantraine (2013:285), they were derived from aforementioned 3pl. ἤιον by a four-part analogy such as, e.g., 3pl. ἔφερον: 3sg. ἔφερε. Peters (1980:104n49) cogently objects that such an analogy is unlikely if only because 3pl. ἤιον, the presumptive base form, is a marginal and infrequent variant. It only occurs in two late passages of the *Odyssey* (23.270, 24.501), in contrast to 3sg. ἤιε(ν) and its disyllabic variants ἦε(ν),

---

[17] The singular of the imperfect of εἶμι was subject to a complete remodeling in Attic, probably under the analogical influence of the imperfect (formally a pluperfect) of οἶδα (Ruijgh 1971:167; Sihler 1995:525): 1sg. ᾖα (later ᾔειν), 2sg. ᾔεις, 3sg. ᾔει; note the homonymy of 3pl. ᾖσαν 'they went' and 'they knew' (later ᾔδεσαν).

[18] The spelling EIE stands for ἤιε /εːie/ or ἤιε /εːi̯e/. A form *ἔιε /eie/ or *εῖε /eːi̯e/ (with a syllabic augment and the zero degree of the root) would be theoretically possible, but parallels are lacking in Greek (Bile 1988:226n293).

which appear 28 times. Peters sides with Watkins (1973:80) in reconstructing a protoform *e-h₁j-e, *h₁ij-e with an old PIE middle ending –e, but this hypothesis seems to me to be as far-fetched as it is unnecessary.

I tentatively propose to interpret 3sg. ἤιε(ν) and ἴε(ν) as the legitimate descendants of 3pl. ἤιεν and ἴεν. The reanalysis of these plural forms as singular occurred parallel to the conversion of 3pl. ἦεν 'they were' (< *h₁e-h₁s-ent) to 3sg. Unlike the –ν of Att.-Ion. 3sg. impf. ἦεν 'he was', which with the only exception of Thess. εἶε remained stable, the –ν of 3sg. ἤιεν and ἴεν 'he went' was reinterpreted as a movable –ν in Attic-Ionic. It is significant in this respect that ἤιεν (ἦεν) and ἴεν tend to occur in prevocalic position,[19] while ἤιε (ἦε) (10 × *Iliad*, 3 × *Odyssey*) (together with Cret. ἔιε) and ἴε (1 × *Iliad*, 1 × *Odyssey*) are almost invariably preconsonantal.[20] While the nasal of ἦεν may have been retained in order to avoid quasi-homonymy with disjunctive ἠέ, the new forms ἤιεν and ἴεν did not incur such a risk. In turn, 3sg. ἤιε(ν) was the basis for new thematic forms to emerge.

It is important to emphasize that the paradigms of εἰμί (Lesb., Thess. ἐμμί, 'strict' Doric ἠμί) and εἶμι shared a similar phonetic and morphological structure, which made them distinctive from all other athematic verbs. For instance, both verbs have thematic-looking participles: cf. ἐών ἐόντος and ἰών ἰόντος.[21] Their affinity made them prone to mutual interference and parallel evolution. A couple of examples will illustrate this point. To judge from the testimony of an inscription from Larisa, the participle of εἶμι in Thessalian had a secondary e-grade of the root (as against the original zero grade of, e.g., Myc. *i-jo-te* /i(j)ontes/ Att. ἰών < *h₁j-ónt-): cf. εἰόντουν ἐν Κραννοῦνα ἀριστερᾶς [χερρός] "on the left hand as one enters Crannon, lit. of those entering Crannon" (*IGC* 9.1.20, late third century). The participle εἰών must have been modeled on the ostensible e-grade of ἐών (< *h₁s-ónt-).[22] Another case in point is the spelling EIMI attested in a significant number of early archaic inscriptions from different regions, where a spelling EMI (/e:mi/) would have been regularly expected. For instance, in the dedication inscribed on the famous monument of Phanodicos of Proconnesos (*IG* 1³.1580, Sigeion, ca. 550?), while the Ionic version has expected ἐμί (l. 2), the Attic text reads εἰμί (l. 12) alongside μελεδαίνεν (l. 19) with E for /e:/. This orthographic anomaly has been plausibly attributed to confusion with εἶμι (/eimi/) prompted by a four-part analogy εἶ 'you go' : εἶμι 'I go' = εἶ 'you are' : x (Ruijgh 1978a:87; 1978b:301).

---

[19] ἤιεν (ἦεν) (2 × *Iliad*, 9 × *Odyssey*), ἴεν (1 × *Iliad*, 3 × *Odyssey*). Exceptionally, there are 4 occurrences of ἴεν before a consonant in the *Odyssey*.

[20] The exception is ἤιε' Ολύμπιος ἀστεροπητής (*Iliad* 1.609).

[21] Actually the suffix had the o-grade: *h₁s-ont-, *h₁i-ont-.

[22] A four-part analogy may have been involved: cf., e.g., ἐστί : ἐών = εἶτι : x. García Ramón (1987:122) opts for an inverse spelling.

Bibliography

Bader, F. 1976. "Le present du verbe 'être' en indo-européen." *Bulletin de la Société de Linguistique de Paris* 71:27–111.

Barber, P. J. 2013. *Siever's Law and the History of Semivowel Syllabicity in Indo-European and Ancient Greek.* Oxford.

Bechtel, F. 1921. *Die griechischen Dialekte,* Bd. I: *Der lesbische, thessalische, böotische, arkadische und kyprische Dialekt.* Berlin.

Bile, M. 1988. *Le dialecte crétois ancien: Étude de la langue des inscriptions, recueil des inscriptions postérieures aux IC.* Paris.

Blümel, W. 1982. *Die aiolischen Dialekte: Phonologie und Morphologie der inschriftlichen Texte aus generativer Sicht.* Göttingen.

Brugmann, K. 1900. *Griechische Grammatik (Lautlehre, Stammsbildungs- und Flexionslehre und Syntax).* 3rd ed. Munich.

Buck, C. D. 1955. *The Greek Dialects: Grammar, Selected Inscriptions, Glossary.* Chicago.

Chantraine, P. 2013. *Grammaire homérique I: Phonétique et morphologie.* Nouvelle édition revue et corrigée par M. Casevitz. Paris.

Dakaris, S., I. Vokotopoulou, and A.-F. Christidis. 2013. *Τα χρηστήρια ελάσματα της Δωδώνης των ανασκαφών Δ. Ευαγγελίδη (Επιμέλεια Σ. Τσέλικα).* 2 vols. Athens.

Dubois, L. 2012. "Thessalika." In *Πολύμητις. Mélanges en l'honneur de Françoise Bader,* ed. A. Blanc, L. Dubois, and Ch. de Lamberterie, 45–55. Leuven-Paris.

García Ramón, J. L. 1987. "Geografía intradialectal tesalia: La fonética." *Verbum* 10:101–153.

———. 2008. "Aus der Arbeit an einer Grammatik des Thessalischen: Einige wichtige neue Verbalformen." *Historische Sprachforschung* 120:195–208.

———. 2017. "La desinencia tesalia de 3pl. -(ι)εν: pretérito y optativo." In *Ελληνικές διάλεκτοι στον αρχαίο κόσμο. Actes du VIᵉ Colloque international sur les dialectes grecs anciens (Nicosie, Université de Chypre, 26-29 septembre 2011),* ed. A. Panayotou and G. Galdi, 233–246. Louvain-la-Neuve.

Hoffmann, O. 1893. *Die griechischen Dialekte in ihrem historischen Zusammenhange, 2: Der nord-achäische Dialekt.* Göttingen.

Kümmel, M. 2000. *Das Perfekt im Indoiranischen: Eine Untersuchung der Form und Funktion einer ererbten Kategorie des Verbums und ihrer Weiterenwicklung in den altindoiranischen Sprachen.* Wiesbaden.

Masson, O. 1978. "La forme verbale ἦς 'erat' dans les dialectes grecs." In *Étrennes de septantaine: Travaux de linguistique et de grammaire comparée offerts à Michel Lejeune par un groupe de ses élèves,* 123–128. Paris.

Méndez Dosuna, J. 2016. "Some Critical Notes on the New Dodona Lead Tablets." *Zeitschrift für Papyrologie und Epigraphik* 197:119–139.

———. 2018. "Thessalian Secondary 3pl. -(ι)εν and the Optative: Dangerous Liaisons." In *Studies in Ancient Greek Dialects. From Central Greece to the Black Sea*, ed. G. K. Giannakis, E. Crespo, and P. Filos, 391–404. Berlin.

Morpurgo Davies, A. 1965. "A Note on Thessalian." *Glotta* 43:235–251.

Peters, M. 1980. *Untersuchungen zur Vertretung der indogermanischen Laryngale im Griechischen*. Vienna.

Rix, H. 1976. *Historische Grammatik des Griechischen*. Darmstadt.

Ruijgh, C. J. 1971. "Review of: P. Chantraine, *Dictionnaire étymologique de la langue grecque. Histoire des mots*. Tome: II E–K. Paris 1970 [p. 307–607]." *Lingua* 28:162–173.

———. 1978a. "Review of: S.-T. Teodorsson, *The Phonemic System of the Attic Dialect, 400-340 B.C.* Goteborg 1974." *Mnemosyne* 31:79–89.

———. 1978b. "Review of: H. Rix, *Historische Grammatik des Griechischen*. Darmstadt 1976." *Mnemosyne* 31:298–307.

Scarborough, M. J. C. 2014. "On the Phonology and Orthography of the Thessalian Mid-Long Vowels." In *11th International Conference on Greek Linguistics (Rhodes, 26-29 September 2013): Selected Papers/Πρακτικά*, ed. G. Kotzoglou *et al.*, 1535–1548. Rhodes.

Schwyzer, E. 1939. *Griechische Grammatik*, 1. Allgemeiner Teil. *Lautlehre, Wortbildung, Flexion*. Munich.

Sihler, A. L. 1995. *New Comparative Grammar of Greek and Latin*. New York-Oxford.

Tziafalias, A., and B. Helly. 2004-2005. "Deux décrets inédits de Larisa." *Bulletin de Correspondance Hellénique* 128–129:377–420.

Tziafalias, A., J. L. García Ramón, and B. Helly. 2006. "Décrets inédits de Larissa (2)." *Bulletin de Correspondance Hellénique* 130:435–483.

Watkins, C. 1973. "Hittite and Indo-European Studies: The Denominative Statives in -ē-." *Transactions of the Philological Society* 1971:51–93.

Wilson, N. G. 2015. *Herodotea. Studies on the Text of Herodotus*. Oxford.

12

Observations on the Linear B Sign a_2- in the Various Chronological Phases of the Knossos and the Mainland Archives

MARIE-LOUISE NOSCH

University of Copenhagen
nosch@hum.ku.dk

Abstract

The Linear B sign a_2 (also known as sign *25) was closely examined and discussed in the years immediately following the decipherment. It was determined that a_2 represents *ha*. While scholars noted that the sign a_2 was rare in Crete, but frequently found on the mainland, they did not explain this unequal distribution. In this contribution in honor of José L. Melena, who has done so much to help us understand how the Linear B syllabary originated, developed, and was used, I reexamine the use of sign *25 through time and space in the Mycenaean palatial period. I take into account the new corpus of Theban tablets (with many attestations of a_2), the new Ayios Vasileios tablets, and the new chronologies of the Knossos archives. I observe that sign a_2 is used in the Room of the Chariot Tablets (RCT) and North Entrance Passage (NEP), but not in the later phases of the Knossos archives, whereas a_2 occurs regularly in words on Linear B documents from the mainland sites of LH IIIB Pylos, Thebes, and Mycenae, and also at Ayios Vasileios. I suggest that sign a_2 is an isograph, a distinguishing feature of the early phase of the Knossos administration, which was abandoned in the late Knossos phase. This isograph continued in use in the scribal traditions of the mainland palaces.

Keywords
Writing, orthography, syllabograms, doublets, scribal conventions, script transmission

JOSÉ MELENA HAS MADE A NUMBER OF SIGNIFICANT CONTRIBUTIONS TO THE SCHOLARSHIP OF LINEAR B.[1] For my work, his seminal book on Knossian textiles has always been fundamental.[2] In this contribution, I focus on an observation stemming from my research on Mycenaean textiles. It concerns a Mycenaean textile type, identified as neuter singular *pa-wo* (KN Wm 8499). In the nominative and accusative plural, it is spelled either *pa-we-a* or *pa-we-a$_2$*.[3] The distribution and alternation of these two forms at first sight seem rather random and, perhaps for this reason, have not yet raised any discussion.

pa-we-a$_2$ is attested twice at Mycenae, and it occurs three times at Knossos, but only on tablets from find place I3 in the North Entrance Passage (= NEP).

MY L 710   (unknown/House of Columns)
.1   ]$_.$ pa-ta $_,$ [
.2   pa-we-a$_2$ $_,$ ko-u-ra [

MY Oe 127   (55/House of Oil Merchant)
pa-we-a$_2$ $_,$ e-we-pe-se-so-me-na $_,$ LANA 20

KN Ld(2) 786   (114/I3)
.A   ] a-*34-ka TELA³+ *PA* 1 [
.B   pa-we-]a$_2$ $_,$ / ke-ro-ta $_,$ *161* ki[

KN Ld(2) 787 + 1009 + 7378   (114/I3)
.A   a-*34-ka TELA³+ *PA* 1 [
.B   pa-we-a$_2$ $_,$ / o-re-ne-ja *161* ki-to-pi[

KN Ld(2) 788   (114/I3)
.A   ]   ti-ri[
.B   pa-we-]a$_2$ $_,$ / ke-ro-ṭạ[

[1]   I am grateful to Richard Firth for discussing this topic with me ever since Athens 2013 and for sharing copies of his forthcoming papers with me. The content of the present paper was enriched by the thoughtful and useful comments and corrections by Hedvig Landenius Enegren, Adamantia Vasilogamvrou, Brendan Burke, Joanne Cutler, Maurizio del Freo, Richard Firth, Torsten Meissner, Vasilis Petrakis, Peder Flemestad, Rachele Pierini, Anna Judson, and John Bennet. I could not have written this paper without all these colleagues. Remaining mistakes remain, however, my own responsibility. My special gratitude also to Tom Palaima, who peer-reviewed the paper and helped me with significant improvements both in style and content, and I am most grateful for his insightful comments and perspectives.
[2]   Melena 1975.
[3]   Nosch 2012:325–329.

It is interesting to observe that the variant form *pa-we-a* only occurs on West Wing tablets from Knossos. Furthermore, the prolific Knossos textile scribes[4] 103 and 113 only write *pa-we-a* and never *pa-we-a₂*.

The two Ld sets both record finished and decorated *pa-wo* cloth:[5] the Ld(2) tablets are by scribe 114, are from the NEP (I3), and record *pa-we-a₂*; the Ld(1) tablets are by scribe 116, are from the West Wing, and record *pa-we-a*. The two sets share several terms for decorative elements of this kind of cloth. These include *o-re-ne-ja* on Ld(1) 579, 583 and Ld(2) 787; *e-ru-ta-ra-pi* on Ld(1) 573, 585, 649 and Ld(2) 785; and *po-ki-ro-nu-ka* on Ld(1) 579, 584, 587, 598, 5845 and Ld(2) 785. However, according to Driessen, there is a difference of one to two generations between the two sets.[6] Moreover, as observed here, the scribes of the two chronological phases spell the cloth name differently.

In the West Wing of Knossos, *pa-we-a* is recorded on tablets by scribe 103 as *ri-ta pa-we-a* in the L(1) set, and by scribe 113 in the *ta-ra-si-ja* target series of western Crete.[7]

KN Lc(2) 481		(113/F6)
.A	] 'pa-we-a' TELA³ 30[	
.B	] , ku-do-ni-ja LANA[	
↓		
		(115)
v.	to-]u-ka LANA[	

It thus seems that *pa-we-a₂* occurs in the early phase at Knossos (NEP) and also on the mainland at Mycenae, but that in the later Main Archive Phase at Knossos (here abbreviated as MAP: the largest assemblage of Linear B tablets, from the West Wing and East Wing primarily, and dated to LM IIIB), the scribes instead write *pa-we-a*.

However, a closer look shows that this pattern of usage is not limited to the word for this specific fabric. The syllabic sign a_2 /ha/ itself is used at all mainland sites (Pylos, Mycenae, Thebes, Ayios Vasileios). But at Knossos, it only occurs in

---

[4] I use the word "scribes" with caution because the persons responsible for writing Linear B seem to have operated differently from scribes using scripts in the surrounding high cultures of the period, e.g. Egyptian, Hittite, Mesopomian, Levantine. See Palaima 2011:112–127. Due to conventions, I here term them Hands at Pylos and scribes at Knossos, Mycenae, and Thebes.

[5] The most important works on the Ld series are by Melena (1975) and Killen (1979).

[6] Driessen 1999; 2000.

[7] Killen 1966; 1974.

the early archival phases: in the RCT and the NEP.[8] In the MAP, this syllabic sign never occurs, and the value it represents (/ha/) is, instead, denoted simply by a.[9]

What Is a_2?

In the early days of Mycenaean studies, it was observed that the vowel /a/ can be written with the sign *08 (a), or sign *25 (a_2), or sign *43 (a_3). In 1954, Chadwick suggested that the sign *25 (a_2) had the value /ha/.[10] In the years after the decipherment, it was then conclusively determined that these three signs had different values:[11] sign *08 is a pure vowel /a/; sign *43 (a_3) has the value /ai/; and sign *25 (a_2) denotes /ha/.[12]

Right after the decipherment, the sign a_2 was closely examined and discussed, especially by Bartoněk,[13] Meriggi,[14] and Milani,[15] who all came to the conclusion that a_2 represents /ha/.[16] It is clear that Lejeune was skeptical at

---

[8] Driessen (1990; 2000) gives evidence for the earliest Linear B tablets at Knossos from the Room of the Chariot Tablets, and the ramifications of the chronological separation of the RCT tablets in Driessen 2001a. Driessen moreover suggested other destructions at Knossos and the formation of the NEP in Driessen 1997 and 1999; discussed fully in Firth 2000–2001.

[9] This was noted by Driessen (1999:216), who, however, did not discuss the ramifications further: "The sign a_2 is rare at Knossos: except for its occurrence in the RCT, there are examples on D 411, perhaps B 806 and several times in the word pa-we-a_2 by hand 114; all these records come from the NEP." Meissner (2008:514) also observes the unbalanced distribution of the spellings with intervocalic a_2 according to sites.

[10] Chadwick 1954:9.

[11] See the discussion in Bartoněk 1957.

[12] Bartoněk (2003:104–105) writes concerning a_2: "Hinweis auf die Existenz einer eventuellem Hauchlautreihe stellt das Zeichen 25 A$_2$ (ohne LA-Parallele) dar, das meistens eindeutig Silbe *ha* bezeichnet, d.h. eine Silbe mit einem Hauchlaut *h*, der als Resultat des frühgriechischen Lautwandels von antevokalischem *s*- und intervokalischem -*s*- entstanden ist. Im Laufe der Zeit hat man das Syllabogramm auch für andere Zwecke zu verwenden begonnen. Das Zeichen kommt vor allem in Pylos vor [...]; doch auch hier wechseln manchmal A$_2$ und A, bzw. A$_2$ oder JA (weniger sichere Variationen: A$_2$/A$_3$, A$_2$/WA)."

[13] Bartoněk 1957.

[14] Meriggi 1955:67.

[15] Milani presented a comprehensive study of these signs in 1958.

[16] Bartoněk (1957:54) notes that, "a considerable number of sign groups terminating in sign 25 and discovered both in Mycenae and in Pylos have one feature in common. Although even here we cannot rely too much on the hitherto suggested interpretations, it appears to be very probable that at least those linear sign-groups ending with sign 25 that may be designated as plurals of neuter s-stems (Nom. or Acc.) have been interpreted correctly (a-ke-a_2, ke-re-a_2, me-u-jo-a_2, me-zo-a_2, no-pe-re-a_2, o-da-a_2, pa-we-a_2, te-tu-ko-wo-a_2). Thus, we meet here transliterations of such Greek forms that once upon a time had an [s] before the final [a] and after a preceding vowel. It is, however, generally accepted that this [s], before it ceased to exist phonetically, passed through an intermediate phonetic stage, characterized usually with the consonant [h], and it may be that the Continental sign 25 gave at least for a certain time expression to this transitional stage." Milani (1958:130): "concluende e riassumendo quanto finora è stato detto, a_2 indicò dapprima il suono *ha*, esito di *sa* e di *ja* (raremente). Attenuandosi poi l'aspirazione di *ha*, in alcuni casi

first.[17] These scholars noted that the sign a_2 is rare in Crete, but frequently found on the mainland;[18] Bartoněk (1957:54) even coined it "the Continental sign 25."[19] However, they did not present any explanation for this unequal distribution. While these remain valid and excellent papers, they were based on a smaller corpus. In the present generation of Linear B scholars, less attention has been devoted to the interpretation of the sign a_2. This is despite the discovery of the new deposit of Theban tablets (with numerous attestations of a_2) as well as the new chronologies of Knossos, which shed new and crucial light on the role played by a_2. Two exceptions are the recent discussions by Anna Judson and the phonological analysis by Rachele Pierini, who sees a_2- as an example of archaic traces in the language.[20]

Our *honorandus* José Melena noted in 2014 that:

> Although ASPIRATION (/h/) is phonemic in Mycenaean, it is not systematically noted. Nevertheless, when the following vowel is /a/, a special sign can be used: a_2-*te-ro* /*hateron*/ 'the other (year)', *pa-we-a₂* /*pharweha*/ 'cloths'. Such a practice seems limited to this vowel, and no sign for aspiration plus another vowel has been identified to date.[21]

The sign a_2 is not attested in Linear A and is therefore classified by some scholars as a "Sonderzeichen" and "Sondersyllabogram" and its relative rarity is emphasized;[22] however, it is also defined as an "innovation" of the Mycenaean Greek scribes.[23] This will be discussed further below, but first, we will survey the attestations of a_2.

    (inizio di parola, in fine di parola e in iato), a_2 espresse anche il suono *a*. D'altra parte, l'evoluzione di **ja* in *ha* e poi in *a* fece si che venisse usato anche *ja* accanto ad a_2."

[17] Lejeune (1956) was not yet convinced of the phonetic value *ha* of a_2: "Rien, non plus, ne prouve qu'elle ait été liée au caractère, aspiré ou non, de la voyelle; l'hypothèse, par exemple, que a_2 noterait, de préférence, *ha* n'est pas démontrée par l'examen des exemples" (Lejeune 1956:48).

[18] Chadwick 1954:9. Lejeune (1956:46): "Le signe 25 est à peu près inconnu à Cnossos. [...] Le signe a, à Pylos, une fréquence nettement supérieure; à Mycènes, la fréquence est du même ordre, semble-t-il, qu'à Pylos." Bartoněk (1957:46) noted: "The most important anomaly requiring explanation is the considerably different frequency of signs 8 and 25 in relationship to the place of occurrence (by far most documents containing sign 25 come from Pylos)."

[19] Bartoněk 1957:54.

[20] Pierini (2014:134): "Alla luce di questo fatto ci si potrebbe chiedere se a_2 non possa essere un tratto arcaico della lingua." On the variation between *a* and a_2, see Judson 2019, and on the usage of a_2 as an additional or extra sign, see Judson 2017:119–120.

[21] Melena 2014:25.

[22] Bartoněk (2003:109): "Der vorauszusetzende mykenische Hauchlaut *h*, der aus dem protogrie-chischen Zischlaut *s* antevokalisch (am Wortanfang) oder intervokalisch (im Wortinneren) entstanden ist, wird besonders in Pylos vor einem nachfolgenden *a* sehr oft durch das Sonder-syllabogram Nr. 25 (A_2=*ha*) bezeichnet; in Knossos benützt man dagegen in solchen Fällen meis-tens das Grundsyllabogram A (Nr. 8)."

[23] Bartoněk (2003:104) classifies a_2- among the "Innovatives Sonderzeichen, die wohl erst nachträg-lich [...] in direktem Zusammenhang mit dem lautlichen Charakter der griechischen Sprache in

Where and how often is sign a_2- attested?

- Pylos: 143 attestations
- Thebes: 24 attestations
- Mycenae: West Houses: 8 attestations
- Knossos: NEP: 5 or 6 attestations[24]
- Knossos: RCT: 2 attestations
- Ayios Vasileios: 2 attestations

Where is the sign a_2- unattested?

- Knossos: MAP (LM IIIB)
- Khania (LM IIIB)
- Pylos: Megaron tablets (LH IIIA)
- Mycenae: Petsas House (LH IIIA2)[25]
- Tiryns (LH IIIB2)
- Midea (LH IIIB2)

It is always dangerous to draw conclusions from missing evidence. That the sign a_2 is unattested in Midea, Tiryns, and Khania may simply be due to the low number of tablets preserved from these places.[26] The absence of a_2 among the Pylos Megaron tablets may also be due to their small number, but they are here singled out from the other Pylos tablets because of their earlier date.[27] However, more importantly, the fact that a_2 is never attested in the very numerous MAP texts at Knossos cannot simply be dismissed as a coincidence of preservation: the many MAP scribes clearly did not use the sign a_2. MAP scribes such as 113

---

das LB-Inventar eingereiht wurden, um spezifische griechische Laute wiederzugeben." Bartoněk 2003:143: "Der Hauchlaut h, der im Mykenischen nur vor Vokal bezeichnet wird (durch das Zeichen A₂ = Nr. 25), scheint kein ursprünglicher urgriechischer Laut gewesen zu sein. Es ist meistens durch die Abschwächung von *s* sowohl am Anfang des Wortes vor Vokal (oder vor *r, l, m, n, w, j*) also auch im Wortinneren zwischen Vokalen entstanden." Bennett 1966:302 noted the following regarding the scribal traditions of Knossos and Pylos: "When the two use different shapes, we may try to distinguish the innovation from the inherited form." See also succinctly Palaima and Sikkenga (1999:604–605) concerning scribal innovations.

[24] The sixth, and uncertain, attestation is KN X 9669; see below for discussion.

[25] Skelton 2006.

[26] From Knossos derive some 4,000 clay tablets/fragments, of which some hundreds from the RCT and the NEP (NEP=514 tablets, according to Driessen 1999:212), but the bulk is from the MAP. From Pylos there are ca. 1,100 documents, from Thebes c. 430, from Mycenae 73, Tiryns 24, Midea 4, Khania 7, Ayios Vassileios with a so far unknown number of tablets. The Pylos Megaron yielded only 16 tablets, and Petsas House in Mycenae 13 tablets.

[27] Skelton 2009.

and 103 write *pa-we-a* and never *pa-we-a$_2$*; scribes 135 and 136 write *ko-ri-ja-do-no* and never *ko-ri-a$_2$-do-no* as it was written on the mainland; and scribe 222 writes *qe-te-a*, and not *qe-te-a$_2$*. This will be analyzed in detail below.

Scribes Who Use the Sign a_2

It is important to investigate whether the use of *a* or *a$_2$*, respectively, may reflect the personal style of certain scribes. The following scribes use the sign *a$_2$*:

- Knossos: "124"[28]
- Knossos: 104, 114[29]
- Pylos: 1, 2, 6, 14, 15, 21, 22, 24, 25, 26, 31, 32, 34, 42, 43, 44, 45, Ci, Cii, Ciii[30]
- Mycenae: 52, 53, 55, 57, 61
- Thebes: 301, 302, 303, 305, 309, 315 and "groupement paléographique γ"[31]
- Ayios Vasileios: scribal hands are not yet identified

Sites, Chronology, and Findspots with the Sign a_2

It is also important to investigate whether the use of *a* and *a$_2$*, respectively, is a matter of chronology. The chronological sequence of the use of the sign *a$_2$* is the following:

- Knossos: RCT (LM IIIA1)[32]

---

[28] Hand 124 and hand "124" were coined as such in Olivier 1967, but are not hands or scribes as the term is applied to other Mycenaean scribes but rather a common denomination for a series of tablets with peculiar features. The denomination has later been discussed and refined in Driessen 1988 and 2000, where further divisions into more than ten groupings and stylus groups were introduced. They are also employed in Firth and Melena 2016a, in Firth and Skelton 2016a, and in *KT⁶*.

[29] The principal works on Knossos scribes are Olivier 1967, now revised in Firth 2000–2001a; 2000–2001b; Firth and Melena 2016b; Firth and Skelton 2016a; Firth and Skelton (2016a:171–172) classify 104 and 114 among the conservative NEP hands.

[30] Palaima 1988. The assignment to Class i, ii, and iii may conceal different Hands.

[31] Aravantinos *et al.* 2005:214.

[32] Driessen 1990:129–130. According to Driessen 1997 and 2000, the oldest surviving Linear B documents at Knossos were preserved in the RCT, dated to the LM IIIA1 period, while the majority of the rest of the archive dates a generation or two later, in early LM IIIA2, although some small groups may date later still (the chronology is summarized in Driessen 1990; 1997; 1999). Olivier (1967:135) already noticed how the more conservative writing styles appear in the RCT and the northern part of the palace. Driessen 1990 followed the same observation and path classifying the RCT scribes among the conservative styles as well as the NEP scribes such as scribes 104 and 120. More progressive styles are found in the West Wing such as scribe 103, 115, and 116. In between, Driessen classifies the centrist styles of for example scribes 114 and 118 (from the NEP)

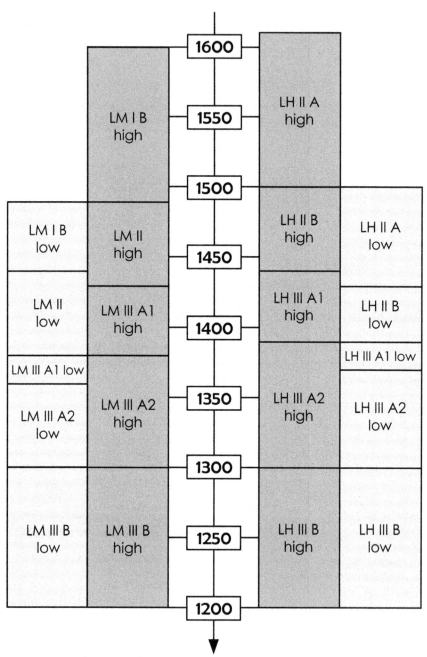

Figure 12.1. An overview of the absolute and relative dates (high and low) relevant here. Based on Shelmerdine 2008 and Firth and Skelton 2016c:219.

- Knossos: NEP: I2, I3 (LM IIIA2)[33]

- Ayios Vasileios: (LH IIIA1–2 early)[34]

- Thebes: Liagas Plot (Wu nodules) (LH IIIB1?)

- Mycenae: House of Oil Merchant, West House, House of Sphinxes (LH IIIB1)

- Mycenae: House of Columns (LH IIIB2)

- Pylos: Archive Complex, Rooms 99, 92, 23, SW Area (LH IIIB2)

- Thebes: Odos Epaminondou, Odos Oidipodos, Odos Pelopidou, Arsenal, Treasury Chamber (LH IIIB2)[35]

The Spatial and Chronological Distribution of a_2

It was noted early on that the sign a_2 occurs most frequently at Pylos, and much more rarely at Knossos. Even before the decipherment, Emmett Bennett observed that a_2 was mainly attested in Pylos.[36] Indeed, nearly all attestations of a_2 come from the mainland palace sites, and this observation has been confirmed by the new finds of tablets from both Mycenae and Thebes, and recently also at Ayios Vasileios, where the sign a_2 is now attested twice. In contrast, a_2 is only attested seven or eight times at Knossos.

The Attestations of a_2 at Knossos

The sign a_2 is attested twice in the RCT:

KN Ai(1) 213   (124-B?/C)[37]
]a_2-ta VIR 2

---

but also scribes 117 and 119 from the east–west corridor (MAP). Thus, his 1990 classification of the scribes does not entirely match the Firth and Skelton's proposed chronological divisions.

[33] Skelton (2008) was the first scholar to apply a phylogenetic analysis to Linear B writing and consequently divided the Knossos archives into three parts, the RCT, the NEP, and the late Knossos archives, and I follow her division in the present paper. See also Firth and Skelton 2016a:162 and Firth and Skelton 2016b:189, who term the three parts "Early Knossian Linear B Style" (RCT), "Middle Knossian Linear B Style" (NEP, Rooms of the Column Bases, Arsenal, and Corridor of the Sword Tablets), and "Late Knossian Linear B Style" (scribes 103 and 117 and most of the tablets found in the West Wing and the East Wing of the palace). In Firth and Skelton 2016c:215 the following dates are given: "Early Knossian Linear B Style" (LM IIIA1), "Middle Knossian Linear B Style" (LM IIIA2), and "Late Knossian Linear B Style" (LM IIIB1).

[34] Aravantinos and Vasilogamvrou 2012. This view was also expressed in Vasilogamvrou 2015.

[35] Aravantinos *et al.* 2001:14.

[36] Bennett 1951:x and 82, believed that sign *25 was only used at Pylos; cf. Bartoněk 1957: n14.

[37] Firth and Melena 2016a:326.

RCT (1)	RCT (2)	RCT (3)	RCT (4)	KN 101	KN 102	KN 103	KN 106	KN 115

KN 116	KN 117	KN 118	KN 120	KN 134	KN 141	KN 104+	KN 128+	KN 201+

KN n.i.	KN n.i.	PY 1	PY 14	PY 15	PY 21	PY 23	PY 26	PY 41

PY 43	PY 2–22	PY 24/5	PY other	MY 51	MY 57	MY 62	MY 52–64	MY n.i.

TH (a)	TH (b)	TH (c)	TH (d)	TH (e)	TI (a)	TI (b)	Z-MY	Z-TI

Figure 12.2. Forms of a_2 from Knossos, Pylos, Mycenae, and Thebes.
Driessen 2000.

KN V(1) 118   (124 stylus 4/C)[38]
  po-ru-da-si-jo , / a_2-ke-te-re 2[
    a_2 over [[a]]

It is important to note that scribe 124 seems to have corrected his first a to a_2 in V(1) 118, as is indicated in the apparatus criticus, which suggests that he knew well the difference between the two signs.[39]

In the NEP, area I3, the sign occurs on D 411, e-ma-a_2-o (*Ἑρμᾱhας, Hermes, theonym) by an unknown scribe. The same name is probably also recorded on X 9669. The cloth word pa-we-a_2 is recorded on the three tablets from the NEP discussed above (Ld[2] 786, 787, 788). The sign a_2 may also be attested in the NEP in the personal name ru-a_2[on B(5) 806.7, written by scribe 104.

---

[38] Firth and Melena 2016a:338; Firth and Skelton 2016a:169.
[39] I thank Peder Flemestad for this observation.

The Attestations of a_2 at Mycenae

The eight attestations of a_2 at Mycenae include the personal names *wa-a_2-ta* in Au 102.7, and *a-ne-a_2* in Fo 101.1 and V 659.6. It is also attested in the nouns *pa-we-a_2* (L 710.2) and *ko-ri-a_2-da-na* (Ge 605.4 and 5).

The Attestations of a_2 at Pylos

At Pylos, the sign a_2 is so abundantly attested that we cannot list all the occurrences here but rather some salient examples. It occurs in personal names such as *a_2-ta* on An 209.2, *a-pi-a_2-ro* /*Amphi-halos*/ on An 192.1, and *au-to-a_2-ta* /*Auto-hātās*/ /*Auto-hāltās*/ on Cn 314.3. The theonym *e-ma-a_2* occurs three times.[40]

It is attested in the geographical designation *o-pi-a_2-ra* /*opi-hala*/ 'coast line/ coastal regions' on An 657.1, and the toponym *wa-a_2-te-pi* on Na 1009 and Mb 1377, which appears in the locative *wa-a_2-te-we* on An 207.9 and Mn 1371.1.[41] The sign a_2 is used in a textile term, mostly attested in the abbreviated form WE in logogram *146, but sometimes spelled out as *we-a_2-no-i* (Fr 1225.2) and *we-a_2-no[* (Un 1322.5).[42] It is also attested in the term *si-a_2-ro*, /*sihalons*/ 'fattened pigs' on Cn 608.1. In adjectival forms, it occurs in *me-zo-a_2* and *me-u-jo-a_2* in the Sh series. Finally, it is frequently attested in the resumptive and/or slightly adversative heading phrase *o-da-a_2* meaning 'thus now' or 'thus in turn'.[43]

The Attestations of a_2 at Thebes

The sign a_2 is attested several times at Thebes in personal names, such as *do-ra-a_2-ja* in the feminine form (Fq 229.12, 254+255.12, 276.7, 277.2, 278.1, 294.3, 311.5, 403.1, by scribe 303) and in the personal name *te-ri-a_2[* on Gp 157.2 (scribe 309). Two other Theban personal names are *ne̹-a_2-ri-da* (Of 39.2, scribe 303?) and *a_2-ta-o* in the genitive form on X 189.7 (scribe 315). Three toponyms use sign a_2: *po-to-a_2-ja-de*, built on **po-to-a_2* /*Ptōihai*/ 'to the region of P',[44] written on Av 104.2 by an unidentified scribe; toponym *a_2-pa-a_2-de* on Wu 94 and toponym *a_3-ki-a_2-ri-ja* /*Aigi-halia*/ (cf. αἰγιαλός 'sea-shore') on Of 25.1, written by scribe 303, who chooses the alternative spelling *a-ki-a_2-ri-ja-de* on Of 35.2. There is also the name of the god Hermes *e-ma-a_2* on Of 31.3 (scribe 303). On sealings in Thebes, there is

---

[40] Tn 316.7 *verso* by Hand 44, Un 219 by Hand 15, and Xn 1357 by Hand 1.

[41] See Pierini 2014. *DMic.*, 397, *s.v. wa-a_2-te-pi*, note 2.

[42] Nosch 2012:335–337. Pierini 2014:122.

[43] Taillardat 1981:34: "Le signe a_2 valant *ha*, *o-da-a_2* se lit nécessairement o- δαhα ou o- δαhα + consonne. Comme le souffle intervocalique *h* repose sur l'affaiblissement soit de la sifflante *s*, soit d'un yod, nous tiendrons pour très vraisemblable que *o-da-a_2* note ὡς-δαhαρ provenant de ὡς-δαy-αρ, c'est-à-dire ὡς δαì ἄρ 'et ainsi' avec δαí coordonnant." But there are several other equally plausible explanations. *DMic.*, 15–16, *s.v.*

[44] Melena 2014:78.

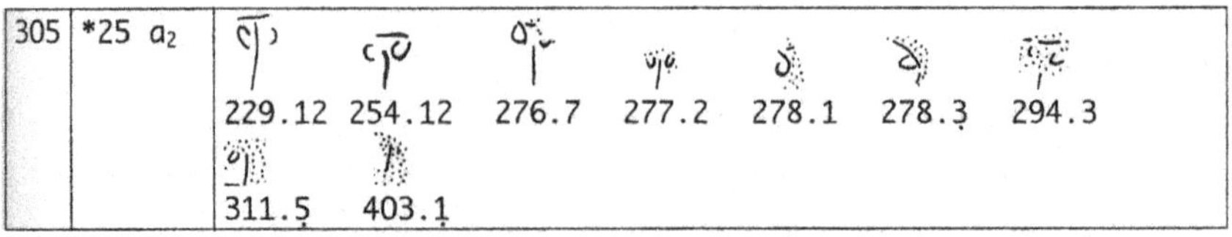

Figure 12.3. Attestations of a_2 at Thebes by scribe 305. From Aravantinos *et al.* 2006:173.

the transaction term *qe-te-a₂* on Wu 51, 65, and 96. Further examples at Thebes include *te-ra-a₂*[on Ug 17 (scribe 302),]*-te-a₂* on Fq 138.4 (scribe 305), *ku-su-a₂*[on Fq 278.3 (scribe 305), and *a₂* is also attested on Ug 424 (scribe 301) and Up 432.[45]

The Attestations of a_2 at Ayios Vasileios

The sign *a₂-* is now also attested at least twice in the new archive at Ayios Vasileios:

X 4   (Sparta Mus. 16341)
.1   e-ni-da̩[
.2   tu-we-a₂ [
.3   ri-za [
     inf. mut.

The excavator Adamantia Vasilogamvrou kindly reminds me that this tablet was found in a Byzantine layer, outside the main settlement area, and thus we cannot be certain of its date. Vasilogamvrou states, however, that sign *25 (*a₂*) also occurs on another unpublished tablet, X 44, in what she plausibly interprets as a male personal name.[46] We must await the full publication in order to assess how frequently this sign occurs in the Linear B texts from Ayios Vasileios.

Alternation of a_2 and Other Signs

Alternation of *a* and a_2 in the Linear B Archives

In our Linear B tablets we may observe a noteworthy alternation between the two signs *a* and *a₂*. This alternation occurs not only between different sites, but, curiously, also within one site and even within one scribal hand. Moreover, as noted above, scribe 124 in the RCT first spells a word with an initial *a* but then erases it

---

[45] Aravantinos *et al.* 2006:3–7.
[46] Personal communication via email from A. Vasilogamvrou, November 12, 2015: "It belongs to what I call the 'main cluster' of documents that we assigned to the LH IIIA1–2 early period, according to the preliminary study of the related pottery."

and changes it to a_2 on KN V(1) 118. In Knossos, as observed above, scribes seemingly only have the choice between a and a_2 in the RCT and NEP phases.

At Pylos, the alternation of a- and a_2 is attested in the adjectives we-a_2-re-jo (Ta 714.1) and we-a-re-ja (Ta 642.1), both tablets being written by Hand 2. Likewise, Hand 21 writes the same personal name as a_2-ne-u-te on Cn 599.2 and a-ne-u-te on Cn 40.7.

The personal name a_2-di-je-u (nominative) in PY An 656.2 might occur in the genitive as a-di-je-wo in Knossos documents D 747[47] and D 5520.[48] The transactional term qe-te-a_2 (PY Un 138, TH Wu 51, 65, 96) is also attested at Knossos as qe-te-a (KN Fp[2] 363.1 by scribe 222 and from E1=Room of the Column Bases).[49]

At Knossos, on MAP tablet As(1) 602.3, a man is called a-ta. The same name is also attested in the nominative form at Pylos on An 39.9 *verso* as a-ta. But at Pylos there is also the aspirated personal name a_2-ta (nominative) on An 209.2.[50] At Thebes, scribe 315 writes a_2-ta-o in the genitive form on X 189. These two male names, a-ta and a_2-ta, are both a-stem masculine forms, and a-ta is possibly to be understood as Ἄνθας, Ἄντας, Ἄρτας, Ἄλτας vel sim.,[51] while a_2-ta is less well explained.[52]

The occupational name a_2-ke-te-re is attested with a_2 at Knossos in the RCT on V(1) 118 and at Pylos as a-ke-te-re on Jn 832.1.

The term tu-we-a is attested in PY Un 267.3,[53] but is spelled tu-we-a_2 at Ayios Vasileios.

Even if RCT and NEP scribes would have the sign a_2 available, they did not always choose to use it. There is man's name (ko-a_2-ta) attested on PY Jn 706.17 by Hand 21. At Knossos, the man's name ko-a-ta is recorded on B 798.8 by scribe 107 from the NEP, and it should be noted that scribe 107 as a NEP scribe would potentially have the option to use a_2, but he did not use it.

---

[47] In Firth 1996–1997:104 the findspot is suggested as H5 (=H6), and in a place that Evans called: "Under blocked doorway of Room N. of Throne"; the scribe is unidentified. I thank Richard Firth for this information.

[48] From Batch C with mainly MAP fragments. See Firth 2000–2001b:345.

[49] Sacconi 2005:433; Pierini 2014:110–112.

[50] Perhaps also attested as a compound name in]-a_2-ta on PY An 172.

[51] DMic., *s.v.* a-ta.

[52] Tom Palaima, per email December 2018, suggests: "If you are looking for a form that might have had aspiration that then disappeared, it would be Ἄλτας > Ἄλτας from the IE root that gives us Latin *salio* and Greek ἅλλομαι 'leap'." I thank him for this clarification.

[53] Bartoněk (1957:54) notes: "But we can scarcely find an adequate sense in the occurrence of sign 8 at the end of the sign group tu-we-a. Here we would much rather expect to find sign 25 at the end, as the other plurals of neuter s-stems [...] have generally this sign for their final letter." The new find at Ayios Vasileios may suggest a sequence of original *θύϝεσα, tu-we-a_2 in LH IIIA, and tu-we-a in LH IIIB Pylos.

Likewise, the word for wool (εἶρος < *werw-os) forms the adjective 'woolen', we-we-e-a /werweheha/, a nominative plural neutral of a stem in –es. It occurs in Knossos on L 178 from the RCT and L 870 from the Area of the Bull Relief in the NEP. The latter tablet, L 870, is tentatively assigned to scribe 114?, and if this identification is correct, it must be noted that scribe 114 writes pa-we-a₂ in the Ld(2) set, also from the NEP. Thus, a₂ was available to the RCT and NEP scribes but they did not always choose to use it in order to indicate the aspiration in this word. At Pylos (Un 853.11), the word for wool might be attested in [? we]-we-e-a₂[by Hand 6.[54]

Alternation of a₂ and ja in the Linear B Archives[55]

As indicated above, the occupational name in the nominative plural form a₂-ke-te-re is attested with a₂ at Knossos in the RCT on V(1) 118, while at Pylos, Hand 2 writes ja-ke-te-re (Mn 11.2) /iakestēres?/ and he writes a-ke-te-re on Jn 832.1. However, it is not certain that these terms indicate the same occupation.[56]

Sometimes, the same scribe alternates between ja and a₂ in his spellings. At Mycenae, on Ge 605, scribe 57 writes ko-ri-ja-da-na in line .3B but ko-ri-a₂-da-na in lines .4B and .5; was he correcting himself? Or did he hear the word differently the second time? Or did he copy this spelling from colleagues?

We also have the form ko-ri-a₂-da-na at Pylos on Un 267.5 by Hand 1, but in Knossos both scribes 135 and 136 of the MAP choose to write ko-ri-ja-da-no in the Ga(1) and Ga(2) sets.

Another example is the personal name te-ri-a₂[on TH Gp 157, and the personal name te-ri-ja on PY Un 443.3.[57]

Alternation of a₂ and je in the Linear B Archives

At Pylos, there is one example of alternation between pi-a₂-ra (Tn 996.2 by stylus Ciii and from room 20) and pi-je-ra₃ (Ta 709.1 by Hand 2 and from the central archives) both denoting phiale-type vessels.[58]

---

[54] I thank Maurizio de Freo for the example and his reminder of the doubts in the apparatus criticus. See Melena 1992–1993:319–320, suggesting instead]pu₂-we-e-a₂[. PTT³ now prefers to conjecture:] pạ-we-e-a₂.

[55] Bartoněk 1957:55: "It is especially the ie. consonant [j] that as an original initial before vowels sometimes resembled in the historical development of the Greek language the original initial or intervocalic [s], both of them being presumably transformed into [h]".

[56] DMic., s.v. a-ke-te: "Igualmente no parece verosímil su consideración como doblete de a₂-ke-te-re / ja-ke-te-re."

[57] A significant observation was made by Vasilis Petrakis, email December 2015: "it seems to me interesting how these ja/a₂ 'alternations' are found only to occur in the environment of liquids, where they theoretically overlap with the range of uses of ra₂ (cf. /lla/ < /lja/, /rra/ < /rja/). Note that ra₂ could also be used for geminate liquids (cf. Melena 2014:66)."

[58] Marazzi 2013:253 notes the vacillation in Mycenaean between e and a in words such as sa-ri-nu-wo vs. se-ri-no-wo (σέλινον) and pi-a₂-ra vs. pi-je-ra (φιάλη) concluding that "si tratta di lessemi derivati da ambiente (sostrato?) non grecofono recipiti variamente sotto il profilo fonologico."

Alternation of a_2 and a_3 in the Linear B Archives

At Pylos, there is one example of alternation between the personal name of a smith a_2-nu-me-no (Jn 389.12 by Hand 2) and a_3-nu-me-no (An 261.3 by Hand 1).[59]

Alternation of a_2 and wa in the Linear B Archives

The name *me-nu-wa* is found in the RCT (Sc 238, V 60, Xd 7702). At Pylos, Hand 1 uses the same spelling in *me-nu-wa* (An 724.2), but two other Pylian Hands, 15 and 21, chose the aspirated and theoretically more archaic version]*me-nu-a₂* (Aq 218.14 by Hand 21),]*ṃẹ-nu-a₂* (Qa 1293 by Hand 15), and *me-nu-a₂* (Qa 1301 by Hand 15). Since the spelling with /w/ represents a glide or semivowel that could only occur after the aspirate (resulting from original intervocalic /s/) had disappeared, this could suggest that psilosis was still an ongoing process in the RCT phase; it may also suggest that the transmission of script between Knossos and Pylos must have occurred in a phase when the aspiration was (partially) still in place, that is, earlier than the RCT, or in the RCT phase during which it is possible that scribes would use both psilotic and aspirated forms.

    This exemplifies the complexity of the process of psilosis, when early Knossos material testifies to the loss of aspiration and change into a /w/, and Hand 1 at Pylos testifies to the same phonetic development, while his colleagues, Hands 15 and 21, maintain the aspiration sign.[60]

Discussion and Conclusion on a_2-

The uniformity of Linear B writing is expressed by several scholars as a kind of Mycenaean *koiné*, especially with regard to the mainland scribal tradition.[61] Despite this uniformity, it has hitherto remained unclear why there is a difference in the use of a_2. Ivo Hajnal and Ernst Risch discuss the few differences in the use of syllabograms in the Linear B archives. They conclude that such differences are due to *spelling rules* and *writing conventions*:

---

[59] According to Bartoněk (1957:56), it is unlikely that these are the same words. Cf. also *DMic.*, s.v. *a₂-nu-me-no*: "No es fonéticamente plausibile que se trate de una variante grafica de *a₃-nu-me-no*." However, Palaima (2020:293) comments on how *iota*-diphthongs do not always have the *iota*-element explicitly represented, cf. *ko-to-i-na* and *ko-to-na*, and *wo-no*. Therefore, a₂ /ha/ may also represent *hai*. There are also the examples of alternation between *a* and *a₃*/*ai* in the Theban toponym spelt by the same scribe 303 *a₃-ki-a₂-ri-ja* on Of 25.1 and *a-ki-a₂-ri-ja-de* on Of 35.2. I thank Tom Palaima for sending me his paper ahead of publication. See also Duhoux 1978:111–112.

[60] Tom Palaima also observes that it is surprising that we do not have the spelling *me-nu-a in the corpus, since the intervocalic /w/ is a non-phonemic glide (email, December 2018).

[61] According to Driessen (2000: nn50 and 57), the term *koiné* was first used by Godart and Olivier in 1975 and later reiterated by Godart, Olivier, and Killen in 1983. The uniformity of the dialect was already emphasized by Chadwick (1954:1).

> Trotz der großen räumlichen, vielleicht auch zeitlichen Distanz [...] ist
> die Sprache aller mykenischer Texte—soweit feststellbar—auffallend
> homogen. Die Unterschiede, welche zwischen den einzelnen Zentren
> festgestellt werden können, sind außerdem zum Teil nur orthogra-
> phischer Natur, also durch die Tradition der Schreibschulen bedingt.[62]

In the linguistic discussions of the sign, a_2 seems to be considered mostly as a
pragmatic choice of rendering the aspiration or not. When a is chosen over a_2, it
is possible that the aspiration may still function to prevent elision of vowels.[63]
Alternatively, some Mycenaean Greeks would pronounce the vowels distinc-
tively and did not need the aspiration to do so. In other words, the alterna-
tion of a and a_2 is perceived as a '*doublet*'[64] or '*doppione*',[65] thus a possible *option*
depending on personal choice, pronunciation, dialect, place, and convention.
Duhoux has discussed the alternation of a and a_2 in terms of *orthographic variants*
in his investigation of the teaching of orthography in Pylos.[66] He observed that
at Pylos, Hands 1, 2, 5,[67] 14, 21, 26, and perhaps 44 use both a and a_2, while scribes
15, 22, 24, 25, 31, 32, 34, 42, 43, and 45 only use a_2. Bartoněk termed it a *habit* or
preference.[68]

Ivo Hajnal and Ernst Risch, however, do propose a *phonetically based theory*
of why a_2- is rare in Crete:

> Andererseits kann die Verwendung bzw. Nichtverwendung eines Sil-
> benzeichens an einem jeweiligen Ort auch lautliche Gründe haben: so
> mag a_2 /ha/ in Knossos so selten sein, da auf Kreta schon früh Psilose
> eingetreten sein könnte (vgl. so etwa pylisches *me-nu-a₂* PY Aq 218.14++

---

[62] Hajnal and Risch 2006:93. However, there is no evidence for scribal schools as institutions, but some scribes display certain similarities in script. Palaima 2011:112-127.

[63] See, for example, Jiménez Delgado 2015:120: "In other cases the aspiration is not graphically rendered, but it does prevent the elision of the preceding vowel."

[64] Lejeune 1976:196. Duhoux 2013:21: "doublets: syllabogrammes pouvant remplacer facultati-vement *un* syllabogramme fondamental et de valeur phonétique plus précise que ce dernier. Nous connaissons actuellement cinq doublets: au (notant /aw/), a_2 (notant /ha/) et a_3 (notant /ay/), tous trois concurrençant le signe fondamental a." Duhoux 2013:31: "Aspiration: /h/. Elle n'est presque jamais notée explicitement. Toutefois, /ha/ peut facultativement être rendu par le doublet a_2-."

[65] Sacconi 2005:433.

[66] Duhoux 1986:149. See also Pierini 2014:110: "variante grafica."

[67] Hand 5 in Duhoux's list no longer occurs among the Pylian scribes in Melena's new electronic version of the tablets. I thank R. Pierini for this observation.

[68] "We may take for granted that with the scribes from the mainland it was habitual to prefer sign 25 to sign 08 in the final position, the same being true also about the medial position (with the exception of compounds)" (Bartoněk 1957:54). In compounds, Bartoněk observed, sign 08 often occurs in the middle position of a word, indicating the compound structure, whereas sign 25 is less used as middle element in compounds; see Bartoněk 1957:50-51.

/*Menuhās*/ vs. kretisches [aber auch pylisches!] *me-nu-wa* KN Sc 238+ /*Menuās*/.[69]

Psilosis is the sound change in which Mycenaean Greek lost the consonantal sound /h/. The Mycenaean spelling variations may have to do with this weakening of /h/ in the initial position as scribes tried to represent in visible speech the words they heard. This weakening may have been stronger and earlier in Crete than on the mainland.[70] The observations in this paper suggest that at Knossos we can observe that the *psilosis* process is underway in the RCT and NEP, and we can date its completion to the phases after the NEP. In LM IIIA2, the aspiration, both initial and intervocalic, is sometimes still rendered graphically in the NEP in Crete and also in LH IIIA2 Ayios Vasileios on the mainland. Thereafter, in Crete, in the MAP documents, either *psilosis* had become generalized and also intervocalic aspiration was no longer recorded, and/or the Knossos scribes chose to abandon the use of the sign a_2.[71] On the continent, aspiration is maintained and this sound change only occurs later, in LH IIIC or in the beginning of the first millennium BCE.

Sign *08 *a* is attested in all archives and stems from Linear A, while sign *25 a_2, instead, is a Mycenaean innovation. In the RCT and NEP, both signs a_2 and *a* are employed; in the MAP at Knossos only sign *08 *a* is in use. At mainland sites, at Pylos, Mycenae, and Thebes, scribes often prefer to use sign *25 a_2 to indicate the aspiration. Sign *08, however, maintains its importance in initial position in the mainland archives, but within a word, the vowel -*a*- is rather expressed through a syllabogram representing a consonant and vowel together. At Knossos, internal -*a*- is used sixteen times (from all phases, RCT, NEP, and MAP); at Pylos there are thirty-five attestations on twenty-two tablets of internal -*a*-. At Mycenae, internal -*a*- is attested only once, and at Thebes, there is so far no attestation of internal -*a*-.

---

[69] Hajnal and Risch 2006:93. Pierini 2014. See also Bartoněk 2003:105: "Die weitgehende Beschränkung von A₂ auf Pylos kann man entweder als eine rein graphische oder als eine mundartliche Differenz erklären (entweder handelt es sich um Einfluss einer anderen Schreiberschule oder um eine hier exklusive Erhaltung des *h* vor *a*)."

[70] See quote above by Hajnal and Risch (2006) and Meissner 2008:514: "Admittedly, the amount of evidence is restricted but we may interpret it as further and powerful evidence for the so-called Knossian psilosis." See also Judson 2017:120.

[71] I thank Maurizio Del Freo and Torsten Meissner for their helpful clarifications about *psilosis*.

The Place and Time of the Origin of Linear B and Its Transmission to Other Mycenaean Centers

In this paper, it has been observed that the distribution of the Linear B sign a_2 with a phonetic value of /*ha*/ is defined both by geography and by chronology. Whereas the alternation a and a_2 is a regular feature in words in LH IIIB Pylos, Thebes, and Mycenae, this alternation only exists in the early phases of the Knossos archive, RCT, and NEP; in the tablets coming from the MAP (the West Wing and East Wing), the scribes exclusively use a. Chronologically a_2 is used in the early Linear B tablets at Knossos of LM IIIA1–2. a_2 is also used on the later mainland Linear B tablets of LH IIIB. But a_2 is not used in the LM IIIB MAP. This suggests an association of writing practices between the early parts of the Knossos archives and the writing tradition of the mainland sites.

Driessen has compared the archival tradition at Pylos and Knossos and suggested that Pylos and the NEP shared a similar practice in having a central location for the gathering of various documents, whereas in the MAP, documents were stored in a number of places within the palace.[72] Another similarity between the Pylos archive and the NEP is their location at the entrance of the palace.[73] Skelton emphasizes common features among the LH IIIA Megaron tablets of Pylos, the RCT tablets, and Linear A.[74] Although the objectives and conclusions in these studies differ, they do seem to support the model of a specific Knossian tradition, which is different from the mainland palace traditions. It seems we should consider the mainland sites initially sharing a scribal tradition with Knossos, which subsequently followed another path.

In Khania (dated LM IIIB1) there is thus far no attestation of a_2 and this would corroborate the present hypothesis that the sign had gone out of use in the latest phase of Knossos. There are, however, so far very few tablets preserved from Khania; therefore this observation is clearly not conclusive.[75]

Concerning inscribed stirrup jars (ISJ), the current corpus numbers ca. 160 items[76] and the ISJs have been found in many places in the Aegean: Attica, the Argolid, Boeotia, Crete, and Thessaly. The inscriptions are normally very short, ranging from one sign to three words. The a_2 sign is not attested on any ISJ. This may be a coincidence of preservation or due to the relatively small number of signs attested on ISJs. However, it is important to keep in mind that these ISJs

---

[72] Driessen 1999:221.

[73] Driessen 1997:121.

[74] Skelton 2009.

[75] Hallager *et al.* 1992. These tablets are very similar to the MAP, especially to scribe 115 in the MAP (Olivier 1993; 1996; Palaima 1993, but not of the same hand).

[76] Sacconi 2012; Van Alfen 1996–1997:252 and 2000:235.

come from Crete and are dated to LM IIIB1 and LM IIIB2.[77] Thus, crucially, they date to a period when the sign a_2 was no longer used in Knossos. We should therefore not expect to find a_2 in these Cretan-made ISJs according to the findings of this paper.

It should also be noticed that a_2- is so far never attested in location E1=Room of the Column Bases (Fh series by scribe 141 and Fp[2] set by scribe 222). Indeed, scribe 222 writes the transactional term *qe-te-a* on Fp(2) 363.1, and not *qe-te-a₂* as it is attested on the mainland.[78] This may be significant since the date of E1 is debated. Driessen suggested that E1-tablets may be dated earlier than the other tablets.[79] This was discussed by Firth.[80] The absence of a_2 in this location could represent a random preservation (there are only twenty-seven tablets associated with this place), or could reflect personal choices of scribes 141 and 222;[81] the absence could perhaps suggest associating this find place with the MAP.

The observations made in this paper provide yet another argument for dissociating the NEP and RCT chronologically from the later phase of the bulk of the Knossos archive (MAP).

If the LM IIIA2 date of the NEP is accepted, this paper suggests that the transmission of scribal traditions between Knossos and the mainland took place at the latest in the final phase of the NEP. It also remains possible that the transmission took place earlier. Moreover, we can now assume that a_2 was used simultaneously on Crete (NEP) and Ayios Vasileios in LM/LH IIIA2. In the following phase, LH/LM IIIB, the two traditions part ways, conforming to the statement by Bennett in 1966 that:

> At some time, probably remote and certainly before the destruction of the first of the two palaces, there must have been a single scribal tradition from which our scribes equally derive, and in which those common prototypes were present. When the two use different shapes, we may try to distinguish the innovation from the inherited form.[82]

Bennett analyzed the differences of signs in Knossos and Pylos; regrettably, his analysis was only a qualitative study which did not quantify the attestations, and he thus overlooked the unequal distribution of sign *25. However, his observations and models of how Linear B was transmitted from one palace to another are still relevant for the present study:

---

[77] Van Alfen 1996–1997; 2008; Hallager 1987; Day and Haskell 1995; Haskell *et al.* 2011.
[78] TH Wu 51, 65, 96; PY Un 138.1.
[79] Driessen 1990.
[80] Firth 1996–1997:13, 22, 95–96; 2000–2001a:203–205.
[81] On scribe 222, see Firth and Melena 2016c.
[82] Bennett 1966:302.

Any indication of the isolation of one palace from the other must be found in the presence or predominance of a significant innovation, and in the significant rarity or absence of inherited traits. If these conditions are found in both sets of inscriptions we may assume that both palaces were destroyed some generations later than the breaking of communications between them. If they are found in only one, we may assume it survived some generations after the break, and that the other fell while still in communication with the other Mycenaeans.[83]

Bennett cautiously hypothesized that, "Pylos, alone or together with other Mycenaean palaces, had for several generations been cut off from communications with Knossos";[84] and he proposed that either "the differences in the script of Pylos and Knossos give some evidence of a period of several generations of little communication or exchange of personnel before their nearly contemporary destructions," or that "Knossos, while still in fairly close communication with the rest of the Mycenaean world, was cut off several generations before the same disaster was seen at Pylos."[85]

I believe that Bennett was right to emphasize the levels of contacts between scribes at the different palaces, and that the degree of contact may be reflected in the Linear B tablets and the choices scribes make about many matters, including our main focus in this paper, how to represent spoken words through written symbols.

The Development of Linear B

In 1976, Lejeune made an important observation concerning the early history of Linear B and how it was spread. Lejeune reviewed the "fundamental signs" and the "accessory signs." His accessory signs, to which a_2 belongs, are optional and also of a supplementary nature.[86] Lejeune argued that, since accessory signs appear in similar number and distribution on all sites, they must have been inserted/adapted at a single moment and place since they occur consistently in several archives and do not appear as local adaptations.[87] Concerning a_2, we

---

[83] Bennett 1966:307.

[84] Bennett 1966:308.

[85] Bennett 1966:309.

[86] Lejeune 1976:196: "On a, d'autre part, par surcroît, des *signes accessoires* ayant le double caractère d'être *facultatifs* dans leur emploi (puisque le répertoire fondamental pouvait suffire à tout noter) et d'être *inorganiques*, c'est-à-dire de ne pas constituer des séries cohérentes" (italics by Lejeune). See also Duhoux 2013:21, and Judson 2017:119–120.

[87] Lejeune 1976:196: "Rien ne nous indique que les signes accessoires aient été ajoutés après coup, au cours du temps, au répertoire fondamental. [...] On considérera ici, faute de présomptions contraires, que le syllabaire B a été constitué en une seule fois (événement B¹ du §1) tel que, plus

have observed here that it belongs to these initial accessory signs invented in the time called B¹ by Lejeune (see below), and that it rapidly spread and was adapted by scribes in all palaces, but then ceased to be used in LM IIIB Knossos.

Lejeune focused on the proto-Mycenaean stage, the period between the invention of Linear B (the moment he termed B¹) and the moment of the preservation of the tablets (B²) and he assumed that they were separated by a considerable period of time.[88]

Lejeune's assumption is challenged by Firth and Skelton and their use of phylogenetic and *r8s* analyses, since they conclude that a rather short period of time passed between the invention of Linear B in LH/LM II (that they date 1452 BCE in high chronology, or 1419 BCE in low chronology) and the earliest tablets.[89]

In recent years, in their three-part seminal study, Firth and Skelton have combined phylogenetic analysis, findspot analysis, and *r8s* analysis. They come to conclusions that touch upon the date of the Linear B archives and their mutual relationship, and it is, therefore, worthwhile to summarize their results briefly.[90] Firth and Skelton compare the Knossos scribes and their chronologies with the mainland scribal traditions, and, in my view, they have gathered some of the most stimulating new data.[91] They observe how the phylogenetic tree separates after the Arsenal and Corridor of the Sword Tablets.[92] Despite the fact that Firth and Skelton classify scribes 104 and 114 among the conservative NEP hands,[93] the phylogenetic analysis and the *r8s* analysis date scribe 104 to between 1305 and 1296 BCE, which is the transition between the latest phases of LM IIIA2 and the earliest phase of LM IIIB.[94] Thus, scribe 104 is the latest of the Middle Knossian NEP scribes.[95]

---

tard, il nous apparaît; tel, faut-il ajouter, qu'il nous apparaît partout, car les signes accessoires, eux aussi, sont identiques sur tous les sites." As an example, *pu₂* occurs as an alternative to *pu* in Knossos, Pylos, Thebes, and Mycenae, and in Knossos it is attested in the RCT, the NEP, and the MAP. See Palaima and Sikkenga 1999:600–605.

[88] Lejeune 1976:194.
[89] Firth and Skelton 2016c:223–225.
[90] Firth and Skelton 2016a; 2016b; 2016c.
[91] Firth and Skelton 2016a:176: "It is worthwhile considering briefly why the phylogenetic analysis consistently places the Late Knossian Linear B hands on a separate *branch* to the hands from the mainland." They identify features, which are common between hand 304 from Thebes and hands 41 and 43 from Pylos but not shared by any Late Knossian hands. They observed how the phylogenetic tree separates late Knossian scribal hands from the hands in Pylos and Thebes.
[92] Firth and Skelton 2016a:176.
[93] Firth and Skelton 2016a:172.
[94] Firth and Skelton 2016c:221–222.
[95] Firth and Skelton 2016c:224.

Firth and Skelton date the emergence of a mainland *koiné* to the early phase of LH IIIB, according to the *r8s* analysis.[96] In Pylos, the earliest evidence of Linear B is by Hand 13, according to Skelton;[97] Hand 13, however, has no attestation of a_2.

From Models to Palaeography

Many scholars of Aegean scripts have discussed the time and place of the transmission of Linear A to Linear B.[98] This paper cannot propose a solution to the place of invention of Linear B.[99] I do, however, propose that the time of transmission of the script between Crete and the mainland took place in LM IIIA1 or earlier, potentially starting in the early phase of the RCT LM IIIA1 and continuing in the NEP LM IIIA2 phase. It would mean that the mainland scribal activity was well established and functioning before LH IIIA2 at the latest. The transmission probably took place from Crete to the mainland in an early phase and the mainland palaces preserved this early graphical tradition consistently. Palaima discusses the time in which the mainland centers would need a script, and suggests LH II.[100] Theoretically, it is also possible to argue that Linear B was invented in the Shaft Grave period on the mainland and immediately transmitted to Crete where we find it in the RCT and the NEP; it then developed on its

---

[96] Firth and Skelton 2016c:225.

[97] The *r8s* analysis in Firth and Skelton 2016c:223–224 suggests the following: "While Skelton (2008) proposes that Pylos Hand 13 represents some of the earliest known examples of Linear B, the *r8s* analysis suggests that Pylos Hand 13 in fact comes less than a generation after the invention of Linear B. The high dates place Pylos Hand 13 at 1435, or seventeen years after the invention of Linear B; the low dates place Pylos Hand 13 only ten years after the invention of Linear B, in 1409. The high dates place Pylos Hand 13 at the very beginning of LH IIIA1, while the low dates place it in LH II. For comparison, the *r8s* analysis places the writing style of the earliest RCT scribe 37 years (high dates) or 25 years (low dates) after the invention of Linear B. The r8s analysis suggests that the writing style of RCT Hand 124-S is 15 to 20 years later than that of Pylos Hand 13. The implication is that Linear B spread throughout the Mycenaean world quite rapidly." Please note that here the low date (LH II) is set higher than the high date (LH IIIA1) due to statistical uncertainty of the method; it does not change the overall conclusion, though.

[98] See, for example, Pope 1962–1963; Palaima 1988b.

[99] See Palaima 1988b:275 for references to the various theories of where Linear B was created.

[100] Palaima 1988b:339: "we must, I think, focus on the mainland centres and try to determine when their activities would have reached the point when their administrations could no longer function or function effectively without the assistance of written records. We shall then have an historical *terminus ante quem* for the use of writing by the Mycenaeans. My own answer is LH II (late and post-LM IB)." Palaima makes the introduction of Linear B script coincide with the construction of tholos tombs and the first phases of monumental architecture, and furthermore notes: "I would then see the Mycenaeans adapting the Linear A script and borrowing Minoan administrative techniques in LH II." The finds in summer 2015 of a rich grave at Pylos with many Minoan prestige objects puts new emphasis on the early power structures in Pylos and the close ties with the Minoans; see Stocker and Davis 2016.

own in Crete until the MAP, while it remained highly conservative and stable on the mainland. This is, however, a more complex explanatory model.[101]

The crucial issue is how far the disappearance of a_2 in the MAP testifies to earlier *psilosis* in Crete, or whether MAP scribes, motivated by phonological changes or not, chose to delete the sign from their repertoire? Does a_2, present or absent, inform us about language or about script developments?

Do these observations simply add to the bulk of theories and models of the transmission of script systems? Can they also be applied concretely to the palaeography of Linear B? I believe they can. The observations in this paper enable us to make new hypotheses concerning the organization of the Knossos archive and assignment of find places.

There is, for example, a record of sheep under the divinity Hermes from the NEP.[102]

KN D 411 + 511   (-/I3)

di-ko-to / e-ma-a₂-o OVIS^f 60 WE 30[

> -ma- and perhaps e- over erasure. Perhaps to be read as *e-ma-a₂*
> o OVIS^f. Perhaps traces after 30[.

Tablet X 9669 from Knossos has no identified scribe or findspot:

KN X 9669   (-/-)

.a   ]-ja̱[
.b   ]ṣi̱-jo / e̱-ma-a₂[
   .a   ]ṛa̱-ja̱[?

The observations made in this paper suggest that the presence of a_2 in Knossos would entail that X 9669 should be assigned to a find place in either NEP or RCT. This spelling, and this divinity, is not attested in the MAP documents. But it appears three times at Pylos as *e-ma-a₂*.[103] While one may argue that there could be a greater tendency for conservatism in a theonym than in a human personal name, a MAP scribe would probably spell the divinity's name **e-ma-a* as the sign a_2- would have been unavailable to him. The tablet may therefore be reclassified as Xd (fragments from the RCT) or as **Xg (fragments from the NEP). Thus, the

---

[101] See also Palaima 1988b:334 for the very scanty evidence of script use in the Shaft Grave period. Palaima concluded in 1988b:339: "I cannot see any way of choosing, or even favouring, Crete or the mainland as the place of origin of Linear B." Palaima 1988b:340–341, with further discussion, and Palaima 2003:192. Bennet (2007:189), however, suggested that, "It is possible that the bureaucratic techniques familiar from Linear B were first developed at Knossos in the second half of the fifteenth century BC and only then introduced on the mainland."

[102] Nosch 2000.

[103] Tn 316.7 *verso* by Hand 44; Un 219.8 by Hand 15; Nn 1357.1 by Hand 1.

identification of a specific graphical feature may enable us to assign tablets to a plausible findspot and, perhaps, scribe.

It could be argued that also the use of the logogram TELA+*PA* follows a similar chronological and spatial pattern. The logogram is attested in the early Knossos phases: in the RCT (L 178) and in the NEP (Ld[2] 786, 787). On two other tablets, scribe and findspot are unknown (KN L 7387) and on KN L 523 from F8 (MAP) the writing of TELA+*PA* is very uncertain.

KN L 7387   (‑)

                ]TELA³ + *PA* 1

KN L 523   (‑/F8)

.a   ]qe-re-jo   [

.b   ]ku-da-ra-ro TELAˣ + *PA*

Thus, logogram TELA+*PA* in Knossos was used in the RCT and in the NEP, but not with certainty in the MAP. It may therefore be more plausible to read TELA+*TE* on L 523 since TELA+*PA* seems no longer to be used in the MAP/F8. I would also tentatively suggest assigning L 7387 to a findspot in the RCT or NEP.

Instead of TELA+*PA*, it seems that MAP scribes ceased to use this logogram and embraced a new graphical convention of spelling the textile term out, *pa-we-a*, which is the most well attested way of recording this type of textile in the MAP. Before adopting this new convention, however, Knossos RCT and NEP scribes must have shared the use of the logogram TELA+*PA* with their Pylos colleagues because we find the logogram TELA+*PA* in the LH IIIA Megaron texts PY La 623, 626, and 630. Alternatively, was it the other way around? Did the Pylians export the logogram to RCT and NEP scribes at Knossos? According to Firth and Skelton, phylogenetic analysis suggests that the Megaron tablets are currently the oldest attestations of Linear B.[104] TELA+*PA* was perhaps a Mycenaean innovation made to represent a Greek clothing item or textile, the *pharos*.

Conclusion

When comparing Linear A and Linear B, we can observe that only forty-two of 172 Linear B logograms have a Linear A parallel,[105] and thus approximately three-quarters, or 75 percent, of the Linear A logograms were eliminated in Linear B.[106]

---

[104] Skelton 2008; Firth and Skelton 2016c.

[105] Duhoux 1985:20, 22.

[106] Palaima 1988b:323. With regard to the interest in textiles that I share with José Melena, it is worth mentioning that many of the maintained logograms denote textiles. Nosch 2016.

For the syllabograms, the situation is the opposite: only fourteen new Linear B phonograms were created for the purpose of the Greek language.[107] These new (e.g., without a Linear A parallel) syllabograms include the signs **12 so*, **14 do*, **15 mo*, **32 qo*, **36 po*, **41 wo*, **62 pte*, **64*, **75 we*, and **72 pe*.[108] They are all attested throughout the Knossos archive, from the RCT, to the NEP, and to the MAP. As we have seen, a_2 counts among the new signs and does not have a Linear A parallel, but in Crete it is only used for a brief period of time in the RCT and NEP, and then abandoned in the MAP.[109]

The phylogenetic analyses suggest some absolute dates for the use of sign a_2. The RCT is dated to 1415 to 1359 (high chronology) or 1394 to 1354 (low chronology). The latest documented use of a_2 in Crete is by scribe 104, whose tablets are dated by phylogenetics to ca. 1300 (both for high and low chronology).[110] At Pylos, Hand 32 (dated 1258 BCE), Hand 21 (dated 1214 BCE), and scribe 1 (dated 1200) write a_2.

The present contribution, therefore, suggests seeing the sign a_2 as an isograph, a distinguishing feature of the early phase of the Knossos administration but abandoned in the late Knossos phase. This isograph was continued and maintained, perhaps even strengthened, in the mainland palace scribal traditions.

Bibliography

Aravantinos, V. L., L. Godart, and A. Sacconi, eds. 2001. *Thèbes: Fouilles de la Cadmée* I: *Les tablettes en linéaire B de la Odos Pelopidou. Edition et commentaire.* Pisa.

———, eds. 2002. *Thèbes: Fouilles de la Cadmée* III: *Corpus des documents d'archives en linéaire B de Thèbes (1–433).* Pisa.

———. 2006. "Commentaires aux nouveaux textes insérés dans le corpus de Thèbes." In *Die neuen Linear B-Texte aus Theben: Ihr Aufschlusswert für die mykenische Sprache und Kultur. Akten des internationalen Forschungskollo-*

---

[107] According to Duhoux (1987), only 19 of 88 Linear B phonograms have no parallel in Linear A. Palaima (1988b:322) narrows the number down to 16 phonograms (although they are attested logogrammatically in Linear A). This number has been lowered to 14, since a Linear A prototype for Linear B sign **48 nwa* was studied on a Minoan bronze axe head by Emmett L. Bennett, Jr., and Tom Palaima, most likely illicitly removed from a site of Crete (Palaima 2003:195) and the sign is now attested in Linear A on SY Za 4. Moreover, Linear B sign **43 ai* is possibly identified on a bronze cauldron from Shaft Grave IV, Mycenae, as A?/B **43*, see Palaima 2003:195.

[108] Driessen 2000:145.

[109] According to Palaima (1988b:322) signs **18*, **19*, **63*, **64*, **83*, **84* were used by Greek scribes to write Minoan names.

[110] Firth and Skelton 2016c:221–222.

quiums an der Österreichischen Akademie der Wissenschaften, 5.-6. Dezember 2002, ed. S. Deger-Jalkotzy and O. Panagl, 1–9. Veröffentlichungen der Mykenischen Kommission 23, Mykenische Studien 19. Vienna.

Aravantinos, V. L., M. Del Freo, L. Godart, and A. Sacconi, eds. 2005. *Thèbes: Fouilles de la Cadmée IV: Les textes de Thèbes (1-433). Translitération et tableaux des scribes*. Pisa.

Aravantinos, V. L., and A. Vasilogamvrou. 2012. "The First Linear B Documents from Ayios Vasileios (Laconia)." In Carlier *et al.* 2012:41–54.

Bartoněk, A. 1957. "The Linear B Signs 8-A and 25-A: Remarks on the Problem of 'Mycenaean' Doublets." *Sborník prací Filozofické fakulty brněnské univerzity. A, Řada jazykovědná* 6, issue A5:45–62.

———. 2003. *Handbuch des mykenischen Griechisch*. Heidelberg.

Bennet, J. 2007. "The Aegean Bronze Age." In *The Cambridge Economic History of the Greco-Roman World*, ed. W. Scheidel, I. Morris, and R. Saller, 175–210. Cambridge.

———. 2008. "Now You See It; Now You Don't! The Disappearance of the Linear A Script on Crete." In *The Disappearance of Writing Systems. Perspectives on Literacy and Communication*, ed. J. Baines, J. Bennet, and S. D. Houston, 1–29. London.

Bennett, E. 1951. *The Pylos Tablets, a Preliminary Transcription*. Princeton.

———. 1966. "Some Local Differences in the Linear B Script." *Hesperia* 35:295–309.

Carlier, P., Ch. De Lamberterie, M. Egetmeyer, N. Guilleux, Fr. Rougemont, and J. Zurbach, eds. 2012. *Études mycéniennes 2010. Actes du XIIIᵉ Colloque international sur les textes égéens, Sèvres, Paris, Nanterre, 20-23 septembre 2010*. Pisa.

Chadwick, J. 1954. "Mycenaean: A Newly Discovered Greek Dialect." *Transactions of the Philological Society* 53:1–17.

Day, P. M., and H. W. Haskell. 1995. "Transport Stirrup Jars from Thebes as Evidence of Trade in Late Bronze Age Greece." In *Trade and Production in Premonetary Greece*, ed. C. Gillis, C. Risberg, and B. Sjöberg, 87–109. SIMA Pocket-Book 134. Jonsered.

Driessen, J. 1990. *An Early Destruction in the Mycenaean Palace at Knossos: A New Interpretation of the Excavation Field-Notes of the South-East Area of the West Wing*. Acta Archaeologica Lovaniensia, Monograph 2. Leuven.

———. 1997. "Le palais de Cnossos au MR II–III: combien de destructions?" In *La Crète mycénienne*, ed. J. Driessen and A. Farnoux, 113–134. *Bulletin de Correspondance Hellénique*, supplément 30. Athens.

———. 1999. "The Northern Entrance Passage at Knossos. Some Preliminary Observations on Its Potential Role as 'Central Archives'." In *Floreant Studia Mycenaea. Akten des X. Internationalen Mykenologischen Colloquiums in*

Salzburg vom 1.-5. Mai 1995. Band II, ed. S. Deger-Jalkotzy, S. Hiller, and O. Panagl, 205–226. Vienna.

———. 2000. *The Scribes of the Room of the Chariot Tablets at Knossos. Interdisciplinary Approach to the Study of a Linear B Deposit.* Suplementos a *Minos* 15. Salamanca.

Duhoux, Y. 1978. "Une analyse linguistique du linéaire A." In *Études minoennes* I: *Le linéaire A*, ed. Y. Duhoux, 65–129. Bibliothèque des Cahiers de l'Institut de Linguistique de Louvain 14. Louvain.

———. 1985. "Mycénien et écriture grecque." In *Linear B: A 1984 Survey*, ed. A. Morpurgo-Davies and Y. Duhoux, 7–74. Bibliothèque des Cahiers de l'Institut de Linguistique de Louvain 26. Louvain-la-Neuve.

———. 1986. "The Teaching of Orthography in Mycenaean Pylos." *Kadmos* 25: 147–154.

———. 1987. "Linéaire B crétois et continental: Éléments de comparaison." In *Tractata Mycenaea. Proceedings of the Eighth International Colloquium on Mycenaean Studies, Held in Ohrid (15-20 September 1985)*, ed. P. Ilievski and L. Crepajac, 105–128. Skopje.

———. 2013. *Le mycénien*. Paradeigmata. Recueil d'Inscriptions Grecques Dialectales I. Nancy.

Firth, R. J. 1996-1997. "The Find-Places of the Tablets from the Palace of Knossos." *Minos* 31–32:7–122.

———. 2000–2001a. "A Review of the Find-places of the Linear B Tablets from the Palace of Knossos." *Minos* 35–36:63–290.

———. 2000–2001b. "The Knossos Tablets: Genesis of the 5000-Series." *Minos* 35–36:315–355.

Firth, R. J., and J. L. Melena. 2016a. "Re-visiting the Scribes of the Room of the Chariot Tablets at Knossos." *Minos* 39:319–351.

———. 2016b. "Re-visiting the Scribes of Knossos: The Principal Hands 101–123, 125–141." *Minos* 39:249–318.

———. 2016c. "The Secondary Scribes of Knossos." *Minos* 39:353–378.

Firth, R. J., and C. Skelton. 2016a. "A Study of the Scribal Hands of Knossos Based on Phylogenetic Methods and Find-Place Analysis. Part I: The Phylogenetic Analysis." *Minos* 39:159–188.

———. 2016b. "A Study of the Scribal Hands of Knossos Based on Phylogenetic Methods and Find-Place Analysis. Part II: Early, Middle and Late Writing Styles and the Dating of the Knossos Tablets." *Minos* 39:189–213.

———. 2016c. "A Study of the Scribal Hands of Knossos Based on Phylogenetic Methods and Find-Place Analysis. Part III: Dating the Knossos Tablets Using Phylogenetic Methods." *Minos* 39:215–228.

Godart, L., and J.-P. Olivier. 1975. "Nouveaux textes en linéaire B de Tirynthe." In *Tiryns: Forschungen und Berichte VIII. Deutsches Archäologisches Institut Athen*, 37–53. Mainz.

Godart, L., J.-P. Olivier, and J. T. Killen. 1983. "Eighteen More Fragments of Linear B Tablets from Tiryns." *Archäologischer Anzeiger*: 413–426.

Hajnal, I., and E. Risch. 2006. *Grammatik des mykenischen Griechisch*, Fassung 1.1: Herbst 2006, Internet publication: http://sprawi.uibk.ac.at/content/grammatik-des-mykenischen-griechisch-0.

Hallager, E. 1987. "The Inscribed Stirrup Jars: Implications for Late Minoan IIIB Crete." *American Journal of Archaeology* 91:171–190.

Hallager, E., M. Vlasaki, and B. P. Hallager. 1992. "New Linear B Tablets from Khania." *Kadmos* 31:61–87.

Haskell, H. W., R. E. Jones, P. M. Day, and J. T. Killen. 2011. *Transport Stirrup Jars of the Bronze Age Aegean and East Mediterranean*. Philadelphia.

Jiménez Delgado, J. M. 2015. "The Etymology of Myc. *ku-na-ke-ta-i*, Ion.-Att. κυνηγέτης, and Myc. *ra-wa-ke-ta*, Dor. λᾱγέτᾱς." *Glotta* 91:116–128.

Judson, A. P. 2017. "Processes of Script Adaptation and Creation in Linear B: The Evidence of the 'Extra' Signs." In *Understanding Relations between Scripts: The Aegean Writing Systems*, ed. P. M. Steele, 111–126. Oxford.

———. 2019. "Orthographic Variation as Evidence for the Development of the Linear B Writing System." In *Writing System: Past, Present (... and Future?)*, ed. T. Joyce and R. Crellin, 179–197. *Written Language and Literacy*, special issue 22.

Killen, J. T. 1966. "The Knossos Lc (Cloth) Tablets (Summary)." *Bulletin of the Institute of Classical Studies* 13:105–111.

———. 1974. "A Problem in the Knossos Lc(l) (Cloth) Tablets." *Hermathena* 118: 82–90.

———. 1979. "The Knossos Ld(1) Tablets." In *Colloquium Mycenaeum. The Sixth International Congress on the Aegean and Mycenaean Texts at Chaumont sur Neuchâtel, September 7-13 1975*, ed. E. Risch and H. Mühlestein, 151–182. Geneva.

Lejeune, M. 1956. "Observations sur le signe 43 (AI)." In *Études mycéniennes. Actes du colloque international sur les textes mycéniens (Gif-sur-Yvette, 3-7 avril 1956)*, ed. M. Lejeune, 39–50. Paris.

———. 1976. "Pré-mycénien et proto-mycénien." *Bulletin de la société de linguistique* 71:193–206.

Marazzi, M. 2013. *Scrittura, epigrafia e grammatica greco-micenea*. Rome.

Melena, J. L. 1975. *Studies on Some Mycenaean Inscriptions from Knossos Dealing with Textiles*. Suplementos a *Minos* 5. Salamanca.

———. 1992–1993. "244 Joins and Quasi-Joins of Fragments in the Linear B Tablets from Pylos." *Minos* 27–28:307–324.

———. 1996–1997. "40 Joins and Quasi-Joins of Fragments in the Linear B Tablets from Pylos." *Minos* 31–32:159–170.

———. 2014. "Mycenaean Writing." In *A Companion to Linear B: Mycenaean Greek Texts and Their World*, vol. 3, ed. Y. Duhoux and A. Morpurgo Davies, 1–186. Bibliothèque des Cahiers de l'Institut de Linguistique de Louvain 133. Louvain-la-Neuve.

Meriggi, P. 1955. "I testi micenei in trascrizione." *Athenaeum* 33:64–92.

Meissner, T. 2008. "Notes on Mycenaean Spelling." In *Colloquium Romanum. Atti del XII colloquio internazionale di micenologia, Roma, 20–25 febbraio 2006*, vol. 2, ed. A. Sacconi, M. Del Freo, L. Godart, and M. Negri, 507–519. Pasiphae 2. Pisa and Rome.

Milani, C. 1958. "I segni a, a₂, a₃ (=ai?)." *Aevum* 32, issue 2:101–138.

Nosch, M-L. 2000. "Schafe unter Potnia und Hermes in Knossos." In *Österreichische Forschungen zur Ägäischen Bronzezeit 1998*, ed. F. Blakholmer, 211–215. Wiener Forschungen zur Archäologie 3. Vienna.

———. 2012. "The Textile Logograms in the Linear B Tablets: *Les Idéogrammes Archéologiques des Textiles*." In Carlier *et al.* 2012:303–344.

———. 2016. "What's in a Name? What's in a Sign? Writing Wool, Scripting Shirts, Lettering Linen, Wording Wool, Phrasing Pants, Typing Tunics." In *TOTh Workshop 2013, The Danish National Research Foundation's Centre for Textile Research, University of Copenhagen: Verbal and Non-verbal Representation in Terminology*, ed. S. Lervad, P. Flemestad, L. Weilgaard Christensen, 91–113. Copenhagen.

Olivier, J.-P. 1967. *Les scribes de Cnossos. Essai de classement des archives d'un palais mycénien*. Rome.

———. 1993. "KN 115 = KH 115. Un même scribe à Knossos et à la Canée au MR IIIB: Du soupçon à la certitude." *Bulletin de Correspondance Hellénique* 117:19–33.

———. 1996. "KN 115 et KH 115: Rectification." *Bulletin de Correspondance Hellénique* 120:823.

Palaima, T. G. 1988a. *The Scribes of Pylos*. Rome.

———. 1988b. "The Development of the Mycenaean Writing System." In *Texts, Tablets and Scribes. Studies in Mycenaean Epigraphy and Economy offered to Emmett L. Bennett, Jr.*, ed. J.-P. Olivier and T. G. Palaima, 269–342. *Minos* Suppl. 10. Salamanca.

———. 1993. "Ten Reasons Why KH 115 ≠ KN 115." *Minos* 27–28:261–281.

———. 2003. "The Inscribed Bronze 'Kessel' from Shaft Grave IV and Cretan Heirlooms of the Bronze Age Artist Named 'Aigeus' *vel sim.* in the Mycenaean Palatial Period." In *BRICIAKA. A Tribute to W. C. Brice*, ed. Y. Duhoux, 187–201. Cretan Studies 9. Amsterdam.

———. 2011. "Scribes, Scribal Hands and Palaeography." In *A Companion to Linear B Texts and Their World*, vol. 2, ed. Y. Duhoux and A. Morpurgo Davies, 33–136. Bibliothèque des Cahiers de l'Institut de Linguistique de Louvain 127. Louvain-la-Neuve.

———. 2020. "Iklaina Traganes *a-pu₂* and Αἰπύ." In *ΚΥΔΑΛΙΜΟΣ. Τιμητικός Τόμος για τον Καθηγητή Γεώργιο Στυλ. Κορρέ*, vol. 2, ed. M. Cosmo-poulos, A. Hassiakou, G. Hatzi, P. Kalogerakou, H. Kountouri, Y. Lolos, E. Peppa-Papaioannou, L. Platon, and G. Stathopoulos, 385–397. *AURA* Supplement 4. Athens.

Palaima, T. G., and E. Sikkenga. 1999. "Linear A > Linear B." In *MELETEMATA. Studies in Aegean Archaeology Presented to Malcolm H. Wiener As He Enters His 65th Year*, ed. P. P. Betancourt, V. Karageorghis, R. Laffineur, and W.-D. Niemeier, 599–608. *Aegaeum* 20. Liège.

Pierini, R. 2014. "Ricerche sul segno 25 del sillabario miceneo." In *Donum Mycenologicum: Mycenaean Studies in Honour of Francisco Aura Jorro*, ed. A. Bernabé, and E. R. Luján, 105–138. BCILL 131. Louvain-La-Neuve.

Pope, M. 1962–1963. "The Date of Linear B." *Kretika Chronika* 15:310–319.

Sacconi, A. 2005. "Il significato der termini *qe-te-jo, qe-te-o, qe-te-a, qe-te-a₂* nei documenti in lineare B." *Rendiconti (Accademia nazionale dei Lincei. Classe di scienze morali, storiche e filologiche)*, serie 9, vol. 16:421–438.

———. 2012. "Il supplemento al corpus delle iscrizioni vascolari in lineare B." In Carlier *et al.* 2012:123–142.

Shelmerdine, C. 2008. "Background, Sources and Methods." In *The Cambridge Companion to the Aegean Bronze Age*, ed. C. Shelmerdine, 1–18. Cambridge.

Shelton, K. 2006. "A New Linear B Tablet from Petsas House, Mycenae." *Minos* 37–38:387–396.

Skelton, C. 2008. "Method of Using Phylogenetic Systematics to Reconstruct the History of the Linear B Script." *Archaeometry* 50.1:158–176.

———. 2009. "Re-Examining the Pylos Megaron Tablets." *Kadmos* 48:107–123.

Stocker, S. R., and J. L. Davis. 2016. "The Lord of the Gold Rings: The Griffin Warrior of Pylos." *Hesperia* 85.4:627–655.

Taillardat, J. 1981. "Homère, *K 408*, et mycénien *o-da-a₂*." *Revue de philologie, de littérature et d'historie anciennes* 55:33–35.

Van Alfen, P. G. 1996–97. "The LM IIIB Inscribed Stirrup-Jars as Links in an Administrative Chain." *Minos* 31–32:251–274.

————. 2008. "The Linear B Inscribed Vases." In *A Companion to Linear B: Mycenaean Greek Texts and Their World*, vol. 1, ed. Y. Duhoux and A. Morpurgo Davies, 235–242. Bibliothèque des Cahiers de Linguistique Louvain 120. Louvain-la-Neuve.

Vasilogamvrou, A. 2015. "The West Stoa Archive at Ayios Vasileios: Archaeological Context, Chronology and Preliminary Study of the Documents." Lecture given at *Aegean Scripts. 14th International Congress on Aegean Scripts, Copenhagen, 2–5 September 2015* (unpublished).

13

pa-ki-ja-ne, pa-ki-ja-na,
and *pa-ki-ja-ni-ja*

Thomas Palaima

Program in Aegean Scripts and Prehistory
University of Texas at Austin
tpalaima@austin.utexas.edu

In a little hilltop village, they gambled for my clothes
I bargained for salvation an' they gave me a lethal dose
I offered up my innocence and got repaid with scorn
"Come in," she said, "I'll give you shelter from the storm"
—Bob Dylan[1]

Abstract

In honor of the rigorous reasoning used by José L. Melena in his scholarly writing, I here continue my investigations of how key word units in the Linear B texts have been interpreted through time and why we have come to have, in many cases, mistaken notions of their meanings. Here we will look at how different forms of the toponym identified correctly as the chief sanctuary district associated with the Palace of Nestor at Pylos (*pa-ki-ja-ne, pa-ki-ja-na,* and *pa-ki-ja-ni-ja*) have been (mis?)interpreted and used in discussions of Mycenaean geography, state formation, regional administration, economy, society, religion, and ritual practices and in relationship to the later historical Greek lexicon. As Melena knows, it is best to know what we do *not* know.[2]

---

[1]   Bob Dylan, "Shelter from the Storm" (copyright © 1974 by Ram's Horn Music; renewed 2002 by Ram's Horn Music). In memory, José, of Jimmy LaFave performing this at our request in the Cactus Café at the University of Texas at Austin sometime in mid-October to early November 1999.

[2]   It will be seen that herein I have put what José Melena elsewhere (personal email 12/02/2015) has called my characteristically "exaggerated adjectives" to accurate use in describing his virtues as a scholar and as a human being. I thank Maurizio del Freo and Vassilis Petrakis for helpful comments on several points in the penultimate draft of this paper.

I propose leaving open how we are to "read" in Greek the clearly pre-Greek *pa-ki-ja-ne* / *pa-ki-ja-na* / *pa-ki-ja-ni-ja*, given that we do not have any sure means to identify the root from which it is formed. Proposed connections with the Greek verbal root *sphag-* ('slit the throat', 'sacrifice through slaughter') are not compelling, nor are connections with the historical island of *Sphakteria* as derived from *sphag-*.

pa-ki-ja-ne / *pa-ki-ja-na* / *pa-ki-ja-ni-ja* are likely from a different root than *sa-pa-ka-te-ri-ja* in the Knossos texts. For *sa-pa-ka-te-ri-ja* a connection with *sphag-* ('slit the throat', 'sacrifice through slaughter') is tenable.

The root for *pa-ki-ja-ne* / *pa-ki-ja-na* / *pa-ki-ja-ni-ja* that I tentatively put forward is the root of ὁ σφάκος, the 'sage apple' or *salvia pomifera* or Cretan sage, because of the prevalence and economic and cultural importance of this shrub in Mycenaean palatial Messenia and by analogy with other phytonymic toponyms attested in Linear B times like **ti-mi-to a-ko*, [*ku*]-*pa-ri-so*, *pi-*82*, and **ne-do-wo*.

Keywords

Linear B, *pa-ki-ja-ne*, Sphakteria, *sphag-*, sanctuary

Part 1. Historical Homage to José Melena

It is hard to do justice in honoring a scholar like José Luis Melena. In the very title of this Festschrift, our editorial triumvirate uses a coining *ta-u-ro-qo-ro* *ταυροπόλος to approximate with less violent connotations his nickname *el matador* (literally ταυροσφάγος)[3] arising from his unique status as a commanding, elegant, and noble scholarly presence among the most notable scholars in the seven decades that Linear B has had the attention of serious students of ancient scripts, languages, and material culture. In recognition of his diverse and singular contributions to the field of Mycenology and to the broader fields of Aegean prehistory, the history of the Greek language, and the study of writing systems that have preserved the stages of their developments for us, we might add as epithets πολύτροπος, πολύτεχνος, πολύμνηστος (in the active *and* passive senses), πολυμήχανος, χαλκέντερος (à la Didymus), χαριδώτης (like Dionysos to his legion of followers), and τριφίλατος (with a pun on the meaning of the prefix as an intensifier and as it might be derived from the tricephalic editorship of this volume).

For over twice as long as Odysseus was away from Ithaca, I have had the benefit of relying upon José Melena's keen intellect, wide-ranging knowledge,

---

[3] Our original title, *ta-u-ro-qo-no*, literally 'bull-slayer', alluded both to the tradition of bull-fighting and to Theseus (Mycenaean *te-se-u*) who was a (*mi-no-*)*ta-u-ro-qo-no* in a labyrinth like the one on the *verso* of Cn 1287 as seen on our cover. We changed the title at the request of a contributor. It now emphasizes Melena's major role in tending attentively to the scholarly needs of the many bulls, and bovines, in the china shop of Mycenology.

remarkable ingenuity, incomparable versatility, uncompromising honesty, cooperative generosity, sound judgment, patient advice, and unwavering dedication to the life of the mind and to the nurturing of the human spirit. His work ethic exceeds that of anyone I know in the academic and public intellectual areas in which I have worked. As a scholar he practices humility and conveys a sense of satisfaction. His genius puts him in a class by himself.

We know José Melena as a master of epigraphy, palaeography, linguistics, textual explication, and the study of human beings in their physical world and how they function as social creatures now and over three millennia ago. If a time machine were to place the polymath Eratosthenes alongside José, Eratosthenes would acknowledge that he himself was rightly nicknamed '*bēta*'.

My first contact with José Melena was over forty years ago, the result of a small Forum note[4] I submitted, as my first foray into scholarship, to the monthly bibliographical (and, at that time, more) newsletter *Nestor* that my mentor Emmett L. Bennett, Jr. had brought into being and then monthly put together and distributed to interested scholars the old-fashioned way, via the postal service. I submitted it just before heading to Greece to study the Pylos tablets in the National Archaeological Museum (October 1979–April 1980) for my Ph.D. dissertation. I was responding to an earlier Forum submission by José Melena.[5] In particular, I was weighing the likelihood that the partially preserved second and third signs of the fragmentary painted inscription in question could be read to provide us with another secure, according to then-existing evidence, instance of the use of a sign with a dummy vowel at the end of a word ending in -κς, in this case *ka-ru-ka.

I dimly remembered this as being a bit of young and impertinent foolishness that our *ta-u-ro-qo-ro*, as he moved into his prime, took in stride. But rereading it now, I see that I held to making palaeographical observations pro and con that formed an *argumentum* in the literal sense of 'shedding light on a topic' and not in the sense that James Boswell uses when he describes Samuel Johnson as 'arguing for victory'. I adopted this manner of writing, from which I have deviated in the last forty-two years only rarely and slightly, yet nonetheless to my regret, following the examples of Bennett and Melena, both of whom deserve to be called true 'gentlemen', καλοὶ κἀγαθοί, in the fullest positive meaning of the phrase.

Since then, it has been my privilege to work alongside José, metaphorically and physically, at times cooperating in the editing of articles and book reviews in *Minos*, at other times being entrusted with reading through and commenting on drafts of his precisely reasoned *opuscula* and his magisterial *opera*, the three

---

4   Palaima 1979.
5   Melena 1979.

most recent major works being (1) the magisterial *KT⁶*,[6] all of the readings in which I checked for INSTAP Academic Press as a cooperative practicum together with graduate students Cassandra Donnelly and Caolán Mac An Aircinn, at the Program in Aegean Scripts and Prehistory (PASP); (2) his definitive overview of Mycenaean writing, commissioned by Yves Duhoux and the late Anna Morpurgo Davies;[7] and (3) his definitive transcription of the Linear B tablets from Pylos that supersedes the two recent competing editions that were largely based upon Melena's work in progress.[8] He has read many of my own papers in draft and offered comments that have brought me back from error or led me to deeper and more sophisticated thinking. I will be forever in his debt—and Jean-Pierre Olivier's—for arranging with lightning speed to publish the Emmett L. Bennett, Jr. Festschrift in the Suplementos a *Minos* series, when intractable conditions concerning the contents of the volume unexpectedly developed with the editors of the originally intended series.[9]

One of the highlights of working alongside Emmett Bennett and José Melena in person was our discovery of "contiguities" (leaf-shaped Linear B clay tablets, forming a set relating to a specific subject, that clearly nested in a group one with another) in the Pylos Sh series in the National Archaeological Museum in Athens on December 4, 1989, when Erik Hallager was also present.[10] A bit later, during the Secondo Congresso Internazionale di Micenologia, José helped me in concocting and then publishing a Mycenaean limerick:[11]

1. te-qa-jo , a-pu *pa* ka-ru-to-jo
2. pu-ro-de , pe-re , *DE* ta-u-ro-jo
3. ta-ra-sa , ta-ra-ku-ja
4. na-u-qe , qa-ra-du-ja
5. i-ke-to , me-ta po-ro-wi-to-jo

Our spoof was so good in its poetics and in its scholarly commentary that it has been cited in a prominent scholarly journal as genuine proof that Linear B was used to write poetry: "le seul poème de l'épigraphie mycénienne,"[12] in and of itself not an impossibility.

Another memorable moment was observing José masterfully employ Socrates' maieutic method in a graduate seminar at PASP in fall 1999 and switch

---

[6] Melena 2019.
[7] Melena 2014.
[8] Melena 2021.
[9] Olivier and Palaima 1988. I still remember Olivier saying to me when I called him from Rome: "We shall go to the third peninsula!" He meant Spain.
[10] Palaima 1996:379–396, especially 379, 391–392 and n1. See also Melena 2021:ix.
[11] Palaima and Melena 1992:2501–2502.
[12] Sergent 1994:370n29.

Figure 13.1. Model of Archives Complex (AC) at Pylos built by José L. Melena at PASP 1999 (or 2000?). Clay tablet label giving name of creator and date of work: *me-re-na, we-ko* 2000. Photo: Thomas Palaima and Garrett Bruner, January 5, 2019.

Figure 13.2. Model of Archives Complex at Pylos built by José L. Melena at PASP 1999 (or 2000?). Entrance to Palace of Nestor with AC at left. Photo: Thomas Palaima and Garrett Bruner.

Figure 13.3. Model of Archives Complex, entrance to Palace of Nestor with AC at left with doors and upper room visible. Photo: Thomas Palaima and Garrett Bruner.

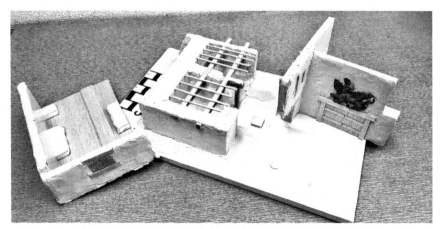

Figure 13.4. Model of Archives Complex, components removed to reveal interior of the AC and the cm. scale. Photo: Thomas Palaima and Garrett Bruner.

Figure 13.5. Model of Archives Complex. Photo: Thomas Palaima and Garrett Bruner.

from linguistic analytical thinking to artistic creativity, producing with materials from the bargain art supply store Hobby Lobby a three-dimensional model of the entrance and Archives Complex of the Palace of Nestor, complete with removable roof. It is still preserved in PASP (figs. 13.1–13.5) and dated in Linear B by the creator as his work (*we-ko*) from or anticipating the year 2000.[13]

I have witnessed José Melena conduct himself with honor many times over the years in situations of considerable diplomatic and personal duress—when

---

[13] The model and the clay tablet indicating the year *might* date from May 2000, when José Melena was also in Austin.

he was out in true storms, what Dylan elsewhere calls "the cruel rain and the wind,"[14] without any shelter—in a manner worthy of the full sense of the adjective ἀγαθός. The principle *nihil nisi bonum et de viventibus* dictates that I not give any particular examples.

I will note here, however, that on April 2, 2003, I received an email with the subject heading *declaration de guerre*. This was eleven days after the president of the United States, citing specious pretexts and inventing and invoking the morally and strategically unsound principle of "preemptive warfare," had ordered the combined military forces in Operation Iraqi Freedom to attack the country of Iraq. Many of us could see that this "purveyance of force," as Martin Luther King would have called it, would cause terrible unjustifiable harm to innocent people and death, destruction, and political destabilization over many years. I had written public commentaries speaking out for restraint and peace, and in this José Melena joined me by letting me voice his own opinions freely and extensively.[15]

Therefore, I thought at first that the email of April 2, 2003, with the subject heading *declaration de guerre*, would contain comments on my public political writing in opposition to the Iraq War. It turned out to be a statement declaring war on me as a scholar for ideas I had expressed in standard scholarly venues that adhered to the scholarly courtesies observed by the editors of and contributors to the publications in which they appeared.[16] In one case, I wrote with considerable reluctance in response to a specific request from the editors of a scholarly journal that I express my viewpoint on the scholarly matters under discussion.[17] To this day, this email letter stands out as an extraordinary aberration from scholarly norms. Unfortunately it is not atypical of other declarations and actions José Melena had to deal with in various high-level positions he has held during his career of service to our field. The letter of April 2, 2003, and the unilateral "war" it declared became even harder to comprehend when a former student and close friend and scholarly collaborator of mine, Col. Ted Westhusing, committed suicide in Iraq on June 5, 2005.[18] José Melena supported me in my resolve to maintain *l'esprit de Gif* and a polite disposition throughout this one-sided *guerre*, which has never been rescinded or suspended. He is still the supreme advocate and most conspicuous practitioner of this spirit inspired by the guiding principles of the United Nations after World War II.

---

14 Bob Dylan, "Percy's Song" (copyright © 1964, 1966 by Warner Bros. Inc.; renewed 1992, 1994 by Special Rider Music).

15 Palaima 2001. The quotation in the title is of a reasoned statement of José L. Melena.

16 Palaima 2002 and Palaima 2003a.

17 Palaima 2003b.

18 Palaima 2007.

Part 2. One More Vocabulary Problem in the History of Mycenaean Textual Studies

In miceneo la sibilante i.e. */s/ mostra vari esiti: a contatto con i suoni occlusivi si conserva come /s/; all'inizio di parola davanti a vocale o davanti a /w/ e in posizione intervocalica si trasforma in un suono aspirato /ʰ/; a contatto con le sonanti, infine, da luogo a suoni geminati.

In lineare B sono presenti notazioni particolari di /s/: (a) di norma nei contesti /sC/ la sibilante non è notata graficamente (p.es. *pa-ka-na* /pʰasgana/ 'spade' (: φάσγανον); fa eccezione la notazione cnossia *sa-pa-ka-te-ri-ja* /spʰaktēria/ 'animali da sacrificio' vs. *pa-ki-ja-ne* /Spʰagiānes/ a Pilo); (b) /-s/ finale non è mai notata graficamente (p.es. *wa-na-ka* /wanaks/, *qo-o* /gʷōns/ (acc. pl.) 'buoi').

José Luis García Ramón (2016:218)

Notation of /s/
The orthographic rule according to which /s/ before consonant is not written, either in syllabic coda (*ti-ri-po-di-ko* Τριποδίσκος) or word-initially (e.g. *pe-ma* σπέρμα), is broken:

A) In names:

> *i-su-ku-wo-do-to* MN KN Fh 348.1 (Hand 141) /Iskʰuʷodotos/.

>]*sa-ka-ri-jo* MN KN V(7) 1523.3 (Hand 101) /(I)skʰaliʲos/ cf. ἀνίσχαλος, ἴξαλος.

B) In contextually supported words:

> *e-sa-pa-ke-me̦.[-na* KN L 7375 (= 508bis).a, L(9) 7401.a (Hand 213?): cloth description, perhaps /espargmena/ 'swaddling clothes' cf. σπάργανα (J. T. KILLEN *per litteras* and *Documents²*, 546) or less likely /espʰagmena/, cf. σφάζω, but in what sense?

> A dubious form *sa-pa* KN L 693.2 (Hand 103) could in theory be interpreted as a metal 'wedge' /spʰān/ followed by a small quantity of 50 g but see below §17.3.4.2.9 for an etymological difficulty and an alternative interpretation.

> *sa-pa-ka-te-ri-ja* KN C(2) 941.B (Hand 112), X 9191.a: livestock description /spʰaktēriʲa/ 'suitable for slaughtering', cf. σφάζω.

> *si-ki-ro* KN U 8210.1 (along with *DIPTE* on line .2) /skirros/ 'gypsum' used for treating parchments?

José L. Melena (2014:104, §17.3.4.2.3)

Here I continue to investigate how we have come historically to commonly accepted interpretations of particular word units in our Linear B texts that influence how we reconstruct the Mycenaean world. I have done something similar with **ti-mi-to a-ko,*[19] *o-ze-to,*[20] *ka-zo-de,*[21] **a-pu₂,*[22] and *ko-re-te,*[23] and, of course, *wa-na-ka* and *qa-si-re-u.*[24] In this case, I will discuss clearly related terms that have long bothered me in regard to how they are used in discussions of Mycenaean geography, state formation, regional administration, economy, society, religion, and ritual practices and in relationship to the later historical Greek lexicon: *pa-ki-ja-ne, pa-ki-ja-na,* and *pa-ki-ja-ni-ja.*

My discussion will also, I hope, make clear the danger of interpreting the Linear B documents by following strands between lexical items occurring in different archaeological and administrative contexts and within different sets of tablets by different scribal hands, without examining each occurrence independently in its peculiar record-keeping environment and without continuing to recognize as hypothetical interpretations originally put forward as such.

Michael Ventris first presented the tentative evidence for the decipherment of Linear B during a BBC broadcast of July 1, 1952. Since then, in standard treatments of how the Linear B script represents Greek words and of the state of the Greek language in the Mycenaean palatial period, the related forms *pa-ki-ja-ne* (clearly a nominative plural masculine consonant stem noun in -ες), *pa-ki-ja-na* (a nominative singular feminine α-stem noun ending in -ᾱνᾱ and potentially other ambiguous case forms) and *pa-ki-ja-ni-ja* (a nominative singular feminine α-stem noun in -ιᾱ and, of course, potentially other case forms as tolerated by Mycenaean "spelling rules") have been interpreted (see citations from García Ramón and Melena above) as related to the later Greek verbal root σφαγ-. σφαγ- has no identifiable cognates outside of Greek and therefore is considered a possible pre-Greek root that may also be seen in the word used for sword in the Linear B texts: φάσγανον reconstructed "as φασγ-/σφαγ-."[25]

---

[19] Palaima 2000. **ti-mi-to a-ko* = *Τιρμίνθων Ἄγκος.

[20] Palaima 2014:85: "*o-ze-to* is from the same root (see historical Gk. ζέω) as *ze-so-me-no* and the second element of the compound *a-re-pa-zo-o* and the phrase is to be interpreted (p. 87) as either (1) aorist ō(s) *dzesto* (for the type of aorist, compare εὗκτο, δέκτο, and γέντο) 'thus he boiled, seethed,' or (2) athematic present ō(s) *dzestoi* 'thus he is boiling, seething'."

[21] Palaima 2020a:127: "*ka-zo-de* should be interpreted as **kalkh-yonde*, from the loan word *kalkhā* (historical Greek κάλχη) used both for the murex, the marine mollusk, and for the purple dye which is extracted from it. The late adjectival formation *kalkhion* is used for the purple dye. A metathesized form of this word, identical then in its stem to *khalk-os*, is attested."

[22] Palaima 2020b.

[23] Palaima forthcoming.

[24] Palaima 2016; 2006; 1995.

[25] Furnée 1972:300; *EDG*, 1426–1427, *s.v.* σφάζω; 1556, *s.v.* φάσγανον; Chantraine 2009:1036–1037, *s.v.* σφάζω. See most recently the characteristically comprehensive and carefully reasoned treat-

In 1953, Ventris and Chadwick discussed the term in a critical part of their fuller argument in support of the decipherment.[26] In trying to convince a skeptical scholarly readership that Ventris's values produced sound results, the showstopper was the list of Cretan place names that could be read in the Knossos texts in tablets related by contents. Emmett L. Bennett, Jr., who was decently reserved in discussing the decipherment of Linear B, in fact once told me that "the Knossos place names were the Rosetta Stone." Indeed, Ventris and Chadwick presented six cases of related terms in the Knossos texts that formed part of Kober's triplets of (1) toponym in noun form, (2) masculine or neuter adjective in -ιος, and (3) feminine singular or neuter plural adjective in -ίᾱ or -ια. Having some corroboration from mainland texts was important, so Ventris and Chadwick continued:

> Apart from *Pu-ro* Πύλος and *Pa-ki-ja-* Σφαγία?, the Pylos place-names (recurring as a group on the Tablets An07–09, 12, 14, 19, Cn02–07, 09–15, Jn09, Kn01, Ma01–19, On01, Vn01–04) appear to refer to local villages whose classical names are unknown. But several of them reflect Greek vocabulary.[27]

What should be noticed here is that Ventris and Chadwick did not deal with the full forms (particularly the noun suffixation) of the plural ethnonym (*pa-ki-ja-ne*), the singular toponyms (*pa-ki-ja-na* and *pa-ki-ja-ni-ja*), and the toponymic adjectives (*pa-ki-ja-ni-jo/-ja*). The question mark that signaled their own doubt about this identification persisted ten years later in the caution used by Anna Morpurgo in her masterful first lexicon of Mycenaean Greek[28] interpreting *pa-ki-ja-na*, among other now-discarded options, as a "topon[ymum] in -ānā exiens" and for *pa-ki-ja-ne* (*s. pa-ki-ja-pi*): "quod ad formam attinet, stirps in -n- exiens videtur: intell. fortasse -ānes, -ānas; gr. Σφαγία conferri potest, sed v. *Docs.* p. 143."

If we follow Morpurgo Davies's cautionary instruction and turn to *Docs²*, 143 in the unchanged main text of the 1956 edition we read:

> We were at first inclined to associate *Pa-ki-ja-* with Σφαγία, a known name of the island of Sphakteria. Two considerations, however, have caused us to question this: the Mycenaean name appears to be alternatively *Pa-ki-ja-na*, *Pa-ki-ja-ni-ja* (fem. *a*-stem?) or *Pa-ki-ja-ne* (= -ānes,

---

ment of Mycenaean terms that might be connected with the root σφαγ- in Petrakis 2021:346–354 *et passim*, who points out: "Tom Palaima has, on numerous occasions, been exceptionally explicit in putting forward the intriguing rendering of the name as 'the place of (ritual animal) slaughter', although he recently questioned his own interpretation" (Petrakis 2021:350 and n30).

[26] Ventris and Chadwick 1953:89–90.
[27] Ventris and Chadwick 1953:90.
[28] Morpurgo Davies 1963:227–228. As it persists in John Bennet's geographical studies (see note 29).

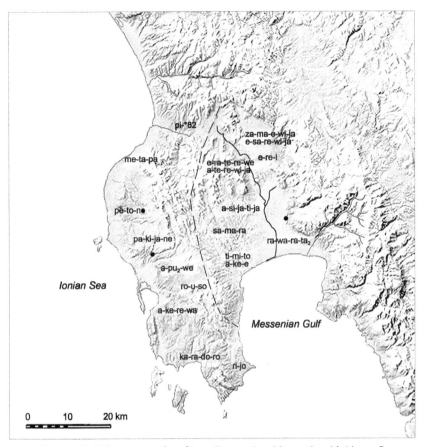

Figure 13.6. The geography of Late Bronze Age Messenia with Linear B toponyms placed in their most likely locations. After figure 4 in Del Freo 2016:639, here reproduced with kind permission of the author.

plural), neither of which corresponds closely with any classical form of the name; and Webster has pointed out that it is an important place and that the amount of land it possesses seems too large for that available on Sphakteria.

We now know that the likely location of the district identified by this complex of forms most likely has nothing to do with the island with the historical name Sphakteria.[29]

---

[29] Bennet (2011:152) identifies it as the fifth of nine second-order districts in the Hither Province. It takes the place of the main center Pylos (= *pu-ro*), which is closely associated geographically, administratively, and ceremonially with *pa-ki-ja-ne*. Bennett cautiously reads it as "possibly Σφαγιᾶνες." Regarding the history of scholarship on correlating the 250 place names attested in the Pylos texts with archaeological sites and areas, see the admirably clear and controlled

We also acknowledge that our source for the alternative name (Σφαγία) given to the island is late (second century CE) and that in the later lexicographical and geographical tradition Σφαγία[30] may itself be the result of a rationalizing folk-etymologizing of what was once a pre-Greek toponym and ethnonym with endings that are typical of pre-Greek.

As is frequently the case in the history of Mycenological scholarship, an attractive original proposal precluded seeking and considering viable alternatives. In fact, Hesychius preserves a gloss §2840[31] σφάκια· τῆς ἀμπέλου τὰ κλήματα ("the branches of the grape vine"). This would provide a suitable root for a phytonymic ethnonym or toponym and one referring to an important agricultural resource in the Mycenaean palatial period. This would be analogous to *ti-mi-to a-ko and *tirminthos < τέρμινθος *Pistacia terebinthus* and the widely accepted Pylian place name [*ku*]-*pa-ris-so*[32] κυπάρισσος = *Cupressus sempervirens* = the cypress tree and cypress wood. See also pi-*82, which, according to Melena (personal communication), means 'Pinewood' (/pitus/ 'Aleppo pine tree' collective /pitu-a/ > pitwa > piswa. There is also ὁ σφάκος, the "sage apple,"or *Salvia pomifera,* or Cretan sage, which grows naturally on low and rocky hills (0–800 m in altitude) in Crete and Greece, preferring strong sunshine and dry, sandy soil: §2841 σφάκος· χόρτος, ὃν τὰ κτήνη ἐσθίει, "a plant, which the cattle eat." Gall wasps produce edible galls on this hardy shrub that were harvested and made into an edible delicacy for human beings.[33]

In addition, Stephanus of Byzantium citing a verse of Lycophron (third century BCE) gives us the following discussion of a toponym Σφήκεια (< Sp^{h}ākeia), πόλις Εὐβοίας. οὕτω δὲ καὶ Κύπρος ἐκαλεῖτο. τὸ ἐθνικὸν Σφῆκες. Σφήκειαν δὲ καὶ Κεράστειαν τὴν Κύπρον, "Sphākeia is a *polis* in Euboea. Thus even Cyprus used to be called. The ethnic is Sphākes. Sphākeia and Kerasteia Cyprus." The *Etymologicum Magnum* gives the same information in more detail. See also Hesychius §2884: Σφήκεια· ἡ Κύπρος τὸ πρότερον.

I have here in transliteration changed to an etymological long *alpha* the *eta* that is used in historical spellings in order to highlight that σφήξ, σφηκός comes from long *alpha* and is compared by Beekes (*EDG, s.v.*) to similar pre-Greek

synthetic treatment by Del Freo (2016:634–643). See p. 639 and figure 4 (here reproduced with Del Freo's kind permission as our fig. 13.6) for his hypothetical map of the provinces and districts of the kingdom of Pylos.

30 Stephanus of Byzantium, *s.v.* Σφακτήρια cites Pausanias as identifying the island with this toponym and Favorinus as the source for the island being called by the alternative place name Σφαγία. The other tradition recorded by Stephanus is that Sphakteria was the place name of a border site between Elis and Messene so named because it is where the Heracleidae concluded treaties attended by animal sacrifices.

31 Hansen 2005:391. All glosses given with identifying numbers are from Hansen 2005.

32 Sainer 1976:44; *Docs*², 416.

33 Plutarch, *Moralia* 662E cites Eupolis: βοσκόμεθ' ὕλης ἀπὸ παντοδαπῆς ... κύτισον τ' ἠδὲ σφάκον εὐώδη.

words in -*ks*[34] like μύρμηξ 'ant' and σκώληξ 'earth worm'. μύρμηξ may be related to the famous toponym and ethnonym discussed in Stephanus of Byzantium: Μυρμιδονία, χώρα τῶν Μυρμιδόνων· οὕτως γὰρ ἡ Αἴγινα ἐκλήθη, "Myrmidonia, the territory of the Myrmidons. For Aegina has been thus [i.e., by this name] called." I mention this information because if we are dealing with clearly pre-Greek ethnics and toponyms in -*ānes* and -*ānā*, we should not have been so quick to "Hellenize"—notice I do not say Indo-Europeanize—the root of *pa-ki-ja-na* and *pa-ki-ja-ne* as connected to the verbal root *sphag-*.

The original reconstructions of *pa-ki-ja-ne, pa-ki-ja-na,* and *pa-ki-ja-ni-ja* linking them to the later Greek root *sphag-* for 'ritual slaughter via throat slitting' were only tentatively put forward. The identification began to be used without any question mark when we established that the region identified as *pa-ki-ja-ne/pa-ki-ja-na/pa-ki-ja-ni-ja* contained many sanctuaries where blood sacrifices *could* have taken place.[35] This was further reinforced when it was proposed to read the key text PY Tn 316 as perhaps recording human sacrifice.[36]

This identification almost defies logic. If regions with developed sanctuaries where sacrificial slaughter could take place were named for the ritual acts that took place there, we would expect toponyms based on the σφαγ-, θῡ-, or φον- roots[37] to be reasonably frequent (as, for example, personal names in *qo-no* and later Greek -φόνος, -φατης, -φοντης[38]) and, if named after the cults had been established, to show, at least in part, Greek naming patterns. They are not and do not.

Further complicating the interpretation here are three other noun forms that have been brought to bear: *pa-ke-te-re, pa-ke-te-ri-[*, and *sa-pa-ka-te-ri-ja*. From Pylos on PY Vn 46.6 and Vn 879.4, it is clear now from context that we are dealing with building materials, probably for ships,[39] interpreted reasonably as 'dowels', i.e., *pāktēres* from the root of πήγνῡμι. These have nothing to do with the root *sphag-* or with ritual practices or animal sacrifice. From Mycenae, the evidence is complicated by the fact that on (1) tablet Ue 611.3 and on (2) inscribed nodule Wt 506, we have respectively (1) an entry of 30 *pa-ke-te-re* among other entries of vases of different kinds and (2) the word *pa-ke-te-ri-ja* alongside the word *ka-na-to*.

Again induced by what we might call *sphag*-mania, the terms at Mycenae have also been connected with the verbal root of σφάζω and interpreted as vase

---

[34] On the pre-Greek origins of words ending in -*ks* in the historical Greek lexicon, see Palaima 2016:141–142 with references.

[35] See Gérard-Rousseau 1968:167–169 for an assessment of the evidence for the locality identified as *pa-ki-ja-ne* (and related terms) and establishing its important religious associations.

[36] Best surveyed and studied now in Notti, Negri, and Facchetti 2015:127–133.

[37] See Petrakis 2021:345–348 for words relating to animal sacrifice.

[38] Von Kamptz 1982:224, 226.

[39] Palaima 1991:295–301 and Palaima and Hocker 1990–1991.

receptacles for blood sacrifice involving ritual slaughter. But they have been interpreted in other reasonable ways: (1) *pa-ke-te-re* as the plural of an agent noun (cf. κρᾱτήρ) standing for a container in which things can be 'fixed' or 'congealed' (later Greek πηκτικος refers to 'curdled' or 'coagulated' liquids like γάλα), namely cheese from milk (Euripides, *Cyclops* line 190) and cream-cheese (Theocritus 11.20) and even wax and salt from brine (all items attested in our Linear B texts);[40] and (2) *pa-ke-te-ri-ja*[41] referring to such containers in the neuter plural by means of a noun form using the 'tool' suffix, ultimately related to the agent noun: *πηκτήριον, plur. *πηκτήρια. Nothing in the archaeological contexts of the tablets and nodules or the textual contexts in which the terms appear makes an interpretation of these texts as references to cultic vases connected with sacrificial slaughter of animals compelling or preferable.[42]

A third term would seem to complicate matters. It is *sa-pa-ka-te-ri-ja* on a tablet that is now identified as Cf 941, from a set of six Cf tablets known securely to come from Knossos area I3. It is fair to say that an *opinio communis* has been reached by a chain of inference that interprets the ethnonymic and toponymic evidence from Pylos and at least the noun forms from Mycenae as derived from *σφαγ-. Using their supposed cumulative weight, *sa-pa-ka-te-ri-ja* is interpreted as an adjective either in the feminine plural modifying the 10 she-goats on line Cf 941.B or in the neuter plural modifying both the 10 she-goats (line .B) and the 8 or so he-goats (line .A) altogether and in either case meaning something like 'animales destinados al sacrificio.'[43]

It should be noted, however, that the six texts definitely forming part of the work of Hand 112 from area I3 at Knossos specify male and female goats and sheep in varying numbers as being *pa-ro* 'under the control of' single individuals specified by name. The only two words not part of this bureaucratic formula for 'who is in charge', are *sa-pa-ka-te-ri-ja* (Cf 941) and *a-ka-wi-ja-de* (Cf 914). The latter is clearly an allative phrase stipulating where animals are going. This then would make it possible for the term *sa-pa-ka-te-ri-ja* in this series and findspot context to be dative-locative locational or even a temporal specifier of a particular event or occasion, e.g., 'at [or within the time period of] the *sa-pa-ka-te-ri-ja*'.

---

[40] Panagl (1972:73, 81) interprets *ka-na-*to in the same context as a receptacle name κάνασθον, an attested variant of κάναστρον = a basket used in manufacturing cheese.

[41] Cf. Leukart, this volume, pp. 110, 111, 114, 115

[42] Gérard-Rousseau (1968:165–166) rightly concludes: "ces interprétations étymologiques de *pake-tere* et *kanato* ne permettent pas conclure à un emploi religieux des termes, car rien ne confirme ces hypothèses dans le context."

[43] DMic., *s.v.* The full argument was first advanced in Killen 1996:74–75 and 79–80, where he discusses *sa-pa-ka-te-ri-ja* on what is now known as KN Cf 941; *sa-pa-ka-*[on KN X 9191.a; and the adjoined *sa* on KN C 394 r. .3, v. .2 and perhaps U 7063.2 [now C 7063] and argues for an interpretation everywhere as /*sphaktēria*/ (or related adjectival forms in the cases of the adjunct abbreviations). See Rougemont 2016:319 and nn. 140–143 for alternatives and complications in interpreting the full word and the adjunct. See also Petrakis 2021:350–354.

The tablet Cf 7064, which seems to "describe" he-goats and she-goats as *a-ki-ri-ja*, most likely ἄγρια 'wild',[44] is only tentatively assigned to scribal hand 112 and its findspot is unknown.

Nonetheless the interpretation of *sa-pa-ka-te-ri-ja* on the Knossos texts as 'for butchery, for sacrifice' makes the best sense and could also make sense for *sa* as an adjunct with OVIS^m and CAP^m on KN C 394. On C 394, *sa* = σηκός 'enclosure' would be equally compelling based on a clear parallel with OVIS+TA relating to /stat^hmos/ (σταθμός) 'in steading'.[45]

Working further through this material, there are many implications and un-addressed questions. First we should note that the identification of *pa-ki-ja-ne* as Σφαγιᾶνες is still considered only a possibility by Bennet.[46] This is admirable and proper caution, given how this entire line of identification started and continued. In contrast, however, the "Glossario" in the most recent comprehensive handbook of Mycenology identifies all the toponymic and ethnonymic forms in the Pylos texts as representing /*Sphagiā-*/.[47] Whatever the root is, the form *pa-ki-ja-ne* must be a consonant declension plural ethnonym of the class that produce toponyms in -ā from the root, analogous to how Κρῆτες yields a corresponding toponymic form Κρήτη.

Let us leave aside *sa-pa-ke-te-ri-ja*, the very spelling of which might differentiate its root from that of the forms of *pa-ki-ja-ne*, *pa-ki-ja-na*, and *pa-ki-ja-ni-ja*. Pre-Greek ethnonyms and toponyms parallel to *pa-ki-ja-ne* and *pa-ki-ja-na* in the Pylos texts are laid out clearly by Sainer, here with details supplemented and/or corrected by me:[48]

	a-pu₂-ka (sg. in -*ān*)	
	a-pu₂-ka-ne	
e-pi-jo-ta-na		*e-pi-ja-ta-ni-ja*
	i-na-ne	*i-na-ni-ja*
me-za-na		
pa-ki-ja-na	*pa-ki-ja-ne*	*pa-ki-ja-ni-ja*
pa-na-pi		
pi-ka-na		
	re-ka-ta-ne	
ta-mi-ta-na		
	te-ta-ra-ne	
	wo-tu-wa-ne	

---

44 Rougemont 2016:318.
45 Rougemont 2016:319 and 335.
46 See above, note 29. Other cautious scholars discuss even the religious aspects of the district of *pa-ki-ja-ne* / *pa-ki-ja-na* / *pa-ki-ja-ni-ja* without translating these Linear B word units, e.g., Hiller 2011:182 and 196–197.
47 Piquero 2016:771.
48 Sainer 1976:62.

(1) *a-pu₂-ka-ne* (in the Pylos *o-ka* texts An 656.13 and An 657.13): singular in -ᾱν *a-pu₂-ka* (PY An 656.20).

(2) *e-pi-jo-ta-na* (Aa 95) and *e-pi-ja-ta-ni-ja* (Ad 687): locations of women cloth workers.

(3) *i-na-ne* (PY An 18.7 and instrumental locative *i-na-pi* PY An 5.8) and *i-na-ni-ja* (An 18.3; also Ae 8 and 72): locations of men for wall-building operation.

(4) *me-za-ne* (PY Fn 50.4 whether dative singular or nominative plural, in allocations of barley to specialists and to *do-e-ro*; cf. singular toponym form *me-za-na* in PY Cn 3.1, a list of allocations of single male bovids).[49]

(5) *pa-na-pi* (Cn 45.10, a record of herds of mainly she-goats and she-sheep associated with notable collectors): *pa-na-pi* is a singleton in the list.

(6) *pi-ka-na* (Na 224): 20 units of flax that the *wanaks* 'holds' 'free': *wa-]na-ka , e-ke e-re-]u-te-ra*.

(7) *re-ka-ta-ne* (An 207.8 and confidently restored on lines .6 and .7): this plural *ethnicon* occurs on each of three lines of entries of men: .6 *a-de-te-re* VIR 2; .7 *ke-ra-me-we* VIR 2; .8 *da-ko-ro* VIR 12. Other localities on An 207 include groups of men designated as *pi-ri-je-te-re, po-ku-ta, ku-ru-so-wo-ko, me-ri-da-ma-te, to-ko-so-wo-ko, ra-pte-re*.

(8) *ta-mi-ta-na* (Na 248): 30 units of flax free for the dog-leaders: *e-re-u-te-ro ku-na-ke-ta-i*.

(9) *te-ta-ra-ne* (An 1.5): one of five communities who provide rowers going to Pleuron.

(10) *wo-tu-wa-ne* (Cn 4.8): a steading location for sheep OVIS in a list headed by the secondary center *a-si-ja-ti-ja* in the Further Province.

We should note that all these localities, unlike *pa-ki-ja-ne/pa-ki-ja-na*, are minor and rural and do not feature prominently in the palatial administrative documents. They are the kinds of sites that we would expect to be identified by ethnonyms and toponyms of pre-Greek form. Compare in historical and Homeric Greek widely attested: Ἀκαρνᾶνες, Τροϊζῆνες, Ἀθαμᾶνες, Δυμᾶνες,[50] Ἀτιντᾶνες, Ταλαιᾶνες, Αἰνιᾶνες, Ἀγρινιᾶνες, Δαιᾶνες, Φοιτιᾶνες.[51]

In the formation of the regional state of Messenia in the late Mycenaean palatial period, the sanctuary locale *pa-ki-ja-na* and community of people *pa-ki-ja-ne* out in the landscape were associated with *pu-ro* when it grew to be the major

---

[49] Cf. *i-qa-ne* likely dative singular personal name of this type in PY Xa 176.1. Not treated in *Docs²* or *DMic*.

[50] Frisk 1960:498, *s.v.* Ἑλλάς.

[51] Von Kamptz 1982:161–162.

center for all of Messenia. Like other place designations in Sainer's list, the place identifiers for this district likewise have pre-Greek form; and the ethnic name *pa-ki-ja-ne* (-*ānes*, sg. -*ān*) seems to have generated the place name forms *pa-ki-ja-na*, "toponymum. in -*ānā* exiens," following Morpurgo Davies (above, note 28). If this were not the case, we would expect a designation of the collective group via an adjectival formation from *pa-ki-ja-na* (ending in -*ānā* = -ήνη) in -ιος. That would give us **pa-ki-ja-na-jo* (i.e., **pa-ki-j-αναῖοι*, which does not occur) as with the ethnics for the citizens of Ἀθήνη Athens and Μυκήνη Mycenae in historical Greek: Ἀθηναῖος, -α, -ον, Μυκηναῖος, -α, -ον, and in Mycenaean Greek the adjectives *di-ka-ta-jo* (KN Fp 1.2) and the personal names *te-qa-ja* (KN Ap 5864.4 and PY Ep 539.6) and *te-qa-jo* (TH Wu 47.β) from place names **di-ka-ta* (in allative *di-ka-ta-de* KN Fh 5467) and **te-qa* (in allative *te-qa-de* MY X 508.a and TH Wu 51.β, Wu 65.β, and Wu 96.β).[52]

Absent evidence in Linear B for forming the toponymic adjective in this way from the ā-stem toponym, it is probable that *pa-ki-ja-na* is the extended distinctive spelling of an original pre-Greek geographical name in -ᾱν -ην of the kind traced by Fick spread over Caria, Crete, Attica, and the Peloponnese: Θήρην, Ρισήν, Ρίττην, Τροιζήν, Ἀραφήν, Ἀραδήν, Βλισσήν for which forms in -ήνᾱ are attested, e.g., Βλισσήνα, Λεβήνα, Σουλήνα.[53] See especially the northern Peloponnesian polis Τροιζήν and the Carian place name Τροιζήνη.[54] Lindner (1995) expands the list: Ἀτρήνη (Thessaly); Κυλλήνη (Arcadia, Elis, Aetolia); Πριήνη (Caria); Κυρήνη (Libya).[55]

In the case of *pa-ki-ja-ne*/*pa-ki-ja-na*, derivation from the pre-Greek roots connected with grape vines σφάκ-, with wasps σφηκ- or with the widespread and economically exploited flowering shrub σφάκος (*Salvia pomifera*) would be tenable. All three are important features of the natural environment. The σφάκος, like the terebinth (**ti-mi-to-*), is important in olive oil production and trade (cf. *pa-ko-we* = **σφακόϝεν* in thirteen entries of olive oil in the PY Fr series[56]) in the late Mycenaean palatial period in Messenia. A derivation from σφηκ- might refer, as in historical Greek, to a wasp-like, i.e., narrow-waisted (narrowing at the center), formation of the terrain with crests or peaks on either side,[57] or to a locality where the gall wasps and the σφάκος (Cretan sage) would be found bountifully. The "wasp" should not be ruled out, especially in

---

[52] See the catalogue of other similar adjectival forms from -ήνη place names in Stephanus of Byzantium, *s.v.* Ἀδράνη, e.g., Ἀδρηναῖος, Κυρηναῖος, Πελληναῖος, Μιτυληναῖος.

[53] Fick 1905:36, and also 25, 30, 37.

[54] Fick 1905:72.

[55] Lindner 1995:697, column 2.

[56] *DMic.*, *s.v. pa-ko-we*.

[57] Hesychius §2890 σφηκὸς λόφου· τὸ ἄκρον τοῦ λόφου, τὸ ἐπὶ τῶν ὤτων ἀποκρεμάμενον τοῦ λόφου.

light of the historical tradition of referring to Cyprus with a toponym from this very root: Σφήκεια (< *Sp^{h}ākeia*).

Regarding the interpretation of *sa-pa-ka-te-ri-ja*, it draws attention for two reasons: (1) the representation of the initial pre-consonantal /s/ that is generally omitted in spellings where /s/ occurs before stop consonants in the Linear B texts; and (2) the spelling with *ka* instead of expected *ke*, for which contrast *pa-ke-te-re* and *pa-ke-te-ri-[ja*. The conspicuous parallel of *wa-na-ka-te-ro* spelled many times (PY En 74, 609; Eo 160, 276, 371; Er 312; KN Le 654, Lc 525, El Z 1, TH Z 839) with sign *ka* by different tablet-writers in different series, including a vase painter, and never with the sign *ke*, which would be the standard Mycenaean spelling, is generally explained as the result of analogical pressure from the spelling of the paradigmatic nominative singular form of the noun with an *a* dummy vowel as *wa-na-ka*.

If the same kind of analogical pressure were to explain the spelling -*ka-te*- versus expected -*ke-te*- in *sa-pa-ka-te-ri-ja*, we might then think of a noun form in the nominative singular that ends in -*ks* and would have some cultural importance. Two candidates would be (1) *σφάξ from the verbal root σφαγ- as attested historically in compounds like διασφάξ 'fente, fissure, gorge, brèche' (Chantraine 2009: s.v. σφάζω) and referring geographically in Herodotus (2.158, 3.117) to a 'river gorge' and in Lycophron (317) to a 'cleft in the earth'; and (2) the already discussed insect σφήξ, σφηκός.

We should not be quick to dismiss the insect option, especially given its association with the sage plant.[58] Two wasps are famously rendered with exquisite accuracy on the gold pendant from the Chrysolakkos tomb at Mallia (MM IIB),[59] implying both close study of the creatures and their symbolic importance in artistic and ceremonial representation. Wasps, σφῆκες, are used as a metaphor for the dangerous and aggressive ferocity of none other than the Myrmidones in Homer, *Iliad* 16.257–267. Elsewhere wasps are characterized as exhibiting positive social behaviors like cooperative nesting and common obtaining and sharing of food.[60] We should notice that these two historical -κς nouns refer to (1) the natural terrain (gorges or clefts geologically cut or sliced into the landscape); and (2) socially well-organized and feisty insects. The peculiar treatment of the initial /s/ might also further differentiate the root of *sa-pa-ka-te-ri-ja* with the root σφαγ- 'slit the throat' or *σφάξ (attested in compounds as, metaphorically, slits in the landscape, i.e., 'gorges' or 'clefts') from the root

---

[58] On wasps in Greek antiquity, see Davies and Kathirithamby 1986:75–83.

[59] LaFleur, Matthews, and McCorkle 1979.

[60] LaFleur, Matthews, and McCorkle 1979:209, 212. See also Koehl 2011:197–201, arguing that the wasp pendant was manufactured in the Levant, but clearly (p. 201) as a highest-quality commissioned piece.

of the ethnonym and toponym (*pa-ki-ja-ne* and *pa-ki-ja-na*) at Pylos, σφάκος, σφάκου 'Cretan sage'.[61]

***

In summary then, although nothing can be concluded with absolute certainty, I would propose leaving open how we are to "read"' in Greek the clearly pre-Greek *pa-ki-ja-ne/pa-ki-ja-na/pa-ki-ja-ni-ja*, given that we do not have any more means to identify the root from which it is formed than when Gérard-Rouseau reached the same conclusion fifty-three years ago.[62] Connections with *sphag-* ('slit the throat', 'sacrifice through slaughter') are wishful thinking and not compelling as are connections with the historical island of *Sphakteria* as derived from *sphag-*.

We should certainly delink the Pylos ethnonym and toponym from discussions of how to read *sa-pa-ka-te-ri-ja* in the Knossos texts, for which a connection with *sphag-* ('slit the throat', 'sacrifice through slaughter') is tenable. Likewise, pending further evidence or stronger arguments, we should not link the names of vases *pa-ke-te-re* and **pa-ke-te-ri-ja* with the root *sphag-* ('slit the throat', 'sacrifice through slaughter') either. This is only done now without any supporting contextual evidence and through a kind of zeal to discover or uncover (or even manufacture) more information about ritual practices in the Mycenaean palatial period.

If forced to choose a most likely suspect to be the root for *pa-ki-ja-ne/pa-ki-ja-na/pa-ki-ja-ni-ja*, I would put forward ὁ σφάκος, the "sage apple" or *Salvia pomifera* or Cretan sage, because of the prevalence and economic and cultural importance of this shrub in Mycenaean palatial Messenia and the analogy with **ti-mi-to a-ko*, [*ku*]-*pa-ris-so*, and locative/dative *ne-do-we-te* /Νεδϝόντει/ and allative *ne-do-wo-ta-de* /Νεδϝοντάδε/, the last two identified with the river Nedōn (Νέδϝων) and the reed plant that grows along it to this day.[63]

---

[61] Del Freo (email Jan. 5, 2019) makes a suggestion in the form of a question. Given that the -*i*- vowel apparently belongs neither to the root nor to the -*anes* suffix, might the -*i*- element in *pa-ki-ja-ne* be compared to the -ι- in historically attested Ταλαιᾶνες, Αἰνιᾶνες, Ἀγρινιᾶνες, Δαιᾶνες, and Φοιτιᾶνες. In any case, the -*i*- vowel is a "problem" to explain even for derivation from *sphag-* ('slit the throat', 'sacrifice through slaughter') since it would require the creation of a Greek noun form in -ία that then would use pre-Greek suffixation.

[62] Gérard-Rousseau 1968:169: "aucune des suggestions avancées ne peut recevoir de preuve decisive."

[63] See https://classical-inquiries.chs.harvard.edu/mastchs-summer-seminar-2021-friday-july-23-summaries-of-presentations-and-discussion/ (last accessed February 23, 2022) §§48.5–48.6; Lamberterie 2017:157–158.

Bibliography

Bennet, J. 2011. "The Geography of the Mycenaean Kingdoms." In *A Companion to Linear B: Mycenaean Greek Texts and Their World*, vol. 2, ed. Y. Duhoux and A. Morpurgo Davies, 137–168. Bibliothèque des Cahiers de l'Institut de Linguistique de Louvain 127. Louvain-la-Neuve.

Chantraine, P. 2009. *Dictionnaire étymologique de la langue grec. Histoire des mots achevé par Jean Taillardat, Olivier Masson et Jean-Louis Perpillou, avec en supplément, les* Chroniques d'étymologie grecque *(1-10) rassemblées par Alain Blanc, Charles de Lamberterie et Jean-Louis Perpillou.* Paris.

Davies, M., and J. Kathirithamby. 1986. *Greek Insects.* London.

de Lamberterie, C. 2107. "Chronique d'étymologie grecque No. 16 (CEG 2017)." *Revue de Philologie* 91:131–229.

Del Freo, M. 2016. "La Geografia dei regni micenei." In Del Freo and Perna 2016: 625–656.

Del Freo, M., and M. Perna, eds. 2016. *Manuale di epigrafia micenea: Introduzione allo studio dei testi in lineare B.* 2 vols. Padua.

Fick, A. 1905. *Vorgriechische Ortsnamen als Quelle für die Vorgeschichte Griechenlands.* Göttingen.

Frisk, H. 1960. *Griechisches Etymologisches Wörterbuch*, Band I: A–Ko. Heidelberg.

Furnée, E.J. 1972. *Die wichtigsten konsonantischen Erscheinungen des Vorgriechischen*, Janua Linguarum, Series Practica 150. The Hague and Paris. [Reprint 2016.]

García Ramón, J. L. 2016. "Il greco miceneo." In Del Freo and Perna 2016:211–243.

Gérard-Rousseau, M. 1968. *Les mentions religieuses dans les tablettes mycéniennes*, Incunabula Graeca XXIX. Rome.

Hansen, P. A. 2005. *Hesychii Alexandrini Lexicon*, Volumen *III Π–Σ.* Berlin.

Hiller, S. 2011. "Mycenaean Religion and Cult." In *A Companion to Linear B: Mycenaean Greek Texts and Their World*, vol. 2, ed. Y. Duhoux and A. Morpurgo Davies, 169–211. Bibliothèque des Cahiers de l'Institut de Linguistique de Louvain 127. Louvain-la-Neuve.

Killen, J.T. 1996. "Thebes Sealings and Knossos Tablets." In *Atti e memorie del secondo Congresso internazionale di micenologia, Roma-Napoli, 14-20 ottobre 1991*, vol. 1: *Filologia*, ed. E. De Miro, L. Godart, and A. Sacconi, 71–82. Incunabula Graeca 98. Rome.

Koehl, R. B. 2011. "South Levantine Middle Bronze Age Gold-Work in the Aegean." In Πεπραγμένα Ι΄ Διεθνούς Κρητολογικού Συνεδρίου, Χανιά, 1-8 Οκτωβρίου 2006, vol. A1, ed. M. Andreadaki-Blazaki and E. Papadopoulou, 189–208. Khania.

LaFleur, R. A., R. W. Matthews, and D. B. McCorkle. 1979. "A Re-Examination of the Mallia Insect Pendant." *American Journal of Archaeology* 83:208–212.

Lindner, Thomas. 1995. "Griechische (incl. Mykenische) Ortsnamen / Greek (and Mycenaean) Place Names / Noms de lieux grecs (et mycéniens)." In *Namenforschung (Name Studies / Les noms propres)*, ed. E. Eichler, G. Hilty, H. Löffler, H. Steger, and L. Zgusta, 690–705. Berlin and New York.

Melena, J. L. 1979. "Note on Spelling with a Dummy Vowel on KH Z 1." *Nestor* 6:5 (May): 1369.

———. 2014. "Mycenaean Writing." In *A Companion to Linear B: Mycenaean Greek Texts and Their World*, vol. 3, ed. Y. Duhoux and A. Morpurgo Davies, 1–186. Bibliothèque des Cahiers de l'Institut de Linguistique de Louvain 133. Louvain-la-Neuve.

———. 2019. *The Knossos Tablets. Sixth Edition. Transliteration by José L. Melena in collaboration with Richard J. Firth*. Philadelphia.

———. 2021. *The Pylos Tablets. Third Edition in Transliteration by José L. Melena with the collaboration of Richard J. Firth*. Vitoria-Gasteiz.

Morpurgo, A. 1963. *Mycenaeae Graecitatis Lexicon*. Incunabula Graeca 3. Rome.

Notti, E., M. Negri, and G. M. Facchetti. 2015. "Linguistic Expression and Ritual Taxonomy in PY Tn 316." *Pasiphae* 9:119–133.

Olivier, J. P., and T. G. Palaima, eds. 1988. *Texts, Tablets and Scribes: Studies in Mycenaean Epigraphy and Economy in Honor of Emmett L. Bennett, Jr.*, Suplementos a *Minos* 10. Salamanca.

Palaima, T. G. 1979. "Note on Vase Inscription KH Z1." *Nestor* 6:6 (September): 1378–1379.

———. 1991. "Maritime Matters in the Linear B Texts." In *Thalassa: L'Égée prehistorique et la mer*, ed. R. Laffineur, R. and L. Basch, 273–310, pl. LXIII. Aegaeum 7. Liège.

———. 1995. "The Nature of the Mycenaean Wanax: Non-Indo-European Origins and Priestly Functions." In *The Role of the Ruler in the Prehistoric Aegean*, ed. P. Rehak, 119–139, plates XLI–XLII. Aegaeum 11. Liège.

———. 1996. "'Contiguities' in the Linear B Tablets from Pylos." In *Atti e memorie del secondo congresso interazionale di micenologia*, ed. E. de Miro, L. Godart, A. Sacconi, 379–396.

———. 2000. "*Themis* in the Mycenaean Lexicon and the Etymology of the Place-Name **ti-mi-to a-ko*." *Faventia* 22:7–19.

———. 2001. "'This Is Not Justice. It Is Retaliation.'" *Times Higher Education*, Sept. 28. https://www.timeshighereducation.com/news/this-is-retaliation-not-justice/165010.article

———. 2002. Review of *Les tablettes en linéaire B de la Odos Pelopidou, Édition et Commentaire*, ed. V. L. Aravantinos, L. Godart, and A. Sacconi. Thèbes: Fouilles de la Cadmée 1 (Pisa and Rome 2001). *Minos* 35–36:475–486.

———. 2003a. Review of *Les tablettes en linéaire B de la Odos Pelopidou, Édition et Commentaire*, ed. V. L. Aravantinos, L. Godart, and A. Sacconi. Thèbes: Fouilles de la Cadmée 1 (Pisa and Rome 2001). *American Journal of Archaeology* 107:113–115.

———. 2003b. "Reviewing the New Linear B Tablets from Thebes." *Kadmos* 42:31–38.

———. 2006. "*Wanaks* and Related Power Terms in Mycenaean and Later Greek." In *Ancient Greece: From the Mycenaean Palaces to the Age of Homer*, ed. S. Deger-Jalkotzy and I. Lemos, 53–71. Edinburgh Leventis Studies 3. Edinburgh.

———. 2007. "Ted's Ghost. The Death of Ted Westhusing Leaves a Widening Circle of Sorrow." *Austin Chronicle*, April 27. http://www.austinchronicle.com/news/2007-04-27/469144/.

———. 2014. "Pylos Tablet Vn 130 and the Pylos Perfume Industry." In *KE-RA-ME-JA. Studies Presented to Cynthia W. Shelmerdine*, ed. D. Nakassis, J. Gulizio, and S. James, 83–90. Philadelphia.

———. 2016. "The Ideology of the Ruler in Mycenaean Prehistory: Twenty Years after the Missing Ruler." In *Studies in Aegean Art and Culture: A New York Aegean Bronze Age Colloquium in Memory of Ellen N. Davis*, ed. R. B. Koehl, 133–158. Philadelphia.

———. 2020a. "*Porphureion* and *Kalkhion* and Minoan-Mycenaean Murex Dye Manufacture and Use." In *Alatzomouri-Pefka: A Middle Minoan IIB Workshop Making Organic Dyes*, ed. V. Apostolakou, T. M. Brogan, and P. P. Betancourt, 123–128. INSTAP Prehistory Monographs 62. Philadelphia.

———. 2020b. "Iklaina Traganes *a-pu$_2$* and Αἰπύ." In *ΚΥΔΑΛΙΜΟΣ: Studies in Honor of Prof. Georgios Styl. Korres*, ed. P. Kalogerakou, A. Hassiakou, M. Cosmopoulos, E. Peppa-Papaioannou, I. Lolos, L. Platon, and C. Marabea, 385–397. Athens University Review of Archaeology Supplement 4. Athens.

———. Forthcoming. "*Koiranos* and *Koirētēr* Among Power Titles in Linear B and Homer." In *Power and Place in the Prehistoric Aegean and Beyond*, ed. S. Allen, M. Lee, R. Schon, and A. K. Smith. Philadelphia.

Palaima, T. G., and F. Hocker. 1990–1991. "Late Bronze Age Aegean Ships and the Pylos Tablets Vn 46 and Vn 879." *Minos* 25–26:297–317.

Palaima, T. G., and J. L. Melena. 1992. "Note in the Section *qu'il est permis de rire entre mycénologues*." *Nestor* 19:6 (September): 2501–2.

Panagl, O. 1972. "*Pa-ke-te-re* und *ka-na-to*: Zwei Gerätetermini der mykenischen Milchwirtschaft." *ZivaAnt* 22:71–84.

Petrakis, V. 2021. "Slaughter, Blood and Sacrifice: Mycenaean *sphag-* in Context." In *ZOIA: Animal-Human Interactions in the Aegean Middle and Late Bronze Age*, ed. R. Laffineur and T. Palaima, 343–371. Aegaeum 45. Leuven and Liège.

Piquero, J. 2016. "Glossario." In Del Freo and Perna 2016:753–782.

Rougemont, F. 2016. "Animali e allevamento." In Del Freo and Perna 2016:305–347.

Sainer, A. P. 1976. "An Index of Pylos Place Names." *Studi Micenei ed Egeo-Anatolici* 17:17–63.

Sergent, B. 1994. "Les petites nodules et la grande Béotie." *Revue des Études Anciennes* 96:365–384.

Ventris, M., and J. Chadwick. 1953. "Evidence for Greek Dialect in the Mycenaean Language." *Journal of Hellenic Studies* 73:84–103.

Von Kamptz, H. 1982. *Homerische Personennamen*. Göttingen.

14

Leukippos
Paralipomena zu einem griechischen Personennamen

OSWALD PANAGL

Department of Linguistics
University of Salzburg
oswald.panagl@sbg.ac.at

Abstract

The first section of this contribution exhaustively lists the epigraphic and literary evidence of the item *Leukippos* and discusses the questions of its morphology and semantics. I investigate all instances of compounds exhibiting either *leuko-* as first member or *-(h)ippo/ā-* as second member. Both the simplex adjective *leuko-* and *Leuko-* as the first member in a personal name are already attested in Linear B. As far as the type of word formation is concerned, *Leukippos* has to be classified as an exocentric possessive compound form. The etymology of the word for 'horse' in Ancient Greek differs in some features from the reconstructed form $*e\acute{k}wos$. The most prominent deviations (namely *i* instead of *e*, initial aspiration) receive a plausible explanation. Employing relative chronology as heuristics, I assume that the compound form chronologically precedes the unexpected initial aspiration in *híppos*. Therefore the form **Leukhippos* is not attested.

Keywords

Possessive compounds, etymology of *hippos*, vowel raising $e > i$, aspiration, personal names

1. Zum Geleit

1.1. Das auf diesen Seiten behandelte sprachwissenschaftliche, genauer lautliche Problem hat mich zunächst im Jahr 1999 punktuell beschäftigt—und zwar auf einem linguistikfernen Arbeitsgebiet. Als Dramaturg einer Salzburger

Produktion der Oper *Daphne* von Richard Strauss (auf ein Libretto von Joseph Gregor) bin ich den männlichen Protagonisten und zugleich Konkurrenten um die Gunst der Titelfigur begegnet: Apollon und Leukippos. Der mächtige olympische Gott tötet im Handlungsverlauf den Schäfer und lädt dadurch Blutschuld auf sich, die er erst durch Verzicht auf die Nymphe und ihre Verwandlung in einen Lorbeerbaum (ein altes, in Ovids *Metamorphosen* exemplarisch behandeltes Motiv!) tilgen kann.

1.2. Wie in der gesamten griechischen Überlieferung lautet das Vorderglied des Kompositums Leukippos auf die Tenuis -*k* und nicht, wie wegen des *h*- Anlauts des zweiten Bestandteils *hippos* zu erwarten wäre, auf die Tenuis aspirata -*kh* aus. Der Beleglage, Forschungsgeschichte und einer möglichen Lösung dieses Zetemas seien die folgenden Kapitel gewidmet.

2. Die Beleglage

2.1. Das *Lexikon der griechischen Eigennamen* von Pape-Benseler (1911/1959) bucht unter dem Lemma Λεύκιππος eine zweistellige Anzahl von Belegen, verteilt über unterschiedliche Autoren wie mehrere Textsorten bzw. Zeitstufen (u.a. homerischer Apollonhymnos, Theokrit, Aristoteles, Pausanias, Diodor, Apollodor, Strabon, Plutarch), die sich nach dieser Klassifikation auf 17 verschiedene Namensträger verteilen. Im *Apollonhymnos* (V. 212) findet sich bereits der im genannten Operntextbuch auftretende *Rivale des Gottes*.

2.2. Das epigraphische Nachschlagewerk von Fraser–Matthews (1987), dessen erster Band den Inseln der Ägäis sowie Zypern und der Kyrenaika gewidmet ist, registriert in dieser Lautung eine Vielzahl von Stellen—durchwegs in der gängigen Schreibung—, die sich vor allem auf die Inseln Chios, Delos, Kalymnos, Kos, Samos, Tenos und Thasos verteilen.

2.3. Die Internet-Plattform *The Lexicon of Greek Personal Names* (*LGPN*) (http://www.lgpn.ox.ac.uk/index.html) verzeichnet 45 inschriftliche Vorkommensfälle (z.T. stark fragmentiert), wobei unter den Fundorten auch Athen, Sparta, Argos, Abdera, Magnesia, Milet und Halikarnass aufscheinen.

2.4. Im gleichen lautlichen Habitus an der Kompositionsfuge findet sich noch das Motionsfemininum Λευκίππη mit einem weitgespannten Skopus der Beispiele vom homerischen *Demeterhymnos* über Platon bis zu den *Ilias*-Scholien sowie (aus der lateinischen Literatur) den *Fabulae* des Hyginus. Erneut sind prosopographisch unterschiedliche Personen (neun an der Zahl, u.a. Tochter des Okeanos, Gemahlin des Thestis, Mutter des Aigyptos von Hephaistos) mit diesem Namen versehen.

2.5. Eine andere feminine Ableitung auf *-id-* begegnet in der Pluralform Λευκιππίδες, welche die beiden Töchter des Messeniers Leukippos mit den Namen Hilaeira und Phoebe bezeichnet, die als Heroinen einen Tempel in Sparta besaßen.

3. Komposita mit alternierendem Vorder- bzw. Hinterglied

3.1. Sucht man unter den griechischen nominalen Zusammensetzungen zunächst nach Bildungen mit *leuko-*, so scheinen im Wortschatz auch etliche Appellativa auf. Unter den 31 bei LSJ zitierten Beispielen nenne ich in Auswahl λευκάμπυξ 'mit weißem Stirnband', λεύκασπις (bereits Hom. *Il.* 22.294) 'weißbeschildet', λεύκιππος 'mit weißen Rossen', λευκοδίφθερος 'mit weißem Leder', λεύκοθριξ 'weißhaarig', λευκόπεπλος 'weißgewandet', λευκόπους 'weißfüßig', λευκόπωλος 'mit weißen Rossen' und λευκόχροος 'weißfarbig'. Im onomastischen Material finden sich u.a. Λευκάνωρ, -άριστος, -ασπις, -γαιος, -θέα, -λοφος, -μαντις, -νοτος, -πετρα, -πολις, -πυρα, -φάνης, -οφρυς, sowie Λευκώλενος und Λευκωπίας.

3.2. Komposita auf das Hinterglied -ιππος begegnen gleichfalls als Appellativa wie als Nomina propria in reicher Zahl; man vergleiche nur aus der ersteren Gruppe (nach Kretschmer–Locker 1965) in Auswahl die Nomina ἡμίιππος, τρί-, φίλ-, ἄμ-, ἄν-, μελάν-, δάμν-, πλήξ-, ζεύξ-, πάρ-, ἄγρ-, ἐλάσ-, δαμάσ-, κτῆσ-, μίσ-, δύσ-, εὔ-, πολύ-, ἄφ-, ἔφ-, ἄμφ-, ἀνάγχ-, κρύψ-. Dabei fallen neben der Vielzahl an verbalen Rektionskomposita vom Typus πλήξιππος, μίσιππος die aspirierten Belege ἀνάγχιππος, neutrales τέθριππον 'Viergespann' und die Hypostasen (präpositionale Ableitungskomposita) ἔφιππος 'beritten' und ἄφιππος 'des Reitens unkundig' auf. Die Behauchung der beiden letzten Beispiele mag ursprünglich gewesen oder von ähnlich gebildetem ἄμφιππος 'Reiter, der von einem auf das andere Pferd springt' analogisch beeinflusst worden sein.

3.3. Zum zweiten Komplex sei auf das rückläufige Wörterbuch von Dornseiff-Hansen (1957) verwiesen, in dem nicht weniger als 227 types mit häufig mehreren tokens verzeichnet sind. Der Sprache des alten Epos gehören neben Λεύκιππος (Hes. fr. 50.52) bzw. Λευκίππη (h.Cer. 418) die Formen Εὔιππος sowie Μελάνιππος an. Ersteres fungiert als Epitheton zu Ἴσχυς (h.Apoll. 210) sowie für die Hyperboreer (Hes. fr. 150.21) und ist auch durch das Motionsfemininum Εὐίππη bezeugt, das die Tochter eines Λεύκων benennt (Hes. fr. 70.10). Das zu unserem Problemwort konträre Μελάνιππος wird in der *Ilias* sowohl für Griechen (15,546 bzw. 5.76; 19,240) wie für Trojaner (8,276; 16,695) verwendet.

Die späteren Formen Ἄνθιππος und Πάνθιππος fallen durch die Behauchung von -*t* im jeweiligen Vorderglied auf.

3.3.1. Die Verwendung des Adjektivs λευκός (= *re-u-ko*) im Mykenischen (vgl. u.a. PY Cn 418.3, MY Ge 603.1, KN Ld 649.b) als qualifizierendes Attribut, aber auch als männlicher Personenname (PY An 615.13, TH Z 849) steht außer Zweifel. Als Vorderglied in der nominalen Komposition begegnet es jedenfalls in der Form *re-u-ko-nu-ka* (= *leukó/ónykha*) als restriktive Kennzeichnung von Tüchern (= *pa-we-a*, u.a. KN Ld 571.b, 572.b, 573.b, 574.a im Gegensatz zu *po-ki-ro-nu-ka* (= *poikiló/ónykha*, KN Ld 579.a, 584.1). Aura Jorro (*DMic., s.v.*) gibt diesen sachlichen Gegensatz durch die verbale Opposition (un tipo de tejido con los hilos de su trama) 'sin teñir' bzw. 'blanqueados' vs. 'tenidos de diversos colores' wieder.

3.3.2. Daneben stellt sich in der Bildungsweise *re-u-ko-ro-o-pu₂-ru* als Männername (PY Jn 415.2), das als *Leukoᵘrus* 'mit weißer Braue' entweder eine fehlerhafte Hinzufügung des mittleren *r* enthält oder als assimilative Erweiterung durch das *r* im Hinterglied (*leukro-* statt *leuko-*) zu verstehen ist.

4. Semantische und morphologische Interpretationen

4.1. Das Wörterbuch von Pape–Benseler (*s.v.*) deutet und übersetzt *Leukippos* als 'Schimmel', was zunächst wie ein Determinativkompositum anmutet, aber in der Anwendung auf einen menschlichen Namensträger auch possessiv 'das Merkmal bzw. das Aussehen eines Schimmels habend, wie ein Schimmel' verstanden werden kann und soll. Das hohe Alter der Bildung legt jedenfalls eine archaische exozentrische Lesart nahe, die neben der optisch-phänomenologischen Gleichung (s.o.) auch den eigentlichen Besitz („ein weißes Pferd bzw. weiße Pferde habend") benennen kann; man vergleiche dazu das berühmte Kompositum ἀργυρότοξος „Silberbogner" als Epiklese des Gottes Apollon. Eine gleichfalls frühe Zusammensetzung mit entsprechendem Vorderglied zeigt sich in λευκώλενος 'mit weißen Ellenbogen', das als schmückendes Beiwort von Frauen, besonders Göttinnen, aber auch Dienerinnen in der homerischen Sprache erscheint (vgl. Risch 1974, *s.v.*).

4.2. Die reichhaltige Doxographie zur Entstehung der Possessivkomposita ausführlich zu referieren, ist hier nicht der Ort. Doch sei immerhin auf den rezenten Beitrag von Lindner (2002:268–273) hingewiesen, der über die Problematik kompakt und exhaustiv informiert. Unter den Ursprungshypothesen (u.a. Synekdoche: H. Osthoff, J. Schmidt; Relativsatzhypothese: F. Justi) scheint die Deutung als Hypostasierung eines Nominalsyntagmas, also die Univerbierung eines Sachverhalts, welche eine prädikative Aussage zu einem zitierfähigen

Attribut macht (K. Brugmann, J. Schindler), heuristisch und typologisch am plausibelsten zu sein.

4.3. Bei der Personennamengebung des Griechischen ist grundsätzlich zu beachten, dass nicht alle, besonders die jüngeren Items *per se* sinnvoll—als Bezeichnungen von objektiven Sachverhalten oder Wunschvorstellungen— sein müssen, sondern aus Namensteilen der Vorfahren mechanisch geklittert werden konnten. Als Musterbeispiel gilt dabei Φειδιππίδης in den Wolken des Aristophanes, dessen Bestandteile nach Aussage des Vaters Στρεψιάδης das aristokratische Nomen ἵππος und das kleinbürgerliche Konzept des Sparens (φείδομαι) bilden. Die Verschränkung der beiden kontrastiven Wörter und Werte deutet die handelnde Person als Kompromiss zwischen dem sozialen Gefälle von Vater und Mutter. Dass der scherzhaft wirkende zusammengesetzte Name aber bereits bei Homer in der Basisform Φείδιππος vorkommt und sich in der Konstellation "der auf Pferde verzichtet" auf die kriegerische Apobaten- Technik, also das Absteigen vom Wagen für den Nahkampf bezieht, hat Panagl (1983) nachgewiesen.

5. Zur Etymologie von ἵππος

5.1. Seit Beginn der etymologischen Erforschung des griechischen Wortschatzes hat die Herleitung von ἵππος der Wissenschaft drei sprachliche Probleme gestellt: (a) die Vertretung einer durch den Sprachvergleich (ai. *áśva-*, airan. *aspa-*, got. *aíhva-*) evidenten Lautfolge -*ḱw*- durch -*pp*-; (b) die Vertretung eines grundsprachlichen *e*- (vgl. lat. *equus*) durch griechisch *i*-; (c) die durch externe Rekonstruktion nicht begründbare Behauchung des Anlauts. Die führenden modernen Etymologica (Frisk 1960/1972, Chantraine 1999², *EDG*, jeweils *s.v.*) müssen sich mit diesen erheblichen lautlichen Problemen kritisch auseinander- setzen und verfolgen dabei ähnliche Erklärungswege.

5.2. Am relativ leichtesten fällt eine Lösung für die Wiedergabe der Abfolge von palataler (in einer Kentum-Sprache velarer) Tenuis und labialem Halbvokal als -*pp*-. Die Nebenform ἵκκος (*Etym. magn.* 474.12) bzw. Ἴκκος (Personenname, tarentinisch) zeigt zunächst einen Variationsspielraum der Vertretung im Griechischen. Falls der Schöpfer des trojanischen Pferdes Ἐπειός auch vom Stamme dieses Nomens gebildet ist, wäre auch eine Lautung mit einfachem -*p*- belegt.
    5.2.1. Die mykenische Schreibung mit *q* (*i-qo* 'Pferd', *i-qi-ja* 'Wagen' usw.) rückt den Lautwert der Phonemfolge in die Nähe eines Labiovelars (vgl. -*qe* 'und', *qo-u-ko-ro* 'Rinderhirt', *su-qo-ta* 'Schweinehirt, -züchter'). Die Gemination

bzw. Längung des intervokalischen -*p*- im alphabetischen Griechisch könnte eine nachmykenische Unterscheidung der Konsonantengruppe vom Resultat eines einfachen Labiovelars markieren.

5.3. Die auffällige Vokalfarbe *i*- im Wortanlaut hat Panagl (1989:129–135) als ein aus „mycénien normal," der aristokratischen Hofsprache ererbtes Merkmal interpretiert. Diese lautliche Veränderung ist vor Labiallauten entstanden (vgl. *a-te-mi-to* : *a-ti-mi-te*; *e-pa-sa-na-ti* : *i-pa-sa-na-ti*; *te-mi-ti-ja* : *ti-mi-ti-ja*; *dépas* : *di-pa*), wobei die Wechselformen auf -*e*- aus „mycénien spécial" (jeweils nach E. Risch), aus der Umgangssprache der Texte und ihrer Schreiber stammen, deren Eigenschaften üblicherweise im alphabetischen Griechisch weiterleben. Dass *hippos* die Ausnahme von dieser Regel darstellt, ist mit dem höfisch-ritterlichen Charakter dieses Nomens plausibel erklärbar. Für die phonetische Seite dieser „labialen Hebung." die auch für *o* > *u* gilt, lassen sich lautphysiologische Argumente anführen und im artikulationsphonetischen Experiment empirisch erhärten (vgl. Panagl 1989:131ff.).

5.4. Das größte, bislang nicht zufriedenstellend gelöste Problem stellt die sekundäre Behauchung des Pferdeworts im Anlaut dar. V. Georgiev (mündlich) dachte an ein lautnachahmendes Phänomen (= etwa /*hiha*/ als Imitation des Wieherns. Ruijgh (1976) schlug eine analogische Übertragung vom Wort für den Wagen in einem Syntagma *hármata kaì íppoi* > *híppoi* vor. Diese Annahme muss den Vorgang allerdings zeitlich in die dunklen Jahrhunderte verlegen, da *hármata* in der Bedeutung 'Wagen' als Synekdoche erst bei Homer aufscheint. In der mykenischen Periode bezeichnete *a-mo* (= /*harmo*/) eindeutig noch das Rad, während 'Wagen' mit komplementärer Verteilung der Fundorte mit *i-qi-ja* (Knossos) und *wo-ka* (Pylos) bezeichnet wurde.

5.4.1. Eine angenommene späte Behauchung erklärt zugleich die fehlende Aspiration in hocharchaischen zweigliedrigen Personennamen wie Λεύκιππος und Ἄλκιππος, bei denen die einmal geprägte Wortform der sekundären Entwicklung des Anlauts im Pferdewort widerstand. Die lockerer gefügten, da aus präpositionalen Verbindungen entstandenen Bildungen wie Ἄνθιππος, Πάνθιππος und Ἔφιππος (letzteres auch als Adjektiv vertreten) folgten der rezenten Gestalt des Anlauts und zeigen daher Tenuis aspirata im Vorderglied.

5.4.2. Unter den späteren Zusammensetzungen weist λευκηπατίας 'mit weißer Leber, verzagt' eine jüngere Nebenform λευχηπατίας (Suda) auf; das Kompositum λευχείμων (zu εἷμα) 'clad in white' (u.a. Philo Mechanicus, Aristides, orphische Hymnen) mit seinem verbalen Derivat λευχειμονέω 'to be clad in white' (u.a. Platon, Strabon, inschriftlich) erscheint ausschließlich in der zur Zeit der Entstehung sprachwirklichen Lautform mit aspiriertem Velar.

5.5. Erwähnt sei noch der attraktive Vorschlag von J. Schindler (Handout eines Vortrags), in idg. *eḱwos im Wege der inneren Ableitung die sekundäre *e*-stufige Thematisierung der Wurzel für 'schnell' (vgl. gr. ὠκύς) zu sehen.

6. Die Bestätigung einer frühen Vermutung

6.1. Die in den vorigen Kapiteln nachgezeichnete Wortgeschichte und Lautentwicklung von griechisch ἵππος wurde bereits im 19. Jahrhundert von einem Pionier der neueren, vorjunggrammatischen Indogermanistik angedacht. August Schleicher (1861:182) geht in seiner Behandlung des Phonems idg. s im Griechischen auch auf die Verhauchung im Anlaut vor Vokal und in intervokalischer Position ein:

> Bisweilen tritt h als späterer zusatz auf, so z. b. in ἵππος aus *ἰϝος, vgl: lat. *equos*, altind. *áçvas*, grundf. *akvas*; daß hier *h* erst spät eintrat, beweisen formen wie Λεύϙιππος, Ἄλϙιππος, die sonst bekantlich *Λευχιππος, *Ἀλχιππος zu lauten hätten. (S. 182)

6.2. Dass in der Rekonstruktion der Urform als akvas das Altindische als Maß aller Dinge und Bezugsgröße der Grundsprache firmiert, gehört freilich zu den Spezifika der Forschungsgeschichte in einer Periode vor der Entdeckung des Palatalisierungsgesetzes von Velaren und Labiovelaren vor hellem Vokal im Indoiranischen.

Bibliographie

Chantraine, P. 1999. *Dictionnaire étymologique de la langue grecque. Histoire des mots.* Nouvelle édition. Paris.

Dornseiff, F., and B. Hansen. 1957. *Rückläufiges Wörterbuch der griechischen Eigennamen.* Berlin.

Fraser, P. M., and E. Matthews. 1987. *A Lexicon of Greek Personal Names* I. Oxford.

Frisk, H. 1960/1972. *Griechisches etymologisches Wörterbuch* I, II und Nachtrag. Heidelberg.

Kretschmer, P., and E. Locker. 1965. *Rückläufiges Wörterbuch der griechischen Sprache*². Göttingen.

Lindner, T. 2002. "Nominalkomposition und Syntax im Indogermanischen." In *Indogermanische Syntax-Fragen und Perspektiven*, ed. H. Hettrich, 263–279. Wiesbaden.

Panagl, O. 1983. "Pheidippides. Etymologische Überlegungen zu einem aristophanischen Personennamen." In *Festschrift für Robert Muth zum 65. Geburtstag*, ed. P. Händel and W. Meid, 297–306. Innsbruck.

————. 1989. "Phonologische Überlegungen zu einem mykenischen Laut-wandel." In *Phonophilia. Untersuchungen zur Phonetik und Phonologie. Festschrift für Franz Zaic*, ed. W. Grosser, K. Hubmayer, F. Wagner, and W. Wieden, 129–135. Salzburg.

Pape, W., and G. Benseler. 1959. *Wörterbuch der griechischen Eigennamen* I, II (Nach-druck der 3. Aufl.). Graz.

Risch, E. 1974. *Wortbildung der homerischen Sprache* (2., völlig überarb. Aufl.). Berlin, New York.

Ruijgh, C. J. 1976. "Chars et roues dans les tablettes mycénniennes: La méthode de la mycénologie." *Mededelingen der Koninglijke Nederlandske Akademie van Wetenskappen. Afd. Letterkunde* 29.1:171–200.

A. Schleicher, 1861. *Compendium der vergleichenden Grammatik der indogermanischen Sprachen* I. Weimar.

15

Quelques réflexions *fiscales* sur la tablette Jn 829 de Pylos

Massimo Perna

Centro Internazionale per la Ricerca sulle Civiltà Egee
"Pierre Carlier"
maxperna59@gmail.com

Abstract

Several scholars have studied the relationships of the numerical quantities on Pylos tablet Jn 829 (dealing with "recycled bronze") and the tablets of the Ma series (dealing with items that are commonly held to be annual taxations), both affecting the principal districts of the two provinces into which the palatial kingdom of Messenia was divided. The generally accepted assumption is that the proportional relationships between the quantities associated with each district in Jn 829 are the same as those in in the Ma series. In this article we will try to demonstrate that this is *not* the case.

Indeed, Killen (1996) also admits that the proportional relationships between the districts in Jn 829 are not the same as in the Ma series ("the higher contributors on Jn 829 being lower contributors on the Ma tablets"). One wonders, therefore, what are the clues that could relate Jn 829 with the Ma series and especially what pieces of evidence support the hypothesis of a subdivision of the taxation of the kingdom of Pylos into 100 units, as suggested by De Fidio.

The Ma series has been linked to other texts that show proportional relationships among the principal districts, for example Cn 608 and Vn 20. De Fidio (1982) underlined not only that these two documents may be linked with the Ma series, but that their numbers follow the same tax procedure as in the Ma series. An analysis of the mathematical process of this hypothesis has shown that the supposed links between these two documents and the Ma series are not demonstrable.

Keywords

Mycenaean fiscality, Ma series, Jn series, bronze, *ta-ra-si-ja*

L ES TEXTES DE LA SÉRIE JN DE PYLOS sont systématiquement évoqués chaque fois que l'on parle de documents de type fiscal.[1]

Les tablettes de cette série enregistrent (à l'exception de PY Jn 829) une distribution de bronze, appelée *ta-ra-si-ja*: (*ka-ke-we ta-ra-si-ja e-ko-te/e-ko-si*, χαλκῆϝες ἔχοντες / ἔχονσι)[2] destinée à des groupes de forgerons qui sont tenus de fournir au Palais une prestation de service, c'est-à-dire un certain nombre d'objets en bronze.

À chaque groupe est attribuée une quantité de bronze qui va d'un minimum de M 1 N 2 (= M 1.5) à un maximum de M 12[pour chaque forgeron.

La série toute entière nous restitue environ 270 noms de forgerons et, si l'on tient compte du caractère fragmentaire d'une partie des documents, aurait même pu comporter selon Lejeune (1971:186) jusqu'à 400 noms.

Certains de ces artisans sont vraisemblablement des esclaves (*do-e-ro*); leur nom n'est pas consigné mais ils sont évoqués à travers le nom de leur maître. S'appuyant sur le fait que les esclaves cités sont toujours *a-ta-ra-si-jo*, Lejeune (1971:195) a formulé l'hypothèse que l'attribution d'une *ta-ra-si-ja* n'est pas à considérer comme "une charge pour les attributaires (c'est-à-dire un τέλος), mais au contraire un privilège probablement recherché" qui devait probablement consister en des dégrèvements fiscaux ou en de petites quantités de matière brute.

D'autres forgerons, en outre, semblent être des personnes affectées au service d'un sanctuaire (*a-pe-ke-e*, *ka-ke-we*, *po-ti-ni-ja-we-jo*, *ta-ra-si-ja e-ko-te*, Jn 431.16).

Dans trois des textes (Jn 431.6, 601.8, 845.7), après la liste des forgerons et juste avant la formule *to-so-de ka-ko* (τόσ(σ)ον δὲ χαλκόν), est cité un personnage important, le *qa-si-re-we* qui s'occupe en quelque sorte de la distribution du bronze. Ces distributions sont pour la majorité destinées au village ou mieux, à des forgerons appartenant à un village. Les districts en effet sont mentionnés seulement dans quatre cas (*a-ke-re-wa*, *a-pu₂-we*, *a-si-ja-ti-ja* et *ro-u-so*) et le sont en tant que centres principaux du territoire.

L'un des textes de la série, Jn 829, se distingue nettement des autres enregistrements. Il concerne en effet un prélèvement (*jo-do-so-si*, *ko-re-te-re*, *du-ma-ta-qe*) de bronze issu de temples (*ka-ko na-wi-jo*)[3] pour la fabrication de javelots (*pa-ta-i-jo-qe*) et de pointes de flèches (*a₃-ka-sa-ma*).

---

[1]   Il existe sur la série Jn une bibliographie considérable: voir en dernier lieu Varias 2016:403–419.

[2]   Pour Lejeune (1971:195) la *ta-ra-si-ja* est "une attribution accompagnée, probablement, d'avantages sensibles qui en faisaient un véritable privilège." Chadwick la considère comme un "amount weighed out and issued for processing" (*Docs*², 583), opinion partagée par Killen (2001:161).

[3]   Del Freo (2005:800–803) traduit *ka-ko na-wi-jo* comme "bronze pour les navires."

Il est possible replacer ce prélèvement, sans que l'on puisse toutefois le prouver absolument, dans le contexte particulier de la situation d'urgence que le Palais connaît probablement à la veille de sa chute, comme l'a souligné P. De Fidio (1982:114). Dans ce cas nous aurions affaire à une réquisition de bronze auprès des sanctuaires, ce qui représente sans aucun doute un acte extrême, dicté par la nécessité de se procurer dans des délais très brefs les armes nécessaires pour équiper le plus grand nombre d'hommes possible. Nous ne croyons pas cependant que cet acte soit nécessairement dû, comme le soutient De Fidio (1982:114), au fait que les canaux de réapprovisionnement aient été interrompus dans ce contexte de menace imminente. Importer du bronze par voie de mer ou de terre aurait seulement pris trop de temps, compte tenu de l'immédiateté des besoins, d'où le choix de trouver rapidement du bronze.

En Jn 829 tous les districts des deux provinces sont énumérés,[4] et pour chaque district sont mentionnés un *ko-re-te* et un *po-ro-ko-re-te*, soit les principales autorités du district, tenues de prélever et de livrer au Palais les quantités de métal exigées pour chaque district.

Presque tous les *ko-re-te-re* prélèvent dans les sanctuaires une quantité égale à 2 M, sauf celui de *ra-]wa-ra-ta₂* qui donne une quantité de 3 N en plus, et ceux de *sa-]ma-ra*, *za-ma-e-wi-ja* et *e-re-i* qui donnent une quantité de M 3 N 3. Tous les *po-ro-ko-re-te-re* en revanche prélèvent le même quota de N 3. Au total, les sanctuaires des neufs districts de la Province Proche fournissent aux *ko-re-te-re* et aux *po-ro-ko-re-te-re* un quota de 11 N de bronze pour un total de 11 N × 9 = 99 N, alors que les sanctuaires des sept districts de la Province Lointaine fournissent 101 N de bronze.

La différence entre ces deux quantités, que nous pouvons évaluer à environ 24,750 kg pour la Province Proche et à 25,250 kg pour la Province Lointaine, est de presque ½ kg de bronze, soit 2 N. Étant donné que la différence entre les deux Provinces (2 N) est du même ordre de grandeur (N) que celui utilisé dans la tablette, on peut se demander pourquoi le Palais n'as pas imposé aux deux provinces une charge égale et pour quelle raison il a laissé une telle différence, négligeable, entre les deux provinces (Province Proche 99, Province Lointaine 101).

Nous estimons que le Palais avait besoin de 200 N de bronze, et en a demandé environ 100 N par province; l'explication de cette petite différence pourrait alors être des plus banales. En effet, en demandant 11 N pour chaque district de la Province Proche, on arrive à 99 N. Aussi, plutôt que de créer des différences entre les districts (en demandant le N de bronze à un seul district), le Palais a préféré demander un N en moins à la Province Proche en le reportant sur la Province Lointaine.

---

[4]   *E-re-i* à la place de *a-te-re-wi-ja* qui apparaît à sa place en Ma 335.1 et Vn 493.6.

Étant donné que le Palais ne voulait pas descendre au dessous de la mesure N, ni avoir affaire à des quantités négligeables, il a été obligé de créer une disparité au détriment de quatre districts. L'un d'entre eux est *ra-wa-ra-ta₂*, c'est-à-dire le district qui paie aussi le plus dans la série Ma. Peut-être était-ce également le district le plus grand, ou peut-être, comme dans les trois autres districts, les temples y étaient-ils plus nombreux et recelaient donc plus de bronze? Il nous semble inévitable que le Palais, obligé de créer une disparité dans la Province Lointaine, ait demandé la différence de bronze aux districts qui en possédaient le plus. Mais il n'existe, à notre avis, aucune preuve dans Jn 829 qui puisse indiquer que cette méthode de subdivision de la charge a un quelconque rapport avec la série Ma, malgré ce que suggère Killen (1996:148).

En effet, Killen lui-même admet que les rapports entre les districts dans Jn 829 ne sont pas les mêmes que dans la série Ma ("the higher contributors on Jn 829 being lower contributors on the Ma tablets"). On se demande donc quels sont les indices qui pourraient mettre en relation Jn 829 avec la série Ma, et surtout quelles sont les preuves soutenant l'hypothèse d'une subdivision en 100 unités de taxation de l'imposition du royaume de Pylos, comme l'a suggéré De Fidio (1982:100). En effet le seul indice réside dans le fait que le Palais a besoin de 200 N de bronze, répartis à peu près également entre les deux provinces. Il faut également rappeler que pour la série Ma, la subdivision de l'impôt en 100 unités de taxation par province est seulement une hypothèse, et que cette hypothèse s'oppose nettement aux données des tablettes. Il ne faut pas oublier enfin que le modèle mathématique élaboré pour soutenir cette hypothèse se fonde sur une démarche mathématique très faible.[5] L'équivoque vient du fait que le Palais demande 200 N de bronze, plus au moins 100 par province: on est donc tenté de mettre en relation ce nombre avec l'hypothèse d'une répartition de l'impôt en 100 unités. Mais si le Palais avait eu besoin par exemple de 250 N, il aurait demandé 125 N par province. En effet la coïncidence des 100 N de bronze (ou mieux 99 et 101) par province avec les 100 unités de taxation imaginées par De Fidio pour la série Ma est seulement due au hasard. La quantité totale de bronze demandée par le Palais ne peut pas être liée aux calculs de l'imposition, mais représente seulement le besoin réel du Palais à un moment donné.

Malgré tout, même s'il n'y a aucune preuve convaincante pour supposer que les produits Ma sont payés par les districts à raison de 100 unités de taxation par province, il n'est peut être pas sans importance de se demander (comme Killen 1996:148) si le fait que le Palais demande aux deux provinces du bronze en

---

[5] Pour une critique detaillée de cette hypothèse, voir Perna 2004:191–198. Même la tentative d'imaginer une subdivision en 100 unités pour la série Mc de Cnossos est discutable; voir Perna 2004:152. Pour une critique détaillée de toutes les hypothèses sur la série Ma, voir Perna 2004:131–202.

quantités plus au moins égales, a un rapport avec l'hypothèse, jamais démontrée mais avancée par Wyatt (1962:21–41), d'une égalité de contribution (originaire) des deux provinces dans la série Ma.

Selon nous, ce n'est pas le cas. En premier lieu comme nous l'avons vu, la répartition de la demande en bronze suit une autre logique parce que les rapports entre les districts sont totalement différents dans Ma et Jn 829. En effet le Palais en Jn 829 a sans doute demandé plus au moins la même quantité de bronze aux deux provinces et il a appliqué aux 16 districts une quantité standard de 11 N. Un petit surplus (de 750 g à 1,750 kg.) est demandé seulement à quatre districts de la Province Lointaine. Ce supplément est évidemment la quantité qui manque (24) pour arriver à 101, si on demande 11 N aux 7 districts de la Province Lointaine (c'est-à-dire 77 N). Les 24 N de bronze qui restent pour arriver à 101 ont été répartis entre quatre districts de la Province Lointaine en tenant compte par exemple du nombre des sanctuaires ou de leur richesse.

Il y a de toute façon une différence remarquable entre la demande des six produits Ma et la demande du bronze. Dans la série Ma la demande est faite aux districts. Dans Jn 829 au contraire, les destinataires de cette réquisition ne sont pas les districts, au sens où ils définissent le territoire, mais les sanctuaires qui se trouvent dans chaque district. La mention du district sert donc seulement à identifier un certain nombre de sanctuaires. Pour cette raison, la capacité de production et de contribution d'un district en Ma n'a rien à voir avec la capacité contributive d'un district en Jn 829, parce que celle-ci dépend seulement du nombre et de la richesse des sanctuaires présents dans le district. Il est donc très dangereux, selon nous, de mettre en relation les chiffres de la série Ma avec ceux de Jn 829, parce qu'ils se réfèrent à deux modes de calcul différents.

La série Ma a été mise en relation aussi avec d'autres textes, tels que PY Cn 608 et PY Vn 20. De Fidio a souligné non seulement que ces deux documents pourraient avoir un lien avec la série Ma, mais que leurs chiffres suivent la même procédure fiscale que la série Ma. Une analyse du procédé mathématique sur lequel se fonde cette hypothèse a cependant prouvé que les liens supposés entre ces deux documents et la série Ma ne sont pas démontrables (Perna 2004:203–207). En effet, PY Cn 608 enregistre une obligation, à laquelle sont assujettis les *o-pi-da-mi*-jo de la Province Proche, à engraisser de porcs (*jo-a-se-so-si* , *si-a$_2$-ro*), et PY Vn 20 enregistre une distribution de vin (*pa-ra-we-wo wo-no*) aux districts de la même province. Nous avons donc affaire à une entrée (sous forme d'un travail dû) et une sortie; or on ne peut pas imaginer que les entrées fiscales et les distributions de biens aux districts aient suivi la même règle mathématique.

En effet la proportionnalité que nous trouvons entre les chiffres des districts, dans les tablettes Ma ainsi que dans PY Cn 608 et PY Vn 20, peut être expliquée de manière plus simple. Il n'y a rien d'étrange à ce que deux districts qui ont une extension, une richesse ou une population semblable soient imposés par le Palais de la même manière, et il en va de même, bien entendu, quand il s'agit pour le Palais de distribuer des produits ou des animaux.

Il est souhaitable, à notre avis, de reprendre l'examen de tous les textes où l'on a pensé retrouver, depuis le déchiffrement du linéaire B, des traces de la procédure fiscale de la série Ma (comme PY Cn 608, PY Vn 20, Jn 829, etc.). Malheureusement, les études récentes sur le monde mycénien, même lorsqu'elles sont concernées par l'économie et la fiscalité des royaumes mycéniens, semblent systématiquement ignorer la seule monographie existante sur la série Ma et les documents connexes, et se limitent à fournir un aperçu d'études qui remontent aux années 1980. Or même si ces analyses ont été établies conformément aux critères de scientificité de leur époque, elles sont aujourd'hui totalement à revoir.

Bibliography

De Fidio, P. 1982. "Fiscalità, redistribuzione, equivalenze: Per una discussione sull'economia micenea." *Studi Micenei ed Egeo-Anatolici* 23:83–136.

Del Freo, M. 2005. "L'expression *ka-ko na-wi-jo* de la tablette Jn 829 de Pylos." In *Emporia. Aegeans in the Central and Eastern Mediterranean. Proceedings of the 10th International Aegean Conference, Athens, Italian School of Archaeology, 14-18 April 2004*, vol. II, ed R. Laffineur and E. Greco, 793–803. Aegaeum 25. Liège-Austin.

Killen, J. T. 1996. "Administering a Mycenaean Kingdom: Some Taxing Problems." *Bulletin of the Institute of Classical Studies* 41:147–148.

———. 2001. "Some Thoughts on *ta-ra-si-ja*." In *Economy and Politics in the Mycenaean Palace States. Proceedings of a Conference Held on 1–3 July 1999 in the Faculty of Classics, Cambridge*, ed. S. Voutsaki and J. T. Killen, 161–180. Cambridge.

Lejeune, M. 1971. *Mémoires de philologie mycénienne. Deuxième série (1958–1963)*. Rome.

Perna, M. 2004. *Recherches sur la fiscalité mycénienne*. Nancy.

Simpson R. H. 2014. *Mycenaean Messenia and the Kingdom of Pylos*. Philadelphia.

Varias, C. 2016. "Testi relativi ai metalli." In *Manuale di epigrafia micenea: Introduzione allo studio dei testi in lineare B*. Vol. 2, ed. M. Del Freo and M. Perna, 403–419. Padua.

Wyatt, W. F. 1962. "The Ma Tablets from Pylos." *American Journal of Archaeology* 66:21–41.

16

Afinidades semánticas entre mic. *do-so-mo* y griego δωτίνη[1]

Rosa A. Santiago

Universitat Autònoma de Barcelona

rosa.santiago@uab.es

Abstract

The noun *do-so-mo*, common in Mycenaean, does not show continuity in later Greek. In this paper I try to underline some semantic parallelisms between Mycenaean *do-so-mo* and historical Greek δωτίνη, both terms coming from the Indo-European root *deh_3- 'give, pay'.

Semantic affinities with the Mycenaean uses of *do-so-mo* are noticeable in the earlier literary uses of δωτίνη and in some Argive inscriptions. Both terms share the idea of 'compulsory, normative payment', pointing first and foremost to the taxes on cultivation of plots that were controlled by sacred and public ownership but where the right of cultivation was granted to private individuals for their exploitation.

Keywords

do-so-mo, δωτίνη, taxes, land cultivation

Resumen

El nombre *do-so-mo*, frecuente en micénico, no tiene continuidad en griego posterior. Pretendo en este trabajo poner de relieve ciertas coincidencias semánticas entre mic. *do-so-mo* y gr. δωτίνη, dos nombres derivados de la raíz ide. *deh_3- 'dar, pagar'.

[1] Trabajo realizado en el marco del Proyecto de Investigación FFI2016-79906-P: "Estudio diacrónico de las instituciones sociopolíticas de la Grecia antigua y de sus manifestaciones míticas" (AEI/ FEDER, UE), dirigido por el Prof. Carlos Varias García. Agradezco al Prof. Julián Méndez Dosuna sus valiosas observaciones a este trabajo, del que soy única responsable.

En los usos literarios más antiguos de δωτίνη y en ciertas inscripciones argivas se observan afinidades semánticas con los usos micénicos de *do-so-mo*. Ambos términos comparten la idea de 'pago obligado, normativo', referido prioritariamente a las rentas por el cultivo de parcelas de titularidad sagrada y pública cedidas a particulares para su explotación.

Palabras clave

do-so-mo, δωτίνη, rentas, cultivo tierra

EN DOS TRABAJOS PREVIOS[2] ME HE OCUPADO DEL ANÁLISIS de los derivados de la raíz indoeuropea *deh₃-* en micénico y en Homero respectivamente. La comparación de los usos de mic. *do-so-mo* con los de gr. δωτίνη me sugirió la idea de una cierta afinidad semántica entre ambos. Aprovecho este merecido homenaje a José Luis Melena para profundizar en la cuestión.

1. Los primeros estudios sistemáticos del léxico micénico derivado de la raíz indoeuropea *deh₃-* son los de Duhoux (1968; 1976) y Lejeune (1975). Los derivados de esa raíz constituyen una de las familias léxicas mejor documentadas en micénico y la más importante en el léxico de la fiscalidad.[3]

El sustantivo *do-so-mo* /dosmós/ 'impuesto, tributo' es el término que cuenta con más menciones: 66. Igual que sus derivados *do-si-mi-jo, do-si-mi-ja* y *a-pu-do-so*[*-mo*[4] se aplica en general a las contribuciones en especie que determinados individuos o grupos laborales deben entregar al palacio o a los templos como tasas sobre sus productos. Esas entregas pueden ser ocasionales, como en PY Un 718, pero en general son aportaciones habituales, probablemente anuales, como indica la expresión *we-te-i-we-te-i* 'anualmente' repetida en todas las entradas de PY Es 644, o la expresión *pe-ru-si-nu-wo o-pe-ro* 'deuda del año anterior'.

Sorprende que, a pesar de su frecuencia en micénico, el término *do-so-mo* no haya tenido continuidad en griego alfabético: solo pervive como segundo elemento de compuesto en dos formas: ἀπυδοσμός y el derivado ἀπυδόσμ[ιον[5] (cf. mic. *do-si-mi-jo/a*). Ambas aparecen en dos inscripciones arcadias del s. IV. La primera, *IPArk* 15.34.35 (Orcómeno, ca. 360–350),[6] es un tratado de *sympoliteia* entre Orcómeno y Euaimon. El contexto induce a traducir el término ἀπυδοσμός como 'reintegro, devolución'.[7] La segunda, *IPArk* 2.28 (Tegea, ca. 400), hace refer-

---

[2] Santiago 2014a y Santiago 2014b.
[3] Una buena presentación en Varias 2006:241–248, 253.
[4] *Hapax* en KN Nc 4484, donde se registra una contribución de 20 kg de lino procedente de Amniso.
[5] Interesantes propuestas respecto a su interpretación en Lejeune 1975:9–11.
[6] Dubois 1986.II:146–163, 155s.
[7] Según propuesta de Thür (1994:136–137).

encia al reglamento del santuario de Atenea Alea, donde fue hallada. El adjetivo ἀπυδόσμιος parece aplicarse aquí a un estiércol[8] 'destinado a la venta'.[9]

2. Las primeras menciones de δωτίνη se dan en Homero. Según Benveniste,[10] ya desde Homero δωτίνη se diferenciaría de los otros términos que significan 'don, regalo', porque connota la idea de obligación o reciprocidad: "le don obligé," "la notion du don en retour ou du don qui appelle retour." Morfológicamente, δωτίνη es un derivado nominal con un antiguo sufijo complejo indoeuropeo *-i-Hn-eh₂*, bien atestiguado en latín (*regina, gallina*), etc., pero residual en griego.[11]

2.1. De los cuatro ejemplos homéricos, dos aparecen en la *Ilíada* y dos en la *Odisea*. Los de la *Ilíada* pueden reducirse a uno, ya que el pasaje se repite en sendos discursos, el primero pronunciado por Agamenón (*Ilíada* 9.115–161) ante los nobles aqueos, y el segundo por Odiseo en la tienda de Aquiles (9.225–306). En dicho pasaje, el último de los presentes ofrecidos es la entrega de siete ciudades (πτολίεθρα) 149–156 (≈ 291–298): "Le daré también siete ciudades bien pobladas: Cardámila, Enopa e Hira la herbosa, la muy divina Feras y Antia de abundantes pastos, la hermosa Epia y Pédaso rica en viñedos. Todas ellas cerca del mar, al fondo de la arenosa Pilo." Y añade: "En ellas viven hombres ricos en corderos [πολύρρηνες] y bueyes [πολυβοῦται], que a él con sus dones [δωτίνῃσι] como a un dios honrarán [θεὸν ὣς τιμήσουσιν], y sometidos a su cetro [ὑπὸ σκήπτρῳ], le pagarán pingües contribuciones [λιπαρὰς τελέουσι θέμιστας]."

La problemática respecto a esas ciudades, su posible realidad y localización es una cuestión largamente debatida y para la que no hay una respuesta unánime.[12]

En un análisis anterior del pasaje,[13] yo proponía entender esos versos como una *hendíadis*, en la que λιπαρὰς θέμιστας concretaría las δωτίνῃσι mencionadas previamente y que en el plano humano se materializarían en las contribuciones normativas (θέμιστας) que los habitantes de esas prósperas ciudades pagarían como rentas a su señor, Aquiles en este caso. Estilísticamente sería un

---

[8]   IPArk 2.27–29: τὰ [δ' ἄλλα τ]]ὸς δαμιοργός ∷ τὸν κόπρον τὸν ἀπυδόσμ[ιον ἐξάγε]][ν] τᾶι hεβδόμαι τõ Λεσχαναϲίο μενός·.

[9]   Cf. Dubois 1986.II:20–34. A partir del s. V el verbo ἀποδίδωμι, especialmente en voz media, tiene a menudo el significado de 'vender'.

[10] Benveniste 1966:318–319.

[11] Chantraine 1933:205, Dieu 2016:208.

[12] Hope Simpson 1957, 1966; Hope Simpson, Lazenby, and John (1971) defienden la realidad micénica del *Catálogo*. García Ramón (1974) la rechaza convincentemente. Análisis de las diferentes posturas en González García 1997:1–44, crítico respecto a la historicidad del *Catálogo* (González García 2007:42–46). Plácido (2002:65–73) ve en los datos homéricos y la arqueología claves para explicar la primitiva historia de Mesenia.

[13] Santiago 2014b:287s.

procedimiento semejante al comentado por Fraenkel[14] a propósito de ciertas yuxtaposiciones en el *Agamenón* de Esquilo: παυσανέμου γὰρ θυσίας παρθενίου θ'αἵματος (214s.), βίᾳ χαλινῶν δ' ἀναύδῳ μένει (238), φύροντα πλοῦτον ἀργυρωνήτους θ'ὑφάς (949). Fraenkel remite a Schadewaldt[15] para ese tipo de yuxtaposición consistente en expresar una misma idea en dos frases coordinadas, una abstracta y otra concreta ("a single idea is expressed both in the abstract and in the perceptible concrete symbol").

2.2. En los ejemplos de la *Odisea* el carácter normativo de δωτίνη hace referencia a los deberes de hospitalidad. En *Odisea* 9.266–268 Odiseo reclama al Cíclope la ayuda mínima debida a extranjeros y suplicantes: ἡμεῖς δ' αὖτε κιχανόμενοι τὰ σὰ γούνα /, εἴ τι πόροις ξεινήιον ἠὲ καὶ ἄλλως / δοίης δωτίνην, ἥ τε ξείνων θέμις ἐστίν ("y nosotros postrados estamos ante tus rodillas, esperando que nos procures algún don de hospitalidad [ξεινήιον] o, al menos [καὶ ἄλλως], el don [δωτίνην] que es norma [θέμις ἐστίν] entregar a extranjeros"). La oposición entre ξεινήιον y δωτίνη parece denotar aquí una cierta diferencia semántica entre ambos: el primero depende de la generosidad del donante, en tanto que δωτίνη parece hacer referencia al 'don normativo' (θέμις ἐστίν),[16] es decir, a la ayuda mínima a quien llega de fuera y la solicita adecuadamente.

En *Odisea* 8.387–389, Alcínoo, después de recibir y agasajar a Odiseo, se dirige a los nobles de la corte feacia instándolos a ofrecerle sus presentes de hospitalidad: "Oíd caudillos y reyes de los feacios: el extranjero me parece ser muy sensato [πεπνυμένος]. Ea, pues, démosle [δῶμεν] nuestro don de hospitalidad [ξεινήιον] tal como corresponde [ὡς ἐπιεικές]."

En *Odisea* 11.351–353, Odiseo ha sido aceptado ya como huésped de honor y ha recibido ricos presentes, pero Alcínoo decide completar (πᾶσαν δωτίνην τελέσω, 352) los regalos entregados previamente a Odiseo, ya que se había comprometido, junto con los demás reyes feacios, a añadir más, accediendo a la petición previa de Arete (335–341).

2.3. El pl. δω[τίναις, reconstruido en un fragmento de Hesíodo (200, 9 M-W), parece indicar contribuciones por la explotación de tierras: Menesteo espera que ningún otro de los pretendientes de Helena pueda competir con él en regalos, dadas sus cuantiosas posesiones (κτήνεσσί) y las rentas (τε δω[τίναις τε) procedentes de su explotación, entendidas esas rentas como don obligado para quienes explotan sus tierras.

---

[14] Fraenkel 1950:123–124.
[15] Schadewaldt 1932:328n3.
[16] Como las θέμιστας del pasaje de *Ilíada*.

3. De gran interés son algunos testimonios epigráficos procedentes de la Argólide, tanto de inscripciones ya publicadas como de otras pendientes de publicación.[17]

3.1. De las publicadas la más explícita respecto al significado de δωτίνη (δωτίνᾱ en este dialecto) es una inscripción (*IG* IV 841) del s. III a. C. avanzado procedente de Calauria, antigua isla situada en el golfo Sarónico en la que se conservan restos de un templo dedicado a Posidón. Las diez primeras líneas de la inscripción están en muy mal estado y no permiten reconstruir su contenido. El texto recoge las decisiones de la asamblea de ciudadanos de Calauria respecto a la administración de la doble ofrenda, en dinero y en tierra cultivable, que un matrimonio, Agasicles y Nicágora, hacen (o habían hecho) a Posidón. Se nombran dos *epimeletes* que deben encargarse de prestar a interés el dinero (15s.) y de arrendar el terreno (καὶ τὸ χωρίον ἐκδωσοῦντι δωτίνας, 18s.). Con los intereses del dinero y las rentas del terreno (πράξαντες τὸ διάφορον τοῦ ἀργυρίου καὶ τὰν δωτίναν τὰν ἐκ τοῦ χωρίου, 20s.) deberán organizar sendos sacrificios de víctimas perfectas en honor de Posidón[18] y Zeus Salvador (21–23), sacrificios que se repetirán cada año (26). Se cuidarán asimismo de que todo lo demás (τὰ λοιπά, 26) en esos sacrificios sea de gran brillantez (ὡς ὅτι χαριέστατα, 27).

3.2. Distinto es el caso de una inscripción de época imperial grabada sobre una tumba en la ciudad caria de Afrodisias (*MAMA* 8.544). En ella su dueño, de nombre romano (Μᾶρκος Ἀντώνιος Μολο[σσός]), establece quiénes tendrán derecho a ser enterrados allí: [ταφήσονται δὲ οἵς ἂν αὐ]τός βουλήλομαι ἢ διατάξομαι ἤ δωτί[νην δώσω], "Serán enterrados quienes yo personalmente desee, disponga o (a quienes) se lo conceda como regalo" (ll. 9–10).

3.3. En una inscripción de época bizantina (post 516 d. C.) procedente de Anazarbos en Cilicia (*IK* Anazarbos 58)[19] aparece el sintagma δωτίναις βασιλῆσι[ν] en un epigrama con una petición a San Menas.[20] El firmante, un notable local, pide al santo para su ciudad una "juventud de hermosa doncella," recordándole el bello templo construido en su honor gracias a los "dones imperiales"[21] (δωτίναις βασιλῆσι[ν]), y mantenido por los cuidados (μερίμναις) de la familia

---

[17] Desde los años ochenta del pasado siglo han ido apareciendo noticias sobre las nuevas inscripciones recuperadas en Argos: Des Courtils 1981; Kritzas 1992, 2006; Bommelaer and Des Courtils 1994; Piérart 1997, 2000; McAuley 2009–2010. Su publicación se ha ido alargando, pero se ha anunciado ya (Chaniotis *et al.* 2010:336) una próxima edición de *IG* IV que incluirá esas nuevas inscripciones.

[18] La importancia del culto a Posidón en Calauria es visible también en otras inscripciones, como *IG* IV, 840, de la misma época que la comentada y muy afín a ella en forma y contenido.

[19] *SEG* 12 (1955), 545; *BE* 1954:238.

[20] Comentado recientemente en Agosti (2010:176–177).

[21] Agosti apunta como probable donante al emperador Anastasio I.

del firmante. Dada la fecha tardía de la inscripción, δωτίναις podría ser aquí un mero cultismo.

4. En cualquier caso, la información más relevante sobre δωτίνη y sus derivados proviene de una de las inscripciones de Argos pendiente de publicación definitiva. Disponemos de un texto, aparentemente parcial, incluido por Kritzas[22] en dos trabajos en los que el autor pone de relieve el interés de las informaciones que transmiten algunas de las inscripciones recuperadas—esta entre otras—para un mejor conocimiento de la historia política y económica de Argos en el s. V a. C.[23]

Kritzas presenta así la inscripción:[24] "Il s'agit d'un décret honorifique pour quelqu'un qui entre autres" y da el texto, pero no lo traduce. He aquí el texto:

> Κατασταθεὶς δὲ καὶ [- - - -] τᾶς ἱερᾶς καὶ δαμοσίας χώρας [- - - -] τοὺς μὲν γύας ἰδιωτικοὺς γεγενημένους [- - - -] τῶν πολιτᾶν, ἔπεισε ἄνευ πραγμάτων ἀποδόμεν τοὺς γύας. Τοὺς δὲ μὴ ἀποδίδοντας εἰσαγωγῶν εἰς τὸ δικαστήριον καὶ παραδείξας τοῖς δικασταῖς ἀδίκως καρπευομένους τοῖς γύαις καὶ μὴ ὀφειλομένους μηθέν, ἀνάγκαξε ἀποδόμεν τᾶι τε Ἥραι καὶ τῷ Ἡρακλεῖ καὶ Πυθαεῖ καὶ Ἀληκτρυῶνι καὶ ἀπεκατέστασε ἑκάστωι τῶν θεῶν τὰν ἱερὰν χώραν.
>
> Κατασταθεὶς δὲ καὶ δωτινατὴρ τᾶς ἱερᾶς καὶ δαμοσίας χώρας, μετὰ Μενεστράτου τοῦ ταμία, ἐποιήσατο δικαίως τὰν δωτίνασιν καὶ εἰσάγαγε τᾶι πόλει καθ᾽ ἕκαστον ἐνιαυτὸν πλεῖον ἤ ταλάντωι τὰν δωτίναν εὑρεῖν παρά τὰν πρότερον οὖσαν δωτίναν καὶ φερομέναν τᾶι πόλει.
>
> Ἐπιμέλειαν δὲ ἐποιήσατο καὶ ὅπως ἀναγράφωντι οἱ γύαι ἐφεξᾶς, καθὼς ἁ χώρα διεκλαρώθε ὑπὸ τῶν ἀρχαίων καὶ κατεμερίσθη κατὰ γύας δωτιναμένας, τὸν προτοῦ χρόνον ὡς ἔτυχε καὶ ἀναγραφομένας ἐν διερριμμένοις τόποις.

Adelanto una posible traducción:

> Y nombrado también [- - - -] de tierra sagrada y pública (ἱερᾶς καὶ δαμοσίας χώρας) [- - - -] a los ciudadanos que habían convertido las parcelas en particulares [- - - -] les instó a devolver las parcelas sin entrar en negociaciones. Y a los no dispuestos a devolverlas, llevándoles ante

---

[22] Kritzas 1992:231–240. Para una presentación más detallada del proceso de las excavaciones en la zona y de sus aportaciones, cf. Kritzas 2006.

[23] Aunque la inscripción mencionada es de finales de la época helenística, Kritzas (1992:237) afirma que hace referencias a períodos anteriores.

[24] Kritzas 1992:237ss.

el Tribunal de Justicia y mostrando a los jueces que estaban disfrutando injustamente de las parcelas sin pagar nada de lo debido,[25] les obligó a pagar lo adeudado a Hera, a Heracles, a Apolo Piteo y a Alectrión, y devolvió a cada uno de los dioses la tierra sagrada.[26]

Asimismo como encargado del arriendo [δωτινατήρ] de la tierra sagrada y pública, acompañado de Menéstrato, el tesorero llevó a cabo con toda justicia el arrendamiento [δωτίνασιν] y propuso ante la asamblea de ciudadanos que cada año la renta [τὰν δωτίναν] tuviese un incremento de más de un talento respecto a la renta real anterior [πρότερον οὖσαν δωτίναν] y entregada a la ciudad.

Se cuidó asimismo de que las parcelas fuesen inscritas ordenadamente, tal como el terreno había sido sorteado por los antiguos y repartido en parcelas destinadas al arriendo [δωτιναμένας], parcelas que, como ocurría en los primeros tiempos, estaban inscritas en lugares dispersos.

La clasificación del texto por Kritzas como decreto honorífico es clave para su comprensión: en el texto se exponen los méritos del personaje honrado que han motivado tal decreto, y que no son otros que sus sucesivas actuaciones para asegurar el cobro de las rentas de parcelas de titularidad sagrada y pública cedidas a particulares para su explotación.

Destacaré los puntos más interesantes de la inscripción para la problemática que nos ocupa:

(1) Aporta los primeros testimonios conocidos de varios derivados de δωτίνα: δωτίνασις 'arrendamiento', δωτινατήρ 'encargado del arriendo', δωτινάω 'arrendar'.

(2) El uso de esos términos muestra que, en la administración argiva, δωτίνα y sus derivados formaban parte del léxico habitual referente a la parcelación y arrendamiento de tierras.

(3) Esta inscripción completa el testimonio de la de Calauria antes examinada (cf. 3.1): en ambas, δωτίνα se aplica a rentas provenientes de terrenos de titularidad sagrada, pero administrados por la ciudad.

---

[25] Es decir, las rentas correspondientes.

[26] Aunque la titularidad fuese de los templos, era el estado el que recibía el dinero de las rentas y velaba por el recto cumplimiento de las normas. Las relaciones financieras entre ambos eran muy estrechas y a menudo los templos hacían de banca del Estado. Iluminador al respecto es el resumen de Dareste, Haussoulier y Reinach (1895-1898, 224s.).

Estos testimonios epigráficos reforzarían el valor testimonial de los ejemplos de *Ilíada* 9.155–156 / 9.297–298 y del fragmento de Hesíodo (200, 9 M-W) antes comentados, lo que induce a pensar que mic. *do-so-mo* y gr. δωτίνη habrían coincidido, al menos originariamente, en su aplicación a obligaciones derivadas del cultivo de la tierra, situación que en Argos habría tenido gran importancia y continuidad, como puede deducirse de las inscripciones analizadas. En consecuencia, creo que podría aplicarse a δωτίνη la afirmación que Perna[27] hace con respecto a *do-so-mo*:

> Le dénominateur commun à tous ces documents (= séries Ma, Na, Es, PY Un 718, Wa 730, 731) serait donc la terre. Quels que soient les produits livrés au Palais, ils réprésentent ou bien une redevance ou bien une taxe dérivant de la possesion d'une terre.

Fuera de Argos, δωτίνη habría adoptado pronto el significado más general de 'don que obliga a un contra-don'.

Bibliography

Agosti, G. 2010. "*Saxa loquuntur*? Epigrammi epigrafici e diffusione della Paideia nell'Oriente tardo antico." *Antiquité Tardive* 18:163–180.

Benveniste, E. 1966. "Don et échange dans le vocabulaire indo-européen." In *Problèmes de Linguistique générale*. Vol. I, 315–326. Paris.

Bommelaer, J. F., and J. Des Courtils. 1994. *La salle hypostyle d'Argos*. Athens.

Chaniotis, A., T. Corsten, N. Papazarkadas, and R. Tybout, eds. 2010. *Supplementum Epigraphicum Graecum (SEG)*. Vol. 60. Leiden.

Chantraine, P. 1933. *La formation des noms en grec ancien*. Paris. [Repr. 1979.]

Dareste, R., B. Haussoulier, and T. Reinach. 1895–1898. *Récueil des inscriptions juridiques grecques: Texte, traduction, commentaire*. 2 vols. Paris. [Repr. 1965.]

Des Courtils, J. 1981. "Note de topographie Argienne." *Bulletin de Correspondance Hellénique* 105:607–610.

Dieu, É. 2016. *L'accentuacion des noms en *-ā (*-eh₂) en grec ancien et dans les langues indoeuropéenes: Étude morphologique et sémantique*. Innsbruck.

Dubois, L. 1986. *Recherches sur le dialecte arcadien*. 3 vols. Louvain-La-Neuve. [Repr. 1988.]

Duhoux, Y. 1968. "Le group léxical de δίδωμι en mycénien." *Minos* 9:81–108.

———. 1976. *Aspects du vocabulaire économique mycénien: Cadastre, artisanat, fiscalité*. Amsterdam.

Fraenkel, E. 1950. *Aeschylus, Agamemnon*. Vol. II. Oxford.

---

[27] Cf. Perna 2004:297.

García Ramón, J. L. 1974. "En torno al *Catálogo de las Naves* homérico (A propósito de un reciente libro de R. Hope Simpson y J. F. Lazenby)." *Cuadernos de Filología Clásica* 7:145–180.

González García, F. J. 1997. *El* Catálogo de las Naves: *Mito y parentesco en la épica homérica.* Madrid.

———. 2007. "Historizando a Homero (y II): Los testimonios épicos y mítico-religiosos." *Habis* 38:41–59.

Hope Simpson, R. 1957. "Identifying a Mycenaean State." *Annual of the British School at Athens* 52:231-259.

———. 1966. "The Seven Cities offered by Agammenon to Achilles (*Iliad* IX 149ff., 291ff.)." *Annual of the British School at Athens* 61:113–131.

Hope Simpson, R., R. Lazenby, and F. John 1971. *The Catalogue of Ships in Homer's* Iliad. Oxford.

IPArk = Thür, G., and H. Taeuber. 1994. *Prozessrechtliche Inschriften der griechischen Poleis: Arkadien.* Vienna.

Kritzas, Ch. B. 1992. "Aspects de la vie politique et économique d'Argos au Ve siècle avant J.-C." In *Polydipsion Argos. Argos de la fin des palais mycéniennes à la constitution de l' État classique,* ed. M. Piérart, 231–240. Athens.

———. 2006. "Nouvelles inscriptions d'Argos: les archives des comptes du Trésor sacrée (IVe s. av. J.-C.)". *Comptes rendus des séances de l'Académie des Inscriptions et Belles-Lettres* 150.1:397–434.

Lejeune, M. 1975. "ΔΟΣΜΟΣ et ΑΠΥΔΟΣΙΣ." *Museum Helveticum* 32.1:1–11.

McAuley, A. 2009-2010. "Ethnicity, the Polis, and the Negotiation of Identity in the Argolid, 500–440 BC." *Hirundo: The McGill Journal of Classical Studies* 8:1–10.

Perna, M. 2004. *Recherches sur la fiscalité mycénienne.* Nancy.

Piérart, M. 1997. "L'attitude d'Argos à l'égard des autres cités de l'Argolide." In *The Polis as an Urban Centre and as a Political Community. Symposium August, 29-31 1996,* ed. M. Herman Hansen, 321–351. Copenhagen.

Piérart M. 2000. "Argos: Une autre démocratie." In *Polis & Politics: Studies in Ancient Greek History Presented to Mogens Herman Hansen on His Sixtieth Birthday, August 20, 2000,* ed. P. Flensted-Jensen, T. H. Nielsen, and L. Rubinstein, 297–314. Copenhagen.

Plácido, D. 2002. "Las protociudades de Mesenia." *Studia historica. Historia antigua* 20:65–73.

Santiago, R. A. 2014a. "La polaridad 'dar' / 'pagar' en el mundo micénico." In *Donum Mycenologicum. Mycenaean Studies in Honour of Francisco Aura Jorro,* ed. A. Bernabé and E. R. Luján, 137–151. Louvain-la-Neuve.

Santiago, R. A. 2014b. "La polaridad 'dar' / 'pagar' en Homero." In *ÁGALMA. Ofrenda desde la Filología Clásica a Manuel García Teijeiro*, ed. A. Martínez, B. Ortega, H. Velasco, and H. Zamora, 283–290. Valladolid.

Schadewaldt, W. 1932. "Der Kommos in Aischylos Choephoren." *Hermes* 67:312–354.

Varias, C. 2006. "The Mycenaean Fiscal Vocabulary." In *Fiscality in Mycenaean and Near Eastern Archives. Proceedings of the Conference Held at Soprintendenza Archivistica per la Campania, Naples, 21-23 October 2004*, ed. M. Perna, 241–253. Paris.

17

Further Thoughts on the Reflex of Syllabic Nasals in Mycenaean Greek

CHRISTINA MICHELLE SKELTON

Center for Hellenic Studies, Harvard University
cskelton@ucla.edu

Abstract

Mycenaean shows an alternation between *a* and *o* as the outcome of syllabic nasals in the vicinity of a labial consonant. Previously, it has been argued that this alternation represents dialect variation or sound change in progress. The current paper argues, on the basis of acoustic and auditory phonetics, as well as data from Arcadian, Cypriot, and Old English, that the outcome of syllabic nasals in Mycenaean was simply unconditioned nasalized *a*, and that the variation between *a* and *o* represents scribes' efforts in representing this perceptually ambiguous segment.

Keywords

Mycenaean, Greek dialects, Linear B, syllabic nasals, Proto-Indo-European

1. Introduction

One long-standing problem in Mycenology is the nature of "special" versus "normal" Mycenaean, a collection of features that show an apparently random alternation in spelling between two variants.[1] These features include the athematic dative singular in -*e* versus -*i*, the outcome of the Proto-Indo-European syllabic nasals as *a* or *o* in the vicinity of a labial consonant, alternation between *i* and *e* in certain words, whether or not *ti* has assibilated to *si*, and whether or not sequences of liquid + vowel have undergone metathesis (Thompson 2002; Palaima 1998–1999). The distribution of some or all of these variants has

---

[1]   V= vowel; Ṽ = nasalized vowel; N = nasal consonant.

been studied at Knossos (Woodard 1986), Pylos (Risch 1966), Mycenae (Varias 1997), and Thebes (Hajnal 2006). The existence of "special" versus "normal" Mycenaean has been explained in various ways, including dialect variation (e.g., Risch 1966, Nagy 1968) and sound change in progress (Thompson 1997).

The present paper discusses one of these features, the outcome of syllabic nasals in the vicinity of a labial consonant, e.g., *pe-ma* and *pe-mo* 'seed', corresponding to Classical Greek σπέρμα, from PIE *spermṇ. It argues that this variation is not, in fact, due to the presence of two speech variants, either through the existence of two dialectal variants or a sound change in progress, but to scribes' efforts in representing a single, perceptually ambiguous segment. This possibility has been mentioned before, but has generally been dismissed by scholars (e.g., Thompson 1997:322). However, there is a strong argument to be made for this position on the basis of acoustic and auditory phonetics. If the reflex of syllabic nasals in Mycenaean was simply unconditioned nasalized *a*, as seems likely on the basis of both Greek and cross-linguistic evidence, phonetic cues from the nasalization and the labial environment could have rendered this vowel in this context perceptually ambiguous between *a* and *o*. According to auditory phonetics, scribes would not have recognized that this vowel was ambiguous between *a* and *o*. Instead, they would have perceived the vowel randomly as either *a* or *o*, and would have transcribed it accordingly.

The hypothesis that the Mycenaean reflex of syllabic nasals in a labial environment represents a perceptually ambiguous segment offers a more compelling explanation for the evidence than the alternatives, dialect variation and sound change in progress. To demonstrate this, I will compare the Greek and Mycenaean evidence to a parallel situation from Old English, the outcome of inherited West Germanic *a before nasal consonants in Old English. Both Mercian and Kentish show an alternation between *a* and *o* in manuscripts. In Mercian, the ultimate outcome was *o*, indicating that a real sound change took place. However, in Kentish, the ultimate outcome was *a*, indicating that the presence of *o* in this dialect was merely an orthographic illusion (Toon 1976). The Greek data, from both Mycenaean and its most closely related historical dialects, Arcadian and Cypriot, matches the Kentish situation much more closely, supporting the position that the Mycenaean situation represents phonetic ambiguity, not the coexistence of two speech variants.

Thus, this paper is divided into two parts. The first part lays out the argument that the outcome of syllabic nasals in Mycenaean was unconditioned nasalized *a*, that this vowel was perceptually ambiguous between *a* and *o* in the vicinity of a labial consonant, and that scribes would have rendered this perceptually ambiguous vowel alternately with *a* and *o*. The second part compares the Greek evidence to the parallel situation from Old English, and argues that the

Greek evidence is a better match for spelling ambiguity than dialect variation or sound change in progress.

2. The Mycenaean Reflex of Proto-Indo-European Syllabic Nasals

The reflex of the Proto-Indo-European syllabic nasals in Greek was ultimately *a*, sometimes *o* in certain dialects, but it is not common for syllabic nasals to develop directly into vowels; they typically pass through an intermediate stage involving nasalized vowels. Cross-linguistically, it is common for syllabic consonants to develop schwa-like prop vowels (Scheer 2004:304–306). Once such a vowel existed, it would be trivial for this vowel to develop along the common pathway VN > ṼN > Ṽ > V (Greenberg 1966; Beddor 2009).

In Greek, this intermediate stage most likely would have been nasalized *a*. The outcome of syllabic nasals in Mycenaean in a non-labial environment was regularly *a*. The outcome of syllabic nasals in two of the major Greek dialect groups, Attic-Ionic and West Greek, is *a*. Furthermore, even in the two dialect groups that do show *o* as the outcome of syllabic nasals, it is still possible to find the outcome *a* (e.g., Dubois 1986:39–41).

If the outcome of syllabic nasals in Mycenaean were nasalized *a*, two factors would have contributed to its occasional misperception as *o* in the vicinity of a labial consonant.

First, the nasalization of the vowel would have contributed to the perception that the nasalized *a* was a central vowel, not a low vowel. Nasalization affects the first formant, which is also the acoustic correlate of vowel height, and, as a result, nasalization tends to centralize the perception of vowels, especially when nasalization is not phonemic in the language and when the vowel is not in a nasal context (Krakow *et al.* 1988). Thus, nasalization would nudge the acoustic properties of the low back vowel *a* in the direction of the mid back vowel *o*.

Second, coarticulation effects between the nasalized *a* and the adjacent labial consonant would have led to the impression that the vowel was rounded. In speech, segments are not articulated independently of one another; instead, the articulation and acoustic properties of a given segment are influenced by the surrounding segments. The results of this kind of interference between adjacent segments are known as coarticulation effects (Farnetani and Recasens 2010). For example, in English, the phoneme [k] is pronounced further forward on the palate than in the word *kit* than the word *cot*, since [i] is a front vowel and [ɑ] is a back vowel.

One notable fact about the alternation between *a* and *o* as the reflex of syllabic nasals in Mycenaean is that it only occurs in the vicinity of a labial consonant; otherwise the outcome is *a*. As it happens, one of the salient differences between the vowel *o* and the vowel *a* is that *o* is pronounced with rounded lips, whereas *a* is not. This distribution is easy to explain as a coarticulation effect; the gesture of opening or closing the lips to produce a labial consonant would likely still be taking place at the time the adjacent vowel was pronounced, leading to the impression that the vowel was rounded (Farnetani and Recasens 2010:317). This would bring the phonetic realization of nasalized *a* in the vicinity of a labial consonant still closer to *o*.

Thus, even though the outcome of the syllabic nasals in Mycenaean would have been nasalized *a*, the nasalization on the vowel would have acoustically contributed to the impression that it was a central rather than a mid-vowel, that is, *o* instead of *a*, and the lip rounding from the adjacent labial consonant would have contributed to the impression that it was a rounded rather than an unrounded vowel, again, *o* instead of *a*. The result would have been a vowel that was perceptually ambiguous between *o* and *a*.

When presented with a perceptually ambiguous segment, the Mycenaean scribes would not have heard it as an intermediate vowel; instead, they would have heard and interpreted it randomly as either *a* or *o*. When listening to speech, listeners do not perceive speech sounds continuously, only categorically. Thus, they hear vowels, including intermediate vowels, as being part of a category they already know, and do not recognize gradations within categories (Liberman *et al.* 1967:442–443). When presented with a set of small steplike changes that vary continuously from one category to another—such as an example of a continuum between the stops [t] and [d], with an audio file, located at the following URL: http://www.vowelsandconsonants3e.com/chapter_10.html#—one does not hear the steplike changes, but instead simply switches from hearing one category to hearing the other. Thus, when presented with a vowel that was perceptually ambiguous between *a* and *o*, the Mycenaean scribes would have perceived it as either *a* or *o*, and written it accordingly.

Note that this argument relies on the idea that nasalized vowels were no longer a phonemic category in Mycenaean; if they had been, this ambiguity would not have existed because nasalized *a* would have been its own category. As improbable as it may seem for speakers to consistently produce a distinction that is no longer phonemic in their language, the existence of this phenomenon, known as a near-merger, is well documented (Labov 1994:357–370). For example, Labov describes a certain Keith, a fourteen-year-old boy from Norwich, who could produce a distinction between the words *toe* and *too* reliably enough that his friend David could always distinguish the two, and yet was not able to hear the distinction himself. As Labov notes, "there is not the least doubt that he had come to the conclusion that the *toe* class and the *too* class were 'the same' in the linguistic sense. He was therefore unable to identify and label the two phonemes on the basis of the regular difference in the sound pattern, a difference that is found regularly in the speech of his best friend as well as his own" (365–366). Thus, it is entirely plausible that nasalized *a* could have persisted as the outcome of syllabic nasals in Mycenaean even after it had ceased to have phonemic status in the language.

To summarize, the argument presented here is that the outcome of the Proto-Indo-European syllabic nasals in Mycenaean was nasalized *a*, though this did not have phonemic status in the language. The nasalization on the vowel, combined with the perception of lip rounding from coarticulation effects with the neighboring labial consonant, caused this vowel to be perceptually ambiguous between *a* and *o*. As a result, scribes heard and wrote it sometimes as *a* and sometimes as *o*.

The idea that the alternation between *a* and *o* represents spelling ambiguity has been criticized by previous scholars. For instance, Thompson argues the following:

> Suppose for example, that the reflex of *M̥ in a labial context was [ɒ], that is to say a back, rounded, open vowel, somewhere between [a] and [o]. Given that there is no series of signs for this vowel, scribes may well attempt to write it either as *a* or *o*. But if this were so, we would probably expect either (i) total randomness: if scribes are completely unsure whether the intermediate vowel is closer to [a] or [o], they would probably pick one or the other at random each time they needed to write it; or (b) randomness between scribes, but uniformity within each hand: this would be the case if each scribe had his preferred convention for the representation of the intermediate vowel. In neither case, however, would we expect to see the distribution which we do see, *viz.* The spelling varying from hand to hand and from word to word within each hand, but the spelling of a given word in a given hand being constant. (Thompson 1997:322)

First, in my scenario, the vowel in question is perceptually ambiguous between two vowel categories, not a separate category intermediate between *a* and *o*. Thus, the alternation happens at the level of speech perception, not as a conscious decision on the part of scribes about how to render an intermediate vowel. Therefore, we would not expect the systematicity of Thompson's scenario (b). Second, it would naturally have been possible for some kind of mild spelling standardization to arise within hands, since it defies belief that scribes would have randomly picked a spelling every single time they came across a word—they would presumably remember how they had spelled the word previously, especially for common words.

3. Alternation Between *a* and *o* in Mycenaean and Old English

It is not sufficient to simply demonstrate the plausibility of the hypothesis that the *o*/*a* alternation represents the scribes' efforts to represent a perceptually ambiguous segment; it is also necessary to demonstrate that this hypothesis offers a more compelling alternative than the existing explanations: dialect variation and sound change in progress. These two sets of hypotheses carry different implications, and unpacking these implications should provide an approach to testing these hypotheses against the existing evidence.

Surely the most salient of the differences between these two sets of hypotheses is that dialect variation and sound change in progress both assume that the alternation between *a* and *o* indicates the existence of some real linguistic difference between the *o* and *a* forms, while spelling ambiguity assumes that it does not. Our ability to conclusively determine the linguistic reality of the *a*/*o* alternation would appear to be hampered by the small sample size and limited vocabulary of the Linear B texts and the highly restricted population of scribes who used Linear B. However, a parallel example from Old English, as described by Toon (1976), presents an illustration of the sort of evidence that can be used to tell these two cases apart.

Between 700 and 1000 CE, certain dialects of Old English show an alternation between *a* and *o* as the outcome of West Germanic **a* before nasals. A series of Latin glossaries provides evidence for one dialect, Mercian. The early eighth-century Epinal Glossary consistently shows *a*. The mid-eighth-century Erfurt Glossary shows an approximately 50/50 split between *a* and *o*. In the later Corpus Glossary, *o* forms predominate. The most reasonable interpretation of this data is that it represents a sound change in progress.

The Kentish data, on the other hand, presents an enigma. The earliest charters, ca. 679–741 CE, show only forms with *a*. However, between 803 and 824, we only find forms with *o*. Between 833 and 850, there is a mix of spellings with *a* and *o*. From 859 through 868, forms with *a* once again predominate. This pattern is unexpected—sound changes should not appear suddenly only to gradually reverse themselves. From the historical record, however, it is clear that the sudden switch from *a* to *o* forms represents a period of Mercian control over Kent. This control extended to scribal practices. As Mercian power waned, the local dialect gradually reasserted itself in the written record.

Further evidence for the differing histories of the two dialects comes from their modern-day equivalents. In Mercia, the outcome of West Germanic **a* before nasals is [ɔ], but in other dialects, the outcome is [ɑ]. Indeed, this approach— checking whether or not the change is present in any surviving descendants of the dialect in question—presents the surest way of determining whether the *a/o* alternation in Mycenaean represents a true linguistic difference or an artifact of scribal practice. If the *a/o* alternation represents a true linguistic difference, we would expect to find a surviving dialect with *o* outcomes in a pattern that can be clearly related to the conditioning in Mycenaean. If the *a/o* alternation is an artifact of scribal practice, we would expect to find only *a* forms in the surviving dialects, or no relation between the *o* forms in the surviving dialects and the *o* forms in Mycenaean.

The descendants of Mycenaean, or at least its nearest relatives, are generally agreed to be Arcadian and Cypriot. It is frequently stated that Arcadian and Cypriot show *o* as the outcome of syllabic nasals (e.g., Colvin 2007:32). However, a closer investigation of the Arcadian and Cypriot data shows that this generalization is not accurate. In Arcadian, the only words that contain *o* as the outcome of syllabic nasals are numerals (δέκο 'ten', εἴκοσι 'twenty', ἑκοτόν 'a hundred', and their derivatives), but the *a* forms of these words are also widely used (Dubois 1986:39–41). In none of these examples do we find *o* in the vicinity of a labial consonant. In Cypriot, the outcome of the syllabic nasals is simply *a* (Egetmeyer 2010:144, 151, 158). Thus, there is no evidence to support continuity between the putative *o* outcomes of syllabic nasals in Mycenaean and the *o* forms of Arcadian. Instead, with only three exceptions, the outcome of the PIE syllabic nasals in Arcado-Cypriot was *a*. This lends support to the idea that the outcome of syllabic nasals in Mycenaean was simply nasalized *a*.

4. Conclusions

This paper has argued that the outcome of the PIE syllabic nasals in Mycenaean was nasalized *a*, and that the alternation between *a* and *o* in Mycenaean reflects scribes' attempt to spell this perceptually ambiguous segment. There are several facts this hypothesis is able to explain that the competing theories, dialectal variation and sound change in progress, cannot. First, this hypothesis is the only one that can explain why the alternation between *a* and *o* occurs exclusively in the vicinity of a labial consonant; the coarticulation effects from the neighboring labial consonant are necessary in order for the scribes to sometimes misperceive the sound as *o* rather than *a*. Second, it explains why Mycenaean shows this apparent conditioning when its closest relatives, Arcadian and Cypriot, do not. Thus, it seems very likely that we can strike the outcome of the PIE syllabic nasals off the roster of potential dialect variation in Mycenaean Greek.

Bibliography

Example of a continuum between the stops [t] and [d]: http://www.vowelsand-consonants3e.com/chapter_10.html.

Beddor, P. 2009. "A Coarticulatory Path to Sound Change." *Language* 85(4):785–821.

Colvin, S. 2007. *A Historical Greek Reader*. Oxford.

Dubois, L. 1988. *Recherches sur le dialecte arcadien, I-III*. Louvain-la-Neuve.

Egetmeyer, M. 2010. *Le dialecte grec ancien de Chypre. Tome I: Grammaire; Tome II: Repertoire des inscriptions en syllabaire chypro-grec*. Berlin.

Farnetani, E., and D. Recasens. 2010. "Coarticulation and Connected Speech Processes." In *The Handbook of Phonetic Sciences*, ed. W. J. Hardcastle, J. Laver, and F. E. Gibbon, 316–352. Malden, MA.

Greenberg, J. H. 1966. "Synchronic and Diachronic Universals in Phonology." *Language* 42(2):508–517.

Hajnal, I. 2006. "Die Tafeln aus Theben und ihre Bedeutung für die griechische Dialektologie." In *Die neuen Linear B-Texte aus Theben. Ihr Aufschlusswert für die mykenische Sprache und Kultur. Akten des internationalen Forschungs-kolloquiums an der Österreichischen Akademie der Wissenschaften, 5.-6. Dezember 2002*, ed. S. Deger-Jalkotzy and O. Panagl, 53–69. Vienna.

Krakow, R. A., P. S. Beddor, L. M. Goldstein, and C. A. Fowler. 1988. "Coarticulatory Influences on the Perceived Height of Nasal Vowels." *The Journal of the Acoustical Society of America* 83(3):1146–1158.

Labov, W. 1994. *Principles of Linguistic Change: Internal Factors*. Oxford.

Liberman, A. M, F. S. Cooper, D. P. Shankweiler, and M. Studdert-Kennedy. 1967. "Perception of the Speech Code." *Psychological Review* 74(6):431–461.

Nagy, G. 1968. "On Dialectal Anomalies in Pylian Texts." In *Atti e Memorie del 1° Congresso Internazionale di Micenologia*, 663–679. Incunabula Graeca 25:1-3.

Palaima, T. G. 1998-1999. "Special vs. Normal Mycenaean: Hand 24 and Writing in the Service of the King?" *Minos* 33–34:205–221.

Risch, E. 1966. "Les différences dialectales dans le mycénien." In *Proceedings of the Cambridge Colloquium on Mycenaean Studies*, ed. L. R. Palmer and J. Chadwick, 150–159. Cambridge.

Scheer, T. 2004. *A Lateral Theory of Phonology: What Is CVCV, and Why Should It Be?* Berlin.

Thompson, R. 1997. "Dialects in Mycenaean and Mycenaean among the Dialects." *Minos* 31–32:313–333.

Thompson, R. 2002. "Special vs. Normal Mycenaean Revisited." *Minos* 37–38: 337–369.

Toon, T. 1976. "The Variationist Analysis of Early Old English Manuscript Data." *Proceedings of the Second International Conference on Historical Linguistics*, ed. W. M. Christie, Jr., 71–81. Amsterdam.

Varias, C. 1997. "A Tentative Analysis of Dialectal Differences in the Linear B Texts from Mycenae." *Minos* 29–30:135–157.

Woodard, R. D. 1986. "Dialectal Differences at Knossos." *Kadmos* 25(1):49–74.

ku-ne y *qo-we* en la tablilla de Micenas Fu 711

Carlos Varias García

Universitat Autònoma de Barcelona

Carlos.Varias@uab.cat

Abstract

This paper reexamines the Linear B terms *ku-ne* and *qo-we* on the Mycenae tablet Fu 711. A thorough analysis of the text of this tablet allows to conclude that MY Fu 711 records different kinds of supplies of agrarian products to individuals, and that *ku-ne* and *qo-we* are most probably two personal names in dative, namely /*Kunei*/ and /*Gʷōwei*/.

Keywords

Mycenae, personal names, Linear B, animals, festival rations

UNA DE LAS TABLILLAS EN LINEAL B más singulares procedentes del yacimiento de Micenas es Fu 711, hallada en 1968 entre los restos de un edificio situado en la zona nordeste de la ciudadela.[1] Su texto, muy fragmentado, es el siguiente:[2]

---

[1] Estudio hecho en el marco del Proyecto de Investigación FFI2016-79906-P del Ministerio de Economía, Industria y Competitividad (España): "Estudio diacrónico de las instituciones socio-políticas de la Grecia antigua y de sus manifestaciones míticas" (AEI/FEDER, UE). Agradezco a José Luis García Ramón sus observaciones a este artículo, de cuyos errores soy el único responsable. Dedico este trabajo a mi maestro José Luis Melena, quien dirigió mi tesis doctoral sobre las inscripciones en Lineal B de Micenas en 1993.

[2] Reproduzco el texto de la edición de Melena and Olivier 1991:57.

MY Fu 711

sup. mut.

```
.1                              ] ṿ [
.2                    ]HORḌ        v 2
.3              ]5̣  HORD   T 7   v 3
.4        ]          HORD         v 2
.5–.6     ]    vacant
.7        ] z 2   ku-ne ,  FAR z 2
.8     ]1̣  ka-ra-u-ja  FAR z 1̣   NI z 1
.9        ]ṿ 3  a-re-ke-se-[•]  [•]   T 2̣[
.10       ]3 z 1          CYP + O  T 1  ⟦5⟧
.11       ] z 2
```

→

v.

sup. mut.

```
.1   ṣẹ-wọ-[
.2   to-wo-ṇạ[
.3   a-re-ke-ṣẹ[
.4   qo-we      [
```

reliqua pars sine regulis

Esta tablilla, escrita por ambas caras, sin escriba asignado para ninguna de ellas, se encontró en un contexto aislado en cuanto a inscripciones en Lineal B, en un edificio formado por un conjunto de almacenes con restos de gran cantidad de vasijas de todas clases, jarras de estribo, marfiles, *pithoi*, etc., destruido por el fuego hacia 1200 a. C., fecha en la que se data MY Fu 711.[3]

Los dos fragmentos que conforman Fu 711 corresponden, *grosso modo*, a algo más de la mitad inferior derecha de una tablilla opistográfica, y registran asignaciones de varios productos agrarios: cebada (logograma HORD en líneas 2, 3 y 4), harina (logograma FAR en líneas 7 y 8), higos (logograma NI en línea 8) y juncia (logograma CYP+O en línea 10) a diferentes destinatarios. En su integridad la tablilla constaría de unas quince líneas en el *recto*, y algunas en el *verso*, que registraban suministros de productos agrícolas almacenados, sin duda, en los *pithoi* hallados *in situ*. Así pues, MY Fu 711 formaría parte de un depósito de tablillas situado en la habitación superior de estos almacenes. Hasta la fecha se trata de la única tablilla de Micenas que registra cebada y harina.

Dado lo fragmentado del texto conservado, no es posible saber con certeza el propósito de este registro, esto es, a quiénes y para qué se suministraban las

---

[3] Reportaje de la excavación de este edificio y del hallazgo de MY Fu 711 en Mylonas 1968 y 1970.

cantidades de estos productos. Solo se conservan siete términos escritos silábi-camente como destinatarios, si bien tras los cuatro del *verso* no se conserva ningún logograma, por lo que, *a priori*, no puede descartarse que el registro del *verso* fuera diferente del del *recto*.

Dos de los términos, *a-re-ke-se-*[•] (línea 9) y *a-re-ke-ṣẹ*[(línea 3 del *verso*), aun acabando el primero con una lectura dudosa y estando incompleto el segundo, tienen la estructura clara de sendos antropónimos, que podrían ser el mismo: *a-re-ke-se-u* /*Alekseus*/, testimoniado en KN Da 1156.B.[4] Como un tercer término, *ṣẹ-wọ-*[(línea 1 del *verso*), también incompleto, solo puede coincidir con un término micénico que es asimismo un antropónimo: *se-wo-to*, en KN Da 1268.B, la deducción primera fue pensar que todos los términos registrados silábicamente eran antropónimos, masculinos y femeninos, que designaban a los individuos destinatarios de las cantidades consignadas de cebada, harina, higos y juncia.[5]

Palmer (1983:283–287 y 292–293) fue el primero en interpretar MY Fu 711 en clave religiosa, asegurando que "all the ideographic clues offered by the new text from Mycenae diagnose it as a record of small quantities of standard food-stuffs and the aromatic CYP+O offered to divinities" (p. 286) e interpretando cuatro términos como divinidades: *ku-ne* /*Kunei*/, dat. sing. 'to the Dog', lo que apoyarían las representaciones de los sellos de Creta; *ka-ra-u-ja* /*Grāwya*/ 'Old Woman', que identifica con Deméter; *a-re-ke-se*[-*we* /*Aleksēwei*/, que interpreta como referencia al 'Shield God', pareja masculina de /*Grāwya*/; *qo-we* /*Gʷōwei*/, dat. sing. 'to the Bull', como pareja masculina de *qo-wi-ja* /*Gʷōwiāi*/, que inter-preta como diosa en PY Tn 316.v.3.

Tanto Chadwick (1988:198–199) como Risch (1987:287–288) se opusieron a esta interpretación de Palmer. Chadwick argumentó que no había ningún nombre divino con seguridad en esta tablilla, que el único término que podía no ser un *hapax*, *a-re-ke-se-*[•], coincidiría con un nombre de varón (*vid. supra*), y que, si bien *qo-we* y *ku-ne* podían ser los dativos de βοῦς y κύων, otras interpre-taciones no se excluían; además, a ninguno de estos dos términos le precede el logograma de la juncia (CYP+O), aducido por Palmer para su interpretación reli-giosa. Por su parte, Risch, siguiendo en gran medida lo ya expuesto por Perpillou (1973:213) sobre el antropónimo *ku-ne-u*, registrado en KN Da 1396.B, y la serie de hipocorísticos en griego alfabético Κυνέας, Κύνης, Κύνων, fem. Κυνώ, incluyó

---

[4] En cuanto a la lectura del último signo de *a-re-ke-se-*[•], Melena and Olivier (1991:57) escriben en el aparato crítico de su edición: "*a-re-ke-se-jạ* perhaps better than *a-re-ke-se-ụ*," en cuyo caso se trataría de un adjetivo pertinentivo en -*e-ja* como *di-we-se-ja*, nombre de mujer en MY Oe 103.2 formado sobre el antropónimo masculino *di-we-so*.

[5] Así, para los dos términos objeto de este trabajo, Chadwick interpretó *ku-ne* como "MN? *Kunes*? [Κύνης]" (*Docs²*, 557) y *qo-we* como "MN," sin interrogación (*Docs²*, 578). En el mismo sentido *DMic., s.v. ku-ne* ("Antr. masc. dat. ... Quizá Κύνης"); *s.v. qo-we* ("Antr. masc.").

ku-ne (y también *ku-ne*[en KN Sc 258.*v.*, si el término está completo)⁶ entre los antropónimos en *-e* que corresponden a apelativos o antropónimos en */-eus/*, lo mismo que *qo-we* (: hom. βοεύς 'correa de piel de buey'), y negó que fueran divinidades por el contexto de la tablilla.

La edición de las tablillas de Tebas halladas en los años noventa del siglo pasado, a cargo de Aravantinos, Godart, and Sacconi (2001), revitalizó la discusión sobre la interpretación de MY Fu 711, que los editores compararon con la serie TH Fq, en donde aparecen varios nombres de animales, entre ellos el 'perro' (*ku-ne, ku-no, ku-si*), que interpretaron en un sentido religioso. La bibliografía al respecto de estos últimos veinte años es copiosa. En síntesis, las interpretaciones propuestas para *ku-ne* y *qo-we* en MY Fu 711, como destinatarios de harina y quizá otros productos, son cuatro:

(1) Divinidades teriomórficas en dat. */Kunei/* 'para el Perro' y */Gʷōwei/* 'para el Buey': Hiller (2011:189 y 194), y Franceschetti (2016:738) siguen esta intepretación original de Palmer (*vid. supra*), mientras que Weilhartner (2005:222 y 224) la plantea con dudas;

(2) Animales en nom. pl. de rúbrica, */kunes/* 'perros' y */gʷōwes/* 'bueyes' o 'vacas', destinatarios de productos alimenticios para ser consumidos en ceremonias cultuales: Aravantinos, Godart y Sacconi 2001:196–197, 201 y 364–365; Rousioti 2001:307; Ruijgh 2003:224–225; Killen 2004:220–221; 2006:100n61, 103n71 y 105, y Lupack 2016:377, que menciona solo *ku-ne*, entre otros;⁷

(3) Grupos de personas designados con nombres de los animales cuya máscara llevan y que participan en un ritual religioso, opinión hoy en día mayoritaria respecto a las tablillas tebanas: Weilhartner 2005:215n560, como posibilidad; 2007:343, donde rechaza que sean divinidades teriomórficas; Ricciardelli 2006:262–263, donde menciona *qo-we* en relación con βουκόλος, título presente en muchas asociaciones dionisíacas del I milenio a. C., y Piquero Rodríguez 2019:145–146 y 305–306, donde recoge también las otras interpretaciones;

(4) Antropónimos designando sendos varones, *ku-ne* en nom. de rúbrica */Kunēs/* o en dat. */Kunei/* y *qo-we* en dat. */Gʷōwei/*: además de Chadwick y Risch (*vid. supra*), Duhoux 2002–2003:184n65; 2008: 376 y 381, respecto a *ku-ne*, y Melena 2014:30, en donde interpreta *qo-we* como */Gʷōwei/*, dat. sg. de un nombre propio.

---

⁶ Por otro lado, si no está completo, el registro podría haber sido *ku-ne*[-*i* /Kuneʰi/, dat. de un antropónimo con nom. en */-ēs/* como *ku-ne* /Kunēs/.

⁷ Uchitel (2004:277 y 279), en cambio, interpreta estos términos como simples animales, no sagrados, estabulados en una "estación de mensajeros" de la red viaria micénica, para lo que invoca paralelos en los textos mesopotámicos.

Por último, *DMic.Supl.*, *s.v. ku-ne* I escribe "término de interpretación dudosa en MY Fu 711.7" y propone dos posibilidades: antropónimo masculino en nom. o zoónimo en dat. sg. o nom. pl. de κύων 'perro', con referencias bibliográficas; además, separan bajo el mismo lema este testimonio del de las tablillas tebanas.

Casi todas las interpretaciones, religiosas o laicas, propuestas para *ku-ne* y *qo-we* en MY Fu 711 están ligadas a las de la serie Fq de Tebas, en donde se registra también *ku-ne* (en Fq 229.9 y, con lectura dudosa, en Fq 292.4) y sus variantes *ku-no* (en Fq 205.3, 236.5, Gf 163.1 y Gp 150.2) y *ku-si* (en Fq 130.4), sobre todo porque un tercer término, *ka-ra-u-ja* en MY Fu 711.8, está testimoniado, con la variante gráfica *ka-ra-wi-ja*, en TH Fq 169.4 y, con lectura dudosa, en Fq 207.1 y 228.2. No obstante, hay ciertas diferencias entre la tablilla de Micenas y la serie Fq de Tebas que me parecen bastante significativas.

En primer lugar, en Fu 711 hay dos líneas no escritas (5-6) que diferencian claramente un párrafo anterior de al menos cuatro líneas (1-4) del párrafo final de la tablilla (líneas 7-11). En ese primer párrafo solo aparece registrada, en la parte conservada, la cebada (logograma HORD), en tres líneas diferentes, mientras que en el segundo párrafo se registran tres productos agrarios, pero no la cebada: harina (logograma FAR, en líneas 7-8), higos (logograma NI, línea 8) y juncia (logograma CYP+O, línea 10). Puesto que, además, como luego se verá, las cantidades de cebada difieren también de las del segundo párrafo, parece probable, a pesar del estado fragmentado del texto, que el carácter del registro de las líneas 1-4 fuera distinto del de las líneas 7-11, lo que lleva a pensar que MY Fu 711 debía de estar constituida por varios párrafos (otro de ellos sería el de las líneas 1-4 del *verso*) con distintos tipos de registros, cuyo único nexo era la distribución de productos agrarios almacenados *in situ*, aunque los destinatarios y/o la finalidad de esas distribuciones fuera diferente.

En cambio, en ninguna tablilla del centenar largo que forma la serie Fq de Tebas se aprecia una división semejante en párrafos. Es cierto que cerca del 80% de esta serie son pequeños fragmentos con tan poco texto conservado que no permiten ninguna conclusión al respecto, pero en las tablillas con diez o más líneas de texto conservadas (Fq 214, 229, 240, 241, 254, 276) la única línea en blanco está en Fq 229, antes de la última línea, que registra el total de las cantidades anotadas mediante el término *ku-su-to-ro-qa* /ksunstrok^{hw}ā/ 'suma total' (: συστροφή 'reunión' Hdt.+), mientras que en las tablillas Fq 214, 254 y 276 ni siquiera hay esa línea de separación de la línea de registro del total. Podría pensarse que esto se debe simplemente a un *usus scribendi* de la mano 305, autora de todas estas tablillas, pero lo cierto es que el total recogido en ellas es solo de cebada, que debe de ser el único logograma registrado en estas cuatro tablillas al menos, a pesar de que los editores han transliterado también el logograma FAR, harina, en algunas líneas de cada tablilla, lectura que se ha puesto razonablemente en cuestión, proponiéndose en su lugar el silabograma **65* con el valor fonético /ju/.[8] Así pues, en la serie Fq de Tebas muy probablemente solo se registre un producto agrario, la cebada, a diferencia de la tablilla Fu 711 de Micenas, donde figuran al menos cuatro productos diferentes.

Por otro lado, las cantidades de cebada registradas permiten constatar una diferencia importante: en las líneas 2 y 4 de MY Fu 711 se conservan sendas entradas de 3.2 litros (v 2) de cebada, una cantidad similar a las registradas en la serie Fq de Tebas, coincidente en varios casos (p. ej., en Fq 254.2 para *a-ko-da-mo*, y .14 para *a-ke-ne-u-si*; en Fq 269.6 para]*o-ro-wa-ṭạ*), pero en la línea 3 hay una entrada de 72 litros (T 7 v 3) de cebada, cantidad solo comparable a varias entradas totalizadoras de la serie Fq: 65.6 litros (T ḅ v 5[) en Fq 214.1̣4̣; 68 litros (]T 7 z 2[) en Fq 252.6; 100.4 litros (HORD 1 v 2[ ]z 3[) en Fq 269.7̣, u 80 litros (T 8 v 2[) en Fq 276.10. Pero nada indica que la línea 3 de Fu 711 sea una entrada totalizadora, sino más bien al contrario: como se ha visto, la línea inmediata inferior (4) tiene la misma pequeña cantidad registrada que la inmediata superior (2), y antes de ese gran registro de cebada en la línea 3 se conserva una cifra justo tras la parte rota (]5), lo que es indicio de otra cantidad registrada, puede que de otro producto; además, sería muy rara una entrada totalizadora en mitad de la tablilla seguida de otra línea con una entrada individual y luego dos en blanco. Este hecho nos previene contra la aserción generalmente aceptada, sobre todo a partir de Killen (2006:103n71, 105), de que Fu 711 registra cantidades muy pequeñas de los productos suministrados, igual que la serie Fq de Tebas, lo que se aduce como otro indicio del contexto religioso del texto de Micenas. Esto no es exacto, no solo por la entrada de cebada de la línea 3, sino también por una entrada individual de la línea 9, en el siguiente párrafo, donde se suministra un mínimo de 19.2 litros de un producto agrario que no puede leerse bien ([•] T 2̣[ ) a *a-re-ke-se*-[•], una cantidad que no recibe ni de lejos ningún receptor de la serie Fq.[9] Lo mismo podría decirse de los 9.6 litros de juncia (CYP+O T 1) de la línea 10, si bien aquí con más reservas, ya que a este logograma no le precede ningún destinatario, sino otra cantidad incompleta.

Por consiguiente, la separación de párrafos, la variedad de productos agrícolas y la divergencia de las cantidades anotadas hacen que MY Fu 711 sea bastante menos uniforme que la serie entera Fq de Tebas. Ahora bien, en el segundo párrafo de la tablilla de Micenas figura *ku-ne* (línea 7) justo encima de

---

[8] Un buen estudio pormenorizado sobre esta cuestión es el de Palaima (2006), cuya postura es seguida, entre otros, por Melena (2012:78).

[9] Esta cantidad o similar solo se registra en la serie Fq tras el término *ma-ka*, cuya interpretación ha suscitado una gran discusión. Lo más probable es que *ma-ka* designe el motivo o acontecimiento por el que se distribuyen las pequeñas cantidades de cebada en las tablillas donde aparecen, como recoge *DMic.Supl.*, *s.v. ma-ka*, con bibliografía abundante.

ka-ra-u-ja (línea 8) con cantidades muy pequeñas de los productos que reciben: 0.8 litros (z 2) de harina para *ku-ne* y 0.4 litros (z 1) de harina y otros tantos de higos para *ka-ra-u-ja*. Son también los dos únicos receptores de harina conservados en la tablilla. Como la línea 7 es la primera de este segundo párrafo conservado, parece razonable pensar que la finalidad de estas pequeñas asignaciones sea la misma, quizá como ofrendas a una divinidad (*ka-ra-u-ja*) y raciones para participante(s) en una festividad religiosa (*ku-ne*), tal como propone Killen (2006:103n71, 105).

Independientemente de si *ka-ra-u-ja*/*ka-ra-wi-ja* es o no una divinidad en los textos de Tebas y Micenas, y aun admitiendo que las entradas de las líneas 7 y 8 de Fu 711 se expliquen en el marco de un contexto cultual, ello no implica necesariamente que *ku-ne* no pueda ser un antropónimo. La interpretación de *ku-ne* como nom. pl. /*kunes*/ 'perros', tanto en MY Fu 711 como en las tablillas tebanas, se apoya en el hecho de que éste y los demás zoónimos de Tebas están en plural, al designar grupos de oficiantes que participan en el culto con la apariencia de esos animales, en la atractiva propuesta de Ricciardelli (2006) y Weilhartner (2007) (así también *DMic.Supl., s.v. ku-ne* II, solo para los textos de Tebas). Sin embargo, tres objeciones pueden hacerse a esta interpretación:

(1) Como ya observó Duhoux (2002–2003:183; 2008:376), en las dos tablillas de Tebas en donde se registra *ku-ne*, Fq 229 y Fq 292, no aparece ningún otro nombre de animal como receptor, sino solo antropónimos y apelativos de persona en dat. pl. (y, según los editores, alguna divinidad). Es cierto que de Fq 292, que es un texto breve muy fragmentado, con solo tres términos conservados enteros (el propio registro de *ku̯-ne̯* no es seguro), no puede deducirse nada, pero en el caso de la tablilla Fq 292, con un registro de catorce líneas y veintiún términos conservados, es un dato muy relevante: un mínimo de trece antropónimos seguros se registran entre las líneas 4 y 12, junto con dos apelativos de persona en plural, *o-ti-ri-ja-i* (línea 7) y *e-pi-qo̯-i̯* (línea 10). El hecho de que ninguno de los otros cinco términos tebanos mayoritariamente interpretados como nombres de animales (*e-mi-jo-no-i*, *e-pe-to-i*, *ka-no*/*ka-si*, *ke-re-na-i* y *o-ni-si*) ni el debatido *ko-ro* figure en las tablillas donde se registra *ku-ne* no puede obviarse.

(2) Tanto en los dos registros de Tebas como en el de Micenas se suministra a *ku-ne* la misma pequeña cantidad de cereal o harina: z 2 = 0.8 litros. Esta coincidencia, tratándose además de dos centros distintos, no puede ser casual. Ahora bien, resulta que *ku-si*, interpretado como dat. pl. /*kunsi*/ 'para los perros', en Fq 130.4, su único registro conservado, recibe una cantidad mínima de v 2[= 3.2 litros, es decir, cuatro

veces más que *ku-ne*. Resulta chocante que, si *ku-ne* es un nom. pl. de rúbrica escrito por la misma mano 305 como variante de la forma en dat. pl. *ku-si* para designar al mismo grupo de animales o, más probablemente, oficiantes, haya tal disparidad en la cantidad recibida, sobre todo porque tanto en Fq 130 (donde figura *ku-si*) como en Fq 229 (donde figura *ku-ne*) se registra el antropónimo *ka-wi-jo* recibiendo la misma cantidad en la dos tablilas (v 1= 1.6 litros), sin que podamos comparar más cantidades de los mismos receptores de estos dos textos (*o-po-re-i*, *ko-wa*, *a-me-ro*), al no haberse conservado las cantidades que reciben en alguna de las dos tablillas. Podría ser que el grupo de *ku-ne* comprenda menos integrantes que el de *ku-si*, pero esta es una hipótesis harto improbable, tratándose de la misma serie de tablillas con una lista regular de receptores que se repiten, y en todo caso indemostrable.

(3) De los otros nombres de animales tebanos ninguno está en nom. pl., sino en dat. pl., como *ku-si* (*e-mi-jo-no-i*, *e-pe-to-i*, *ka-si*, *ke-re-na-i*, *o-ni-si*) o en gen. pl. *ku-no* /*kunōn*/ 'de los perros' (como *ka-no* /*kʰanōn*/: 'de las ocas'), cuestión en la que no entraré aquí (vid. *DMic.Supl.*, 196). En cuanto al término *ko-ro*, aunque algunos autores lo interpretan como otro nombre de animal: χοῖρος /*kʰoiros*/ 'cochinillo', en dat. sg. como receptor, debe de ser el término κόρος /*koros*/: 'forraje', en nom. sg. describiendo el alimento registrado para animales (vid. García Ramón 2010:82–83).[10]

Todas estas razones me llevan a considerar como hipótesis más probable que *ku-ne* sea un único receptor registrado en dat. sg., tanto en Tebas como en Micenas. Y en tal caso me parece improbable que sea el apelativo 'perro', dado que los nombres de animales tebanos están en plural por designar grupos de personas. Así pues, propongo interpretar *ku-ne* como el dat. sg. /*Kunei*/ de un antropónimo */Kunēs*/ o incluso */Kuōn*/, teniendo en cuenta la existencia de una abundante serie de antropónimos griegos en el I milenio a. C. con este mismo lexema (*vid. supra* y Perpillou 1973:213; Risch 1987:288; Duhoux 2002–2003:184; 2008:376, entre otros). Son, además, numerosos los ejemplos de antropónimos en griego formados a partir de zoónimos, tanto en micénico (vid. García Ramón 2011:228, para una selección) como a partir del I milenio a. C. (vid. Bechtel 1982:581–592): Δράκων, Ἔριφος, Λύκος, Ταῦρος, etc.

Esta interpretación de *ku-ne* como antropónimo no obsta para que las líneas 7 y 8 de MY Fu 711 puedan registrar asignaciones de harina e higos a

---

[10] Para una relación bibliográfica completa de ambas interpretaciones vid. *DMic.Supl., s.v. ko-ro.*

los participantes en una fiesta religiosa, como he dicho antes. En la siguiente
línea del mismo párrafo (9) figura un antropónimo, *a-re-ke-se-*[•], que recibe una
cantidad de un producto no identificado, que puede ser cebada, harina o higos,
según el aparato crítico de Melena y Olivier (1991:57), suministro que tendría
el mismo motivo que las dos líneas anteriores (¿raciones para participantes en
una fiesta religiosa?), aunque las cantidades son mucho mayores, como ya he
comentado. La siguiente línea (10) registra 9.6 litros de juncia (CYP+*O* T 1) sin
que se conserve su destinatario, que, por el comienzo fragmentado de esta línea,
recibiría también otro producto. Si bien el registro de CYP+*O* se ha puesto en
relación con tablillas de ofrendas religiosas en Pilo, Cnoso y Tebas, esto no es así
en todos los casos, como bien ha demostrado Weilhartner (2005:215), mencio-
nando al respecto las tablillas KN F(2) 852 y F(1) 157; es un alimento que se
registra en escasas cantidades en comparación con otros, servido como comple-
mento a los alimentos básicos. En Micenas hay otra tablilla que registra CYP+*O*:
Ue 652.3, en cantidades mucho mayores (672 litros), texto que anota la entrega
al palacio de la producción agraria del año anterior (*pe-ru-si-nwa*, en línea 2) de
una explotación agrícola.[11]

En cuanto a *qo-we*, *hapax* en MY Fu 711.*v*.4, resulta aún más improbable
su interpretación como nom. pl. /$g^w\bar{o}wes$/ (: βόες), puesto que este animal no
se registra en escritura silábica en ninguna tablilla de Tebas, y en el texto de
Micenas figura debajo de tres líneas que registran, casi con toda seguridad, otros
tantos antropónimos (*ṣẹ-wọ-*[(línea 1), *to-wo-ṇạ*[(línea 2) y *a-re-ke-ṣẹ*[(línea 3)).
En la tablilla de Pilo PY Jo 438.17 se registra un antropónimo *qo-wo* en nom.
que propongo interpretar como /$G^w\bar{o}w$-$\bar{o}n$/: Βόων, nombre de varón atestiguado
seis veces (la primera en Atenas, siglo V a. C.), formado, como *qo-we*, sobre βοῦς
(*$g^w\bar{o}w$-), que subyace en una serie de nombres con otros sufijos, e.g., Βοΐων
(Bitinia, s. III a. C.), fem. Βοιώ, Βόϊλ(λ)α y Βοΐσκος (Rodas, s. III a. C.), Βοΐσκα.
Por tanto, cabe entender *qo-we* como dat. /$G^w\bar{o}wei$/, de */$G^w\bar{o}us$/, antropónimo
con correlato perfecto en Βοῦς, atestiguado como nombre de cuatro hombres
(el más antiguo con fecha segura en Éfeso, s. I d. C.) y dos mujeres (la primera en
Cízico en época helenística).

---

[11] Para la interpretación de MY Ue 652 vid. Varias 2019. Por otra parte, el contexto arqueológico
y lugar de hallazgo de MY Fu 711 no aporta indicios en apoyo de una interpretación religiosa
de este texto. La tablilla se encontró en la zona nordeste de la acrópolis de Micenas, alejada del
Centro de Culto, que se halla en el sudoeste de la acrópolis, y, si bien delante de los restos de
almacenes donde se halló había un camino de una anchura media de 2.50 m, no puede saberse si
esta era una vía utilizada sólo para ir al Centro de Culto o simplemente para salir por la puerta
norte de la ciudadela, por donde quizá entraran y salieran los receptores de los productos de Fu
711. Además, ninguno de los receptores de Fu 711 aparece en la serie de tablillas Oi encontrada
en el Centro de Culto de Micenas, que registra con claridad un suministro regular del producto
*190 a una divinidad y a los participantes en una ceremonia cultual.

Bibliography

Aravantinos, V. L., L. Godart, and A. Sacconi, eds. 2001. *Thèbes: Fouilles de la Cadmée I: Les tablettes en linéaire B de la Odos Pelopidou. Édition et commentaire.* Pisa-Rome.

Bechtel, F. 1982. *Die historischen Personennamen des Griechischen bis zur Kaiserzeit.* Hildesheim. [Orig. pub. Halle 1917.]

Chadwick, J. 1988. "What Do We Know about Mycenaean Religion?" In *Linear B: A 1984 Survey*, ed. A. Morpurgo Davies and Y. Duhoux, 191–202. Louvain-la-Neuve.

Deger-Jalkotzy, S., and O. Panagl, eds. 2006. *Die neuen Linear B-Texte aus Theben: Ihr Aufschlußwert für die mykenische Sprache und Kultur. Akten des internationalen Forschungskolloquiums and der Österreichischen Akademie der Wissenschaften 5.-6. Dezember 2002.* Vienna.

Del Freo, M., and M. Perna, eds. 2016. *Manuale di epigrafia micenea: Introduzione allo studio dei testi in lineare B.* 2 vols. Padua.

Duhoux, Y. 2002-2003. "Dieux ou humains? Qui sont *ma-ka, o-po-re-i* et *ko-wa* dans les tablettes linéaire B de Thèbes?" *Minos* 37–38:173–253.

———. 2008. "Mycenaean Anthology." In Duhoux and Morpurgo Davies 2008–2014, vol. 1:243–393.

Duhoux, Y., and A. Morpurgo Davies, eds. 2008-2014. *A Companion to Linear B: Mycenaean Greek Texts and Their World.* 3 vols. Louvain-la-Neuve.

Franceschetti, A. 2016. "La religione micenea." In Del Freo and Perna 2016, vol. 2:725–751.

García Ramón, J. L. 2010. "Reconstructing IE Lexicon and Phraseology: Inherited Patterns and Lexical Renewal." In *Proceedings of the 21st Annual UCLA Indo-European Conference*, ed. S. W. Jamison, H. Craig Melchert, and B. Vine, 69–106. Bremen.

———. 2011. "Mycenaean Onomastics." In Duhoux and Morpurgo Davies 2008–2014, vol. 2:213–251.

Hiller, S. 2011. "Mycenaean Religion and Cult." In Duhoux and Morpurgo Davies 2008-2014, vol. 2:169–211.

Killen, J. T. 2004. "Names in *-e* and *-e-u* in Mycenaean Greek." In *Indo-European Perspectives. Studies in Honour of Anna Morpurgo Davies*, ed. J. H. W. Penney, 217–235. Oxford.

———. 2006. "Thoughts on the Functions of the New Thebes Tablets." In Deger-Jalkotzy and Panagl 2006:79–110.

Lupack, S. 2016. "Spezie, oli profumati e offerte religiose." In Del Freo and Perna 2016, vol. 2:373–402.

Melena, J. L. 2012. "Filling Gaps in the Basic Mycenaean Syllabary." In *Donum Mycenologicum. Mycenaean Studies in Honour of Francisco Aura Jorro*, ed. A. Bernabé and E. R. Luján, 75–85. Louvain-la-Neuve.

Melena, J. L. 2014. "Mycenaean Writing." In Duhoux and Morpurgo Davies 2008–2014, vol. 3:1–186.

Melena, J. L., and J.-P. Olivier. 1991. *TITHEMY. The Tablets and Nodules in Linear B from Tiryns, Thebes and Mycenae. A Revised Transliteration.* Salamanca.

Mylonas, G. E. 1968. "Ἀνασκαφή Μυκηνῶν." *Πρακτικά της εν Αθήναις Αρχαιολογικής Εταιρείας του έτους* 1968:5–11 + pls. 1–7.

Mylonas, G. E. 1970. "A New Tablet from Mycenae, MY Fu 711." *Kadmos* 9:48–50 + pl. I.

Palaima, T. G. 2006. "*65 = FAR?* or *ju?* and Other Interpretative Conundra in the New Thebes Tablets." In Deger-Jalkotzy and Panagl 2006:139–148.

Palmer, L. R. 1983. "Studies in Mycenaean Religion." In *Festschrift für Robert Muth zum 65. Geburtstag am 1. Januar 1981*, ed. P. Händel and W. Meid, 283–296. Innsbruck.

Perpillou, J.-L. 1973. *Les substantifs grecs en -εύς.* Paris.

Piquero Rodríguez, J. 2019. *El léxico del griego micénico. Index Graecitatis. Étude et mise à jour de la bibliographie.* Nancy.

Ricciardelli, G. 2006. "I nomi di animali nelle tavolette di Tebe: Una nuova ipotesi." *La Parola del Passato* 61.4:241–263.

Risch, E. 1987. "Die mykenischen Personennamen auf -e." In *Tractata Mycenaea. Proceedings of the Eighth International Colloquium on Mycenaean Studies Held in Ohrid, 15–20 September 1985*, ed. P. Hr. Ilievski, and L. Crepajac, 281–298. Skopje.

Rousioti, D. 2001. "Did the Mycenaeans Believe in Theriomorphic Divinities?" In *POTNIA. Deities and Religion in the Aegean Bronze Age. Proceedings of the 8th International Aegean Conference, Göteborg University, 12–15 April 2000*, ed. R. Laffineur, and R. Hägg, 305–314 + plate XCVI. Liège-Austin.

Ruijgh, C. 2003. "Review of Aravantinos, Godart and Sacconi 2001." *Mnemosyne* 56.2:219–228.

Uchitel, A. 2004. "Theban Fq Series and Ancient Near Eastern Messengers' Stations." *Studi micenei ed egeo-anatolici* 46.2:271–279.

Varias, C. 2019. "Un posible testimonio de tierra comunitaria en Micenas: La tablilla MY Ue 652 + 656." In *Nunc est Bacchandum. Homenaje a Alberto Bernabé*, ed. J. Piquero, P. de Paz, and S. Planchas, 329–336. Madrid.

Weilhartner, J. 2005. *Mykenische Opfergaben nach Aussage der Linear B-Texte.* Wien.

———. 2007. "Die Tierbezeichnungen auf den neuen Linear B-Texten aus Theben." In *Keimelion: Elitenbildung und Elitärer Konsum von der Mykenischen Palaszeit bis zur Homerischen Epoche. Akten des internationalen Kongresses vom 3. bis 5. Februar 2005 in Salzburg*, ed. E. Alram-Stern and G. Nightingale, 339–351. Vienna.

19

Missing Numerals

A Neglected Phenomenon in the Linear B Documents

Jörg Weilhartner

University of Salzburg

joerg.weilhartner@sbg.ac.at

Abstract

There is some general agreement that the most important pieces of information on the Linear B tablets, which all focus on registering economic information relevant for the administration of Mycenaean palaces, are the numerals. The fact that a couple of entries do not show any numerals has received little attention up to now. This paper demonstrates that in dealing with those texts, in which logograms are not followed by numerals, there is no easy solution for supplementing the missing information.

Keywords

Linear B logograms, Mycenaean administration, numerals.

PARTICULAR ENTRIES ON LINEAR B TABLETS consist of: (a) lexical information such as personal names or place names written with syllabic signs; (b) a logogram representing the commodity, material, product, plant, or living being according to the subject recorded on the document; and (c) a numeral referring to the quantity. If required, these numerals are specified by signs indicating subunits of dry measure, liquid measure, or weight. Due to their nature as economic accounting documents of the inputs and outputs of palatial storerooms, inventories, lists of human beings and animals, and detailed records of landholding, the numbers and quantities of humans, animals, plants, agricultural products, and finished goods recorded are of primary interest for the palatial administration. Tom Palaima puts it in a nutshell: "The most important pieces of information entered in documents of account are the numbers."[1] However, a substantial number of entries in the Linear B documents do not show any numerals. This contribution deals with this phenomenon, being inspired by the thought-provoking work that the recipient of this Festschrift has done on Linear B logograms.

Along with clay tablets and clay vessels (primarily, but not exclusively, transport stirrup jars), Linear B inscriptions regularly appear on small three-sided nodules, which frequently bear the impression of a seal. It is for this reason that they are referred to as sealings. If inscribed, one or more facets of the sealings show an inscription consisting of a logogram (usually over the seal impression) and/or a syllabic entry. In most cases the inscription on this type of document lacks numerals. As a general rule, Mycenaean inscribed sealings are of a type known as two-hole hanging nodules, also called regular string nodules by Erik Hallager:[2] these lumps of clay are formed around a knotted string thought to be tied to a single animal or object. As a consequence, it is assumed that one sealing refers to one animal, one container, or one bundle vel sim. For example, a collection of sealings from Thebes (assigned as TH Wu series), most of which refer by logogram to domesticated livestock, are taken to record contributions of single animals provided by individuals for a communal feast.[3] A typical example of a sealing from this series is shown below. It records a (single) male sheep by means of a logogram (OVIS^m) and an individual named *a-e-ri-qo*, designating the person who is responsible for the contribution:

TH Wu 70

.α   OVIS^m
.β-γ.1   a-e-ri-qo
    .2   *vacat*

The information provided by this kind of textual data is likely to have been collected and compiled on clay tablets such as Un 2 or Un 138 from Pylos. Among those texts, which are assumed to serve a similar purpose, i.e., to record animals (and other foodstuffs) destined for use at centrally organized banquets, is tablet C 902 from Knossos.[4]

---

[1]   I used the following text editions: For Knossos *KT*⁶, for Pylos *PTT*², and for Thebes *ADGS* 2005. Palaima 2004a:233. See Killen 1987:319 with reference to John Chadwick.

[2]   Hallager 2015:145–146. This paper demonstrates the typological diversity of (and the differences between) Minoan and Mycenaean sealings.

[3]   Piteros, Olivier, and Melena 1990:171–184; Killen 1996; Palaima 2004a:219–226.

[4]   Godart 1999:251–254; Weilhartner 2005:78–79; Killen 2015:1128–1131.

KN C 902

.0	*supra mutila*	
.1	mi-ru-ro / si-pe-we	BOS *ne* *170 12
.2	o-du-ru-wi-jo / ko-re-te	BOS *ne* *170 12
.3	wa-to / ko̞-re-te	BOS *ne* *170 12 , wa-to / da-nu-wo 'BOS' *170 12
.4	si-ra-ro / ko-re-te	BOS 1 *ne* *170 12
.5	*56-ko-we / e-ra-ne	BOS 1 *ne* *170 12
.6	o-du-ru-we / u-wo-qe-we	BOS 1 *ne* *170 12
.7	ri-jo-no / ko-re-te	BOS 1 *ne* *170 12
.8	ru-ki-ti-jo	BOS 1 *ne* *170 12
.9	a-pa-ta-wa / ko-re-te	BOS 1 *ne* *170 12
.10	ku-ta-i-to / ko-re-te	BOS 1 *ne* *170 12
.11	re-ri-jo / e-re-ta	BOS 1 *ne* *170 12
.12	] wa-to / we-re-we	BOS 1 *ne* *170 12
.13	*infra mutila*	

This page-shaped tablet has in each line the logogram for cattle (BOS) followed by twelve units of an unidentified commodity referred to as *ne* *170. Conspicuously, the entries on lines .1 to .3 have no numeral after the logogram for cattle. Since lines .4 to .12 show BOS 1, it is tempting to suggest that the numeral 1 has been omitted in the first three lines.[5] If one assumes, on the basis of the interrelationship between the Wu sealings from Thebes and some of the Ua and Un tablets from Pylos, that the data of this tablet is likely to rely on information furnished by inscribed sealings, the reason for this omission seems clear: in compiling this list the scribe has been affected by the fact that the textual data on the nodules usually do not mention numerals.[6] A similar explanation is likely to hold true for the lack of a numeral on another tablet from Knossos, M 724. On the basis of other tablets from the findspot Gallery of Jewel Fresco (G1), which seem to record single pieces of the simple textile *146,[7] there are some reasons to believe that the entry on this tablet stands for *146 1. Does this indicate that the data recorded on this tablet have been derived from a sealing?

---

5   See, for example, Chadwick 1976:43.

6   For a similar suggestion, see Godart 1999:251–252.

7   However, it cannot be ascertained if the numbers on the fragmentary tablets KN M 719 (*146 1[) and KN M(1) 720 (*146 1[) are complete. The same holds true for KN M 729 (*146 1[), which was found in the Small Room to the East of the Gallery of Jewel Fresco (G2). KN M(1) 1645, which records a single piece of *pe* *146, may also derive from findspot G1; see Firth 2000–2001:236. In this article (pp. 233–236) Firth suggests that all tablets found in this area have fallen from the upper floor. On these tablets, see Weilhartner 2005:59–62.

KN M 724

.1   ]me-no *146

.2   ] *vacat*

Some tablets from Knossos list male personnel by personal names. These texts provide further examples where the numeral 1 is to be understood even though the information for this kind of tablet seems not to be derived from individual sealings. A group of mostly fragmentary tablets written by Scribe 104[8] and referred to as set KN B(5) in *KT* V and as KN Bk series in *KT* VI, respectively, are characterized by an extensive use of the word divider, which is represented in the transliterations by a comma. Within this series, the word divider regularly appears before the logogram for man (VIR) as well as after it. These punctuation marks, which are written as short vertical strokes placed in the lower half of the line, resemble numeral 1, which is written as a long vertical stroke. It may be for that reason that Scribe 104 chose to omit the numeral after the logogram VIR.

KN Bk 803

supra mutila

.0   ]*vestigia*[

.1   ]-u , VIR , ko-ku-ro , VIR , to-na-ta , VIR ,

.2   ]u , VIR , a-so-qi-jo , VIR , pi-ri-u̬-wo , VIR

.3   ]V̬I̬R̬ ‚ko-ru-[   ]*vestigia*[

.4   *infra mutila*

Another clear example of the logogram VIR without a following numeral is provided by the Pylian text An 39. Since each entry on lines .3–.9 of the *verso* of this tablet records a personal name, it is difficult to doubt that here, too, VIR is to be read as implying VIR 1.[9] On the *recto* of this tablet, line .6 shows a comparable entry. The anthroponym *ka-sa-to* is followed by the logogram VIR without any numerical entry. Since a checkmark (×) has been written after the personal name, it seems unlikely that the numeral has been omitted accidentally.[10] The remainder of PY An 39 *recto* and the first line of the *verso* show occupational designations[11] in the nominative plural followed by numerals between 3 and 23.

---

[8] On the tablets of Scribe 104, see Melena 1975:64–81 (chapter III). Within Melena's chapter there is no comment about the fact that the logogram VIR is usually not followed by a numeral on the tablets of this series.

[9] Chadwick 1988:45.

[10] See Olivier 1960:17–19. On the contrary, the lack of a numeral on line .8 of PY An 129, written by a different scribe (Hand 22), looks like an unintentional omission.

[11] On arguments for viewing occupational designations such as *pu-ka-wo* /*purkawoi*/, *mi-ka-ta* /*miktai*/, and *o-pi-te-u-ke-e-we* /*opiteukhehēwes*/ as referring to palatial culinary personnel (in the sense of 'fire kindlers', 'mixers of water and wine', and 'F&B managers') and not to *desservants de*

PY An 39

Recto

.0		*margo*
.1	pu-ka-wo ×	VIR 16
.2	me-ri-du-ma-te	VIR 10 ×
.3	mi-ka-ta ×	VIR 3
.4	o-pi-te-u-ke-e-we	VIR 4 ×
.5	e-to-wo-ko ×	VIR 5
.6	ka-sa-to ×	VIR
.7	pu-ka-wo ×	VIR 23
.8	me-ri-da-ma-te ,	VIR 6
.9	o-pi-]te-u-ke-e-we ,	VIR 5 ×
.10	mi-ka-]ta ,	VIR 6 ×
.11	e-]to-wo-ko , VIR 4 a-to-po-qo VIR 3	
.12	] *margo*	

⇒

Verso

.0		*margo*
.1	po-ru-da-ma-te	VIR 4
.2	*vacat*	
.3	qa-ra₂-te ,	VIR
.4	pu-ko-ro ,	VIR
.5	a-ko-so-ta ,	VIR
.6	pi-ri-ja-me-ja	VIR
.7	e-ni-ja-u-si-jo	VIR
.8	pte-jo-ko VIR , qo-ta-wo VIR[	
.9	a-ta-ro VIR te-o-po-[	
.10	*vestigia*	
.11		*margo*

Other texts, which contain similar lists of occupational designations and anthroponyms, do show the numeral 1 after the personal name. See, for example, text PY An 594, which has on its first line the personal name *ma-ri-ti-wi-jo* followed by a checkmark and VIR 1.[12]

PY An 594

.1	ma-ri-ti-wi-jo × VIR 1	pu-ka-wo × VIR 10

---

sanctuaire/cult personnel, see Weilhartner 2017a:222–225. On the assumption that these occupational designations refer to *desservants de sanctuaire*, see Olivier 1960:37–74, 122–125, 138–147.

[12] See Olivier 1960:19–20.

.2   me-ri-du-ma-te   VIR 4   mi-ka-ta   VIR 1 ×
⇓

Although in all cases referred to so far the missing numeral is easily understood to represent a single person or animal, it is important to note that the lack
of numerals does not automatically imply a missing single unit.[13] This is made
clear by the following examples:

PY Ad 697 deals with the sons (*ko-wo* /*korwoi*/ VIR) of female linen or flax
workers (*ri-ne-ja-o* /*lineiāhōn*/) from the location *da-mi-ni-ja*. Irrespective of
whether these sons are described as either 'serving as/being rowers' (*eretai kʷelo-
menoi*) or, less likely, 'willing/wishing to row' (*erehen gʷēlomenoi*),[14] the absence
of any numeral after the logogram for man (VIR) seems to indicate that the
young men in question are temporarily absent. As a consequence on this tablet
ko-wo VIR is likely to represent *ko-wo* VIR 0.[15] This interpretation is likely to be
accepted also for other cases within this series where either *ko-wo* (PY Ad 290,
685, 689, 700) or *ko-wo* VIR (PY Ad 678) is written without a numerical entry.[16]

PY Ad 697

.a   e-re[ ]qe-ro-me-no
      da-mi-ni-jaᴌ ᵣi̯-ne-ja-o ko-wo VIR

It is interesting to note that within the corresponding PY Ab series, which
was written by some other scribe (Hand 21) than the PY Ad series (Hand 23),
logograms written without following numerals do not refer to absent persons.
Within this series the optional entries *DA* and/or *TA* may occur (in either
order). These logograms are likely to denote *external* male (*DA*) and *internal*
female (*TA*) supervisors.[17] If they occur within the PY Ab series, they are usually
not followed by a numerical entry (the single exception is PY Ab 584). On the
contrary, if they occur within the parallel PY Aa series, written by two different
scribes (Hand 1 and Hand 4, respectively), *DA* and *TA* are always followed by
the numeral 1. At first sight, then, this seems to suggest that *DA* and *TA* always

---

[13] On an entry where not only the numeral (1) but also the logogram (*204^VAS) is missing, obviously
      due to lack of space, see PY Ta 711.2. I owe this reference to the kindness of Tom Palaima.

[14] The original text has a lacuna between *e-re*[and]*qe-ro-me-no*. On its possible restoration as *e-re*[*-ta*]
      qe-ro-me-no, see Chadwick 1987:77n3, 87–88; Killen 2012:174n16.

[15] Chadwick 1987:77n3; Killen 2012:174n16.

[16] Chadwick 1988:45–46; Palaima 1988:88. *Pace* Palaima 1988:88n127 (following Tritsch 1957:154),
      PY Ad 380 and Ad 663 do have numerals. On the quasi-join PY Ad 663 [+] Ad 674 see Melena
      2000–2001:368. Another explanation for the blank spaces after some logograms on the tablets
      of the PY Ad series is offered by Tritsch (1957:154–157). On arguments that speak against this
      explanation, see Palaima 1988:88.

[17] Killen 1983; Chadwick 1988:71–73.

refer to single individuals even when no numeral is recorded. However, taking into account that the presence of *DA* and *TA* within the PY Ab series results in varying amounts of supplements (T 7 or, occasionally, T 9) to the basic monthly rations of wheat (GRA) and figs (NI), there are some reasons to believe that *TA* without numeral implies either *TA* 1 or *TA* 2.[18] As a consequence, comparing the rations of wheat (GRA) and figs (NI) with the numbers of women (MUL) and children (*ko-wa* /korwai/, *ko-wo* /korwoi/) is the only means of determining the number of *TA* present. For what reason the numeral is not explicitly stated we cannot guess.

PY Ab 189

.A   GRA 6 T 7 *TA DA*
.B   pu-ro ki-ni-di-ja MUL 20 ko-wa 10 ko-wo 10 *NI*   6 T 7

PY Na 924 provides another example where the omission of a numeral after the logogram seems to indicate a zero. Tablets of the Na series from Pylos appear to record the taxable capacity of individual plots of flax-growing land.[19] The flax from these plots at various places in both provinces of the Pylian kingdom is presumably used by the central administration for the manufacture of linen cloth. These texts also list various exemptions from the payment of taxes. Among these records is tablet PY Na 924:

PY Na 924

.A   to-sa   *SA* 10
.B   ri-sa-pi , *SA*   me-to-re , e-re-u-te-ro-se

According to John Killen[20] the verb *e-re-u-te-ro-se* /eleutherōse/ refers to (permanent) exemptions granted. On this tablet the exemption is granted by a person called *me-to-re*.[21] Unlike tablet PY Na 568, the beneficiaries are not explicitly mentioned. Usually, the first entry, which begins with a toponym written in large characters, followed by a majuscule *SA* and a number, indicates the quantity that the central administration expects to receive. On tablet PY Na 924, however, the *SA* entry following the toponym *ri-sa-pi* is written without a

---

[18]   *TA* 1 is likely to be understood on PY Ab 186, 189, 194, 217, 277, 372, 379, 388, 515, 558, and 578. *TA* 2, instead, on PY Ab 382, 553, and 573 (and maybe also on Ab 190 and 586). See Killen 1983:121 and Chadwick 1988:68–71. Chadwick points out that *TA* is followed by either 1 or 2 in the KN Ak series, which is comparable to the PY Ab series in structure and contents. Bennett (1983:119) offers an alternative explanation of the supplements of T 9 (i.e., not the usual quantities T 5 and T 2 for *DA* <1> and *TA* <2>, but T 6 and T 3 for *DA* <1> and *TA* <1>) without subscribing to it.

[19]   See, for example, Foster 1981, esp. 76–91 with further references.

[20]   Killen 1992–1993:114–121.

[21]   For *me-to-re* being a nominative case, see KN Da 5295.

numeral. As has been observed "[t]he first *SA* entry and the amount(s) of the exemptions(s) must be added together to obtain the gross assessment for the town."[22] For example, the total assessment for the village *e-ri-no-wo* amounts to 30 units of *SA*. For some reason, 6 units are discounted because an exemption (*e-re-u-te-ra* /eleuthera/) is granted to the smith (*ka-ke-we* /khalkēwei/).[23] Therefore, the palace expects to receive 24 units.

PY Na 106

.A   e-re-u-te-ra *SA* 6
.B   e-ri-no-wo *SA* 24   to-sa-de , ka-ke-we

Subsequently, the total assessment for the village recorded on PY Na 924 seems to amount to 10 units and the entry *ri-sa-pi SA* is likely to stand for *SA* 0.[24]

In some other cases, the logographic entries written on the tablets without numerals are not to be read as implying any of the numerals 0, 1, or 2. This can be demonstrated by a tablet belonging to the Ma series from Pylos. This series records taxation assessments of six different commodities or raw materials in proportional amounts expected from the major towns in the various districts of the Hither and the Further Province of the Pylian kingdom. The six items are listed by logograms (**146* = some sort of simple textile, **152* = oxhide) or syllabograms (*RI, KE, O, ME*) standing for logograms. The latter function as phonetic abbreviations of (presumably Greek) words, the identification of which is a matter of discussion.[25] Some amounts have already been delivered (*a-pu-do-si* /apudosis/, 'delivery'); certain proportions are still owed (*o* standing for *o-pe-ro* /ophelos/, 'debt'). In addition, these tablets also refer to workers (most notably bronzesmiths, *ka-ke-we* /khalkēwes/), who receive exemptions (or postponements) from contributions (*o-u-di-do-si* /ou didonsi/, 'they do not give').

PY Ma 123

.1   ti-mi-to-a-ke-e **146* 24 *RI* M 24 *KE* M 7   **152* 10   *O* M 5 *ME* 500
.2   a-pu-do-si **146* 21 *o* 2 *RI* M *KE* M   **152*   *O* M   *ME*
.3   o-da-a₂ , ka-ke-we , o-u-di-do-si **146* 1 *RI* M 1   *ME* 10

On PY Ma 123 the first line states the assessment of the amount of the six standard commodities of what is due from the site of **ti-mi-to-a-ko*. The third line records how much of this assessment needs not be delivered due to exemptions

---

[22]   Foster 1981:69.
[23]   Or, less likely, to the smiths (*ka-ke-we* /khalkēwes/).
[24]   *Docs²*, 468; Chadwick 1988:45. In addition, it has been suggested that on PY Na 248 and Na 334 *SA* 0 is to be understood after the place name, see *Docs²*, 468.
[25]   See, for example, Killen 2008 with further references.

granted to the smiths. Line 2 is introduced by the word *a-pu-do-si* indicating the amount that has actually been contributed by the district of **ti-mi-to-a-ko*. While there are some shortfalls in the delivery of **146* (there is a deficit of 2 units indicated by the abbreviation *o*), none of the other commodities are marked as outstanding. Quite unusually, the scribe has not indicated any numerals after the logograms *RI*, *KE*, **152*, *O*, and *ME* in this line. The reason usually assumed for this absence of numerals after the last five logograms in line .2 is that the payments expected had come in full.[26] However, although the missing quantities can easily be figured out by subtracting the amounts 'the smiths do not give' in the third line from the assessment recorded in the first line (i.e., *RI* M <23>, *KE* M <7>, **152* <10>, *O* M <5>, and *ME* <490>),[27] the notation of the specific quantities would be more in line with the usual habits of the central administration, as is documented, for example, on PY Ma 222, Ma 346, and Ma 393. Whatever the reason for the scribe not indicating the numerals after the logograms on line .2 of tablet Ma 123, their absence without doubt impedes the direct reading of the numerical information of these entries.

Other groups of tablets document the omission of numerals on a more regular basis. The Knossos Do series lists female sheep (OVIS[f]), invariably 100 on each record. Usually, the syllabic sign *se* is written before the logogram. Those tablets where *se* does not appear have the place-name *se-to-i-ja* instead (KN Do 1054, 7087, 7613, 7740) indicating that this word has regularly been abbreviated by its first syllable.[28] Consequently, all tablets of this series seem to record flocks of a single location. Along with the female sheep other animals are listed, each qualified by an adjunct. On the basis of KN Do 927, which shows the adjunct *ki* (𐀑) as extending well above the center of the tablet (Fig. 19.1), one may suggest that this adjunct, which is usually taken as a designation for young animals (of either sex),[29] qualifies the entries that follow. Subsequently, the animals listed as *pe* OVIS[m] and *za* OVIS[m] (and maybe also *o* OVIS[m]) are likely to refer to young animals, which are further specified by the adjuncts in question.[30]

---

[26]   *Docs*[2], 293; Killen 1984:178–179, 182n11.

[27]   See, for example, *Docs*[2], 293 and the table in Hooker 1980:173.

[28]   On the interpretation of *se* as an abbreviation of the place name *se-to-i-ja* or an adjectival derivative of this toponym, see Killen 1964:89–93.

[29]   On the interpretation of *ki* OVIS[m] as 'young animal of either sex', see Killen 1964:78, 80n28, 84.

[30]   See Killen 1964:81: "On this text, there can be little serious doubt that *ki* qualifies both *pe* and *za*. The base of this sign is drawn just above the lower edge of the tablet, and its upper section extends well above the level of the tablet's central dividing line." Killen views *pe* as an abbreviation of *pe-ru-si-nu-wo* (and referring to last year's sheep) and *za* as an abbreviation of **za-we-te-jo*, or the like (and referring to this year's sheep).

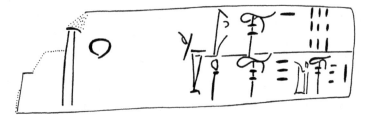

Figure 19.1. KN Do 927 (after *CoMIK* I, 383).

KN Do 927

.A   ]   *pe* OVIS^m 19

.B   ]ṣẹ OVIS^f 100   *ki za* OVIS^m 30 *o* OVIS^m 31

This tablet records 19 *pe* OVIS^m, 30 (*ki*) *za* OVIS^m, and 31 *o* OVIS^m. Other tablets of this series show no numerals after these logograms, as can be shown *inter alia* by tablet KN Do 919.

KN Do 919

.A   *ki pe* OVIS^m *o*[OVIS^m

.B   wi-da-ma-ro / *se* OVIS^f 100   *za*   OVIS^m [

Since this omission of numerals is documented on various tablets there is no question of an oversight.[31] Is this lack of numerals related to the fact that the first entry of these tablets is invariably 100? Does the scribe skip numerals that he views as standard-sized?

A similar phenomenon may be observed within the KN Sc series, which is of uniform character. This series lists suits of armor (TUN), chariots (BIG), and horses (EQU), along with men's names.[32] At times, the logograms of these texts are not accompanied by numerical entries. This omission may be viewed as reflecting a situation where some information was not available. Alternatively, the scribes may on occasion not have written down what seems to be self-evident for them. If this assumption is correct, BIG may stand for BIG 1, TUN for TUN 2, and EQU for EQU ZE 1.[33]

---

[31] Next to KN Do 919 the following tablets show an omission of numerals after one or two entries: KN Do 924, 929, 5010. Other texts are too fragmentary to allow for a clear assessment.

[32] On this series, see Driessen 1996:489–492.

[33] An omission of one or more numeral(s) is to be observed on the following tablets: KN Sc 103 (EQU), Sc 221 (TUN) (?), Sc 236 (BIG), Sc 251 (TUN), Sc 5061 (EQU), Sc 5066 (EQU), Sc 5068 (TUN), Sc 5083 (BIG), Sc 5086 (EQU), Sc 5139 (EQU, TUN), Sc 5141 (EQU), Sc 5142 (BIG), Sc 5146 (BIG), Sc 5155 (TUN), Sc 5165 (BIG), Sc 7469 (TUN), Sc 7471 (ZE), Sc 7506 (BIG) (?), 8467 (TUN), Sc 8470 (TUN), Sc 8476 (BIG), Sc 8478 (BIG), Sc 8479 (BIG) (?), Sc 9113 (TUN), Sc 9142 (EQU) (?), Sc 9156 (BIG) (?). As only a small number of Sc records are complete there may have been even more original records which contain a logogram not followed by a numeral.

KN Sc 236
ku-ru-me-no ⟦TUN⟧ BIG

On other documents, the attempt to figure out the envisaged number has no reasonable chance. For example, on PY Un 1322 *146 is specified twice as we-a₂-no [ri]-no re-po-to /wehanoi linon lepton/, i.e., as robes of fine linen.[34] On line .3 the logogram is immediately followed by GRA 2 NI 2, on line .5 by GRA 5, and on line .6 by GRA 15, respectively. Since this tablet records o-no /onon/ transactions, which seem to denote some kind of 'benefits' or 'payments', it has been suggested that the value of *146 is expressed in terms of wheat (GRA) (and figs (NI)).[35]

PY Un 1322

.1   ]vest.[   ] GRA [
.2   ]no-[•]-o-no[ ]   GRA 6   NI [
.3   de-ku-tu-wo-ko[ ]o-no *146 GRA 2 NI 2
.4   i-te-we , o-no[   ] GRA 12
.5   we-a₂-no[ ]-no , re-po-to *146 GRA 5
.6   we-[   ]-no , re-po-to *146 GRA 15
.7   vest.

If GRA 2 NI 2, GRA 5, and GRA 15 represent the 'price' to be paid for the textiles (*146) in question, one wonders why the numbers of *146 are not recorded.[36] On the other hand, if one reads *146 to imply *146 1, as has been suggested by Michel Lejeune,[37] it is difficult to explain: (a) the great amount of wheat (ca. 480 l–1,440 l) or of wheat and figs (ca. 192 l each) as the 'price' for a single simple textile; and (b) the different amounts of wheat or of wheat and figs given as payments in exchange for one piece of textile in each case. A possible solution of this conundrum has been tentatively suggested by John Chadwick,[38] who states: "possibly there was a standard payment per garment which would have allowed the officials to calculate the number."[39] If this is the correct explanation of this

---

[34] On this tablet, see Chadwick 1964. For an updated transcription of this tablet, see PTT².
[35] Chadwick 1964:25; Killen 1988:181–183.
[36] See Chadwick 1964:25: "It appears therefore that Un 1322 records in lines .4 and .5 (i.e. .5 and .6) the equation of quantities of wheat with *unspecified* numbers of garments. [...] It is curious that the number of garments is not given" (my emphasis). See Docs², 505. *146 was not read on line 3 at that time.
[37] Lejeune 1964:116, 121n15.
[38] Chadwick 1964:25. Interestingly, another tablet of class Cii, PY Ua 158, shows the same combination of logograms (GRA, NI, *146) as well as the term o-na /ona/ plural of o-no /onon/. On this tablet, however, all logographic entries are followed by a numeral.
[39] On another occasion Chadwick proposes that the person who was responsible for issuing the wheat was not interested in the goods received in exchange; see Docs², 505–506. However, from

text, the correct numbers of *146 in each line can only be achieved by a scribe directly involved in the transactions in question. The same holds true for the numerals to be supplemented on the Do series from Knossos referred to above.

***

On the whole, the presence of logograms without following numerical entries, which appears on a more regular basis than is usually acknowledged, indicates that the information recorded on the tablets serves only a very limited number of administrators. For those not directly involved in the recorded transactions, it would be, at least occasionally, almost impossible to figure out the unrecorded numerical data. This seems to reinforce the idea that the main purpose of these documents is their use as mere *aide-mémoires* for the particular official in charge of the relevant transaction.[40] In my view, individual scribes do usually not attempt to make the information summarized onto clay tablets easily comprehensible to other scribes.

Appendix: Juxtaposition of Logograms

Of a different nature are those examples that show an intended combination of two logograms. In these cases there is no question of supplementing a number after the first logogram. The best-known examples are provided by tablet PY Tn 316, on which the material of three different types of vessels, specified by the logograms *213^{VAS} (a simple bowl without handles), *215^{VAS} (a cup with small handles identified as a kylix), and *216^{VAS} (a plain conical bowl on a high cylindrical stem resembling a chalice), is indicated by another logogram, *141/AUR, most probably gold.[41] Another example is the juxtaposition of *161 and TELA on several texts of the Lc, Ld, and L series from Knossos. Although there is no general consensus on the meaning of *161, its function as an additional qualifier

---

the point of view of the central administration, which is interested in quantities, I view this explanation as less likely.

[40] See, in general, Palaima 2004b: esp. 286–288, 294. However, there are some indications that the status of at least some of the clay documents was higher than that of impermanent records; see Bennet 2001:27–29. In this paper, Bennet argues persuasively for taking *scribes* as administrators and members of the palatial élite.

[41] In a recent study, Louis Godart (2009) argues that the variant forms of logogram *141 represent two different metals, gold (AUR) and silver (ARG). However, as scribal variations of logograms usually do not indicate any difference in meaning (on that topic see Weilhartner 2017b), it was agreed on the 14th Mycenological Colloquium at Copenhagen to suppress for the time being a transcription of the variant form as either ARG or *141bis. As the Signary Committee acknowledges the need for further discussion, it was suggested to make a final decision on *141 and *141bis at the next colloquium; see Nosch and Landenius Enegren 2017:837. For a detailed discussion on logogram *141/AUR, see Weilhartner, in press.

for the cloth logogram TELA is beyond reasonable doubt.[42] A comparable combination of logograms is documented by the juxtaposed logograms for female (OVIS^f) and male (OVIS^m) sheep on the one hand and wool (LANA) on the other within the Dp series from Knossos.[43] This juxtaposition indicates that the wool recorded is from either female or male sheep.[44]

KN Dp 7280

.1   ]OVIS^m LANA 50   [

.2   ]OVIS^f LANA 36[

Like logogram *141/AUR on PY Tn 316, which is not written to record a specific amount of gold but to specify the material of which the vessels are made, the logograms for female and male sheep in this series do not function as a logographic character for recording numbers of individual animals. Rather, they qualify the wool listed to derive from either female or male sheep. More typically, specifications of logograms are phrased by syllabic words.[45] However, a similar juxtaposition of two logograms is to be observed on tablet KN D 7252. Its text reads as follows:

KN D 7252

.1   ] OVIS^m VIR 1 [

.2   ]OVIS^x VIR[

In dealing with this tablet John Killen has asked the following question: "If the reading here is correct, does this indicate that the men in question are shepherds?"[46] If his assumption is correct, and I can see no argument against it, this would mean that on occasion a Mycenaean scribe could have written OVIS^m VIR instead of the more familiar *po-me* /*poimēn*/ VIR. If one assumes that on the second line of KN D 7252 one should read OVIS^f, the scribe may have come up with this exceptional solution because he had to differentiate between a shepherd of male sheep (OVIS^m) and another one of female sheep (OVIS^f). Whether this interpretation is correct or not, the examples shown in this paper clearly document that the usage of logograms within the Mycenaean writing systems allows for a greater variability than is usually assumed.

---

[42] A detailed discussion of all texts where *161 occurs and of the problems raised by this logogram is given in Melena 1975:94–117. See Nosch 2012:310, 338–339.

[43] This juxtaposition of OVIS^m LANA or OVIS^f LANA is attested on the following tablets: KN Dp 43, 699, 937 (?), 1061, 2004, 7135, 7280. See also KN Dp 997.

[44] Killen 2006:103n73. See *Docs*², 505. Another example is provided by KN Wb 5527, which has on its first line]OVIS^f LANA[.

[45] See, for example, the syntagma *ko-wo* /*korwoi*/ VIR for recording 'young men' in the Pylian A series.

[46] Killen 2006:103n73.

Bibliography

Bennet, J. 2001. "Agency and Bureaucracy: Thoughts on the Nature and Extent of Administration in Bronze Age Pylos." In *Economy and Politics in the Mycenaean Palace States. Proceedings of a Conference Held on 1-3 July 1999 in the Faculty of Classics, Cambridge,* ed. S. Voutsaki and J. T. Killen, 25–37. Cambridge.

Bennett, E. L. Jr., ed. 1964. *Mycenaean Studies. Proceedings of the Third International Colloquium for Mycenaean Studies Held at "Wingspread," 4-8 September 1961.* Madison.

———. 1983. "Notes on the Pylos Tablets: Aa and Ab." In Oliva and Frolíková 1983:115–120.

Chadwick, J. 1964. "Pylos Tablet Un 1322." In Bennett 1964:19–26.

———. 1976. "Mycenaean *e-re-ta*: A Problem." In *Studies in Greek, Italic, and Indo-European Linguistics Offered to Leonard R. Palmer,* ed. A. Morpurgo Davies and W. Meid, 43–45. Innsbruck.

———. 1987. "The Muster of the Pylian Fleet." In *Tractata Mycenaea. Proceedings of the Eighth International Colloquium on Mycenaean Studies, Held in Ohrid, 15-20 September 1985,* ed. P. Hr. Ilievski and L. Crepajac, 75–84. Skopje.

———. 1988. "The Women of Pylos." In Olivier and Palaima 1988:43–95.

Driessen, J. 1996. "The Arsenal of Knossos (Crete) and Mycenaean Chariot Forces." In *Archaeological and Historical Aspects of West-European Societies. Album Amicorum André van Doorselaer,* ed. M. Lodewijckx, 481–498. Leuven.

Firth, R. J. 2000-2001. "A Review of the Find-Places of the Linear B Tablets from the Palace of Knossos." *Minos* 35–36:63–290.

Foster, E. D. 1981. "The Flax Impost at Pylos and Mycenaean Landholding." *Minos* 17:67–121.

Godart, L. 1999. "Les sacrifices d'animaux dans les textes mycéniens." In *Floreant Studia Mycenaea. Akten des X. Internationalen Mykenologischen Colloquiums in Salzburg vom 1.-5. Mai 1995,* ed. S. Deger-Jalkotzy, S. Hiller, and O. Panagl, 249–256. Veröffentlichungen der Mykenischen Kommission 18. Vienna.

———. 2009. "I due scribi della tavoletta Tn 316." *Pasiphae* 3:99–115.

Hallager, E. 2015. "Mycenaean Administrative Sealing Practice: A World of Its Own?" *In Tradition and Innovation in the Mycenaean Palatial Polities. Proceedings of an International Symposium Held at the Austrian Academy of Sciences, Institute for Oriental and European Archaeology, Aegean and Anatolia Department, Vienna, 1-2 March, 2013,* ed. J. Weilhartner and F. Ruppenstein, 141–153. Mykenische Studien 34. Vienna.

Hooker, J. T. 1980. *Linear B: An Introduction.* Bristol.

Killen, J. T. 1964. "Some Adjuncts to the SHEEP Ideogram on Knossos Tablets." *Eranos* 61:69–92.

———. 1983. "*TA* and *DA*." In Oliva and Frolíková 1983:121–126.

———. 1984. "Last Year's Debts on the Pylos Ma Tablets." *Studi micenei ed egeo-anatolici* 25:173–188.

———. 1987. "Notes on the Knossos Tablets." In *Studies in Mycenaean and Classical Greek Presented to John Chadwick*, ed. J. T. Killen, J. L. Melena, and J.-P. Olivier, 319–331. *Minos* 20–22. Salamanca.

———. 1988. "Epigraphy and Interpretation in Knossos WOMAN and CLOTH Records." In Olivier and Palaima 1988:167–183.

———. 1992–1993. "*Ke-u-po-da e-sa-re-u* and the Exemptions on the Pylos Na Tablets." *Minos* 27–28:109–123.

———. 1996. "Thebes Sealings and Knossos Tablets." In *Atti e memorie del secondo congresso internazionale di micenologia, Roma-Napoli, 14-20 ottobre 1991*, ed. E. De Miro, L. Godart, and A. Sacconi, 71–82. Rome.

———. 2006. "Thoughts on the Functions of the New Thebes Tablets." In *Die neuen Linear B-Texte aus Theben: Ihr Aufschlußwert für die mykenische Sprache und Kultur. Akten des internationalen Forschungskolloquiums an der Österreichischen Akademie der Wissenschaften, 5.-6. Dezember 2002.* Mykenische Studien 19, ed. S. Deger-Jalkotzy and O. Panagl, 79–110. Vienna.

———. 2008. "The Commodities on the Pylos Ma Tablets." In *Colloquium Romanum. Atti del XII colloquio internazionale di micenologia, Roma, 20-25 febbraio 2006*, ed. A. Sacconi, M. del Freo, L. Godart, and M. Negri, 431–447. Pasiphae 2. Pisa.

———. 2012. "The Two Provinces of Pylos Revisited." In *Actas del simposio internacional: 55 años de Micenología (1952-2007), Bellaterra, 12-13 de abril de 2007*, ed. C. Varias, 155–181. Faventia Supplement 1. Barcelona.

———. 2015. "The Language of Religious Texts: Some Fresh Thoughts on Old Problems." In *Economy and Administration in Mycenaean Greece. Collected Papers on Linear B, Vol. 3 (2004-2012)*, ed. M. del Freo, 1109–1134. Incunabula Graeca 104. Rome.

Lejeune, M. 1964. "Observations sur l'idéogramme *146.*" In Bennet 1964:111–124.

Melena, J. L. 1975. *Studies on Some Mycenaean Inscriptions from Knossos Dealing with Textiles. Minos* Supplement 5. Salamanca.

———. 2000–2001. "24 Joins and Quasi-joins of Fragments in the Linear B Tablets from Pylos." *Minos* 35–36:357–369.

Nosch, M.-L. 2012. "The Textile Logograms in the Linear B Tablets: *Les idéogrammes archéologiques - des textiles.*" In *Études mycéniennes 2010. Actes du XIIIᵉ Colloque international sur les textes égéens, Sèvres, Paris, Nanterre, 20-23 septembre 2010*, ed. P. Carlier, C. de Lamberterie, M. Egetmeyer, N. Guilleux, F. Rougemont, and J. Zurbach, 303–344. Pisa.

Nosch, M.-L., and H. Landenius Enegren, eds. 2017. *Aegean Scripts. Proceedings of the 14th International Colloquium on Mycenaean Studies, Copenhagen, 2-5 September 2015*. Incunabula Graeca 105. Rome.

Oliva, P., and A. Frolíková, eds. 1983. *Concilium Eirene XVI. Proceedings of the 16th International Eirene Conference, Prague 31.8.-4.9. 1982*, vol. 3. Prague.

Olivier, J.-P. 1960. *A propos d'une 'liste' de desservants de sanctuaire dans les documents en linéaire B de Pylos*. Brussels.

Olivier, J.-P., and T. G. Palaima, eds. 1988. *Texts, Tablets and Scribes. Studies in Mycenaean Epigraphy and Economy Offered to Emmett L. Bennett, Jr. Minos* Supplement 10. Salamanca.

Palaima, T. G. 1988. *The Scribes of Pylos*. Rome.

———. 2004a. "Sacrificial Feasting in the Linear B Documents." *Hesperia* 73: 217–246.

———. 2004b. "Mycenaean Accounting Methods and Systems and Their Place within Mycenaean Palatial Civilization." In *Creating Economic Order. Recordkeeping, Standardization, and the Development of Accounting in the Ancient Near East. A Colloquium Held at the British Museum, November 2000*, ed. M. Hudson and C. Wunsch, 269–301. Bethesda.

Piteros, C., J.-P. Olivier, and J. L. Melena. 1990. "Les inscriptions en linéaire B des nodules de Thèbes (1982): La fouille, les documents, les possibilités d'interprétation." *Bulletin de correspondance hellénique* 114:103–184.

Tritsch, F. J. 1957. "PY Ad 684." *Minos* 5:154–162.

Weilhartner, J. 2005. *Mykenische Opfergaben nach Aussage der Linear B-Texte*. Mykenische Studien 18. Vienna.

———. 2017a. "Working for a Feast: Textual Evidence for State-Organized Work Feasts in Mycenaean Greece." *American Journal of Archaeology* 121:219–236.

———. 2017b. "'Les idéogrammes archéologiques': Does Variation Matter?" In Nosch and Landenius Enegren 2017:169–192.

———. In press. "Gold in the Linear B Tablets." In *KO-RO-NO-WE-SA. Proceedings of the 15th Mycenological Colloquium, September 2021*, ed. J. Bennet, A. Karnava, and T. Meißner.

Afterword

How Far We Have Come in Mycenology in Seventy Years

THOMAS PALAIMA AND GARRETT BRUNER

Program in Aegean Scripts and Prehistory
University of Texas at Austin

tpalaima@austin.utexas.edu
garrettbruner@utexas.edu

"APRIL IS THE CRUELLEST MONTH, BREEDING" is how T. S. Eliot draws us into his landmark poetic thoughts and feelings on the human condition after the carnage and waste, really mass butchery, that we now refer to as World War I (1914–1918). It was then so singular in its scale and impact upon human lives that it was called either "The Great War" or "The War to End All Wars."

The second great war (1939–1945) played a significant role in the history of Mycenology. Its outbreak caused the some six hundred Pylos Linear B tablets unearthed by Carl Blegen (1887–1971) in 1939 to be hastily, but fortunately securely, stored in the vaults of the National Bank of Greece in Athens for the duration of the war. The war and the Nazi occupation of Greece also caused the closing of the Herakleion Museum on Crete, making the Knossos tablets inaccessible. The Museum opened again to the public only in 1952, tragically after the death on May 16, 1950, of Alice E. Kober (1906–1950), the greatest scholar of Aegean scripts during the first half-century of the 1900s.[1] Kober's death impelled Emmett L. Bennett, Jr. (1918–2011) to go and study the tablets by special arrangement in the summer of 1950.[2]

---

[1] Fox 2013; Palaima 2017.

[2] The abridged chronology, based on the correspondence among Bennett, Blegen, Ventris, and Myres is as follows. MAY 17: letter sent to Bennett by Kober's family informing him of her death and her wishes that he be sent her papers. MAY 20: Myres's letter to Bennett regarding

Where readings of the Linear B tablets and analytical identification of the standard elements of the script were concerned, Bennett essentially took over Kober's role in trying to help Sir John Myres (1869–1954) produce a more scientific edition of *Scripta Minoa* II. Myres was a retired professor of ancient history, a distinguished field archaeologist, especially in Cyprus, and a champion of anthropology. Although a past Gladstone Professor of Greek, he had but a passing general interest in Aegean linear scripts before being entrusted with seeing the project begun by Sir Arthur Evans (1851–1941) through to publication, following Evans' death on July 12, 1941.[3] What would become *Scripta Minoa* II was in piecemeal manuscript form when Myres inherited it.

In the end, Kober's and Bennett's help was a failure, as we can read in the correspondence of April 1952 between Bennett and Michael Ventris. Myres was driven by his loyalty to the original pre–World War II conceptions of Sir Arthur Evans, although many were woefully outdated. Myres was also constrained by the postwar economic exigencies of the Clarendon Press. The press could not afford to redo plates and sign charts—and create new script-character fonts—that it had already made for Sir Arthur's version. *Scripta Minoa* II when it appeared early in 1952 maintained the old Evans system of identification of the signs, instead of the Kober-Bennett system adopted by Ventris. It also contained what were known by Ventris and Bennett (and in some cases by Kober before them) to be misreadings of signs and mistakes in making references to tablets.

In the Herakleion Museum in July and August 1950, Bennett autopsied the tablets, making new readings and joins and also correcting inventory numbers and the like. He then had an absolute mastery of the material and generously went about making indices of all the "word" occurrences both for Knossos and for Pylos. These he shared with Michael Ventris, the eventual decipherer of Linear B, just as Bennett and Kober had swapped her knowledge of the Knossos

---

Kober's death and asking if Bennett knows anybody who could take her place in Greece for the summer in order to proof the Knossos tablet readings for *Scripta Minoa* II (*SM* II). MAY 29: Bennett writes Carl Blegen, quoting Myres's letter verbatim on the sudden Knossos tablets/ *SM* II problem. JUNE 26: Bennett writes Blegen that he has secured funding for the trip and has booked a flight to be in London on July 8, and is in the middle of filing for a passport. JUNE 27: Bennett writes to Ventris about this trip. JUNE 27: Bennett receives word from Myres that necessary Herakleion museum resources are approved by director Nikolaos Platon and are in place for Bennett's arrival. AUGUST 12: Bennett reports to Myres in detail regarding his work on the Knossos tablets in the Herakleion Museum. AUGUST 27: Bennett writes to Myres about leaving Greece on September 3 and mentions that he has created a concordance of the Knossos tablets with improved readings.

[3]   Robinson 2002:44–45. On Myres's general knowledge of Linear A, Linear B, and Cretan Hieroglyphic, see Myres 1933:285–289, 300.

material and his knowledge of the Pylos material after Bennett finished his landmark dissertation in 1947.

The Second World War also redirected two of the three main figures in the story of the decipherment of Linear B, Bennett and Ventris, into military service. Michael Ventris navigated bombers in missions over Europe. He was lucky to survive—the odds of doing so and living were 50–50. Bennett went into wartime code-breaking, working with pattern analysis of intercepted Japanese messages. As we have mentioned, he finished his groundbreaking dissertation in 1947, the year in which Kober set aside her own absolutely fundamental work on the scripts in order to begin helping Sir John Myres publish Sir Arthur Evans' *Scripta Minoa* II. When published early in 1952 with an appendix of Bennett's new readings and improvements, the volume was seriously flawed as a scientific instrument because of many complex practical and psychological reasons alluded to above and because Kober's end-of-life extended illness removed the positive influence she was having in bringing the text up to date (1947–1950). But its appearance in the Spring of 1952 still provided frustrating help to the two remaining lead figures in the attack on Linear B, Bennett and Ventris.

For our purposes here, the second great war also created the devastated world into which José Luis Melena was born on December 1, 1946. A reading of George Orwell's *Nineteen Eighty-Four* or W. H. Auden's "The Shield of Achilles" captures the atmosphere in Europe as Melena was growing up. In Spain, three great figures, Francisco R. Adrados (1922–2020), Martín S. Ruipérez (1923–2015), and Antonio Tovar (1911–1985) had firmly laid down the foundations for Spain and for José L. Melena to play leading roles in Mycenological research now for over seventy years. Tovar founded the journal *Minos* to explore the obscure scripts and languages that had fascinated him for years.[4] And Tovar, Adrados, and Ruipérez explored the dialect makeup of Greek in historical and prehistoric times, helping to create a fervent interest in texts that would give us insight into how the Greek language looked in the second half of the second millennium BCE.[5]

As Melena wrote on July 4, 2015, notifying the Aegean-scripts scholarly world of the death of his mentor:

> Martín Ruipérez was the first Spanish classicist to achieve international prominence and recognition in modern times. He opened new routes in Greek linguistics and played a crucial role in the development of Mycenaean studies. He was the editor of *Minos* from 1956 to 1981.[6]

---

[4] Volume 1 appeared in 1951 with a necrology of Kober written by Bennett.
[5] Tovar 1944; Adrados 1952; Ruipérez 1953 (1954).
[6] At which point Melena took over active and inspirational editorship for the next thirty years.

If we turn back the clock seventy years to April of 1952, we will see that Michael Ventris in "Work Note 19" (20 March 1952)[7] and in his personal correspondence with Bennett (18 April 1952; 26 April 1952, cf. Fig. A1a and A1b[8]) was still wedded to the idea that the main language represented in the Linear B inscriptions was somehow related to Pelasgian/Etruscan.[9] In the letter of 26 April 1952, Ventris is using Kober's analyses and Bennett's indices to speculate whether variations in the shapes of particular signs are significant for their values (as when we write *c* or *ç*, *e* or *ē*). He uses Kober's categories of sign groups and is speculating which groups are verbal forms (finite and participial). He has hunches about how endings convey gender and cases (with their corresponding grammatical functions).

In "Work Note 20" (1 June 1952), Ventris asks the question "Are the Knossos and Pylos tablets written in Greek?"[10] He notified Bennett and Myres of the "decipherment" of Linear B as Greek in separate letters dated June 18, 1952. The public announcement was famously a BBC broadcast of July 1, 1952. But, in the letter of 26 April 1952, Ventris is employing Kober's idea of the grid[11] to good effect.

Bennett once told me, "The place names were the Rosetta stone." Only in reading through his April correspondence with Ventris in order to write this afterword, have I come to realize how significant this comment was. Ventris, in his letter of 26 April (Fig. A1b), is still using Etruscan vocabulary (and phonetics) to "read" the Linear B signs and texts that Kober and Bennett had done so much to make precise. Nonetheless in the handwritten section that ends his letter, by using Kober's evidence for primary nouns and derivative adjectival inflections, he already has isolated the three-sign sequence for 'Knossos' and the four-sign sequence for 'Amnisos'. He also speaks of the now famous "Pylos '9'" place names (particularly the place name with the sequence we now read as *pa-ki-ja-na*) in what we now know as the Hither Province. Yet he still is using Etruscan values to try to identify the group of people now transliterated as *ki-ri-te-wi-ja-i* via the Etruscan word for 'peasants, locals'.

When we move forward seventy years to April 2022, we see how sweepingly masterful and centrally important José Melena's work with tablet joins, tablet reading, text transcription, the representation of language by the Linear B script, and the state of the Greek language 1400–1170 BCE has been. His

[7] Ventris 1988:321–326.
[8] https://repositories.lib.utexas.edu/handle/2152/20893.
[9] Ventris 1988:322: "Vaguely analogous are those instances, in Etruscan, where singular and plural forms of an oblique case are differentiated by the choice of variant endings which in themselves carry no suggestion of number." He then cites two Etruscan phrases.
[10] Ventris 1988:327–332.
[11] Palaima 2017:771–772, 777 and figs. 3 and 4.

47 Highpoint,
North Hill,
Highgate,
LONDON, N.6.

26 April 1952

Dear Bennett,

Your index arrived this morning. It is an excellent
piece of work, and I am most grateful to you for it. I had not
realized that this version was to include the Pylos sign-groups with
the Knossos sign-groups, but this makes it doubly useful.

On glancing through it, I notice that a number of the
Evans/Myres forms which seemed suspicious have been suitably amended;
though I expect that there will also be a few less welcome emendations,
such as ones which knock the bottom out of little theories one had
built up. I had already realized that ⟨sign⟩ — on the chariot tablets
has to be divided off as a separate word, and that therefore no amount
of ingenuity will connect together ⟨signs⟩ and ⟨signs⟩ as I tried
to do in my last Note (p 170). If the theory which regards ⟨sign⟩ and
‡ as closely similar sounds is correct, then ⟨sign⟩ might I suppose
be connected with the adverbial (?) ‡⟨sign⟩ of Jn04.7. (— and ⟨signs⟩
with ‡⟨signs⟩ ???).

I am baffled by the last sign of ⟨signs⟩ and ⟨signs⟩
on the Chariot tablets. I had hoped that checking of the tablets would
have revealed a clear choice of — ⟨sign⟩ or of — ⟨sign⟩ throughout these
cases. For the tidiness of the grammatical forms, — ⟨sign⟩ would be
very much more welcome, but if — ⟨sign⟩ is certain we shall have to try
and fit it in. I note you give ⟨signs⟩ (04.22) but ⟨signs⟩
(04.02 etc), but both ⟨signs⟩ and ⟨signs⟩. Your criterion is, I
expect, whether the sign has one or two horizontal strokes above the
"crook". Is it your opinion that there really is a deliberate distinction here, or that all Kober's "verbal" forms in fact are only badly-
written — ⟨sign⟩ s ? In your list of rejected sign-groups, a mistake
has I think crept in in ⟨signs⟩ and ⟨signs⟩, which in Myres'
reference to 04.16 and 04-05.2 do not have the internal-⟨sign⟩- (and
should not, if ⟨sign⟩ is only the alternative vocalisation of the same consonant as ⟨sign⟩ ?).

⟨signs⟩ (04-16) is rather surprising: —⟨sign⟩ can't be
genitival, I suppose, since it follows Vowel 2, and I suspect that
⟨signs⟩ may stand to ⟨signs⟩ as ⟨signs⟩ does to ⟨signs⟩

Myres' idea that the chariot tablets contain just a random list of craftsmen's names is not very imaginative, and cannot be
right. I do not, either, entirely agree with his argument that the
chariots of 04-19 etc are a different sort from those of 04-01 etc.
After all, there's no yoke on them: they look far more like the same
chariots in an early state of manufacture: and this ties up
with the fact that a different "verb" is used with the two theories.

My guess is that two stages are recorded (leaving out a
possible previous stage recorded by ⟨signs⟩ of 04-28).

1) The provision of the ⟨signs⟩ (main farming) governed by the word
   (verb ?) ⟨signs⟩, and qualified by ⟨signs⟩ (plural ? — ⟨signs⟩ king?).
2) The provision of the ⟨signs⟩ (equipment: mounting rail, floor,
   yoke, traces etc) — a word constructed like ⟨signs⟩, but made
   verbal: ⟨signs⟩ [the -⟨sign⟩- forms seem to argue against a compound
   form with -⟨sign⟩-?].
3) Whether the "wheel" tablets record an inventory of wheels, or the
   fitting of them, isn't clear, but as they aren't all in pairs
   it must be a separate part of the process. Myres' suggestion that
   the wheels were changed frequently ties in with this.

Parallel, apparently, in root to ⟨signs⟩ and ⟨signs⟩ are the
two entities ⟨signs⟩ and ⟨signs⟩ (unless the former is connected
rather with ⟨signs⟩). The latter recurs in slightly different spelling
as ⟨signs⟩ on most of the "sword" tablets 1541 etc, which ties up
with some idea of 'equipping' or 'armoury' etc, and makes it unlikely
that the "sword" formula is one of Myres' lists of names either.

Figure 1a. Letter from Michael Ventris to Emmett L. Bennett, Jr.,
26 April 1952, page 1. By permission of Thomas G. Palaima and the archives
of the Program in Aegean Scripts and Prehistory.

26 IV 52

A form which puzzled me for some time is the ⟦Linear B⟧ which
is shown in 04-09.1 on page "Junctions" in SM. I see
you index this as ⟦Linear B⟧ , which removes the difficulty. ⟦Linear B⟧ in K 04-15.2 is presumably a misprint
similarly for ⟦Linear B⟧ . The occurrences of ⟦Linear B⟧ on
04-01 and 04-15 are puzzling, too. I had thought that
there must be some connection between the -⟦sign⟧ and the
-⟦sign⟧ in the verb on 04-01, but 04-15 disproves this.
It would have been nice if there had been 1 chariot
following the -⟦sign⟧ , and a larger number after -⟦sign⟧ : but
there seems to be no perceptible difference in context
at all, any more than between ⟦Linear B⟧ and ⟦Linear B⟧ on
903-907. I am completely baffled by the -⟦sign⟧ of the
"verbal" forms, at Knossos (04-01) and Pylos (Bb01, Sb20 eto)
unless they are intended to be more partizdial than the
others, which might help to bridge the gap to the numerous
endings in -⟦sign⟧ which seem to be part of personal names,
whether or not the endings are in any way connected. -⟦sign⟧
does not seem to be used in these other situations.

Miss Kober evidently made a very good start at listing the
'Category 3' sign-groups which show an "adjectival" form in
-⟦sign⟧/-⟦sign⟧. I'm beginning to think that while -⟦sign⟧ seems regularly
used as the *feminine* form (eg. with ⟦sign⟧ or ⟦sign⟧), and apparently
the general plural, some of the -⟦sign⟧ forms must be *masculine plural*
in sense, not singular (eg:— the senseless alternations of -⟦sign⟧ and -⟦sign⟧
mentioned above). At least they don't alternate on the *same* tablets,
only on separate ones of the same series.

⟦Linear B⟧ is presumably "adjectival" from ⟦Linear B⟧ (Tunnija – Tunan ??) =
two consonants of the same kind sometimes seem liable to be telescoped,
as in ⟦sign⟧ – etc. The chief Knossos 'adjectivals' seem to be these:—

1. CATEGORY 3 (Placenames?) Recurring together like the Pylos "8" (⟦signs⟧ etc)

[handwritten table of Linear B sign-groups in categories, including:]
✓ shared with Pylos or M.

also ⟦Linear B⟧

2. CATEGORY 3, 4a or 4 Not part of the main series. "Adjectivals" in Vowel 3 as well as 1.

[handwritten table of Linear B sign-groups]

I expect you've fully sorted these out already. It would be a wonderful thing if one could sit down
on the hill at Knossos & know just what the names of all the surrounding towns & villages were in
LM; because I'm sure some of them must occur in this series. I'm still rather intrigued by AMNISOS
for ⟦signs⟧ which is the only B group with initial ⟦sign⟧ – and ⟦sign⟧ as 3rd except ⟦signs⟧ – &
this name too should occur, surely. Amnisos is generally spoken of as if it was the port of
Knossos, but I gather there was a "harbour at the mouth of the valley"? The frequent
⟦signs⟧ – AT AMNISOS?, i.e. a(t) a separate royal depot ?? Who are the ⟦signs⟧ who are
mentioned after ⟦signs⟧ (Knossos ⟦sign⟧) and who recur at Pylos & — ci ⟦signs⟧ ija – "peasants, locals,
??" (στρ cilθ, "land, country").

Yours, Michael Ventris

Figure 1b. Letter from Michael Ventris to Emmett L. Bennett, Jr.,
26 April 1952, page 2. By permission of Thomas G. Palaima and the archives
of the Program in Aegean Scripts and Prehistory.

interpretations of the texts as historical documents have been ingenious and inventive—but still fundamentally sound.[12] It is truly a colossal achievement to produce the definitive authoritative transcriptions, with exacting apparatuses, of the Linear B tablets from both Pylos and Knossos and to have co-authored the authoritative transcriptions of tablets from Tiryns, Thebes and Mycenae.[13]

He has furthered the rich tradition of Mycenological studies in Spain and thus fulfilled his pious duties to his native mentors and founding fathers. He has also helped bring to fruition the ground-breaking work of the decipherment trio Bennett, Kober, and Ventris.

The entire field of Mycenology is now and forever in his debt.

Bibliography

Adrados, F. R. 1952. *La dialectología griega como fuente para el estudio de las migraciones indoeuropeas en Grecia.* Salamanca.

Aravantinos, V. L., M. Del Freo, L. Godart, and A. Sacconi, eds. 2005. *Thèbes: Fouilles de la Cadmée IV: Les textes de Thèbes (1–433). Translitération et tableaux des scribes.* Pisa.

Fox, M. 2013. *The Riddle of the Labyrinth: The Quest to Crack an Ancient Code.* New York.

Melena, J. L. 2014. "Mycenaean Writing." In *A Companion to Linear B: Mycenaean Greek Texts and Their World*, vol. 3, ed. Y. Duhoux and A. Morpurgo Davies, 1–186. Louvain-la-Neuve.

———. 2019. *The Knossos Tablets. Sixth Edition. Transliteration by José L. Melena in collaboration with Richard J. Firth.* Philadelphia.

———. 2021. *The Pylos Tablets. Third Edition in Transliteration by José L. Melena with the collaboration of Richard J. Firth.* Vitoria-Gasteiz.

Melena, J. L. and J.-P. Olivier 1991. *TITHEMY. The Tablets and Nodules in Linear B from Tiryns, Thebes and Mycenae: A revised transliteration.* Salamanca and Lejona.

Myres, J. L. 1933. "The Cretan Labyrinth: A Retrospect of Aegean Research." *Journal of the Royal Anthropological Institute of Great Britain and Ireland* 63:269–312.

---

[12] See especially the joint vision of the Mycenaeans as a society composed of living and breathing human beings co-authored by Melena and his mentor: M. S. Ruipérez and J. L. Melena 1990.

[13] Melena 2019 and 2021. Melena and Olivier 1991. Privately circulated are Melena's and Olivier's corrected and true readings (2003) of the Thebes tablets discovered in 1994 and after. It displaces Aravantinos, Del Freo, Godart and Sacconi 2005, especially in reading *65 instead of FAR.

Palaima, T. G. 2017. "Emmett L. Bennett, Jr., Michael G.F. Ventris, Alice E. Kober, Cryptanalysis, Decipherment and the Phaistos Disc." In *Aegean Scripts*, ed. M.-L. Nosch and H. Landenius-Enegren, vol. 2, 771–788. Rome.

Robinson, A. 2002. *The Man Who Deciphered Linear B*. London.

Ruipérez, M. S. 1953–1954. "Sobre la prehistoria de los dialectos griegos." *Emérita* 21:253–266.

Ruipérez, M. S. and J. L. Melena 1990. *Los griegos micénicos*. Madrid.

Tovar, A. 1944. "Ensayo sobre la estratigrafía de los dialectos griegos." *Emérita* 12:245–335.

Ventris, M. 1988. *Work Notes on Minoan Language Research and Other Unedited Papers*, ed. A. Sacconi. Rome.

Personal Comments on José Luis Melena from the Contributors

Francisco Aura Jorro

PROFESSOR EMERITUS, DEPARTAMENTO DE PREHISTORIA, ARQUEOLOGÍA, HISTORIA ANTIGUA, FILOLOGÍA GRIEGA Y FILOLOGÍA LATINA UNIVERSIDAD DE ALICANTE

Es difícil condensar en pocas palabras la peripecia afortunada de una amistad cimentada sobre una relación profesional. Solo diré que me considero muy afortunado de tener como amigo a José Luis Melena («Jose», para mí), un maestro del que he aprendido y disfrutado, incluso abusado, de una generosidad sin límites. Siempre lo he encontrado dispuesto a resolver cualquier duda o ignorancia y a remediar mis carencias, poniendo a mi disposición y sin límites el enorme bagaje de su saber y el no menor de su trabajo, así como el mejor de los consejos. De ahí la verdad de la dedicatoria de mi contribución en su más que merecido homenaje. Gracias por todo, Jose, y, por encima de todo, por tu amistad.

It is hard to distill into a few words the fortunate turns of events of a friendship founded upon a professional relationship. I will only say that I consider myself very fortunate to have as a friend José Luis Melena ('Jose', for me), a mentor from whom I have learned and whose limitless generosity I have enjoyed and even taken advantage of. I have always found him willing to solve any doubt or ignorance on my part and to remedy my shortcomings, as he puts at my disposal, again without any limits, the enormous storehouse of his learning and not least of his scholarly work, as well as the best of his advice. On such reasons is based the truth of the dedication of my contribution to this volume in more than deserved tribute to him. Thank you for everything, Jose, and, above all, for your friendship.

Alberto Bernabé

PROFESSOR EMERITUS, DEPT. OF CLASSICAL PHILOLOGY UNIVERSIDAD COMPLUTENSE MADRID

José Luis Melena and I were born on the same day of the same year. We come from different 'schools', he from Martín Ruipérez's (Universidad de Salamanca and Universidad Complutense Madrid) and I from Francisco R. Adrados's (Universidad Complutense Madrid). This has not prevented us from having cordial relations; and he has always been a point of reference for me, especially in his capacity as editor of texts and in his long dedication, almost exclusively, to Mycenology. It is impossible to work in this field without coming across José Luis's—always pertinent—contributions. I hope that we can continue to enjoy new and excellent contributions from him for a long time to come.

Maurizio Del Freo

DIRECTOR OF RESEARCH, CONSIGLIO NAZIONALE DELLE RICERCHE (CNR), ISTITUTO DI SCIENZE DEL PATRIMONIO CULTURALE (ISPC)

For me, as for many others, José has always been a model of method and a source of inspiration. He was so during my university years, when I did not yet know him personally, and he still is. The exchanges of views I have had with him over the years on many different subjects have enabled me to appreciate not only his scientific value, but also his human qualities, above all his generosity and openness to dialogue. Personally, I owe a lot to José, from the offer to collaborate with *Minos* to the concrete support for many of my projects. But above all, I am grateful to him for having always cultivated our relationship in the name of frankness and authenticity. My wish is that his exceptional work as a philologist and epigraphist can continue for a long time and that all his projects can be realized soon and in the best possible way.

Yves Duhoux

PROFESSEUR ÉMÉRITE FACULTY OF PHILOSOPHY, ARTS AND LETTERS UNIVERSITÉ CATHOLIQUE DE LOUVAIN (LOUVAIN-LA-NEUVE)

José, my friend José, has been and still is an example, and an unsurpassable one. Of course, I try to come nearer and nearer his formidable achievements. I fail. And I try again. And I fail once more. But what a pleasure to measure myself against such an outstanding colleague! Muchísimas gracias, querido José.

Richard Firth
WOLFSON COLLEGE, UNIVERSITY OF OXFORD, UK

The influence of José Melena on me and my work is too great for me to describe in brief.

But I will try. José has been my close friend and mentor for over twenty years. He has opened up a wide range of interests for me. These include not only the Mycenaean period and the wider aspects of the Linear B texts but also the more recent history surrounding Knossos during the years of its excavation, through a fascinating investigation of the diaries of Christian Doll. José has encouraged me to strive to higher goals and has given me space to develop my own ideas. In recent times, I was pleased to have collaborated with José on his publication of the transliterations of the Linear B tablets from Knossos and Pylos. These were the culmination of many years of his work and I am particularly grateful to José for giving me the opportunity to work on these projects.

Michael Lane
ASSOCIATE PROFESSOR OF ANCIENT STUDIES UNIVERSITY OF MARYLAND BALTIMORE COUNTY

When I was a young student, before personal acquaintance with Professor Melena, the breadth of his scholarship astonished me. His meticulous close readings of the Linear B corpus also encouraged me, unperturbed, apparently, by social theoretical trends and fashions. When afterwards I made his acquaintance, his generosity in both material and spirit both impressed and humbled me. He answered my entreaties and commented on my work, while reciprocating with his own drafts, soliciting my commentary. He never seemed concerned to hold center stage or relegate me to a supporting role. He appeared instead dedicated to reproducing the next generation of scholars. For good or ill, he convinced me to pursue Linear B further. This *Festschrift* is a rare and happy occasion to celebrate the legacy of the scholar and the person of José Luis Melena Jiménez.

José Luis García Ramón
DOCENTE A CONTRATO "FILOLOGIA MICENEA" DIPARTIMENTO DI FILOLOGIA CLASSICA, PAPIROLOGIA E LINGUISTICA STORICA UNIVERSITÀ CATTOLICA DEL SACRO CUORE, MILANO

Con José Luis Melena he compartido reflexiones e ideas prácticamente a diario en la Universidad Complutense (1971–1977), cuando trabajábamos con nuestro maestro Martín S. Ruipérez. Los intercambios, ya centrados exclusivamente en la micenología, han continuado, por desgracia desde la distancia, a partir del Coloquio de Atenas (1990). Mis trabajos se han beneficiado siempre en gran medida de las observaciones y críticas de José Luis y, en particular, de su ayuda en cuestiones de tipo epigráfico o de interpretación de los textos, así como de sus ediciones de las tablillas, que ha compartido conmigo a medida que su trabajo progresaba, y de sus informaciones sobre novedades epigráficas.

With José Luis Melena I have shared reflections and ideas practically daily at the Complutense University (1971–1977), when we were working with our teacher Martín S. Ruipérez. The exchanges, already focused exclusively on Mycenology, have continued, unfortunately from a distance, since the Colloquium in Athens (1990). My scholarly works have always benefited to a great extent from the observations and criticisms of José Luis and, in particular, from his help in matters of an epigraphic nature or in interpretation of the texts. My scholarship has benefitted as well as from his editions of the tablets, which he has shared with me. as his work progressed, as well as his sharing of information on new developments in epigraphy.

Eugenio R. Luján

PROFESSOR OF INDO-EUROPEAN LINGUISTICS, DEPT OF CLASSICS, SCHOOL OF LANGUAGES AND LITERATURES UNIVERSIDAD COMPLUTENSE DE MADRID

Juan Piquero

ASSISTANT PROFESSOR DEPT OF CLASSICS, SCHOOL OF LANGUAGES AND LITERATURES, UNED (UNIVERSIDAD NACIONAL DE EDUCACIÓN A DISTANCIA) MADRID

Professor José L. Melena's work has been for us a standing source of inspiration and a model of fine scholarship in the domain of Mycenaean and Aegean studies. We have been able to appreciate his profound knowledge of the intricacies of the Linear B script, his insights into the interpretation of the Mycenaean tablets, and his philological accuracy especially when working on Mycenaean lexicography and systematically checking readings of the tablets. We are indebted to him for his excellent editions of the Mycenaean texts, which are the foundation for undertaking an appropriate work on other areas of Mycenaean studies—no progress can be made unless the textual basis is solid. And because of José, it is.

Marie-Louise Nosch
PROFESSOR, CENTRE FOR TEXTILE RESEARCH & SAXO INSTITUTE UNIVERSITY OF
COPENHAGEN

When I wrote my Ph.D. dissertation in the 1990s on Mycenaean textiles, José
Melena's 1975 monograph *Studies on Some Mycenaean Inscriptions from Knossos
dealing with Textiles* became my dearest reading and source of inspiration,
together with the works by John T. Killen. Each chapter in Melena's book closely
studies a set or a series of Linear B tablets and offers new and original interpretation of them. Later during my postdoc, I corresponded with José about plant
dyes, especially about CROCus, saffron. I wanted to know: Was it a spice or a
plant dye, or both? What technical knowledge of temperatures and mordants
was available for dyeing textiles with plants in the second millennium BCE? I
still recall José's kind and true comment: *Well, chemistry starts in the kitchen.*

Thomas G. Palaima
ROBERT M. ARMSTRONG CENTENNIAL PROFESSOR OF CLASSICS AND DIRECTOR,
PROGRAM IN AEGEAN SCRIPTS AND PREHISTORY, THE UNIVERSITY OF TEXAS AT AUSTIN

I am in the same lucky position as José of having met many of the luminaries
of the first generation of Linear B scholars who assembled at Gif-sur-Yvette
in April 1956 and formally launched the discipline of Mycenology. There are
many Mycenological ghosts whom I revere and try to keep with me. But three
spirits have guided me and still keep me moving forward and always trying to do
better in my own scholarly work the next time. They are Alice Elizabeth Kober,
Emmett L. Bennett, Jr. and José Luis Melena. In my judgment, José is the greatest
Mycenaean scholar of the last sixty-five years. He is a master across the board
as a reader and editor of texts, as a pioneer in the art and practice of making
joins and mastering palaeography, as long-time editor of *Minos*, during which I
was fortunate to be assistant editor and see firsthand his unique form of kindly
and encouragingly conveyed exacting criticism, as a true genius in imagining
what texts mean and exploring historical parallels, as a linguist, and even as
an artist in two and three dimensions. He is quite simply the Leonardo da Vinci
of Mycenaean studies. He is also thoroughly and humanly moral and ethical.
I share with all other contributors our feeling that we are lucky to have as a
colleague and friend and model for our aspirations, José L. Melena.

Oswald Panagl
PROFESSOR EMERITUS, DEPARTMENT OF LINGUISTICS, UNIVERSITY OF SALZBURG

As the representative of Austria in the CIPEM since the eighties, I met José Luis at all relevant colloquia beginning with Nürnberg 1981. In September 1985, when — for personal reasons — I arrived in Skopje one day late, he took me from the airport and during our drive to Ohrid, the venue of the symposium, we had a nice discussion and a lot of fun together. Furthermore, I remember his fine paper at the Salzburg conference (1995) on the Knossos fragments found in 1984. For my own research on problems of Mycenaean morphology and etymology, José Luis has always proved to be a reliable guide for intricate questions in the field of epigraphy. Thanks for your help, Don José!

Massimo Perna

Sono molto lieto e onorato di partecipare a questo *Festschrift* per José L. Melena. Per i miei studi sulla fiscalità micenea, finalizzati alla tesi di dottorato e alla realizzazione di una monografia sullo stesso tema, di grande aiuto e ispirazione sono stati alcuni suoi lavori. Innanzitutto il mio interesse sulla serie Mc di Cnosso è nato proprio grazie agli articoli che riguardavano i prodotti registrati in questa serie e uno dei primissimi articoli che ho letto è stato proprio "On the Knossos Mc Tablets" di Melena, apparso in *Minos* nel 1972, seguito da quello sull'ideogramma *142 negli *Studies Bennett* del 1988, senza contare le sue analisi sul termine *o-pa*, sulla *ta-ra-si-ja* e sui tessili.

E' stato per me, inoltre, un grande onore firmare i miei due primi articoli nel 1988 (*BCH*) e 1989 (*Minos*) su alcuni joints fatti sulle tavolette in lineare B di Cnosso insieme a Melena e gli altri membri del leggendario team che hanno portato alla pubblicazione dei 3000 frammenti di tavolette in lineare B rinvenuti nelle riserve del museo di Herakleion.

I am very pleased and honored to participate in this *Festschrift* for José L. Melena. For my studies on Mycenaean fiscality, aimed at the doctoral thesis and the eventual publication of a monograph on the same topic, some of his works were of great help and inspiration. First of all, my interest in the Mc series of Knossos was born thanks to the articles concerning the products registered in this series. One of the very first articles I read was "On the Knossos Mc Tablets" by Melena, which appeared in *Minos* in 1972, followed by that on the ideogram *142 in *Studies Bennett* of 1988, without counting his analyses of the terms *o-pa* and *ta-ra-si-ja* and of textiles. It was also a great honor for me to sign my first two articles in 1988 (*BCH*) and 1989 (*Minos*) on joins made in the Linear B tablets of Knossos together with Melena and the other members of the legendary team who eventually published the 3000 fragments of Linear B tablets that were found in the storage areas of the Herakleion museum.

Christina Skelton
ASSOCIATE IN HISTORICAL LINGUISTICS AND AEGEAN PREHISTORY, CENTER FOR
HELLENIC STUDIES, HARVARD UNIVERSITY

I have always been deeply grateful to José for his painstaking work on tablet joins (really, what an eye!) and for shouldering so much of the burden of ensuring that the tablets are kept up-to-date in well-edited editions. I'm sure I speak for everyone in saying that all of our work would be far less secure without his diligent efforts. I've recently begun collaborating with a group of computer scientists, and José's generous act of sharing electronic copies of his text editions with us is what will make our future work possible. Thank you so much for everything, José.

Carlos Varias García
ASSOCIATE PROFESSOR OF GREEK PHILOLOGY, DEPARTMENT OF SCIENCES OF
ANTIQUITY AND THE MIDDLE AGES, UNIVERSITAT AUTÒNOMA DE BARCELONA

When in October 1988 Rosa Santiago, whom I had asked to supervise my MA thesis on Mycenaean Greek, introduced me through a letter to José Luis Melena, then cultural attaché of the Spanish embassy in Athens, I did not imagine that the most momentous relationship in my academic life would begin. José Luis wrote me a handwritten letter proposing to me the subject and structure of this work: an in-depth study of the textile tablet KN Ln 1568. After I presented my MA thesis in October 1989, he accepted to supervise my PhD dissertation, proposing to me again its topic (letter of January 11, 1991): a full study of the Linear B inscriptions from Mycenae. I owe him my entire research career for more than thirty years now. Besides being my friend, he has been my best guide as a scholar. His recent publications on Mycenaean, the chapter "Mycenaean Writing" in the third volume of *A Companion to Linear B: Mycenaean Texts and Their World 3* (2014) edited by Yves Duhoux and Anna Morpurgo Davies and the transliterated editions of the Knossos and Pylos tablets, testify that he is a unique Mycenologist.

Jörg Weilhartner

CLASSICAL AND AEGEAN ARCHAEOLOGY, UNIVERSITY OF SALZBURG

José Luis Melena and I met only once, at my first Mycenological conference in Austin, TX, in May 2000. Ever since then we have stayed in contact, assisted each other with bibliographical references, and shared our thoughts on the interpretation of logograms. Among his many contributions to Linear B studies, I would like to highlight his comprehensive chapter on Mycenaean writing in the third volume of *A Companion to Linear B: Mycenaean Texts and Their World* 3 (2014) edited by Yves Duhoux and Anna Morpurgo Davies. This work is not only an indispensable point of reference for me, but also an ongoing source of inspiration for my own work on logograms.

Carlos Varias, Rosa Santiago, José Fortes, Antonio López Eire, Francisco Aura
Jorro, Thomas G. Palaima, José L. Melena, and Jean-Pierre Olivier.
Universitat Autònoma de Barcelona, Sept. 1993. Photo © Carlos Varias García.

Carlos Varias García, José L. Melena, José Luis García Ramon,
and Alex Leukart. Salzburg, May 1995. Photo © Carlos Varias García.

Emmett L. Bennett, Jr., Thomas G. Palaima, José L. Melena.
Austin, May 2000. Photo © Thomas G. Palaima.

José L. Melena, John Bennet, Jean-Pierre Olivier, Thomas G. Palaima, Carlos Varias.
Austin, May 2000. Photo © Thomas G. Palaima.

Jan Driessen, José L. Melena, John Bennet, Jean-Pierre Olivier, Carlos Varias.
Austin, May 2000. Photo © Thomas G. Palaima.

Marie-Louise Nosch, Stefan Hiller, Oswald Panagl.
Austin, May 2000. Photo © Thomas G. Palaima.